PENGUIN BO

DIANA

Diana

SARAH BRADFORD

PENGUIN BOOKS

PENGUIN BOOKS

Published by the Penguin Group
Penguin Books Ltd, 80 Strand, London WC2R ORL, England
Penguin Group (USA) Inc., 375 Hudson Street, New York, New York 10014, USA
Penguin Group (Canada), 90 Eglinton Avenue East, Suite 700, Toronto, Ontario, Canada M4P 2Y3
(a division of Pearson Penguin Canada Inc.)
Penguin Ireland, 25 St Stephen's Green, Dublin 2, Ireland (a division of Penguin Books Ltd)
Penguin Group (Australia), 250 Camberwell Road, Camberwell, Victoria 3124, Australia
(a division of Pearson Australia Group Pty Ltd)
Penguin Books India Pvt Ltd, 11 Community Centre, Panchsheel Park, New Delhi – 110 017, India
Penguin Group (NZ), 67 Apollo Drive, North Shore 0632, New Zealand
(a division of Pearson New Zealand Ltd)
Penguin Books (South Africa) (Pty) Ltd, 24 Sturdee Avenue, Rosebank, Johannesburg 2196, South Africa

Penguin Books Ltd, Registered Offices: 80 Strand, London WC2R ORL, England

www.penguin.com

First published by Viking 2006
Published in Penguin Books with a new introduction 2007

2

Typeset by Rowland Phototypesetting Ltd, Bury St Edmunds, Suffolk
Printed in England by Clays Ltd, St Ives plc

ISBN: 978-0-140-27671-8

For William

Contents

List of Illustrations

Picture Credits

Diana –The Last Word

'She won't go quietly', Diana warned in the famous television interview she gave eighteen months before her death. Nor has she. The mention of her name still generates news; the repeated printing of her photograph brings back instant images of the most famous woman of her time, adored and reviled in equal measure. In death she is still as controversial as she was in life. A great many people would prefer her to remain dead, buried and forgotten, seeing her as a threat to the Royal Family, even though, as the mother of Princes William and Harry, that is the last way she would want to be remembered. Some people hate her as a symbol of the new sentimentality in public life; others cherish her for her 'emotional intelligence'.

It is now ten years since the Mercedes limousine carrying Diana and Dodi Fayed crashed into the thirteenth pillar of the underpass at the Place d'Alma in Paris, fatally injuring her and killing her companion. The circumstances of her death on 31 August 1997 have given rise to the greatest conspiracy theories since President Kennedy's assassination in Dallas. Millions of pounds and thousands of man hours have been expended to provide evidence that the crash was a straightforward accident caused by speed and a drunk driver with prescription drugs in his bloodstream, impelled to his death by a pursuing horde of paparazzi. Mohamed Fayed, shadowed by responsibility for the events of that night, has spent several fortunes in an attempt to prove that the Royal Family, in league with British and foreign secret services, had Diana and her Muslim lover murdered because they were planning to marry and she was pregnant with his baby. Diana was not pregnant, evidence given weight by the testimony of her friend Rosa Monckton, and at least two others in whom Diana confided that she was having two periods a month at the time of her death.

Lastly, and perhaps most importantly, tests on her blood found in the Mercedes proved that she was not pregnant. The fact that none of the conspiracy theories stands up makes no difference: people will continue to suspect an Establishment cover-up, and as many Muslims believe it as give credence to the theory that President Bush was behind 9/11.

Diana's life story was so extraordinary that it is worth looking back to its simple beginnings to discover how it was that in sixteen years, between her glittering marriage to the heir to the British throne and her violent death in a Paris underpass, a young, unsophisticated girl shook the British monarchy to its foundations and became a worldwide celebrity. Diana was just twenty when she married, not yet twenty-one when she became the mother of the future king, an international celebrity at only thirty-six when she was so sensationally killed.

In 1981, when Diana Spencer married the Prince of Wales, watched by a worldwide TV audience of millions, she was just another teenage English rose, a typical Sloane Ranger. By the time of her death, she was an icon and a royal rebel, increasingly glamorous, 'the most hunted woman in the world', as her brother put it at her funeral service. In the days after her death the Royal Family – even the popular and respected Queen herself – became the target of a tidal wave of quasi-revolutionary feeling. No one who was in London during the week following her death, who watched the run-up to the funeral on television, or was reminded of that extraordinary time by *The Queen*, the film released in 2006, will ever forget the experience or the irrational, dangerous emotions which the death of Diana had stirred in the British people. For the Royal Family, its twentieth-century history could be seen as pre-Diana and post-Diana, such was the impact this young woman had upon the ancient institution and people's attitudes towards it.

Why should this be so? Why so much fuss about a Sloaney girl with no O levels and a prize for hamster husbandry? She was beautiful, charming and witty but when her dark side was uppermost even her friends would admit she could be a fiend. So why the fame? What was she really like? Was Diana, as she herself once said in a memorable piece of self-denigration, 'thick as two planks'? Or was she, as her enemies – even some of her friends – would have it, a blonde fruitcake, self-obsessed, disloyal, manipulative and dangerous to know?

Exceptionally resistant to formal education from an early age, she had an almost mystical belief in her destiny and in her own instincts as a guide in life. Unfortunately for her future emotional wellbeing, her favourite reading was the novels of Barbara Cartland, hardly the ideal handbooks for a modern marriage. Poor Prince Charles, a spoiled bachelor set in his ways, was unsuited to the role of romantic husband and Cartland had not scripted a role for a Camilla Parker Bowles. Camilla had orchestrated the engagement and Diana was deeply suspicious of her from the first but fondly imagined that, when she became Charles's wife, his former mistress would fade into the background. When she did not, Diana was unable to accept it. Who could blame her?

When it became apparent to Diana that Camilla had reappeared in Charles's life, and that she was expected not only to tolerate the situation but to go on waving and smiling as if nothing had happened, she made it clear she was not going to suffer in silence, as Queen Alexandra had suffered during Edward VII's liaison with Camilla's great-grandmother, Alice Keppel. The scene was set.

Did Diana leave anything concrete beyond an archive of glamorous images? Was she worth anything as a person? Did she leave a significant mark on her age? Her luminous presence and undoubted gifts of empathy with the suffering held up a mirror to a monarchy which appeared stuffy, remote and out of touch. She did not want to be confined to the 'charity figurehead' role – one reason why she sold her old wardrobe in the summer of 1997.

She wanted to be a modern woman creating a career on her own merits. Her plans included making carefully researched television programmes into subjects or causes which interested her – along the lines of the TV documentary she made on her landmines trip to Angola in 1997 – and she had intended taking media training in New York that autumn to enable her to do so. She was also passionate about advancing the cause of the illiterate – possibly stimulated by her own weakness – something which was not on the fashionable agenda a decade ago.

Diana brought up her sons to be in touch with the age: she had a clear view of how William should set about his royal task when the time came. Her boys were the centre of her life and their royal future was important to her. She saw her role as enabling them to live as normally as possible, fully conscious of the implications and demands of their position. She was determined that they would not be brought up as their father had been, spoiled by courtiers and servants, and remote from everyday experience. By the last months of her life, she and Prince Charles were on cordial terms and in their own ways were excellent parents to their sons. If and when Prince William becomes King, his success will be his mother's enduring legacy.

June 2007

1. The Country Girl

'In the Spencer family the gender issue is a big one . . . Women are very much second-class citizens' (a Spencer cousin)

Diana Spencer was born to the sound of applause. Her birth took place at 7.45 p.m. on a warm summer evening, 1 July 1961, in the bow-fronted bedroom where her mother had been born before her, overlooking the lawn where the annual cricket match organized by her father was nearing its end. Yet far from being a cause for applause, Diana's birth was regarded as a disappointment. As a girl she could not be the heir to the Spencer name that her parents so desperately wanted. Moreover, she was the third girl born to her parents, Frances and Johnnie Althorp, heir to the Spencer earldom, and had confidently been expected to be a boy, so much so that at the time of her birth the local newspaper reported her father as saying 'they had not yet decided on a name'. Since all Spencer male heirs were traditionally christened John or Charles this was understandable in the circumstances. The new girl's Spencer namesake, Diana (1735–43), was the short-lived sister of the 1st Earl Spencer.

Diana's father's family, the Spencers, was one of the most aristocratic in England; her extraordinary bloodline included the children of two Kings, a Duke, and a saint. A web of titled ancestors made her an eleventh cousin to the heir to the British throne, Charles, Prince of Wales; she was even distantly connected to the first President of the United States, George Washington. (Through her grandfather's marriage to American heiress Frances Work she was a seventh cousin to both Humphrey Bogart and Rudolph Valentino.)

Diana's family connections and the location of her birthplace could be said to have determined her royal future. Park House, where she was born, was the property of the Queen, and had been leased to Diana's maternal grandfather, Maurice Fermoy, in 1931 by King George V. It stood on the Sandringham estate in Norfolk about half a mile from the main house where the Royal Family frequently spent their holidays and the church where they worshipped. Diana had connections on both sides with the Royal Family: Lord Fermoy had been friend and shooting companion to Kings George V and VI, her father had been equerry (a privileged position as royal dogsbody reserved for members of the armed forces) to the Queen, Elizabeth II, and was a frequent guest at Balmoral shooting parties. Both her paternal grandmother, Cynthia Spencer (born Lady Cynthia Hamilton), and her great-aunt, Lady Delia Peel, were close friends and ladies-in-waiting to Queen Elizabeth, the Queen Mother, as was her maternal grandmother, Ruth, Lady Fermoy. Another Spencer great-aunt, Lady Lavinia White, who died in 1955, had been a close childhood friend of Queen Elizabeth. Park House could even be seen from the top windows of the Big House at Sandringham. She was, in a very real sense, 'the Girl Next Door'.

The Spencer family estate was Althorp in Northamptonshire but Diana rarely went there as a child; her fierce grandfather, Jack Spencer, the 7th Earl, and his heir, Diana's father Johnnie (Viscount Althorp at the time of Diana's birth), did not get on. She grew up with her roots in north Norfolk, a remote corner of one of the most isolated and rural parts of England, a county of gently rolling countryside under a vast sky. The Sandringham estate surrounding her birthplace is, in contrast, a sandy heath dotted with towering pine trees. The cold grey North Sea with its sand dunes and reeded marshes lies a short distance from Park House. North Norfolk is the territory of large estates and ancient families living the sporting and social life of a closed circle, largely barred to outsiders. Diana's parents, Frances and Johnnie Althorp, fitted perfectly into this background.

On Diana's mother's side the family were Anglo-Irish from County Cork: their name was Roche and their title Baron Fermoy.

Diana's great-great-grandfather, Edmund Burke Roche, was elected to Parliament and made a baron in the mid-nineteenth century; his second son, James Boothby Burke Roche, 3rd Baron Fermoy, married, in 1880, an American 'Dollar Princess', Frances 'Fanny' Work, daughter of a successful Wall Street broker. It was the usual alliance of American money in exchange for European title which became current practice in the nineteenth century and, as so many of such marriages were, it was unhappy and ended in divorce in 1891. Fanny's father, Frank Work, had little use for Europeans and after the divorce he told his daughter that her children would only inherit his fortune if they became Americans. Fanny's twin elder sons, Maurice and Francis, were sent to the cream of American schools and colleges, St Paul's School, Concord, New Hampshire, and Harvard, but despite this they refused to become Americans on their grandfather's death in 1911 and successfully challenged the conditions of his will. With $2.9 million (roughly £28–30 million today) apiece they turned their back on America and in 1921 left for England where Diana's grandfather, Maurice, now 4th Baron Fermoy, settled in Norfolk, becoming Member of Parliament for King's Lynn; a position he held from 1924 to 1935 and later from 1943 to 1945. On a trip to Paris, he met the beautiful, talented and ambitious Ruth Gill, a paint manufacturer's daughter from Aberdeenshire. Ruth was studying to be a concert pianist at the Paris Conservatoire but without much hesitation she gave up her career to marry Maurice, who was attractive to women, extremely wealthy and had a title to boot. They married in 1931, when she was twenty-six and he forty-six, and had three children: Mary, born in 1934, Frances, Diana's mother, born in 1936, and Edmund, born in 1939.

Maurice and Ruth Fermoy settled at Park House, a convenient base for Maurice because of its proximity to his constituency. He was outgoing, jovial and much liked by his constituents, a notable communicator, willing to burst into a speech at any time; on visits to local hospitals he would sit on the side of patients' beds and chat happily away with them. Ruth, backed by the Fermoy money, was a generous and skilful hostess. 'They had wonderful tennis

parties and things like that which nobody else had in those days,'
a Spencer relation recalled. 'Because of the American money they
lived in a style that nobody else seemed to then.' There were
rumours that some of the Norfolk grandees sneered at the couple,
at Maurice for his 'American trade' connections and at Ruth for
her modest background. 'The sort of Norfolk hierarchy – dubbed
"county-bound" by a Spencer contemporary [Lady Margaret
Douglas-Home] – wouldn't have anything to do with them, and
rather rejected them,' said an aristocratic contemporary of Ruth's.
'And because they lived at Park House [so close to Sandringham]
the King and Queen took them up. Queen Elizabeth never liked
that sort of ostracism and snobbery.'[1] Diana's mother, Frances,
was born on 20 January 1936, the day of King George V's death
at Sandringham; even at that stressful time, his widow, Queen
Mary, noted 'the birth of Lady Fermoy's baby' and sent Ruth a
congratulatory note.

Diana never knew her grandfather, who died in 1955, but her
grandmother, Ruth Fermoy, was to play an important part in her
life, not least for her close royal connections based on her valued
friendship with the Queen Mother whose woman of the bedchamber she became. Like her friend the Queen Mother, Ruth
had a Scottish steel about her. 'She was a very, very mysterious
woman,' the Spencer relation said, 'always very elegant and gentle
and quiet but there was another side to her – less gentle.' Ruth
Fermoy was socially ambitious, adopting the attitudes of the aristocratic circles she had joined on her marriage. She was delighted when
her daughter Mary married Anthony Berry, the son of Viscount
Kemsley, ecstatic when Frances became engaged to Johnnie,
Viscount Althorp, only son and heir to the 7th Earl Spencer, with
vast acres of Northamptonshire, and an historic stately home,
Althorp. Now titled herself, very rich and outstandingly beautiful,
she turned her back on her middle-class Aberdeenshire background
to cultivate her royal and aristocratic connections. Her rigid adher-
ence to the conventions of her adopted class and of the courtier
circle was to have dramatic repercussions on Diana's early life.

Frances Burke Roche, whom Diana was to resemble both in

looks and character, was a beauty with fine features, luminous blue eyes, long, slim legs and blonde hair. She was also as strong and independent minded as her mother, Ruth, if not quite as tough. Frances herself said of Ruth, 'I don't think I've ever known anyone with as much confidence. She made up her mind and went for it. She didn't waver over anything.' The same words were echoed of Frances by her friends. 'Frances was the strongest character of anyone I've ever known,' said one. 'She was forcible, dynamic, energetic and very intelligent – had she had a better education she would have been a very contributive person – she had leadership qualities. She had terrific power over men – she was funny but one of the most dominating female characters I've ever known and she was like that at seventeen.' And at seventeen, what Frances wanted was Johnnie Althorp as he then was; she had first seen him when he visited her school, Downham, when she was just fourteen. At seventeen and just after leaving school, her parents launched her on the marriage market for upper-class girls known as the London Season, a daily round of balls, cocktail parties, house parties at weekends and certain sporting events such as the unmissable Royal Ascot. During that Season, Frances met Johnnie again, they fell in love and became engaged, despite the fact that Johnnie had been expected to marry the beautiful and charming Lady Anne Coke, daughter of the Earl of Leicester, owner of a great estate, Holkham, in Norfolk. As head of the great Norfolk family, neighbours of the Royal Family at Sandringham and close friends of the late King and of Queen Elizabeth, the Leicesters were leading lights in the hermetic world of north Norfolk royal and aristocratic society. Lady Anne confessed that she 'adored' Johnnie, though many of her friends did not, finding him 'unkind'. Still less did they like Frances who ruthlessly cut Anne out and took her man.

Johnnie Althorp liked dominant women. Tall, handsome in a bucolic way, charming and impeccably bred, he was a catch in social terms despite the tight financial lead on which his father, the 7th Earl, kept him. Any available money – and there was not a great deal – was devoted to the maintenance and restoration of Althorp. (The exception was the sale of one of the jewels of the

Spencer collection, a magnificent Holbein portrait of Henry VIII, which paid for Johnnie's Eton education, and is now in the Thyssen collection in Madrid.) As was the case in many aristocratic families (and indeed, historically, the British Royal Family) the heir and his father did not get on. Jack Spencer was irascible, difficult and eccentric: his nickname in society was the ironic 'Jolly Jack'. His passion for the family house, Althorp, seemed to have left him little room for other affections and the thought of passing on his treasure to his son was painful in the extreme. Althorp was his temple, and as its custodian he regarded himself as the temple priest, spending hours polishing the silver in the butler's pantry although he had a butler to do it for him. Unlike his son, he disliked human contact, particularly with those he regarded as 'the lower orders'. Among the numerous bees in his bonnet was an aversion to his driver looking round when he got into the car, the signal for departure being the sound of his door slamming shut. As Lord Lieutenant of Northamptonshire he used an old Rolls-Royce with chauffeur; on one occasion after an official dinner, Spencer got out to relieve himself, the wind slammed the door before he could get back in and the driver, knowing perfectly well what had happened, gleefully drove off leaving him in open country in the dark. He was a crashing snob with a dread of anything middle class. Once, lunching at Clarence House, he told Queen Elizabeth that he would never go into a house where people ate fish with fish knives because it was so middle class. 'Whenever he came to lunch after that,' said one of Queen Elizabeth's circle, 'we always had fish with fish knives.' 'He induced respect in many, and fear in almost all,' his grandson Charles Spencer wrote.[2] Unsurprisingly, Johnnie's childhood memories were not happy ones. He used to dread the train journey home and would hide in the shadow of the carriage, hoping his father had forgotten to collect him. At Althorp, when he felt the atmosphere thickening, he would climb into the false ceiling of a bathroom and hide there with his terriers as companions. 'I fear these solitary moments were relatively frequent,' his son wrote.[3]

Jolly Jack's wife, Cynthia, daughter of the Duke of Abercorn, was his complete opposite, beautiful, sensitive, charitable and greatly loved. 'I have never heard anyone say a word against her memory,' her grandson wrote, 'and she is still very much alive as a paragon of sweet nobility ... The word most often used to describe her is "saintly".'[4] She had served the Queen Mother as lady of the bedchamber but even more the local people for whom she had done an enormous amount of voluntary work. When she died in 1972 of a brain tumour, the county's hospice was named after her. Johnnie, who had loved her deeply and seen her too little because of his difficult relationship with his father, was devastated. Some of Diana's gentleness and empathy with the sick and suffering came from Lady Cynthia, whom she resembled in looks. Diana, aged eleven, came to believe that her grandmother Cynthia watched out for her as her guardian angel.

Diana's father was a typical product of his age and class. He was educated at Eton, served as an officer in the Royal Scots Greys and, on the strength of his family connections, had acted as equerry to both King George VI and Queen Elizabeth II and accompanied the Queen on her post-Coronation Commonwealth tour in 1953. By then he was engaged to Frances; they married on 1 June 1954 in a grand society wedding at St Margaret's, Westminster, attended by one thousand guests including the Queen, the Duke of Edinburgh, the Queen Mother and Princess Margaret. The young couple were very much in love but their circumstances were unequal from the start. Frances would have to finance the marriage. Johnnie, once described by his commanding officer in the Royal Scots Greys as 'very nice but very stupid', tried to find a job as a banker but was turned down by his old friend and partner in Hoare's on the grounds that 'mathematics was never his strong suit'. He then enrolled as a student at the Royal Agricultural College at Cirencester, the traditional option for the landed gentry and aristocracy (unkindly dubbed 'clotted cream': rich and thick). They lived first at Rodmarton, Gloucestershire, in a rented cottage and then at Orchard Cottage on the Althorp estate in uncomfortable proximity to Jolly Jack.

Happily for them, after the death of Frances's father, Maurice

Fermoy, in 1955, his widow Ruth had offered to let them take over the lease of Park House. At the same time Frances, having inherited her share of her father's fortune, generously bought Johnnie a 600-acre farm at nearby Snettisham for £30,000. While Johnnie farmed at Snettisham and the family land at North Creake and looked after his charities, particularly the National Association of Boys' Clubs, Frances set about the business of producing babies. The pressure was on her to bear the male heir but her first two children were girls: Sarah, born in March 1955 nine months after the wedding, and Jane born in February 1957. She had a miscarriage but when finally a son was born, on 1 January 1960, it was not a triumph but a tragedy. John Spencer was born malformed: he died ten hours later, unable to breathe, having been taken away from Frances before she could hold him. It was a pain she never forgot.

Something in the relationship fractured after John's death. Johnnie Spencer insisted that Frances was responsible for her continuing failure to bear a healthy boy and she was sent to a Harley Street gynaecologist for humiliating tests and treatment. 'It was a dreadful time for my parents,' Charles Spencer said, 'and probably the root of their divorce because I don't think they ever got over it.' A Spencer cousin and a friend of Frances, said: 'The death of John was a deep tragedy in their lives. Afterwards there was a sadness in both of them which had not been there before.'

Diana was intended to be the replacement child, the longed-for heir. By the time she was born, her parents' marriage was in trouble, which the arrival of yet another girl did nothing to improve. The Norfolk married life which may have suited Frances as a young bride became confining for a woman with wider horizons. Her dashing husband had become considerably less dashing as time went by, settling all too comfortably into his country squire surroundings. 'Johnnie was the best company when he was a young man,' his former fiancée Lady Anne Coke said, 'but then he just became boring, wrapped up in his children and his country life.'

Diana convinced herself that she should have been a boy and

that, being a girl, she was a disappointment and regarded as a lesser being. 'I do know that in the Spencer family the gender issue is a big one and even when there was a son and no pressure to produce an heir, the female children are of less account than the male. Women are very much second-class citizens in the Spencer family,' a Spencer relation said. By the time the longed-for heir, Charles Spencer, was born in May 1964, the marriage was beyond repair. Johnnie, as long as his irascible, eccentric father lived, had virtually no role to play beyond gentlemanly farming, cricket and shooting. Essentially a weak man, he resented the intellectual and financial dominance of Frances. There were rows, sometimes, it is said, descending into violence. Frances was bored with her husband and her life in staid, enclosed, predictable Norfolk society. She was only twenty-eight and wanted to spread her wings.

The inevitable happened: she fell in love with another man, Peter Shand Kydd, whom she had met at a London dinner party in 1966. They met again on a joint skiing holiday with their respective spouses early in 1967. This time interest turned into powerful attraction and they began a secret affair. In the summer of 1967 Frances and Johnnie agreed on a trial separation: with the two older girls now at school, Frances would take Diana, aged six, and Charles, aged four, to London for the weekdays. Both were enrolled in London schools and returned to Park House and their father for weekends. The family were reunited at half-term in October and again for Christmas. By then the thought of continuing with life at Park House had become intolerable to Frances. She was headstrong, a character trait that Diana would inherit, and at Christmas 1967 she confronted Johnnie with a request for a divorce. An affair, however, was one thing, divorce quite another. It was a tradition in English upper-class families at the time that everything should be done to keep the family together and to avoid the scandal and humiliation which the request for a divorce by the wife would involve. Johnnie was not merely hurt but bitterly angry, determined that Frances should be punished and seen to be so. She would not be allowed to profit from her crime by keeping the children. She could leave, but as an outcast. He declared that the children would be sent to school in King's Lynn, that they would stay with him and not return to London.

In the subsequent custody case, Ruth Fermoy took her son-in-law's side and gave evidence against her own daughter. The deep-seated reason for this apparently cruel action seems to have been a combination of shock at her daughter's behaviour and extreme snobbishness, manifested in her determination to take the Spencer side: 'It was the name and the shame,' a Spencer relation who knew Ruth well said.[5] 'When I asked her why she did that,' a friend said, 'she said it was because Charles must be brought up at Althorp . . .' 'She had a very ruthless streak. It was the most extraordinary thing to do. It split her family. Ruth's funeral was one of the saddest and creepiest I have ever been to. We sat on one side of the church with Charles and Diana – who had separated, I think, but came together for the day – and on the other side of the aisle was the Fermoy family, and there was Frances, and they didn't talk to each other, husbands and cousins who were all not talking to her. It was the most terrible thing.'[6] Ruth, she said, in a phrase which was to become a litany in court circles later on, blamed the 'bad Fermoy blood' for Frances's behaviour. 'I remember Ruth saying that the trouble was her husband's family. They are what you call "bolters". They were all American bolters. A very unfortunate gene.'[7]

Diana, six at this time, was old enough to sense the strained atmosphere and, as she later recalled, to overhear the bitter rows. Opinions are divided as to whether an overwrought Johnnie actually hit his wife or not. Both are now dead so the truth cannot be known; the rumour that he did may have arisen because Frances later based her grounds for divorce on a plea of cruelty. Frances had come back for Christmas with the intention of having the children with her in London but, when she left this time, she left for good. Years later Diana, pouring out her heart on tapes for Andrew Morton's explosive book, *Diana: Her True Story*, remembered as a defining moment the crunch of tyres on the gravel as her mother drove off. 'I'll be back,' Frances told her, but she never did return to Park House.

The happy, undemanding childhood life at Park House fell apart. Diana saw her father unhappy and withdrawn, couldn't understand why her mother was no longer there, heard her little brother Charles sobbing for his mother in the night. Her longing for love and her fear of abandonment, her horror and fear of divorce and determination that it should not happen to her and to her children was born at that moment. Torn between love for her devastated father and her absent mother, Diana suffered what was to turn out to be a deep and psychologically crippling wound.

2. A Norfolk Childhood

'She has been accused of making too much of losing her mother through divorce in the late 1960s, but in truth the loss ran deep within her'
(William Deedes[1])

Diana's despair at the departure of her mother would be at the root of her later view of herself as a 'victim', something to which she returned over and over again, particularly when faced with a television camera or a tape recorder. She had a strong streak of fantasy and self-dramatization in her make-up, and as a child had a reputation for lying: one day on the school run, a local vicar's wife told her: 'Diana Spencer, if you tell one more lie, I'll put you out of the car.' Even her brother Charles Spencer later agreed that as a child she had a tendency to lie. Some people, including the Spencer family, tended to dismiss Diana's claims of unhappiness. 'I think in her perception it seemed like that but it wasn't the reality. It was much happier than she felt it was in retrospect,' a cousin said. Yet a man who was close to her before she began her relationship with Prince Charles was convinced that the departure of her mother 'had a very severe, dramatic effect on her'.[2]

People who witnessed the early days after Frances's departure tend to bear out Diana's view. A cook, engaged by Lady Fermoy, who arrived shortly after Frances left when Diana was six, had a very different impression of life at Park House at the time. 'It was not in my recollection a happy household. Lord Althorp was absent a lot of the time and not cheerful . . . Diana was very quiet, kept herself to herself. The children never cried [during the day] but did sob at night when they had gone to bed.' A Norfolk neighbour remembers giving a birthday party for one of her sons at the time: 'It was July and all the children were enjoying themselves in the garden except for poor Diana – she refused to join in and I said to the young nanny who was with her, "What can we do to encourage her to join the other children?" Her answer was: "Nothing, she is a very sad little girl." This was just after her mother had bolted.'[3]

Years later, in 1992, Diana would claim in tapes recorded by Peter Settelen, 'My father told me about five years ago that he would find me on the doorstep: "You didn't speak. You just sat there. You just, you know, you just never spoke."' Diana, at six, was just the age when her mother's unexplained disappearance hit hard: her sisters, aged ten and thirteen, were better equipped to cope; Charles, at only three, cried for his mother at night but was unable to understand or rationalize her departure from his life as Diana did.

But if Diana was shocked and confused by her mother's unexplained disappearance from her life, her father was equally so. When he was at home he shut himself away: 'He was really miserable after the divorce, basically shell-shocked,' Charles Spencer said. 'He used to sit in the study the whole time.' Frances's name was never mentioned. Emotions were raw on both sides: 'Frances went through agonies when she lost her children,' a contemporary recalled.[4]

Luckily for Diana, she was initially unaware of the bitter behind-the-scenes battles between Frances and Johnnie both over the terms of the divorce and the custody of the children. Frances lost all the way down the line: in two custody cases when Ruth Fermoy sided with Johnnie against her and in the divorce case in which her cause was not helped by Mrs Shand Kydd, whose own divorce petition cited Frances as the co-respondent. When Frances petitioned on the grounds of cruelty, Johnnie countersued by reason of her adultery. Frances lost and costs were awarded against her. She was publicly branded an unfit mother, a 'bolter' (after a character in Nancy Mitford's *The Pursuit of Love*, 1945) and an adulteress. The Althorp divorce caused an upheaval in Norfolk society where Frances was widely condemned for what was seen as her desertion of her children.

Diana was not, however, too young to be sensitive to people's curious stares when they attended church at Sandringham or were taken by Ruth Fermoy to Ladyman's tea rooms in King's Lynn. Although there was nothing beyond bald announcements in the London newspapers about the proceedings, all north Norfolk from top to bottom of the social scale knew about it and most of them sympathized with the deserted father and his children.

A Norfolk neighbour left a widower with a number of children around the time of the Althorp divorce used to employ house-keeper/nannies who had previously been at Park House. 'They had usually left Johnnie Althorp and were full of stories about the awful [atmosphere] . . . how Frances would ring the children up every night just as they went to bed, and always upset them. It was a very unhappy set-up.'⁵

Whatever Diana's recollections of her sadness in the first year after her mother left, as time went on that view became a distortion of the truth. Mary Clarke, whom Diana's father engaged to look after the two younger children in February 1971, remembered: 'When I look back to life at Park House, I do think to myself what a wonderful free and easy life we had. Always I remember just laughter and jokes. Diana was a real tease.'⁶ Diana spent the first fourteen years of her life at Park House, a solid Victorian mansion built of the rust-coloured local carrstone with large bow win-dows, a servants' wing and stabling. It was no architectural gem, but the Spencer children remembered it as 'lovely'. The house was large and roomy with open fires in every main room including the nursery, while background heating was provided by huge Edwardian radiators. The entrance led into a flagged hall with huge stone slabs, from which a stone staircase with wrought-iron balustrade led to the upper floor. Off the hall there were big, light rooms with marble fireplaces, bow windows and cornices with tongue and egg moulding. A large cedar tree, planted at the time the house was built, still stands on the lawn in front of the house, cattle graze in the fields beyond and surrounding trees provide shelter from the icy winds blowing in from the Wash to the north and the North Sea to the east. The windows look out beyond the lawn to green fields and to the south over Sandringham Park.

Mary Clarke's memory of life at Park House was very different from the unhappy household of a previous employee's recollection. 'I was impressed from the start by how happy and self-contained the children were,' she wrote, 'and how they always found so much to do to amuse themselves.'[7] A cousin remembers Park House as 'a great family house, everything was family about it, nothing daunting. You felt it was well used and enjoyed but predictable. Not opulent, nothing of that kind, just cosy and predictable.' Diana kept a huge collection of stuffed furry animals in her bedroom; poignantly, she referred to them as 'my family'. There were lots of live animals: Johnnie's black Labrador gun dog, Jill the springer spaniel, Diana's bad-tempered cat Marmalade, and her collection of hamsters, rabbits and guinea pigs. 'She loved animals when she was a child,' her mother said. 'I think you want something to love, and she loved everything that was small and furry or had feathers. She had rabbits, guinea pigs, hamsters; a long succession of animals to care for. She outgrew it and took on people . . . But the animals were super-comfortable and rather well catered for – well looked after, well cleaned out. She had a great consciousness they were dependent on her. She did the dirty work.' There were ponies in the fields and stables, Diana could ride by the time she was three, although after an accident in which she broke her arm her enthusiasm for horses disappeared. There were swimming and tennis parties with the children of the local gentry when Diana liked to show off her diving skills. The family owned a beach hut at Brancaster where they picnicked, and also played and paddled on the huge beach at Holkham.

Diana became used to playing to the camera at an early age. Her father was a passionate photographer, snapping away on every occasion to fill the albums which he dedicated to each of his children. His early pictures registered Diana's shy habit of looking upwards from under her fringe, a habit which never left her. But, like all stars, she never took a bad picture: the camera loved her and she instinctively responded to the lens levelled at her. She had the capacity to pose but yet make the pose look natural, a lifelong characteristic. Wherever she was, she communicated with the camera.

The Spencer children were, with the exception of Diana, all bright academically. Her failure to keep up with her siblings in this area gave Diana a secret inferiority complex which she balanced by her belief in her own instinct. 'Diana was not stupid,' a cousin said of her. 'She was intelligent with this very, very quick wit.' Sarah, six years older than she was, the elder sister whom she hero-worshipped, was named after the Spencers' formidable ances- tor, Sarah Jennings, Duchess of Marlborough, and had many of her namesake's qualities. 'She is a most interesting character,' a cousin said of her. 'The most complex of them all I would have said. Very strong, very alive and alert, intelligent. Not terribly nice. An interesting woman but tough, without Diana's gentle side. She knows what she wants.' Sarah had that foxy look inherited from the red-haired Spencers and the overwhelming confidence of her mother. Jane, the least assertive of the four, managed to spend more time with her mother and Diana did not become close to her until later. Charles, another red-headed Spencer and academi- cally the brightest, was an equally strong character but wary, con- trolling and complex in his relationships. When he grew up, a relation was to say that he was a control freak and that they all, even his mother, were 'terrified of him'. But during their child- hood Diana mothered him and the two were very close. 'I've always seen him as the brains in the family,' Diana told Morton in 1991. 'I still see that. He's got S levels and things like that. I think that my brother being the youngest and the only boy was quite precious [to the family as the heir to Althorp] ... I was the girl who was supposed to be a boy. Being third in line was a very good position to be in – I got away with murder. I was my father's favourite, no doubt about that.

'I longed to be as good as Charles in the schoolroom. I was never jealous of him. I so understand him. He's very like me as opposed to my two sisters. Like me he will always suffer. There's something in us that attracts that department . . .'[8]

In the absence of their parents, the children congregated in the big kitchen begging for treats from the cook. It was a pattern in Diana's behaviour: even when she grew up and married she preferred the company of her staff to that of the 'grown-ups'. The kitchen or the butler's pantry was where she felt at home. The children had a nanny who was so young and inexperienced that she was more of a childminder than a nanny; they ignored her for the company of the cook. Ruth Fermoy, living four miles away at nearby Hillington, was the distant power in the household, hiring the staff and supporting Johnnie. The staff was headed by a couple, Johnnie's former army batman, Mr Smith, and his wife, who lived over the stables and ran the house, doing most of the work, including the shopping, except the nannying and the cooking. They were devoted to Johnnie and aloof with the other staff, the nanny and the cook, whom they treated as outsiders. They all lived off the estate so venison and pheasant featured largely on the menu. 'Bought food', food from the regular shops, was rarely allowed. Vegetables came straight from the garden. The children complained – 'Can't we have lamb chops' – but to no avail.

The children reacted differently to their situation: although Sarah and Jane, being older and at boarding school when the separation happened, were less affected, Sarah at least reacted by being naughty, as indeed to some extent they all did. Sarah was the worst behaved, 'a horror' an employee recalled: she would bring her pony into the kitchen and ride it round the table despite the cook's protests. Diana remembered being extremely badly behaved towards the young and inexperienced 'nannies' who were imposed on them, sticking pins into their seat cushions and throwing their clothes out of the window. Both parents were so traumatized by feelings of guilt (on Frances's side), humiliation and despair (on Johnnie's), that they spoiled the children and exercised little parental control. Like many children of divorce, the Spencers manipulated their parents to get what they wanted. Diana became extremely adept at pushing and cajoling for what she wanted in the certainty that no one would say no to her Machiavellian behaviour, which she would indulge in with devastating effect years later.

Ostracized as a bolter, Frances never came back to Norfolk. Park House, for all its amenities, conspicuously lacked a maternal figure. Ruth Fermoy and Cynthia Spencer did their best to cheer the children, teaching them bridge and card games. Lady Margaret Douglas-Home, Jolly Jack's sister, was a stimulating presence in the children's life; known as 'Aunt Margaret', she was in fact their great-aunt. As Charles remembered, 'Aunt Margaret was a life-enhancing force, her deep and generous laugh always at the ready, a passion for gossip evidence of an enquiring, rather than a malicious mind. To visit her in her small cottage in Burnham Market . . . was to experience humour of the greatest breadth, and intelligence of a rare intensity . . . Few were not bewitched by her mischievous chuckle.'[9]

After her divorce was made final in April 1969, with Johnnie granted a divorce on the grounds of her adultery and given custody of the children, Frances had married Peter Shand Kydd in May 1969. Before that there had been agonizing weekend visits by the two younger children to their mother in London: 'I remember Mummy crying an awful lot and every Saturday when we went up for weekends, every Saturday night, standard procedure, she would start crying. On Saturday we would both see her crying. "What's the matter, Mummy?" "Oh, I don't want you to leave tomorrow . . ."' It was, as Diana said, 'devastating' for a nine-year-old. 'Holidays were always very grim because we had a four-week holiday. Two weeks Mummy and two weeks Daddy and the trauma of going from one house to another and each individual parent trying to make it up in their area with material things rather than the actual tactile stuff, which is what we both craved for but neither of us ever got. When I say neither of us my other two sisters were busy at prep school and were sort of out of the house whereas my brother and I were very much stuck together.'[10] A year before she died, Ruth Fermoy, looking back, told a cousin, 'I feel those two younger ones have been very, very damaged by the separation, divorce, which the older two hadn't.' Years later Diana told one of her mother figures how difficult it had been for her because 'her mother would buy her a dress [then] her father would buy her another one. And there were always these disputes. And for holidays, for ever. Torn between the two . . . she loved her father but I don't think she really loved her mother, she felt sorry for her mother sometimes . . . but she didn't trust her . . .'[11] The children, according to people who knew them, had an 'awful upbringing' with no rules beyond eating everything on their plates and writing thank-you letters.

Again Diana was exaggerating: the sadness of the early years after the divorce blotted out the happy times of her Norfolk childhood. As Mary Clarke wrote: 'A child who was truly, deeply traumatized, would not be able to maintain the contentment Diana continually displayed, apart from those occasional hiccups, throughout the time I knew her.' These 'hiccups' were prompted by the children's returning from their time with their mother: Charles took the situation quite naturally but Diana behaved strangely, the result perhaps of her mother's emotive farewell: 'Don't worry, you'll be all right, you'll settle, don't forget what I said, please ring me.' When Mary Clarke told them how happy their father would be to see them, Diana glanced sideways at her and said how sad her mother would be to be all on her own. Charles, used to his sister's dramatizations, said sharply, 'You know Mummy is not on her own, Diana, and you always say that about Daddy too.' When they reached Park House, Diana's bubbly self was replaced by a shy, deliberately withdrawn, little girl. She thought that if she appeared too excited to see him he might think that she was happier with him than with her mother. When Johnnie held out the prospect of a tea party at Sandringham with Princes Andrew and Edward, Diana said she didn't want to go, pleading a headache; showing a strength of will characteristic of her, she resisted all her father's attempts to persuade her.[12] Whether this was a misguided attempt to show loyalty to her mother by punishing her father, or whether she felt that the distress caused her by their split deserved to be demonstrated, is impossible to tell. Similar incidents were to occur later in life when she behaved in the same way to her husband.

According to Mary Clarke such royal invitations were rare; the

two families did not often socialize. The Spencer children took
their royal neighbours for granted and were not in awe of them.
Among the few occasions when they did see the Royal Family
was Sunday church which they attended only when the Queen
was in residence; Johnnie thought that the Queen would notice
their absence and think it odd. 'We were all shunted over to
Sandringham for [sic] holidays. Used to go and see *Chitty Chitty
Bang Bang*, the film. We hated it so much. We hated going over
there. The atmosphere was always very strange when we went
there and I used to kick and fight anyone who tried to make us
go over there and Daddy was most insistent because it was rude,'
Diana recalled.[13]

The Reverend Reginald Sweet, Latin teacher and chaplain at
her second school, however, had a different story to tell: 'Diana
was very keen on Prince Andrew,' he recalled. 'He was her great
holiday friend. She had all these photographs on her desk and . . .
she said, "Mr Sweet, when I grow up I'm going to marry Prince
Andrew." I said, "Really, Diana?" "Yes, I'm going to marry him
and he's my friend." The impression I got is that they knew
each other very well and used to spend time together during the
holidays.'[14] Diana's nanny, Janet Thompson, remembered walking
into the drawing room at Sandringham to find the Queen playing
hide and seek with the six-year-old Andrew and five-year-old
Diana. At tea, Charles walked in, very much the elder brother.
'Everything all right? Looks like a good party to me.'[15]

In reality Diana knew that both her parents loved her and that
she was her father's favourite. When the children got to know
Peter Shand Kydd they liked him very much. 'Peter was humorous,
generous, spontaneous and exciting,' Charles recorded. Diana and
Charles's first meeting with him was in 1969 at Liverpool Street
Station when they arrived off the train from Norwich. Diana
remembered saying to Frances, 'Where's your new husband? "He's
at the ticket barrier." And there was this very good-looking,
handsome man and we were longing to love him and we accepted
him and he was great to us and spoilt us rotten.'[16] It was Peter
Shand Kydd who first christened Diana 'Duch', short for 'Duchess'.

The name, prompted by Diana's at times haughty behaviour, stuck: not only her family but all her Sloaney friends used it. When Peter and Frances moved to Itchenor in West Sussex, the children spent happy holidays there sailing with him and his three children. His presence made their time with their mother more relaxing and normal. When, after the second custody case, it was agreed that Johnnie and Frances should share the children's time together, Frances and Peter started looking for a proper home with plenty of space. They found an eighteenth-century farmhouse, Arden-caple, on the Isle of Seil off the west coast of Scotland, with 1000 acres of wild farmland and spectacular views. Diana and Charles loved their visits, the freedom, the beauty and the wild landscape – sailing, fishing, lobster-potting. Diana kept a Shetland pony called Soufflé there. At her boarding school, West Heath, she pinned a poster of the island above her bed. Charles Spencer recalled Ardencaple as 'a magical place which Diana and I adored'. Later the Shand Kydds bought a 2000-acre ranch at Yass in New South Wales where they spent six weeks each summer, and the children joined them there.

Diana's education was of the undemanding nature which in those days applied to girls of her age and class. She was first taught by her mother's governess, Gertrude Allen, known as 'Ally', who lived in the nearby village of Dersingham. Ally would collect Diana from Park House and take her to a neighbour's house for morning lessons with the children of the local gentry; while the children ate their packed lunches in the nursery with the owner and the children's nanny, Ally ate hers in isolated splendour in the dining room, her lunch specially prepared by the resident cook. Afterwards she would take the children for a walk accompanied by her ferocious dog.

In January 1968 Diana was enrolled at Silfield private school, a day school for girls and boys in Gayton, on the outskirts of King's Lynn. The school, housed in a large early twentieth-century sub-urban family house in a variety of architectural styles, was, as a notice board still proclaims, 'founded in 1955 for 5–11-year-olds'. There was a good-sized garden dominated by a large monkey puzzle tree contemporary with the house, and rambling wooden outbuildings including a 30-foot room with wooden panelling and false timbering and a fireplace which served as an assembly and games room. A small school with forty pupils, attended by the children of local farmers and gentry (including Diana's best friend, Alexandra Loyd, daughter of the Queen's estate agent at Sandringham), it was a cosy place with a family atmosphere. Diana was remembered by the headmistress, Jean Lowe, for her kindness to younger children, her love of animals and 'general helpfulness' but not for her academic potential. Later, she was shown up by her younger brother, Charles, who revenged himself for her superior strength and height in their sibling fights by calling her 'Brian' after the slow-witted snail in the children's programme *The Magic Roundabout*. It was here too, the first closed organization outside her home of which she had experience, that she found she was the only child of divorced parents. Sadly, she used to dedicate her work in art class 'To Mummy and Daddy'.

When she was nine Diana went to board at Riddlesworth Hall, some one and a half hours' drive from Sandringham. At first she had resented being made to leave her father, towards whom she had become very protective since the divorce but, despite her complaints – 'if you love me you won't leave me here' – she confessed that she 'loved being at school'. She boasted about being naughty and wanting to laugh and muck about, of taking a dare and escaping from her dormitory to run down the drive in the dark. Riddlesworth was a rectangular classical-style house, standing high with many windows and views over the surrounding gardens and fields. It had the feel of a lived-in house; elaborate light fittings, glass cases of stuffed birds and rather gloomy trophies of large animals were traces of the previous occupants. There were plaster and gilt ceilings in the larger rooms which were light and well proportioned; the general atmosphere was cheerful and friendly. Diana was not among strangers; several of the girls she knew from the surrounding families were there with her: Alexandra Loyd, her cousin Diana Wake-Walker, and Claire Pratt, daughter of her godmother, Sarah Pratt. Pupils were encouraged to bring pets, which were housed in 'Pets' Corner' in the garden within sight of the house. Diana became head of Pets' Corner and brought her treasured guinea pig Peanuts with her. She never carried off any academic prizes but she did win a prize with Peanuts for 'Best Kept Guinea Pig' and the Leggatt Cup 'for helpfulness'. She won prizes for swimming and diving: 'But in the academic department, you might as well forget about that!' she laughed. 'I ate and ate. It was always a great joke – let's get Diana to eat three kippers and six pieces of bread. I did all that,' the future bulimic said proudly. What with the pets and the Norfolk friends, school was merely an extension of her normal life and simple, restricted horizon.

Johnnie Althorp always drove Diana back to Riddlesworth, much as he had joined in the school run to Silfield, and where he was remembered for his easy manner and interest in people. At Riddlesworth, the headmistress, Patricia Wood, said that all the kitchen staff and grounds people particularly remembered him. 'When you talked to the kitchen ladies they couldn't remember much about Diana because she was just one of the little girls, but they could all remember her father. He was a very conspicuous gentleman . . . very tall and noticeable and almost the first thing he did when he brought her to the school after the holidays was to go down in the kitchens and talk to them.'[17] Johnnie was interested in everybody he met, regardless of background, a quality Diana inherited from him. 'My father,' Sarah told an interviewer, 'had an instinctive way with people . . . People would talk to him and he was gripped . . . He loved people. And Diana did too. I don't think that quality has got anything to do with upbringing. I think you've either got it or you haven't . . . it's either in you when you're born, or it's not.'[18]

Aged twelve, in September 1973, after three years at Riddlesworth, Diana followed Sarah and Jane to a new school, West Heath, near Sevenoaks in Kent. Located in another splendid country house, West Heath was the natural progression from Riddlesworth: small – there were only 120 girls – friendly, with the emphasis on happiness and good behaviour rather than academic achievement. In many ways such schools were throwbacks to the fifties, when girls of good family were not expected to do much more than prepare themselves for marriage. 'Hamsters and knitting were what they were about,' a contemporary remembered. 'Everyone came out confident and happy,' a schoolmate recorded, 'and there was very little angst . . . It was a relaxed place.' When Diana arrived, Jane, 'the good Spencer' then aged sixteen, was a prefect with an excellent academic record. Sarah was no longer there, having been expelled for drunkenness two years earlier. She had been a success both academically and in sport, winning prizes and appearing in the school plays. But, brilliant, forceful and wilful, she was bored at West Heath. Somehow, according to her own admission, she laid hands on an astonishing variety of drink. 'I used to drink because I was bored,' she said. 'I would drink anything: whisky, Cointreau, gin, sherry or, most often, vodka because the staff couldn't smell that.'[19] But one day in 1971 the staff did notice: she was drunk and instantly expelled. A few years later there were to be further signs of trouble when she was affected by serious eating disorders.

In her own way Diana was a success at West Heath, although she liked later on to emphasize her image as a rebel. The head-mistress, Ruth Rudge, a keen observer, recorded that when Diana first arrived she was 'wary of adults, often prickly with her peers . . . but was lucky enough to find herself in a group of lively, talented, caring individuals, some of whom she already knew, and soon gained confidence in her new surroundings and found her niche socially'.[20] The friends she made at West Heath, notably Carolyn Pride and Laura Greig, were to become part of her loyal inner circle, supporting her through thick and thin, through the depths of despair and beyond. The trauma of her parents' divorce never quite left her: '. . . she came and talked to me quite a lot,' the matron, Violet Allen, said. 'Of course she missed her mother and father. The other [girls] who had divorces felt the same way. Some accepted it and some had more difficulty with it. No doubt about it, Diana found it difficult to accept. She was vulnerable in some things. I can't put a finger on it, but it probably all had to do with the insecurity and break-up of [her parents'] marriage.'[21]

She learned to play the piano, took lessons in ballet, tap and ballroom dance – her greatest relaxation. She won the school dancing competition one year and cups in swimming and diving every year. She developed her strong sense of sympathy for the suffering and the needy when she visited the mentally handicapped in the local hospital: when there were dances she would manoeuvre the wheelchairs from the front, facing the patients as if she were dancing with them, instead of, as was more usual, pushing from behind. In her day-to-day life Diana was at times fierce in her emotional responses, unforgiving to people who had offended her. 'She had a very strong character,' her headmistress said. 'She went about getting what she wanted . . .' In her last year Diana was named a prefect, and carried out her role so successfully that she was awarded a special prize for service – 'for anyone who has done things that otherwise might have gone unsung,' Ruth Rudge said. 'She was dependable in her own doings, reliable, and went out of her way to help people. She was generous with her time.'[22] When she was not being dutiful and dependable, Diana immersed herself in the romantic world of Barbara Cartland's novels in which strong men wooed virgin brides and love triumphed over all. It was perhaps the worst preparation for life in general and her own life in particular that she could have had.

Just as Diana was creating her own stable world on her own terms at West Heath, life at Park House and her relationship with her father there, the hitherto immutable centre for her since childhood, was about to change forever. The one thing the children had always dreaded happened. A new, powerful woman came into their father's life – Raine Legge, then Countess of Dartmouth. The first inkling they had of Raine's existence had come in the summer of 1972 when Johnnie invited Raine to lunch at Park House. Raine Dartmouth, or Legge as she was always then known, was a formidable woman, a beauty, immaculately dressed, made-up and coiffed, with a sharp intelligence and a will as determined as any of the Spencer children. She and Johnnie had met and fallen in love although Raine was still married to her first husband and was the mother of four children. She was also the daughter of another formidable character, the immensely successful Barbara Cartland, Diana's favourite novelist.

Sarah, it seems, who now had a London life, had heard gossip about her father's friendship with Lady Dartmouth which she had passed on to Diana and her siblings. The children were determined that no one should come between them and their beloved father whom they regarded as their property. When Johnnie told them he had invited Lady Dartmouth to lunch, the children's hackles were immediately raised. Diana's reaction to this immaculate vision, so far removed from the county ladies of their experience, was suppressed giggles. Raine was charming and gracious but oblivious to the children's covert hostility or, if she was not, determined not to let it bother her. In the end Sarah, with no other outlet for her enmity, burped loudly and deliberately. Johnnie said 'Sarah!' to which she cheekily replied that in Arab countries a burp was recognized as a sign of appreciation. Her father was so appalled that he told her to leave the table, which she did. Diana attempted to defend her, only to be told, 'That's enough, Diana.' Loyally, Diana riposted that she did not feel well and asked permission to leave, a request which her father readily granted. It had not been a good beginning.

The children's antennae were quivering at the prospect of this new woman in their father's life. 'We didn't like her one bit,' Charles said. 'As a child you instinctively feel things and with her I very much instinctively felt things.' The next encounter was to be at Sarah's coming-out party for her eighteenth birthday the following year, a fabulous occasion arranged by Johnnie at Castle Rising, a Norman ruin in Norfolk. Raine was among the four hundred guests and had taken a hand in its organization, finding a costume for Johnnie as Henry VIII and for Sarah a dress worn by Geneviève Bujold as Anne Boleyn in the 1969 film *Anne of the Thousand Days*. Sarah was in her element dancing with her boyfriend, Gerald Grosvenor, heir to the Duke of Westminster, and driving off in her father's birthday present to her, a green MGB GT sports car.

Sarah may have been too happy to notice the growing relationship between her father and the Countess of Dartmouth. Raine was determined to land Johnnie as her second husband. Her first, Gerald Legge, was already on his way out as far as she was concerned: she frequently gave dinner parties without him. Raine was dogged, ambitious and devastatingly efficient: by the time she and Johnnie met again for the first time since his marriage, she had already led a successful and high-profile public life as a councillor for Westminster for eleven years, for eight as the LCC member for Lewisham West, then as a member of the newly formed Greater London Council, when she had made her name opposing the licensing of the film of James Joyce's *Ulysses*, which she described as 'disgusting and degrading'. 'I like things that present life and sex in a glamorous way,'[23] she declared, true to the theme of her mother's novels. She had been a great success as chairman of the Historic Buildings Board; in 1971 she became a member of the English Tourist Board and headed an advisory committee to the government on the environment. When she resigned from the committee in protest at the Covent Garden development scheme, she became a national figure and a surprising heroine to the liberal left. 'It is all too easy to dismiss this particular woman . . . as a good-looking, immaculately dressed, effusive member of the aristocracy who somehow gets offered positions of power', the *Guardian* wrote, '[but] behind the saccharine image there stands an extremely able politician, a feminine but tough bargainer . . .' In 1972 she was asked to become Chairman of the United Kingdom Executive Committee for European Architectural Heritage Year 1975. Her mission was to preserve historic towns and buildings; she wrote a book, *What Is Our Heritage?*, and co-opted Johnnie Spencer to the Youth Panel to promote the cause in his capacity as chairman of the National Association of Boys' Clubs. She also asked him to help with photographs for her book: it was obvious to colleagues that the couple were in love.

Johnnie was attracted to strong women and, if anything, Raine was even more forceful and dynamic than Frances. He had been lonely ever since Frances left: Raine's looks, wit and physical attraction bowled him over. Being rather slow and diffident he left

3. 'I'm Lady Diana'

'I remember being a fat, podgy, no make-up, unsmart lady but I made a lot of noise and he [Prince Charles] liked that' (Diana to Andrew Morton)[1]

On 9 June 1975, Jack, 7th Earl Spencer, died and Diana's cosy family life at Park House came to an end. At first she was excited by her new title, Lady Diana, so much grander than the former Hon[ourable], and ran round West Heath shouting, 'I'm Lady Diana . . .' It was when she got home for the holidays that the real impact of the change in the family's circumstances hit her. Park House was being packed up in preparation for the move to the Spencer family home, Althorp. Her father was no longer Viscount Althorp but the 8th Earl Spencer. Diana's reaction to all this was to binge on peaches with her friend Alex Loyd at the beach hut at Brancaster.

Diana recalled: 'When I was 13 [actually fourteen; Diana was born 1 July 1961] we moved to Althorp in Northampton and that was a terrible wrench, leaving Norfolk, because that's where everybody who I'd grown up with lived. We had to move because grandfather died and life took a very big turn because my stepmother, Raine, appeared on the scene, supposedly incognito. She used to sort of join us, accidentally find us in places and come and sit down and pour [sic] us with presents and we all hated her so much because we thought she was going to take Daddy away from us . . .'[2] Leaving the house in which she had been born and spent all the years of her life so far was like another abandonment, another stage in her life like the departure of her mother. They had rarely visited Althorp and their feared grandfather and they had not liked it. Charles described it as 'a difficult phase in all our lives: uprooted from our childhood haunts and friends, and marooned in a park the size of Monaco', while the 121-room house seemed to them 'such an old man's house, reflecting my grandfather's Edwardian tastes, in a chilling time warp complete with the permeating smell of Trumper's hair oil and the ubiquitous tocking of grandfather clocks – their ticking always seemed too subtle a sound, getting absorbed in the oak of the floorboards and the fabric of the tapestries'.[3]

While Althorp was never to be 'home' to Diana as Park House had been, it reconnected her to her ancestors in a way which was to make her able to stand up to and even look down on the Royal Family. Even to someone as uninterested in history as Diana, the grandeur of Althorp, and the serried ranks of five centuries of distinguished forebears looking down on her from its walls, could not fail to impart a sense of the historic importance of her bloodlines. A historian friend of Diana's put it this way: 'Diana had sort of vaguely grasped, although being historically ignorant had not completely grasped, that those old Whig families like the Cavendishes and the Russells and her lot and one or two others, they in a way felt they were older and grander than the royal house, that they had put the House of Hanover on the throne when they were just German princelings, absolutely nothing, come from nowhere, couldn't speak a word of English . . . Parliament made George I monarch under the direction of the Whig oligarchy of which her family was a very important constituent founding member. So that in some way she had not married above her by marrying Prince Charles, if anything she'd married beneath her. Now I'm not sure that she ever formulated this view precisely in her mind, but it was sort of there I felt. "Who is he [Prince Charles] to look down on me and to say 'They're praising you because you're married to me, not because they like you'. 'You know, "Who is he to say this?" '[4] Traditionally, the Spencers and their aristocratic connections like the Cavendishes (Dukes of Devonshire) were Whigs who upheld the rights of the people against the overweening power of the monarch, as opposed to the Tory tradition of loyalty to the throne. 'The Tory tradition in the aristocracy,' said the historian Ben Pimlott, 'was deeply loyal to the monarchy; the Whig tradition was basically rather contemptuous. This difference can be exaggerated but there's a grain of truth, not necessarily in their traditions but in their style, and how they related to those traditions. The Whigs were individualists.'[5]

Althorp is not a beautiful house – the warm brick of the original Tudor great mansion was covered over in the late eighteenth century with silvery white tiles which give it a cold appearance – but it is surrounded by idyllic English countryside, the rolling acres of grassland which nurtured the sheep whose wool was the source of the original Spencer fortune. Spencers had occupied Althorp for nearly five centuries since the original John Spencer, known as 'the Founder', had acquired the land in 1507 and begun to build his mansion, acquiring more land, planting trees and creating the surrounding park. The family also owned the magnificent eighteenth-century Spencer House in London overlooking Green Park, but this was rented out in Diana's day. Spencer wealth and possessions had increased over the centuries, some of the more splendid through the first Diana Spencer, daughter of Lady Anne Churchill, whose parents were John Churchill, 1st Duke of Marlborough and his wife, Sarah Jennings, one of the most remarkable and difficult women of her day. The Spencer tendency for falling out with members of the family – it is said Sarah changed her will fifty times – may well have been passed down from her. The Churchill connection was much cherished by the family who were extremely proud of being related to the 1st Duke of Marlborough, whose great victories over the French in the first decade of the eighteenth century had brought him fame and riches and the great palace of Blenheim, named after his most celebrated victory and built for him by a grateful nation. Winston Churchill was born Winston Spencer Churchill: one day Diana's grandfather, Jack Spencer, found Winston Churchill in his cherished Muniment Room, smoking a cigar while researching the life of their mutual ancestor, the 1st Duke of Marlborough. Peremptorily he ordered Churchill to douse his cigar in a glass of water. Sarah, the 1st Duchess, had left her Spencer heirs her great collections of paintings and jewellery and the Marlborough Silver, the reward for the 1st Duke's campaigns, including the lavish gold and silver pieces bestowed on him by Queen Anne after Blenheim.

Diana's ancestors included not only Sarah Jennings, whose pride led her to snub even her sovereign and former friend, Queen Anne, but also another outstanding woman, Georgiana, Duchess of Devonshire, the headstrong beauty whose reckless exploits in Whig politics and at the gaming tables made her the most famous woman of her day. The blood of these distant ancestors meant that Diana was never going to be the mousy little girl some people thought – or perhaps hoped – that she would be. 'Spencers are very difficult and complicated people,' a Spencer relation said. 'The Queen Mother once said to me, "You know the Spencer women are extremely unusual and difficult!" and that's how they are. They also have an unforgiving side to them which seems to run through the family a bit. And I think that that way she had with the inability to sustain friendships and relationships seems to be one of the characteristics of them.' She said of her own Spencer mother: 'She was incredibly like Diana. In the same things. The sort of manipulation of reality, as I call it, and the conflict and then reunion and so on.'[6]

At first life at Althorp when Diana and Charles moved there seemed like a continuation of their childhood, although on a grand scale. Although latterly there had been a butler named Betts at Park House, his services had been abruptly dispensed with when the house was closed. At Althorp, however, there was not only a butler, Ainsley Pendrey, who had served the previous Earl, but a footman as well and seven other indoor servants. 'The early days were very happy ones and jolly good fun, with no bowing and scraping,' Betty Andrews, who started work at Althorp in 1975, told Angela Levin, author of a joint biography of Johnnie and Raine. The children would rush into the kitchen to find something to eat. 'Diana even used to cook for the staff. She loved to make bread and butter pudding for us and rice or milk pudding for herself,' Betty Andrews recalled.[7] Diana, always so domesticated, did her own washing and ironing and often Charles's too. This nurturing, almost domestic slave, side of Diana repeated itself in later life: she would do all the household chores for her sister Sarah, iron shirts for her platonic boyfriends before her marriage and, in the year of her death, do the ironing for Annabel Goldsmith and Jemima Khan on their trip to Pakistan. It was never a Marie Antoinette act, rather a response to a need in herself, to be useful, to show her skills, and to be 'tidy', another of her favourite words. At school people noticed her obsessive tidiness. She even used the word 'tidy' about keeping her virginity for the right man. The atmosphere at Althorp, according to Andrews, was 'happy-go-lucky – all three sisters got on well together'. Diana would toboggan down the grand front staircase on a tea tray, and dance by herself in the great Wootton Hall, designed as the entrance to the house in the early eighteenth century, with pictures and plasterwork reflecting the family passion for hunting.

Raine's presence radically changed the atmosphere. She had always wanted a grand country house, which Gerald Dartmouth had not possessed. Although not yet married to Johnnie, she was ever-present, staying in the India Silk Bedroom across the corridor from Johnnie's room. She began to redecorate the house, paying the cost herself. Johnnie was cash poor, as always, and now faced with a £2 million bill for death duties. She was desperate to marry Johnnie and began to fear that his hostile children would eventually frustrate her. None of them, and Sarah in particular, made any secret of their dislike. Sarah, never averse to talking to reporters, used their inquisitive telephone calls to drop acid into the newspapers about Raine. To one inquiry about Lord Spencer's relationship with Lady Dartmouth, she replied that her father was in bed with Lady Dartmouth and she wasn't going to disturb them. She told another: 'Since my grandfather died last June and we moved from Sandringham to Althorp, Lady Dartmouth has been an all too frequent visitor . . .'[8] When asked why Lady Dartmouth was spending so much time at Althorp, she replied, 'She is helping my father to open the house on a commercial basis. In my grandfather's time he did not care for the idea of the public walking around his house. Lady Dartmouth is writing a guide for it with my father.' Diana's protest was characteristic: a member of the paying public remembered seeing her 'acting the part of Cinderella' sitting beside the fire as the public walked past. The children used to chant 'Raine, Raine, go away' intending that she should hear them.

But Raine did not go away. In May 1976 Gerald Dartmouth obtained a divorce on the grounds of her adultery; two months later, on 14 July 1976, Johnnie and Raine married at Caxton Hall register office in London. He did not tell his children beforehand what he was going to do. Their fury knew no bounds, as he had anticipated. In 1992 Diana told Peter Settelen: 'Sarah rang me up, she said, "Have you seen the newspapers?" So I said, "What?" "Daddy's married Raine." I said, "My God, how do you know that?" "It's in the *Express*." We were so angry, but Sarah said, "Right, Duch" — my nickname was Duch — "you go in and sort him out."

'He said, "I want to explain to you why, um, I've got married to Raine." And I said, "Well, we don't like her." And he said, "I know that, but you'll grow to love her, as I have." And I said, "Well, we won't." I kept on saying we not I . . . I was the little crusader here . . . and I got really angry and I, if I remember rightly, I slapped him across the face, and I said, "That's from all of us, for hurting us", and walked out of the room and slammed the door. He followed me and he got me by the wrist and turned me round and said, "Don't you ever talk to me like that again." And I said, "Well, don't you ever do that to us again", and walked off.'[9]

The four Spencer children had always stood together, metaphorically and physically. 'They were always very close as young people. Always did everything together, on any family occasion they were always in a group together, quite daunting for other people — it seemed like they were protecting each other . . .' a Spencer relation said. For anyone less concentrated on her goal than Raine Dartmouth, the hostile Spencer children gathered like a praetorian guard round their father would have been deeply intimidating. There had even been moments when she feared Johnnie's devotion to his children would prevent him from marrying her. After the wedding, when Raine became undisputed mistress of Althorp, things became even worse. The children's proprietorial attitude towards their father had not changed, and now they felt excluded. They remained impervious to Raine's charms. When friends were invited to stay at Althorp by Johnnie and Raine, they noticed 'a terrible air of strain between all three girls' which was 'very, very awkward' and that the sisters avoided saying a word to Raine if they could. On one social weekend in Yorkshire where there was a ball for the young at Haddon Hall, a friend of Johnnie's and Raine's sat next to Diana at lunch. 'Suddenly her eyes glinted, and she said, "You're a friend of my stepmother's, aren't you?" He replied, "I hope I'm a friend of your father's too."' – 'It was very unpleasant,' he commented. Sarah, who was in touch with the media, was more active in her enmity – leaking disagreeable stories about Raine to a tabloid reporter.[10] Even Jane, the quietest and least unstable of the Spencer quartet, 'the best of the lot' in a family friend's opinion, could not entirely restrain her hostility. On being asked at a dinner how often she went to Althorp, she replied loudly in Raine's hearing – 'When I'm asked.'

So Diana, like the others, felt a kind of estrangement from her father. She loved him but she saw less of him. He remained a loving father but in her view he belonged to Raine and not to her. It did not help the following year when she took her O levels. She took them twice and failed them twice and as a result had to leave West Heath at the age of sixteen. Diana said, 'At the age of fourteen I just remember thinking that I wasn't very good at anything, that I was hopeless. My brother was always the one who was getting exams at school and I was the dropout . . .'[11] 'I was always told by my family that I was the thick one and that my brother was the clever one and I was always so conscious of that.' 'I used to go to the headmistress,' she added, 'crying, saying, I wish I wasn't so stupid,' she said later.[12] Ruth Rudge denies her ever having done this: 'I never remember walking around with her and feeding her aspirins the night before, which I have done a number of times with other girls, [but] I didn't see any signs of panic when she took exams.'[13] Friends of Diana's have attributed it to 'sheer laziness and the fact that she was never pushed'. She excelled in the things she liked doing but, when it came to academic work, she simply gave up even before she started. A relative explained it: 'I think she was not stupid, she was intelligent and she had this very, very quick wit, but I think it reflected on her lack of confidence, her inability to achieve at school and sometimes if you're emotionally damaged in some way you can't sustain concentration or learning, and I think a certain part of you cuts out the ability to absorb and process and construct, and I think that's what happened to her. She certainly wasn't stupid.' The same relation attributed Diana's backwardness in formal education to her status as a 'replacement baby', the girl born after the death of John: 'I have noticed in other families where there has been what's called a replacement baby, that the baby that's been born after a death has certain things imposed on it which are not really relevant and they seem to feel things which have perhaps been in other people's minds . . .' In compensation, Diana developed an almost mystical belief in the power and rightness of her own instinct which was to guide her, for better or for worse, through her entire life. She had, or so she later claimed, a sense of her own destiny, that she was apart from the rest, designed for higher things. If so, who needs exams?

Things were changing in all their lives: Raine was extremely social. There were constant house parties, balls, shooting parties: the children were banished to the nursery floor to leave room for the guests. Entertaining became more formal, and under Raine, demanding and a perfectionist, staff turnover was high. A senior employee told Angela Levin of the children's reaction to their stepmother: 'With the exception of Jane, who wasn't too bad, the children could not have been more difficult and cold to Raine. There was open hostility, not just to her as a person. They also disliked the way she dominated and became so possessive of their father which made them feel they had to compete with her for his attention.'[14] Rupert Hambro recalled his impression: 'It was as if she had put an iron fence around him. She also had a way of making people who played a part in his life before she arrived feel small. She was totally insensitive to Johnnie's family, his life and his interests. When you did see him she was his mouthpiece and if you asked him anything, she would answer. A lot of people are incredibly happy in an environment that takes any pressure away from them. I would describe Lord Spencer as being pretty close to that . . .'[15] Johnnie Spencer's aunt, Lady Margaret Douglas-Home, who knew the children well, saw to the heart of the problem: 'I don't think Raine went about it the right way,' she said. 'I don't think she is made to be a stepmother. She must be the only pebble on the beach and wasn't willing to take second place to Johnnie's children. She used to claim all of him the whole time and didn't like them interfering in her life with Johnnie. The children never liked it and they were old enough to know. I was very sorry for them. They looked miserable.'[16]

According to a friend of Raine's the great strength in the Althorp household during this time of strain was Pendrey the butler whom he described as 'droll and amusing and a great pillar'. He and his wife Maudie, the housekeeper, a Norfolk farmer's daughter, were a refuge for Diana, as Mrs Pendrey recalled:

When she came to live at Althorp, she was always shy. She used to blush ever so easily too, used to go scarlet. My husband adored Diana, we all did. She would come and see her father about every six or seven weeks. When we knew Diana was coming for the weekend my husband would get all her favourite food in and make sure she had everything up in her bedroom. She used to sleep in the nursery, in a little black iron bed . . . When she came to Althorp the first thing she did was come and find my husband, because she was a very lovely, very polite little girl – always called him Mr. Pendrey – . . . of course he used to spoil her.

After her father remarried, she used to come and talk to us quite a lot. She sometimes used to come and have lunch with us. She never had airs and graces. Diana was just an ordinary lovely girl. She was very sweet and all the staff loved her. They used to put flowers in her bedroom when she used to come to Althorp. We used to make a fuss of her and make sure she was someone important. My husband said to me, when he saw her start growing up . . . 'You wait. She's going to be someone very special'.[17]

Staying with friends in Norfolk one September weekend Diana had a premonition about her father. By her own account she told her friends that she felt her father was going to 'drop down' and that 'if he dies, he'll die immediately, otherwise he'll survive'. Next day, 19 September 1978, Johnnie collapsed as he was crossing the courtyard at Althorp: he had suffered a massive cerebral haemorrhage. He was taken unconscious to Northampton General Hospital where he developed pneumonia. Raine, despite the danger, insisted that he be transferred to the National Hospital for Nervous Diseases in Queen Square, London, where the facilities would be better. In a deep coma he was put on a life-support machine, and subsequently underwent a four-hour brain operation. Raine was heroic: sitting beside his bed as he lay unconscious, willing him to live. He appeared to recover, then four weeks after the operation he contracted pseudomonas, a rare virulent bacterium unresponsive to normal antibiotics, and was transferred to the Brompton Hospital. There he remained on the critical list and almost died eight times. Raine saved his life. Desperate, she asked her friend Bill Cavendish-Bentinck, later Duke of Portland and a director of the German pharmaceutical company Bayer, whether the company had any drug under testing that might help his condition. Cavendish-Bentinck told her that there was indeed one, Azlocillin, but that it was not yet on the market and that she needed the approval of Johnnie's doctors before it was tried out on him. She bullied them into agreement: 'I'd rather he died my way, doing something, than your way, doing nothing.' Samples were flown from Germany and given to Johnnie. Almost miraculously he recovered. Later he gave Raine a magnificent parure of rubies from Van Cleef & Arpels for saving his life.

Gratitude does not seem to have been among the feelings Raine's devotion to Johnnie provoked in his children. At one point Raine instructed nurses at Queen Square to prevent the children from disturbing their seriously ill father while she was with him. They waited for her to leave before sneaking in. A nurse remembered that they would have Sarah going up in the lift as

Raine was coming down. Unsurprisingly, they were rude to her, Jane being the only one to say hello. Diana, devastated, was in tears, although by her own account she was 'frightfully calm'. 'We saw another side of Raine which we hadn't anticipated,' she recalled, 'as she basically blocked us out of the hospital, she wouldn't let us see Daddy ... Anyway he got better and he basically changed character. He was one person before and another person after. He's remained estranged but adoring since.'[18]

Meanwhile, Diana's destiny had been taking her away from school and childhood towards a new and unexpected life. Since the previous summer Prince Charles had become involved with her sister Sarah. The two had met when Sarah, as an eligible twenty-two-year-old, was invited to join the house party at Windsor Castle for the racing week at Royal Ascot, at the insti-gation of Henriette Abel Smith, her godmother and one of the Queen's ladies-in-waiting. Prince Andrew, whom she had known as a child, introduced her to Prince Charles. Despite asking her tactlessly, 'Do you have anorexia?' — she was obviously very thin but denied the illness — the two got on. Sarah Spencer was recovering from a traumatic two years, suffering from the eating disorders anorexia nervosa and bulimia, setting a pattern for Diana's own reaction to stress. Years later Diana told patients at the Priory, a private clinic treating addictions on the outskirts of London, that she had first had symptoms of bulimia in the mid-seventies, attributing it to Sarah's experience: 'It started because Sarah was anorexic and I idolized her so much that I wanted to be like her.' If this is so — and Diana's statements are not always the truth of a situation, but sometimes her rereading of it from a distance in time — it certainly did not affect her seriously. While Sarah, who was 5 foot 7 inches tall, went down to 5 stone 10 pounds, photographs of Diana at the time show no signs whatever of serious slimming. Sarah suffered for two years: it was so severe at first that Frances had her taken to hospital. Frances attributed the illness to Sarah's break-up with Gerald Grosvenor after returning from a three-month stay with the Shand Kydds in Australia. This may be so but

Sarah had already shown signs of addiction problems when she drank to alleviate her boredom at school: the split with Grosvenor may well, however, have precipitated it.

Prince Charles enjoyed Sarah's sparkiness and irreverent wit and they made each other laugh. By mid-July the press were following their relationship: Sarah was seen with the Prince at polo and – always a test of the seriousness of one of Prince Charles's relationships – invited by the Queen to Balmoral. Sarah was extremely attractive, vital and witty: Prince Charles was amused by her but not, it seems, physically attracted. Diana later asserted that Sarah had been surprised that he had never tried to go to bed with her. Sarah invited Charles to a shoot at Althorp in November 1977. Diana was given the weekend off from West Heath to attend, meeting the Prince for the first time in a ploughed field near Nobottle Wood when Charles, according to his official biographer, found her 'jolly' and 'bouncy', a pretty, unaffected teenager. Diana herself recorded, perhaps with the benefit of hindsight, that her first impression was 'God, what a sad man'. Sarah, she said cattily in one of her favourite phrases, was 'all over him like a bad rash'.

At the dance that night at Althorp, Charles showed that he was attracted by the sixteen-year-old's high spirits. Diana said, 'I remember being a fat, podgy, no make-up, unsmart lady but I made a lot of noise and he liked that and he came up to me after dinner and we had a big dance and he said: "Will you show me the gallery [the Picture Gallery, a notable feature of Althorp] and I was just about to show him the gallery and my sister Sarah comes up and tells me to push off and I said, "At least let me tell you where the switches are because you won't know where they are", and I disappeared. And he was charm itself and when I stood next to him next day [out shooting], a 16-year-old for someone like that to show you any attention – I was just so sort of amazed. "Why would anyone like him be interested in me?" And it *was* interest.'[19]

Even her siblings began to notice that Diana had changed. 'She suddenly became sort of magnetic and people were interested in her as a character when she hit about 16,' her brother Charles,

who had gone up to Eton that year, 1977, remembered. 'Before
then she was quiet – I mean always up to something . . . never dull
– but quite quiet and shy. But I think as she started to become a
pretty young woman as opposed to a girl, she got some confidence
then. That started to open her up quite a lot and I think she realised
then that she had a knack for being the life and soul of the party.
People really enjoyed being around her.'[20]

Diana always gave it to be understood in her later accounts that
it was Prince Charles who made the running, but her piano teacher
and form mistress at West Heath, Penny Walker, gave a different
version:

She was always talking about Prince Charles . . . I can remember the
weekend she came back after she'd met him, because she couldn't talk
about anything else. She said: 'I've met him! At last I've met him' . . .
She had pictures of him up in her cubicle. It wasn't entirely unusual for
a girl from that kind of background, but it was unusual because it was
so consistent all the time she was at school. Her only talk was of him
and meeting him. I'm not sure there was any talk about marrying, but
she just seemed completely besotted, dreaming of escape, I should think,
into fairytale.[21]

Early the next year, 1978, Diana was dispatched to a finishing
school, the Institut Alpin Videmanette, in Switzerland, where she
was homesick. Always an obsessive letter writer, she wrote 120
letters in her first month there. She learned to ski but felt out of
her depth with the other girls, who were mostly Spanish or Italian.
At the end of one term, it was recognized that there was no point
in keeping her there and she was allowed to come home. She was
back in London for her sister Jane's wedding. Jane had become
engaged in 1977 to a Norfolk neighbour, Robert Fellowes, son of
the Queen's Sandringham land agent Sir William 'Billy' Fellowes,
and they were married in April 1978 with Diana as chief bridesmaid. Jane was only twenty, Robert Fellowes thirty-six, only five
years younger than Jane's mother. He too had been taught by Ally
as a young boy and had moved in exactly the same Norfolk circles

as the Spencer children when they lived at Park House. He was
also, like many of their relations, a courtier and member of the
royal household as the Queen's assistant private secretary. Tall,
slim and discreet, he had the perfect Establishment credentials,
then considered a prerequisite for royal service. He was an Etonian
and had served in the Scots Guards. As Jane put it somewhat un-
romantically, 'We have known each other all our lives and have
gradually grown closer.' Sarah, typically, stated, 'We had been
trying to trap him for years.'

The wedding itself took place at the Guards Chapel, Wellington
Barracks, a few hundred yards from Buckingham Palace, the bridegroom's 'office', and the reception was held at the old royal palace
of St James's, again part of the royal enclave. The Queen Mother
arrived with Ruth Fermoy, and the Duchess of Kent and Duke
and Duchess of Gloucester were among the guests, underlining
the fact that the young couple were part of the 'magic circle' round
the Crown. Frances paid for everything but, as a friend said, 'she
was almost a guest at her own daughter's wedding'. The fact that
she and Johnnie were not on speaking terms was obvious to
everyone who knew them. Raine was very much in evidence and
one of the wedding organizers had to be deputed to keep her out
of the family photographs. At the wedding, Diana bounced up to
one of the best known of the royal press gang, James Whitaker,
then of the *Daily Mirror*, one of Sarah's chief media contacts, and
introduced herself saying, 'You're James Whitaker, aren't you? I
know all about you. I'm Sarah's baby sister.' It was the beginning
of Diana's lifelong affair with the media.

Diana's approach to James Whitaker, perhaps the best known
of the 'rat pack' of tabloid reporters, was almost certainly prompted
by his recent role in her sister's life, specifically the ending of her
close friendship with Prince Charles. Sarah, according to Diana,
had by now 'got frightfully excited about the whole thing'. Over-
excited, perhaps. She had been invited to spend a weekend at
Sandringham, and in February Charles asked her to join his skiing
party for a ten-day holiday in Klosters, Switzerland. By now the
tabloids had Sarah in the frame as Charles's girlfriend, following

her on the slopes and taking photographs. Sarah, according to Whitaker, enjoyed flirting with the media and reading about herself in the press. She subscribed to Durrants cutting service, not only the English cutting service but Durrants worldwide, in order not to miss a word, and kept albums of cuttings about herself. On her return from Switzerland she unwisely lunched with two reporters from the *Sun* and the *Daily Mail*, two of the most widely read popular papers, and talked about her relationship with Charles. One month later she made matters worse by giving Whitaker an extended interview to be published as a long article in the magazine *Woman's Own* (Whitaker wrote it under the pseudonym Jeremy Slazenger in order not to upset his regular employer, the *Sun*). She had told Whitaker of her drinking and expulsion from school and her anorexia, even exaggerating it by saying that her gynaecologist had told her she would never be able to have children (she later had three), and that she had lost virtually all the enamel on her teeth. She had also offered to provide photographs revealing her painful thinness which were so upsetting that the publishers for her sake decided not to print them. She boasted of having had 'thousands of boyfriends'. More seriously, she went on to discuss Prince Charles, 'a romantic who falls in love easily', and denied she was in love with him: 'I'm not in love with Prince Charles. I'm a whirlwind sort of lady, as opposed to a person who goes in for slow-developing courtships. I can assure you that if there was to be any engagement between Prince Charles and myself, then it would have happened by now. I wouldn't marry anyone I didn't love – whether it was the dustman or the King of England. If he asked me I would turn him down. He doesn't want to marry anyway. He's not ready for marriage yet . . . Our whole approach has been a brotherly-sisterly one, never anything else . . . There's no question of me being the future Queen of England. I don't think he's met her yet.'

Poor Sarah compounded her foolishness, as she later told Whitaker, by then picking up the telephone and calling Prince Charles: 'I think I've just done something very stupid, Sir.' 'What have you done?' he asked. She replied, 'I've just given an interview to James Whitaker for *Woman's Own*.' Charles just said, 'Yes, Sarah, you have done something extremely stupid.'[22] Talking to the tabloids was a cardinal sin in royal eyes; talking about Prince Charles to the tabloids was to prove fatal to their relationship.

Despite her own faux pas over the Prince, Sarah was not pleased when Diana came into the picture, as she recalled: 'then she [Sarah] saw something different happening which I hadn't twigged on to, i.e. when he had his 30th birthday dance [on 14 November 1978] I was asked too . . .'[23] From that dinner at Althorp Diana had fallen for Charles with all the passion of youthful love, and with a youthful conviction that she was going to get him.

Diana was completely unsophisticated: she had never moved outside her narrow social circles, never been abroad apart from the vain sojourn in Switzerland, never been to university or indeed read a book beyond Barbara Cartland. Looking after children was the only career Diana had envisaged at that time. While Jane and Sarah both had the credentials to land jobs at *Vogue*, the family considered that looking after children was indeed all Diana was capable of. Some of them, like her great-aunt Lady Margaret Douglas-Home, were concerned that Diana had no aim in life. Indeed, for Diana at that time, her dream was to go to London and share in the independent lives of her sisters and her friends there. After three months of pressure, she was allowed to share her mother Frances's Cadogan Square flat with two other girls, Laura Greig, her West Heath school friend and the most long-lasting of her school-day friendships, and Sophie Kimball, whom she had met at Videmanette. Privileged, living in her mother's flat and paid for by her parents, she did not feel the need to try for a well-paid job: a three-month cookery course in Wimbledon was followed by a stint as an apprentice teacher at Miss Vacani's ballet studio in Kensington which she left when she felt intimidated by the parents. She then took various low-paid jobs, house cleaning and child care, for employers whom she later derided as 'velvet hair bands', a reference to the prim Alice-band style in fashion among a certain class of unimaginative, rather prissy English girls since the fifties.

Looking after children remained the focus of her working life.

She went to work as a part-time assistant at the Young England kindergarten run by Kay King, a West Heath old girl, where, according to Miss King, she showed 'this incredible ability' to get down to the children's level. 'They responded so well to her, [and] she was completely at ease with them.' She also worked part-time as a nanny recruited by an agency, Occasional and Permanent Nannies, which recommended her as 'sweet-tempered, good with children, willing to do whatever she's asked'. There was only one condition: Diana would only work in the smartest, safest areas of London within easy reach of where she lived. And when she went to work for an American couple, Patrick and Mary Robertson, she indicated another: she would not work at evenings or weekends so that her social life could continue unimpeded.

Mary Robertson found her beautiful ('an English rose'), shy, polite and helpful in the extreme but even in those days very private and guarding that privacy. Mrs Robertson had no idea of Diana's aristocratic background and Diana never said anything about it. When asked if she had had a nice weekend she would simply say she had been 'in the country' or, if she had been to see her sister Jane at Kensington Palace, she would say only that she had been 'to see my sister's baby in Kensington'. When Mrs Robertson once admired her haircut and asked who the hairdresser was, she referred vaguely to 'a little hairdresser near my flat'. 'I knew I couldn't push,' Mrs Robertson commented. Diana never mentioned her mother and only rarely her family. If Charles, to whom Mrs Robertson said Diana was 'devoted', came up from Eton, she would ask permission to leave early, forbearing even to say that he was at Eton. Along with Diana's discretion about her social life, Mrs Robertson wrote, she was 'aware of a natural delicacy or refinement that guarded her innermost feelings. I considered her emotional distance as a sign of respect for her own privacy and that of others . . . I thought this aura was her most intriguing quality.' In 1980, she said, Diana was a 'happy normal teenager, enjoying her first experience of independence, busy with her two child-care jobs, and having fun with her friends'.[24]

In May 1980, Sarah married Neil McCorquodale, a Coldstream

Guards officer and gentleman farmer who happened to be a distant connection of Raine, described by a friend as 'solid, very steady, private, quiet; with a good sense of humour'. He was, in short, exactly the type of man whom Lady Diana Spencer could, and perhaps should, have married and never been heard of again. McCorquodale had need of these qualities for Sarah, mercurial as ever, had called off the wedding in February. Finally it took place in the Spencer parish church, St Mary the Virgin, Great Brington, with the reception at Althorp. Again, Frances paid for the wedding, and again Raine and her mother, Barbara Cartland, were well to the fore. Diana was a bridesmaid. She still appeared, according to one observer, 'this rather shy, really very mousy-haired creature'.

By this time, Diana had moved (in July 1979) to 60 Coleherne Court, a smart £50,000-mansion block flat on the borders of South Kensington and Chelsea, found for her by Sarah, who was working for the estate agent Savills, and given to her by her mother as a coming-of-age present. She shared it with three girlfriends: Carolyn Pride, her friend since West Heath, Anne Bolton and Virginia Pitman. Among her other jobs she used to be employed to do the chores for Sarah in her mews house in Elm Park Lane, Chelsea. According to a friend who shared the flat, 'Diana hero-worshipped her [Sarah] but Sarah treated her like a doormat'. She was paid £1 an hour and if she didn't do the job properly she had to do it again.[25] Nor was her social life any more exciting. Diana disliked parties and had turned down her parents' offer of a coming-out ball. She attended quite a few dances during country house weekends with her friends but mostly she preferred sitting at home, watching television and giggling with her friends or careering about London in her Mini Metro, playing silly tricks on their men friends. Diana's male friends were typical upper-class, rather conventional young men; several of them were officers, others undergraduates, most of them with a county background. None of them, apparently, was allowed to become more than just friends, however much they might have liked to get closer. One of her men friends, Rory Scott, who found her sexually attractive, never made the distance. 'She was always a little aloof,' he said. 'You always felt that there was a lot you would never know about her.' She had a dirty laugh and liked lavatorial jokes, said one friend. Men found her very sexy, tactile, flirtatious: she laughed at their jokes but drew the line at serious flirting. In that she was, a friend said, 'unusual at a time when her contemporaries would "go like rabbits"'. The friend thought it was 'rubbish all that stuff about saving herself for something'. Diana, she divined, was afraid of sex. Other friends, like Carolyn Pride, later Bartholomew, perhaps rationalizing after the event, took the view which Diana herself propagated when she said, 'I knew I had to keep myself tidy for what lay ahead.' Bartholomew told Andrew Morton in 1991, 'I'm not a terribly spiritual person but I do believe that she was meant to do what she is doing and she certainly believes that. She was surrounded by this golden aura which stopped men going any further; whether they would have liked to or not, it never happened.'[26]

It may be that Diana secretly thought of herself as special and destined for higher things in compensation for the ordinariness and limited horizons of her everyday life. It is a quality of icons that they have a focused vision of themselves and their future. Grace Kelly and Jackie Bouvier dreamed of being stars and of marrying special men. So did Diana. Behind the jolly English-rose façade, she nurtured extraordinary qualities, but they were not apparent yet. Nothing could have prepared her for the royal future which suddenly appeared on her horizon.

4. Enter the Prince

'I believe in a case like yours that a man should sow his wild oats before settling down. But for a wife he should choose a suitable and sweet-charactered girl before she meets anyone else she might fall for' (Earl Mountbatten to Charles[1])

At the age of thirty, Prince Charles Philip Arthur George was slim, muscled, shy, kind and deeply confused. He had been born on 14 November 1948 at Buckingham Palace, official seat of the ruling dynasty of Great Britain, as befitted the future heir to the throne. And as such he had been the focus of interest from the moment his life began.

His mother, then Princess Elizabeth, was only twenty-two when he was born, and had been married to the former Prince Philip of Greece, now Prince Philip, Duke of Edinburgh, for just a year. In 1952, when he was three and a half years old, his grandfather, King George VI, died and his young mother became Queen of Great Britain and Northern Ireland, Defender of the Faith and Head of the Commonwealth. As Queen she had the weight of her duties to cope with – in the year of her Coronation, for instance, when Charles was four, she and the Duke of Edinburgh undertook a six-month tour of the Commonwealth. In the circumstances Charles saw far less of his parents than did other children of his age. When he did see them – and both made a great deal of effort to make his life as 'normal' as possible, playing with him and trying to be there when he had his evening bath and supper – there was still no escaping the fact that his mother was the Queen, Head of State, Head of the Armed Forces and Governor of the Established Church, the apex of a large royal household dedicated to serving her every wish. She saw her duty first and foremost as her 'job', following her father's footsteps as sovereign, with all the hard work and dedication which that entailed. As Queen, she was inevitably surrounded by an aura, blocking all real intimacy: Prince Charles has remained in awe of her all his life.

He was (and still is) equally in awe of his father, Prince Philip, who, despite a difficult childhood, had emerged as a success in every field he tackled, at school, in the navy and as consort to the Queen. Extremely handsome and formidably strong-willed, the Duke of Edinburgh dominated the family: it was he who decreed the course of Charles's education which largely followed the steps he himself had taken. A preparatory day school in London, Hill House in Knightsbridge, where the shy boy came into contact with unknown children of his own age for the first time, was followed by a preparatory boarding school, Cheam in Surrey. Charles was nine years old when he was sat down in front of the television by his headmaster to watch himself declared Prince of Wales (the hereditary title of the heir to the throne) to a cheering crowd of thousands of Welshmen. It came as an unexplained shock and only served to increase the difficulty of maintaining the illusion that he was 'just another schoolboy'. He was desperately homesick and made no friends at Cheam.

Cheam was followed by a far more harrowing experience – Gordonstoun, the tough educational establishment on the north-east coast of Scotland which his father had attended, and which had been founded by the German educationalist Kurt Hahn, on the model of his original establishment in Germany. Gordonstoun was intended to produce self-reliant leaders in the mode of Charles's father, who had excelled at everything sporting and became Captain of Cricket. Charles, shy and vulnerable, was bullied all the more because he was 'different' and royal; boys lined up for the distinction of roughing up the heir to the throne at rugby. Most kept their distance from him for fear of being labelled as toadies: some went in for active physical bullying, shoving his head down the lavatory or beating him with pillows. The physical discomfort was extreme: snow drove in horizontal from the North Sea through the open windows of the unheated wooden dormitories. There were obligatory cold showers, runs and stormy sessions in open sailing boats on the North Sea. Again, he made no friends; his parents rarely visited, often sending the Dean of Windsor, the Right Rev. Robin Woods, in their stead. His only glimpse of home comforts was staying with his beloved maternal grandmother, Queen Elizabeth, at her Scottish home, Birkhall, on the royal Balmoral estate, which he ever after referred to as 'the most wonderful place in the world'. His refuge was music, to which he was introduced by his grandmother, and the stage, always a home for people who are not totally sure of their own identity.

At home in London his refuge was his nanny, Mabel Anderson. 'Mabel saved my life,' he used to say. Mabel was his guardian angel, ever present in his young life. When he contracted infectious diseases such as chicken pox, he would be sent away to preserve the Queen's health, accompanied by Mabel, often to Holkham, the Leicesters' stately home on the Norfolk coast not far from Sandringham. And home life, much as he cherished it in comparison with his school experiences, could be tough and demanding. His parents believed that being the heir to the throne involved rigorous training. His sister, Anne, outgoing, determined and tomboyish, was always much closer in character to his father, who was often dismayed by Charles's 'wimpishness' and made no secret of it. He could be a bully and often was to Charles, embarrassing him and putting him down in front of other people. His mother, although loving him, was non-confrontational and left the overseeing of his education largely to his father.

With his future involvement with the Commonwealth in mind, Charles was given a year off from Gordonstoun to attend Timbertop; this he liked because of its location in the Australian bush and its connection with nature, which he both enjoyed and revered. Gordonstoun had been followed by university, Trinity College, Cambridge, under the wise guidance of Rab Butler, a distinguished former Conservative minister, and by a brief and uncomfortable period at the Welsh university Aberystwyth, designed to familiarize him with the distant country which was his 'principality'. Charles dutifully learned Welsh and showed courage

in facing up to the hostility of the Welsh nationalists who threatened to disrupt his formal installation as Prince of Wales in 1969.

Under the guidance of his father and his great-uncle, Earl
Mountbatten, he was launched on a series of military training
courses, piloting aircraft, parachute jumping, and Dartmouth
Royal Naval School, culminating in a five-year spell in the navy.
As a result of these macho heroics, the newspapers dubbed him
'Action Man'. Charles drove himself hard physically in a bid to
show his father he was not the wimp he thought he was. He rode
hard to hounds and at polo, pushing himself to the limit although
his horsemanship was not of the highest standard. He faced physical
danger as if it were a challenge to be overcome, but at heart he
was not as tough as he appeared. On one occasion when he
telephoned his mother to express his distress at the death of one of
his sailors, the Queen was heard to remark, 'Charles really must
toughen up'. He remained shy, sensitive and insecure, a good,
kind person who became increasingly spoiled by the indulgence
of those around him. He was loved and cosseted by his mother's
household, notably Lady Susan Hussey, one of the Queen's
Women of the Bedchamber and only eleven years his senior. His
grandmother, the Queen Mother, adored him, as did his aunt, the
vivacious and intelligent Princess Margaret. Once he was given his
own household, he was spoiled by his entourage, principally by
his valets, a tradition which was to continue. This cosseting and
ministering to his every need had, by the time he left the navy in
1976, had its effect on his character. He began to resent the
relentless demands of 'duty', of having his every day planned, of
being told what to do by senior courtiers.

Squadron Leader David Checketts, who had been Charles's
mentor and adviser since 1966 when he had accompanied the
young prince to Timbertop, was the first victim of Charles's determination to assert his independence. Checketts, an urbane, grammar school-educated public relations man with a distinguished
RAF record, had been, as Charles's biographer Anthony Holden
put it, 'a pillar in the young Prince's uncertain public life, rarely
more than six feet away, always ready to help him through

difficulties and defuse awkward situations. Through the end of his schooldays, his time at Cambridge, his investiture and his Service career, Prince Charles owed Checketts a huge debt for the smooth progress of his day-to-day administrative needs and the grand strategy of his emergence into public life.'[2] Checketts had acted as a brake on the Prince's more headstrong impulses and public statements and had expressed occasional disapproval of his private life. Prince Charles had become increasingly unwilling to accept criticism whether direct or implied, or, indeed, opposition to his ideas. To Checketts's despair Prince Charles now seemed bent on pleasing only himself. He had developed a passion for blood sports, shooting and particularly hunting, despite warnings from the Palace that the popular tide was running against them. In summer he ardently pursued another 'elitist' sport, polo, encouraged by his father, who had been an enthusiastic player until injury forced him to retire. In 1979, now aged fifty, Checketts had resigned his post as Charles's private secretary. His departure was much regretted by Michael Colborne, a former naval petty officer who had served with the Prince on HMS *Norfolk* and whose appointment in 1974 as the Prince's personal secretary had been arranged under Mountbatten's unparalleled influence. A grammar school boy like David Checketts, Colborne's appeal to Charles had been his directness, his willingness to say what he thought. 'He desperately needed somebody who could sit in his office and speak common sense to him, and say no. We had these wonderful ten years together of lots of arguments, but he asked me not to change so I thought I'll show him the greatest respect but if I don't agree, I'm going to say so.'[3]

The truth is that the Prince had changed a great deal from the dutiful, biddable young man who left the navy in December 1976. As his official biographer, Jonathan Dimbleby, wrote:

Unable to find a suitable challenge for his ill-focused energy, the Prince had more time on his hands than he either wished or cared to admit. To his friends he seemed troubled by anxiety and discontent, which he sometimes allowed to affect his behaviour towards his staff. Easily provoked by minor irritations, he became uncharacteristically impatient and peremptory. Whereas a decade earlier his comments about the official programmes put before him had been innocent and dutiful, by the late seventies his response to yet another 'Away Day' could seem reluctant and jaundiced.[4]

Charles had inherited the capacity to blow up into sudden fierce fits of temper which his grandfather George VI had displayed to an alarming extent and which were known in the family as his 'gnashes'. 'For no apparent reason,' Dimbleby wrote, 'the Prince would suddenly give way to an alarming display of uncontrolled anger, his face suffused with intense emotion.' Invariably the anger was disproportionate to its cause, usually some minor mistake or annoyance, and vented on his closest aides, Checketts and Colborne.

Hitherto, in the absence of a strong relationship with his parents, his great mentor had been his father's uncle, Earl Mountbatten, who was in effect a surrogate father to him. Charles used to call Mountbatten 'Grandpapa' and address him as 'honorary grandfather': Mountbatten responded by referring to Charles as his 'honorary grandson'. By the time Charles was twenty-three Mountbatten had become his closest confidant and the greatest single influence on his life.

Mountbatten, who had had first-hand experience of the Abdication Crisis of 1936 when Edward VIII, Charles's great-uncle, had chosen to abdicate the throne in order to marry the American divorcee Wallis Simpson, had lately begun to worry about the Prince's wilfulness and lack of direction, comparing him with his great-uncle Edward VIII, always known in the family as David. Observing the Prince's thoughtless, often selfish and inconsiderate behaviour, Mountbatten sternly warned him: 'I thought you were beginning on the downward slope which wrecked your Uncle David's life and led to his disgraceful Abdication and his futile life ever after.'[5] Mountbatten criticized a sudden change of plan by Charles which would have entailed the cancellation of a US Coastguard crew's Easter vacation: '. . . how unkind and thoughtless – so typical of how your uncle David started,' Mountbatten wrote.

'. . . I spent the night worrying whether you would continue on your uncle David's sad course or take a pull.'[6]

Ironically, it was Mountbatten who pointed Charles down the road which led to Camilla and eventually to Diana. 'I believe in a case like yours,' Mountbatten wrote, 'that a man should sow his wild oats before settling down. But for a wife he should choose a suitable and sweet-charactered girl before she meets anyone else she might fall for.' Significantly, he added, 'I think it is disturbing for women to have experiences if they have to remain on a pedestal after marriage.'[7] Unfortunately for his recipe for a successful dynastic marriage, Charles had already met and fallen in love with a girl who did not quite fit the bill. He had met his 'ideal woman' seven years earlier when he was twenty-three: Camilla Shand, introduced to him by his university girlfriend Lucia Santa Cruz. Camilla, a pretty, witty, confident blonde, was the perfect answer to a vulnerable young man like Prince Charles, still very young and unsophisticated for his age. 'Camilla has great sexual power,' a friend affirmed. A courtier related to the family intimated that Camilla was sexually aware quite early: 'she was quite a little goer at fifteen and well organized by her mother'.[8] She was warm and uncomplicated and, importantly, shared his love of the countryside, dogs, horses and hunting. Ironically, the closest link between Camilla and Charles was a sexual one even before they began an affair. Camilla's great-grandmother on her mother's side was the notorious Alice Keppel, wife of Colonel the Hon. George Keppel and mistress of Charles's great-great-grandfather, King Edward VII. Camilla was fascinated by her powerful great-grandmother's career and the thought of emulating her must have been in the forefront of her mind when she famously remarked to him, 'My great-grandmother was your great-great-grandfather's mistress . . .'

Camilla was fifteen months older than Charles but he had always liked the company of older women, with whom he felt more at ease than he did with young girls. He was emotionally lonely and lacking in self-confidence. Camilla's parents were well-connected county people but far from being a part of the high aristocracy.

Camilla's mother, the Hon. Rosalind Cubitt, was Mrs Keppel's granddaughter; her mother, Sonia, had married into the Cubitt family, descendants of the Cubitt builders of Belgravia who had been ennobled with the title Barons Ashcombe. Her father, war hero Major Bruce Shand, became Master of the local hunt, the Cottesmore. Both, and Camilla's mother in particular, were socially ambitious, with a wide circle of upper-class friends in Sussex and London. Camilla and her brother Mark and sister Annabel were brought up in a close-knit family. Confident, good-looking and exceptionally attractive, the three children were destined for social success. Camilla rode to hounds with bravery and skill: she had had a conventional education with the emphasis on social graces rather than intellectual achievement: undistinguished school, finishing school abroad, Queen's secretarial college – almost a prerequisite for debutantes – followed by the Season. Like many girls of her background, her main aim in life was the getting, pleasing and keeping of a man, and in this she was certainly following in her great-grandmother's footsteps. 'I think she sees herself as her great-grandmother, Mrs Keppel,' one of the Queen Mother's ladies-in-waiting told the author in 1993.

Charles and Camilla first met in the summer of 1970, on the polo ground, Smith's Lawn, in Windsor Great Park, where most of his romances began. Their rapport was instantaneous. The romance was encouraged by Mountbatten who saw Camilla as ideal mistress material who could pave the way for his grand-daughter, Amanda Knatchbull, who was still in her early teens, to take over as the virgin bride. The couple spent weekends together at Mountbatten's country house, Broadlands. After a while, the sharp-eyed Mountbatten became aware that Charles was becoming very attached to Camilla and warned him not to get too fond of a girl, who, for all her attractions, he saw as insufficiently aristocratic and insufficiently virginal to be acceptable as a royal bride. There seemed no future in the relationship and, moreover, Camilla was in love with Andrew Parker Bowles with whom she had been having an on and off affair since 1967. Parker Bowles, a handsome Guards officer, was notoriously attractive to women and repeatedly unfaithful to Camilla, who, however, had never given up on him. She was fond of Charles but in love with Parker Bowles. Andrew himself was having an affair with Princess Anne: unkind friends suggested that getting her own back on Andrew by bedding the Princess's brother was a factor in Camilla's relationship with Charles. An older friend of Camilla's remembers an evening at Annabel's, the nightclub which was at the centre of London society: 'I can remember the triangle when Andrew Parker Bowles was there. Princess Anne was in love with Parker Bowles, Camilla was in love with Andrew, Charles was in love with Camilla, Camilla was having some of it but she was also potty about Andrew – and all this intrigue was going on. They were younger than me so I remember watching it all, the whole thing. It was just bad luck. And then off Charles goes to sea and I think Camilla wouldn't have been quite as sad as he was because she was mad about Andrew. But even if she hadn't been, would she have been allowed to marry Charles?'[9]

The answer was undoubtedly no. Camilla's affairs were known in society and at court. The Parker Bowles family moved in royal circles: Andrew's father Derek, charming, witty and a good gossip, was a close friend of the Queen Mother. His mother, Dame Ann, was the daughter of the rich Sir Humphrey de Trafford, twice steward of the Jockey Club, whose wife was a member of the equally rich and aristocratic Cadogan family. Everybody liked Camilla, whom a friend described as having 'laughing eyes . . . warm and full of fun', but she was not considered in those days aristocratic enough for the Prince of Wales and her reputation would certainly have prevented any thought of marriage.

Charles was powerfully attracted to Camilla but three weeks before Christmas 1972 he was posted to the frigate HMS *Minerva* and later left for the Caribbean. It has been suggested by one of Mountbatten's close circle that he arranged for Charles to be posted overseas to get him away from Camilla and to pave the way for a possible engagement to his own granddaughter, Amanda Knatch-bull.[10] Before Charles left he invited Camilla and Mountbatten to tour the ship. She returned the following weekend. Afterwards he wrote sadly to Mountbatten that it was 'the last time I shall see her for eight months'. But if Charles was not ready for marriage, Camilla and Andrew Parker Bowles were. Parker Bowles's romance with Princess Anne ended when she fell for Captain Mark Phillips. On 15 March 1973 he and Camilla were engaged and married in a huge society wedding in July. Camilla had got her man.

After Camilla, Prince Charles played the field. According to his valet, Stephen Barry, who had worked for him since 1970 and knew all the intimate details of his life, Charles's recipe for the perfect woman was that she should be tall, blonde, curvaceous and with an English rose complexion. His first serious involvement was in fact with Mountbatten's granddaughter, Amanda Knatchbull (a brunette), on and off over a period from 1974 to 1979. Mountbatten actively promoted the match: Charles proposed; Amanda, unwilling to step on to the royal treadmill and well aware of what it entailed, refused him.

During this period Charles dated a number of beautiful upper-class and not so upper-class girls. 'All his romances seemed to start at polo matches,' Stephen Barry wrote.[11] Among them were Lady Jane Wellesley, daughter of the Duke of Wellington, a family friend rather than a romance; Georgiana Russell, who got fed up with standing in cold Scottish rivers and married someone else; and Sabrina Guinness. Two of them were important to him: Davina Sheffield and Anna Wallace. Davina, a delightful, tall blonde, was rather in the Diana mode but, Barry said, 'more grown up'. They had seemed set for marriage, she had received the royal seal of approval, being invited to lunch with the Queen at Windsor, and cheerfully passed the Balmoral test, when a former boyfriend ungallantly revealed in the press that he and Davina had lived together. Rumours of an engagement died down after that. Charles could not afford to marry anyone who could create any kind of scandal. The Royal Family had been keen for him to marry the lovely and artistic Lady Leonora Grosvenor, sister of Sarah Spencer's former boyfriend, Gerald, but in 1975 she married the Queen's cousin, Patrick, Earl of Lichfield, instead.

Charles met Anna Wallace, another tall, beautiful blonde, described by Barry as 'a marvellous-looking girl with a sparkling personality and presence' on the hunting field. Like Davina Sheffield, she had had the honour of lunching with the Queen, a sure sign that the relationship was taken seriously. She ended their friendship after quarrelling publicly with the Prince at a Windsor ball in honour of the Queen Mother's eightieth birthday and again at a polo ball at Stowell Park, the home of Lord and Lady Vestey. The cause this time was the Prince's ignoring Anna to spend the entire evening with Camilla Parker Bowles. Anna, who was well aware of the importance of Camilla in Charles's life, walked out on him and shortly afterwards married the Hon. John Fermor-Hesketh. There were others less serious: the actress Susan George, US admiral's daughter Laura-Jo Watkins, and, of course, Sarah Spencer.

The 'World's Most Eligible Bachelor' had become the 'Playboy Prince'. As Sarah Spencer had said, Charles was a romantic and fell in love easily, but in fact his sexual libido was low, he was frightened of and shy with young women and unable to make a commitment. Like most weak men he was capable of behaving worse than if he had been sure of his own mind. These qualities and the fact that most of the women he pursued, like Amanda Knatchbull, Lady Jane Wellesley and Anna Wallace, who moved in the same circles as he did, were only too aware of the stultifying nature of royal life and were repelled by it, made the finding of a bride difficult. Moreover, Charles himself in the mid-seventies was happy as a bachelor: he enjoyed the freedom of being able to do as he pleased and kept his girls at a distance. He made the dates when it suited him, never collected the girls beforehand. They were expected to arrange their own transport unless they were special friends. He never gave them presents and only rarely sent flowers. It was made quite clear that he controlled the relationship so that things could not get out of hand. Only three women were truly important in Charles's life: his mother, the Queen, his grandmother, 'Grannie', and his nanny, Mabel Anderson.

He was only really at ease with confident married women

older than himself: two of them in particular, the boisterous Australian Dale Harper, later Lady Tryon, nicknamed 'Kanga', and, supremely, Camilla Parker Bowles. A friend remembers how she first met Dale at a weekend house party at Lord Tryon's house: 'There was this Australian girl, rather vulgar, great fun, to whom Anthony Tryon had lent his Volvo estate to drive down and she had crashed it – not fatally – so she was in a great state of semi-hysterics . . . "That's all right," said Anthony. "That's all right." So Dale came along and absolutely exploded on the scene and Anthony was a friend of Prince Charles so of course Dale immediately got onto Prince Charles and would often tell stories of what she had taught Prince Charles. Can you believe that? On the Queen's Flight flying to Australia. She would report what she had taught him. Mind boggling . . .'[12]

At the Cirencester Polo Ball in the summer of 1980 the physical passion of Charles for Camilla was obvious to everyone. 'Charles spent the whole evening with Camilla,' Jane Ward, a former girlfriend of the Prince, recalled. 'Charles and the Parker Bowleses shared the same table, and Charles spent the whole evening dancing with Camilla. They were kissing passionately as they danced – on and on they went, kissing each other, French kissing, dance after dance.'[13] Andrew Parker Bowles apparently could not have cared less. He had, as a friend put it, 'other fish to fry', and the fact that his wife was having a passionate sexual affair with the heir to the throne flattered him rather than otherwise.

Royal reporter James Whitaker remembers how, when Prince Charles was going through a period of two years' enthusiasm for cross-country events in 1975–6, 'virtually always there were Camilla and Dale Tryon and so was Stephen Barry. He would bring the boots out of the car and he would carry all HRH's clobber and gear . . . and helped him dress, and the two other girls fussed around and made sure he had a drink and made sure the organizers knew where he was, made sure people got out of his way when he went to the starting lines . . .'[14] Barry, who as Charles's valet since 1970 had acted as his virtual wife, had in return been outrageously indulged. 'He dressed beautifully, his shirts and ties were all from Turnbull & Asser, he was a very amusing, outrageous homosexual who was so extrovert he was absurd, and he got more and more confident as it went on.' 'He was exotic and extravagant and behaved disgracefully. He would give parties at Ascot where he would roll about the lawn fighting with other gays and serving Dom Perignon champagne.'[15] A lady-in-waiting to the Queen remembered Barry: 'He modelled himself on Prince Charles and looked just like him ... And at some intellectual party I went to, I happened to meet somebody who had found out who I worked for and said, "I wonder if you know Stephen Barry?" And I said, "Yes, of course I know him. I walk down the corridor with him every day." "Oh, he's a great friend of mine. He's shown me all the pictures at Clarence House [then the London home of the Queen Mother] and he's very interested in the Arts." So next morning I walked down the corridor with him [Barry] and I said, "I met a friend of yours last night. He said he did enjoy seeing the pictures at Clarence House." And Stephen went bright purple.' When she reported this to a senior courtier, he advised her, 'Be careful. The Queen Mother's probably given him permission to do so.' According to a lady-in-waiting, Barry gave 'very noisy parties' with 'loud music' in the room beneath the one she used at the Palace. 'But Prince Charles liked him,' she added. 'He always stood up to him and didn't make too many mistakes.'[16] According to Whitaker, Barry was on friendly terms with Camilla but when Diana, whom he perceived as a threat to his position, arrived, he left.

Charles had apparently resumed his sexual relationship with Camilla in 1979 but as she was married it was considered – in those days – unthinkable that the relationship should be legitimized. The Parker Bowleses – at least from Andrew's point of view – had an open marriage. He did not feel obliged to give up his pursuit of women despite the fact that he was now married and the father of two children. He condoned his wife's relationship with Charles and the two men were friends but, in military circles, the heir to the throne's relationship with the wife of a brother officer was considered to break the rules, so much so that the Queen's former private secretary felt bound to inform the Queen of their disquiet. 'Ma'am,' he said, 'the Prince of Wales is having an affair with the wife of a brother officer and the Regiment don't like it.' She looked down and said nothing, determined to continue her policy of non-intervention in her children's lives.

Camilla's role in the Prince's life was more than purely physical; she was also his intimate adviser, usurping Mountbatten's role as his mentor. The Prince had ceased to pay as much attention to his 'honorary grandfather' as he had in his younger days. He found other mentors − he was 'an intellectual pillow', his father said scornfully, while a courtier commented, 'Prince Charles goes through gurus like other people do socks'. In his search for self-fulfilment and the meaning of life he had come under the influence of Laurens van der Post, a protagonist of Jungian ideas. In 1977 he and van der Post had spent five days in the Aberdare Mountains of Kenya, exploring the natural world around them in long walks, followed by evenings of intense discussion of the 'inner world'. He then formed a deep emotional and spiritual relationship with a young Indian woman who had sent him a book called *The Path of the Masters*, a guide to the spiritual wisdom of the Eastern gurus. When her influence manifested itself in vegetarianism and above all opposition to the killing of animals which led him to cancel his shooting, his new private secretary, Edward Adeane, became alarmed. 'It's got to be stopped,' he declared. In the event, this enthusiasm was as short lived as many preceding ones, although his interest in non-Christian faiths remained.

Then, in August 1979, Mountbatten was blown up in his fishing boat by the IRA off the coast of Sligo. Charles was devastated. He had been dreading the moment when Mountbatten might die: now that it had come so suddenly and violently he was desolate. 'I have lost someone infinitely special in my life,' he wrote. '. . . In some extraordinary way he combined grandfather, great-uncle, father, brother and friend . . . Life will *never* be the same now that he has gone . . .'[17] As Charles realized, no one could replace Mountbatten in his role of friend and counsellor, and above all his willingness to tell him things he didn't want to hear. Charles accepted criticism from Mountbatten that he would never have taken from anyone else. Mountbatten's death occurred at a critical moment in Charles's life when, dissatisfied with himself and with the course his life was taking, he was seriously contemplating marriage. 'I must say I am becoming rather worried by all this talk about being self-centred and getting worse every year. I'm told that marriage is the only cure for me – and maybe it is!' he had written to a friend on 15 April 1979.[18]

The trouble with Charles was that he did not want to marry. He had everything he needed without a wife (including Camilla). 'He was a loner, he liked silence,' said one of his staff. 'And later when he found he had a wife to talk to and to consider, it threw him.' Charles had led an entirely self-centred life: when he went away for a weekend he did not have to lift a finger: 'Stephen would be ready with the Range Rover, loaded up with everything he needed, his painting brushes . . . everything.' The shock at the loss of his beloved mentor, and the memory of Mountbatten's strictures, were no doubt a crucial influence on Charles's increasing conviction that he must do his duty and take a wife. Camilla's influence on his life even increased with the loss of Mountbatten. She was to play a dominant role in Charles's choice.

5. 'Whatever Love Means'

'Diana was very simple, rosy cheeks, a schoolgirl. Totally sort of innocent . . . They were all delighted' (a courtier describing Diana on her first visit to Birkhall in 1980)

Lady Diana Spencer, tall and blonde, curvy (as she then was) with a clear English-rose complexion, very young, impeccably born and with no scandal attached to her name, perfectly fitted all the criteria for a royal bride. Given that the Prince had to marry and seemed to be attracted to Diana, Camilla, in a spectacular misreading of Diana's true character, saw it as in her own interest that Charles should choose such a shy young girl who would pose no threat to her position in his heart and mind. It suited her to befriend Diana and encourage Charles towards the girl she truly believed to be the best choice available. She had already effectively seen off Anna Wallace. Diana, younger, less fiery, seemed infinitely more malleable.

Indeed, Diana must have remained at the back of Charles's mind, since when he met her again at a house party at Petworth in July 1980, his reaction to her took her by surprise:

. . . Charles came in. He was all over me again and it was very strange. I thought 'Well, this isn't very cool'. I thought men were not supposed to be so obvious, I thought this was very odd. The first night we sat down on a bale at the barbecue at this house and he'd just finished with Anna Wallace. I said: 'You looked so sad when you walked up the aisle at Lord Mountbatten's funeral.' I said: 'It was the most tragic thing I've ever seen. My heart bled for you when I watched. I thought, "It's wrong, you're lonely – you should be with somebody to look after you."'

The next minute he leapt on me practically and I thought this was very strange too, and I wasn't quite sure how to cope with all this. Anyway we talked about lots of things and anyway that was it. Frigid wasn't the word. Big F when it comes to that. He said: 'You must come to London with me tomorrow. I've got to work at Buckingham Palace, you must come to work with me.' I thought this was too much. I said, 'No, I can't.' I thought 'How will I explain my presence at Buckingham Palace when I'm supposed to be staying [the weekend] with Philip [son of the hosts].'[1]

Diana was a lovely young girl, 'high-spirited and larky and fun' as a royal relation put it; 'she had a lot of good in her, a lot of natural good that was not a pose.' It was, above all, her extraordinary powers of empathy, her ability, as she later put it, 'to smell out suffering', which attracted the Prince. Her empathy with him over Mountbatten's death and his own deep sadness and need for consolation touched the Prince deeply. Charles, it would seem, was strangely interested in this young girl who had actually had the self-possession to turn him down. He invited her to join him on the royal yacht *Britannia*, for the annual Cowes week sailing holiday. This time he did not expect her just to turn up on her own but, significantly, asked his assistant private secretary, Oliver Everett, to look after her: '. . . he [Charles] had lots of older friends there and I was fairly intimidated but they were all over me like a bad rash. I felt very strange about the whole thing, obviously someone was talking,' Diana later recalled.[2]

That 'someone' was Charles himself. According to his official biographer, he 'surprised one of his closest confidantes [unnamed] . . . by intimating to her that he had met the girl he intended to marry'. The 'confidante' had responded that if that was the case he should keep quiet about it. Charles, however, went on to praise Diana's open and easy manner . . . her warmth . . . her enthusiasm for rural life, and her background through which she knew a little of his family and certainly enough, he presumed, to have few fears of marrying into it.[3] As an insider, Charles seems to have had little conception of what marrying into the Royal Family would actually mean, and was never properly to understand the pressures Diana underwent when she did enter the royal circle.

In *Britannia*, however, the open and easy manner which Diana had acquired from her parents when talking to strangers made her instantly popular with the crew who, according to Barry, 'fell in love with her to a man'. The royal servants liked her and the general impression was 'Isn't Lady Di lovely?' and that she might well be in line for 'the job'. Yet, whatever Charles may have confessed to his confidante, he was careful not to show anything in public. 'The Prince himself didn't seem to take too much notice of her at the beginning, but *her* eyes followed him everywhere,' Barry recorded.[4]

Unaware as yet of Camilla Parker Bowles's role in her destiny, Diana was invited to stay at Balmoral in September while her sister Jane and brother-in-law Robert Fellowes were there. 'I stayed back at the Castle because of all the press interest,' Diana remembered, '. . . Mr and Mrs Parker Bowles were there at all my visits. I was the youngest there by a long way. Charles used to ring me up and say "Would you like to come for a walk, come for a barbecue?" so I said: "Yes, please." I thought all this was wonderful.'[5] Charles's old friends warmed to her as she was so obviously happy and he seemed so attracted to her. Patty Palmer-Tomkinson, married to Hampshire farmer Charles Palmer-Tomkinson, and one of Charles's closest friends, remembered how enchanted she had been with Diana: 'We went stalking together, we got hot, we got tired, she fell into a bog, she got covered in mud, laughed her head off, got puce in the face, hair glued to her forehead because it was pouring with rain . . . she was a sort of wonderful English schoolgirl who was game for anything, naturally young but sweet and clearly determined and enthusiastic about him, very much wanted him.'[6]

One of the Queen Mother's guests at Birkhall remembered an occasion when the house party from Balmoral came over for drinks. Nicholas Soames, a friend of the Prince's since childhood who also acted as his equerry, and Camilla Parker Bowles, were among them, with Diana. 'I was somewhat surprised to see Diana

in purple stockings seated on the floor in front of Queen Elizabeth
– Camilla Parker Bowles was obviously there to vet this poor girl
who had no idea what she was letting herself in for,' the guest
commented.[7]

Diana was invited up to Scotland again in October, this time to
Birkhall itself, one of Charles's favourite places from his school
days. While Charles went out stalking, Diana remained at the
house, doing her needlepoint. The fact that the Queen Mother
had herself invited Diana to stay was significant; she was clearly in
favour of Diana as a possible bride for her beloved grandson. Some
authorities have it that Ruth Fermoy pressed Diana's claims on
Queen Elizabeth. Others close to Queen Elizabeth deny that she
played a leading role: 'Ruth wasn't against it,' said a courtier; 'to
tell the truth she was rather for it, and no doubt had said something
to Queen Elizabeth. [But] I think Queen Elizabeth came from a
different angle and that is that Cynthia Spencer, Diana's grandmother, had been a great friend and the Spencer family were
"friends of the royal family".' 'It was so surprising,' she went on,
describing Diana's Birkhall visit: 'She [Diana] was very simple, rosy
cheeks [like] a schoolgirl. And charming. Totally sort of innocent
. . . They were all delighted. Before she came up, one of the
Queen's ladies-in-waiting had rung me up and said, "Do take care
about this one, I think it's serious." And there was no doubt that
the Queen Mother was anxious about it, she checked the bedroom
and all that sort of thing which she wouldn't normally have done
for a nineteen-year-old girl. So one sort of knew that it was being
planned or being hoped for . . .' After Diana and Charles had left,
she recalled, 'Ruth was at the airport on her way to go into waiting
and she came running towards me and said, "How did the visit
go? Was she all right? Was it all right?"'[8]

In pushing the claims of Diana, Ruth Fermoy was at the very
least guilty of a cynical act. She of all people would have known
of the Camilla situation and she of all people would have known
what she was getting Diana into. Undoubtedly she must have
found the temptation of being the grandmother of the future
Queen too much to resist, despite knowing her granddaughter's

character and, equally, being aware of the nature of the court. During the engagement, when a friend said to her how wonderful it was that the bride loved music, she did volunteer enigmatically 'She'll need that', but the closest she ever came to warning Diana of what lay ahead was to tell her that she would find the Royal Family's sense of humour very different from her own. In the end she collaborated with the Spencer family – and indeed Diana's own feelings – in pushing her into the marriage.

In true courtier fashion, Ruth Fermoy was swiftly to change her tune when the marriage began to reveal its fault lines. Indeed, when Jonathan Dimbleby was writing his authorized biography of the Prince, conscious of her role in history she told him that in private she had been against the marriage but (as a courtier) had 'thought it wrong to share her doubts'. According to a private source she made a deathbed statement to Dimbleby along the same lines. She also told him, ingenuously: 'If I'd said to him [Charles], "You're making a very great mistake", he probably wouldn't have paid the slightest attention because he was being driven'[9] – 'driven' not only by his family but by the counsels of Camilla, still an important part of his life, and the weight of public expectation that he should do his duty.

Barry, a close and interested observer, thought that 'things seemed to be blossoming' from the time of the Birkhall visit. Charles invited her to Highgrove, his new house in Gloucestershire, the first he had personally owned. Charles was delighted with it, but Diana, according to Barry, was unimpressed. It was a standard Cotswold manor house, small by Althorp standards, in a mess and with only three habitable bedrooms. Diana did not yet know it, but the principal appeal of Highgrove for Charles was that it was only fifteen miles' drive from Bolehyde Manor, home of Andrew and Camilla Parker Bowles. It was also within easy reach of one of his favourite hunts, the Beaufort, where Charles's relationship with Camilla was well known to members, who described her as riding 'in his pocket'. Just at that time, Prince and Princess Michael of Kent were negotiating to buy their country house, Nether Lypiatt, in the same area. They were surprised to find Charles bitterly opposed to their proposed purchase, and it was only through the intervention of another member of the Royal Family that he was persuaded to give up his opposition. Friends surmised that the only reason for his opposing the Kents' buying Nether Lypiatt was that they might become aware of his closeness to Camilla, Princess Michael herself being a keen rider to hounds.

Diana was driven down to Highgrove by Barry three times that autumn, where she would hang around the house and gardens waiting for Charles to return home from hunting, a foretaste of her life to come. After tea and a simple early dinner together, Charles drove her back to London. The mere fact of his presence seemed to him to be enough for her and to compensate for hours of dreary waiting. Perhaps Diana liked it like that: it was a very old-fashioned courtship along the lines prescribed by Barbara Cartland, now her step-grandmother.

Public interest in the possibility of Diana as Charles's future bride was reaching fever pitch. 'HE'S IN LOVE AGAIN! LADY DI IS THE NEW GIRL FOR CHARLES' blared the headline in the *Sun* on 8 September 1980. James Whitaker, stationed at Balmoral, had been the source of the tip-off. Watching from a vantage point above the River Dee, where Charles was fishing, he had spotted Diana looking back at him from behind a tree, using her make-up mirror: 'What a cunning lady, I thought,' he later wrote. 'This one was clearly going to give us a lot of trouble . . . You had to be a real professional to think of using a mirror to watch us watching her.'[10] That same month, Nigel Dempster, the gossip columnist of the *Daily Mail*, broke the story that Diana was Charles's new girlfriend and that his choice had been approved by 'the two happily married women who influence [him] most on personal matters, Lady Tryon and Camilla Parker Bowles'.[11] In London reporters laid siege to Coleherne Court, posting themselves near Mary Robertson's mews house and outside the Young England kindergarten. It was there that one day, in an effort to persuade them to go away, Diana allowed herself to be photographed against the sun in a Madonna-like pose, holding one child in her arms and another by the hand. The sun streamed through her long, flimsy skirt revealing the stunning legs which were among her principal features and inflaming male passions all over the world. The tabloid reporters besieging her flat fell in love with her: by invariably being polite, tolerant and good-tempered, she made them her friends. She flirted with them, giving them the famous 'shy Di' look with lowered eyes. 'You knew deep down it was a game she played, and a very clever one . . . not cynical, but by doing this, she won everybody over,' said tabloid reporter Harry Arnold.[12] Worse still for Diana than the relentless lenses outside the flat were the midnight telephone calls from the press; she concealed the strain it caused her, but in private she wept.

Charles took elaborate precautions so that he and Diana could meet in London without attracting press attention. Diana would ring Barry, say simply 'It's Diana' and tell him where she could be picked up – from Ruth Fermoy's Eaton Square flat or from Jane Fellowes' house at Kensington Palace. Returning home she would be dropped behind the block of flats at Coleherne Court to escape the media stationed at the front. To Barry she appeared still as a simple, giggly teenage girl with an addiction to sweets – Yorkie bars and bags of toffees. But she was already showing signs of trying to influence the Prince's appearance, buying him sweaters and ties in his favourite blue and replacing the formal shoes custom-made for him by Lobb of St James's with more modern slip-ons. 'You'll never get away with those,' Barry warned her. 'He's always had his shoes made to order.' Diana just grinned and that evening he saw the Prince walking around trying to get used to them.

Diana was invited to celebrate Charles's thirty-second birthday (14 November 1980) with an intimate Royal Family gathering at Wood Farm, the ten-bedroom house on the Sandringham estate which the family use when the Big House is closed. Saturday was spent shooting but the gathering hordes of media at the gates curtailed Diana's visit. Their attentions meant that Charles and Diana could not even take a walk together so a stratagem for her escape to London was arranged, cutting short the planned long weekend. She was safely back at Coleherne Court while the media mob remained freezing in Norfolk at the gates of Wood Farm.

Both the press and the royal staff were convinced that an engagement would be announced. In Norfolk the Duke of Edinburgh grumbled about the 'bloody press' spoiling his shooting.

While Diana was still at Sandringham the 'Royal Love Train' scandal broke: on 16 November the *Sunday Mirror* printed a story that on 5 November Diana had slipped into the royal train as it stood in a Wiltshire siding to spend the night with Charles. The story was patently untrue as far as Diana was concerned; that night, with Charles, she had attended a party for Princess Margaret at the Ritz and was photographed arriving there. She had gone home to Coleherne Court at about 1 a.m.; Charles, however, had left earlier around ten or ten thirty and had taken the train to an official engagement; the mystery woman was supposed to have boarded the train at about midnight. The report created a furore: the Queen was furious and her press secretary, Michael Shea, was deputed to write to the editor of the *Sunday Mirror* denying the incident. 'The Woman on the Train' was certainly not Diana, but many people believed – and still do – that it was Camilla. The official line has always been that there was nothing whatever in the story. James Whitaker, however, then writing for the *Daily Star*, followed up the story which had first come through a local press man. 'I went down to the siding . . . I went up into the signal box and I paid the signal man some money and I saw his log book, and they'd logged a person getting on the train . . . down the road at the station . . . they had an official log of somebody going on that train, a woman.'[13] A respected media commentator found the Palace reaction fishy. 'Diana was definitely in London at the time with witnesses; all the Palace had to do was to simply say "Diana was in London, she never went near the train and this is the proof." Why didn't they do it? Because Diana herself would have been spooked by that story. Who was on the train? So they had to deny the train incident altogether.'[14] In the face of repeated official denials, the editor of the *Sunday Mirror*, Bob Edwards, came to believe that he had made a mistake over the story, certainly as far as Diana was concerned. At Christmas 1986, however, he received a Christmas card from Woodrow Wyatt, later Lord Wyatt of

Weeford, the Labour politician and journalist who, despite his politics, moved in royal circles. The message was: 'It was Camilla.'

The Royal Love Train incident added fuel to the Duke of Edinburgh's 'ultimatum', as Prince Charles interpreted it, that he should either propose to Lady Diana Spencer or stop seeing her as he would damage her reputation and expose her to persecution by the press if he continued to do so. To the Royal Family, and indeed to Charles, Lady Diana seemed the answer to their prayers. 'Characteristically,' Dimbleby wrote, 'the Queen refrained from tendering her opinion but Queen Elizabeth the Queen Mother, who was a significant influence, counselled strongly in favour of marriage, as did her lady-in-waiting, Ruth Fermoy . . . Diana Spencer's grandmother.'[15] The Queen Mother is said to have told Charles one day at Royal Lodge, 'There's Diana Spencer – that's the girl you should marry. But don't marry her if you don't love her. If you do, grab her because if you don't there are plenty of others who will.' Ruth Fermoy added to the general pressure for the marriage by putting it about that if Charles did not marry Diana after all this fuss, she would be ruined. One of the Queen Mother's courtiers was overheard to say over tea at Clarence House, when the question of the engagement seemed to be hanging fire, that 'Charles must make his mind up, if he discards Diana she's got no future at all . . .' One of his colleagues told him, 'You must be joking – a pretty girl of nineteen, just because the Prince of Wales doesn't want to marry her, you're living in another world.' Ruth Fermoy, she said, had been putting it about that 'she'll be finished if the Prince of Wales discards her now'. 'Arrant rubbish,'[16] the courtier commented.

After Christmas at Althorp, where, according to her stepmother, Diana spent much of her time walking in the park crying over Charles's failure to propose, she joined her flatmates for New Year's Eve before driving down to Sandringham to join the royal house party, using her grandmother's silver VW Golf instead of her own well-known Mini Metro. Once again the press mob turned up in force, disrupting the Duke of Edinburgh's shooting party and rendering him apoplectic, while Charles bitterly told the

press pack that he wished their editors 'a nasty New Year'. Diana
spent the time waiting for Charles to return from shooting, and
slipping away to visit her old home, Park House, now standing
empty and deserted. But the feelings between the couple were
becoming stronger, and obvious to the court insiders watching
them. At Sandringham that January a lady-in-waiting remembered
that they turned back the carpet to dance and 'they danced like
mad, Prince Charles and Diana – there was this electric thing
between them'. Later she asked the couple, 'That was the moment
you fell for each other, wasn't it?' Both of them, she said, agreed.[17]
A second visit to Sandringham had to be abandoned because of
press attention but instead Charles and Diana had a secret rendezvous at Highgrove. Diana spent the night there and on the return
journey to London Barry, who was as usual driving her on a 'dawn
dash' to get back to her kindergarten job, recalled, 'She was a very
happy young woman . . . relaxed, smiling – and not chattering.'
Charles had not actually proposed, but something must have happened to make Diana think that he would. Diana later told friends
that Charles had proposed to her in Camilla Parker Bowles's garden
at Bolehyde.[18] Whether he actually proposed to her there, or gave
her a very strong indication that he would like to marry her, is
open to speculation.

Close friends of Charles's (later among Diana's foremost
enemies) became alarmed at the possibility. Norton and Penny
Romsey, Mountbatten's grandson and his wife, were against Diana
from the beginning. They thought that she was in love with the
idea of being Princess of Wales, rather than with the Prince himself.
They noticed her friendly relationship with the press pack pursuing
her and that she seemed to pose for their cameras. According to
Dimbleby, in January 1981 both of them raised their doubts with
the Prince, to no avail. Close observers such as Barry denied their
allegation: 'She was most certainly in love with her Prince,' he
stated. 'She was always available when he called, and she always
fitted in with his plans. She obviously adored being with him, and
in January the Prince wrote a memo to his office telling them to
give her a copy of his weekly engagements so that she would

know where he was'[19] – the first time he had ever done so for a girl. Whatever the world may have thought, Diana was deeply in love with Charles and continued to love him even after he had rejected her. 'She hero-worshipped him,' one of her staff was to say. He was the older man in whom she thought she could place her trust, who would love her and look after her as her own father never had.

Nicholas Soames, for one, dared not raise the subject with the Prince but told the Duke of Edinburgh's private secretary, Lord Rupert Nevill, what he thought about the Duke of Edinburgh's 'ultimatum', calling the proposed engagement 'a mismatch'. Soames, Winston Churchill's grandson, was the same age as Charles whom he had known in his early teens fishing in Scotland. He had first met Diana at Birkhall, when he had come away 'amazed' at the possibility that Charles might marry 'this very sweet teenager'. 'She was very sweet,' he said, '[but] it was just like talking to a teenager and not a very clever one either.' Soames and the Romseys were part of Charles's inner circle of friends and absolutely devoted to him. They were quite sincere in their views that this marriage would be a disaster: they were right in the end but not just for the reasons they gave.

Charles himself was, he confessed, in a 'confused and anxious state of mind'. 'It is just a matter of taking an unusual plunge into some rather unknown circumstances that inevitably disturbs me but I expect it will be the right thing in the end.' 'It all seems so ridiculous,' he added, 'because I do so very much want to do the right thing for this Country and for my family – but I'm terrified sometimes of making a promise and then perhaps living to regret it.'[20] And so Charles dithered on, as indeed he well might. He was in love with Camilla, who satisfied his every need. She was, as she herself said, his 'Girl Friday' as well as his lover. And he was attracted to Diana but not in love with her. Everyone, meanwhile, was getting impatient for an outcome. Charles went for his annual skiing holiday in Klosters, accompanied by the Palmer-Tomkinsons, who were initially in favour of Diana and who bolstered his wavering resolve.

'The feeling was,' Diana recalled, 'I wish Prince Charles would hurry up and get on with it. The Queen was fed up. Then Charles rang me up from Klosters and said: "I've got something to ask you." Instinct in a female, you know what's coming. Anyway, I sat up all night with my girls [her three flatmates], saying "What do I say, what do I do?" bearing in mind that there was someone else around.' 'Anyway, next day I went to Windsor and I arrived about 5 o'clock and he sat down and said: "I've missed you so much." But there was never anything tactile about him. It was extraordinary, but I didn't have anything else to go by because I had never had a boyfriend. I'd always kept them away, thought they were all trouble – and I couldn't handle it emotionally, I was very screwed up, I thought. Anyway, so he said, "Will you marry me?" and I laughed. I remember thinking, "This is a joke", and I said, "Yeah, OK", and laughed. He was deadly serious. He said: "You do realize that one day you will be Queen." And a voice said to me inside: "You won't be Queen but you'll have a tough role." So I thought OK, so I said: "Yes." I said, "I love you so much, I love you so much." He said: "Whatever love means." He said it then. So I thought that was great! I thought he meant that! And so he ran upstairs and rang his mother.'[21]

To Diana, Camilla seemed to be ever present and increasingly she had begun to question Camilla's role in Charles's life. 'By that time,' Diana recalled of the period of her secret engagement, 'I'd realized that there's somebody else around. I'd been staying at Bolehyde [Manor, the Parker Bowleses' home] an awful lot and I couldn't understand why she [Camilla] kept saying to me, "Don't push him into doing this, don't do that." She knew so much about what he was doing privately . . . if we were going to stay at Broadlands, I couldn't understand it. [Broadlands was now the property of Mountbatten's grandson, Norton Knatchbull, Lord Romsey, and his wife, close friends of Charles and also of Camilla.] Eventually I worked it all out and found the proof of the pudding and people willing to talk to me.'[22]

Nevertheless, in a state of euphoria, Diana went off to Australia to spend three weeks with her mother planning the wedding.

Frances was determined that on this last holiday on their own before the wedding, Diana should have some real peace and privacy. While the press besieged the Shand Kydd ranch at Yass and Peter Shand Kydd asserted that Diana was 'on a different continent', Frances and Diana were together in a rented beach house at Mollymook, 200 kilometres south of Sydney. Diana spent peaceful days incognito, swimming and surfing on the beautiful beach, not even daring to accompany her mother shopping in case she was recognized. Her stay at Mollymook was, she recalled later, 'the last time I walked alone'. She later alleged that, during her time in Australia, Charles never once telephoned her and that when she rang him he was always out and never called back. This was another instance of her later embroidering the facts to make the picture more dramatic. In truth, according to Barry, Diana and Charles spoke 'constantly but guardedly on the telephone' when she was in Australia, and Charles himself said in a television interview that the first time he tried to call her the Shand Kydd household was so wary of the press that at first they refused to let him speak to her and he had considerable trouble establishing his identity. When she got back home, however, he was not there to welcome her: Michael Colborne sent Sergeant Lewis round with what Diana described as 'this huge, huge bunch of smelly flowers'. 'I knew they weren't from Charles,' she said bitterly, 'because there was no note. It was just somebody being very tactful in the office.'

On 24 February the engagement of the Prince of Wales and Lady Diana Spencer was publicly announced. The couple were interviewed in the garden of Buckingham Palace with the Palace looming in the background. Diana looked very young, her thick blonde hair unbecomingly cut, her figure in a mumsy blue suit looking distinctly chubby, but despite her shyness she seemed more self-possessed than Charles, who was always embarrassed when faced with personal questions and uneasy with television interviews. The occasion seemed more awkward than happy. 'Can you find the right words to sum up how you feel today?' they were asked. 'Difficult to find the right sort of words,' Charles replied, glancing at Diana as she nodded. 'Just delighted and happy. I'm amazed that she's brave enough to take me on.' 'And I suppose in love?' said the interviewer. 'Of course,' said Diana, grimacing shyly and rolling her eyes. 'Whatever in love means,' Charles famously replied. Around the world, people who watched the interview drew in their breath. It seemed to bode ill for the future. Four days later, Diana wrote in her round childish hand, in answer to a letter of congratulations: 'Reading through all the letters, it's amazing how many people have said that married life is the best – I wonder if I'll be saying that in twenty years' time!'[23]

The letter was headed 'Clarence House, February 28th' on plain notepaper in her own hand. On the evening of the day her engagement was announced, Diana moved into the Queen Mother's London home, Clarence House, to protect her from the press. Coleherne Court had become untenable. It was, as her Scotland Yard police protection officer told her: '. . . the last night of freedom ever in the rest of your life . . .'. Diana, in dramatic mode, later said that his words were 'like a sword went in my heart'. On the bed of her first-floor bedroom was a note from Camilla, congratulating her and suggesting lunch. (When, later, the lunch took place during Charles's absence in Australia and New Zealand, Camilla, Diana said, questioned her closely as to whether she intended to hunt or not, the implication being that if not, Camilla would have the hunting field – and specifically the nearby Beaufort Hunt – to herself to meet Charles.) Whatever Diana may have said later, she was in a state of euphoria on the evening of her engagement. After a dinner consisting of her elders – the Queen Mother, Ruth Fermoy and the Queen Mother's private secretary and great friend, Sir Martin Gilliatt – when everyone else had gone to bed, she ended up in the office of William Tallon, the Queen Mother's trusted page, where, spotting a folding bicycle, she seized it and spent the rest of the evening riding round the room singing, 'I'm going to marry the Prince of Wales, I'm going to marry the Prince of Wales . . .'[24]

One seasoned royal observer, Hugo Vickers, had his reservations, however:

Prince Charles is a weak man who doesn't really know what he wants. It is not unknown that he prefers the company of older married ladies. This is almost the royal disease. He was for ages in the arms of Lady Tryon . . . But Camilla Parker Bowles is the one. She has had a hold for some time.

One can only imagine the corner into which the Prince has painted himself. His father no doubt had some choice words on the subject and instructed him to pull out his finger and get hitched. But to whom. If it is known that he [prefers women] of mature years he is in a pickle. For he can't marry anyone with a past. 'Tis said that he didn't even screw [xx] which is ludicrous as surely that is the only point of [xx]. Yet it is not ludicrous if he really loves Mrs P-B . . .

. . . The Prince has got the heat on him & he must wed. Mrs P-B reckons that Lady Diana is sufficiently moronic that we can have our Princess of Wales and she can go on having our Prince . . . ages ago [x] told [x] that the delay for the engagement was due to Mrs PB's reluctance to hand him over.

As for Lady Diana, well she wanted it . . . Evidently she knows all about it & is so in love with him that she is determined to win him over. The verdict is that they have not slept together yet ('Not before the wedding, remember' this P-B perhaps). But to be fair all augurs well because she is a kind girl and I have no doubt she will make him happy . . .[25]

'In my immaturity, which was enormous,' Diana later recalled, 'I thought that he was very much in love with me, which he was, but he always had a sort of besotted look about him looking back at it, but it wasn't the genuine sort. "Who was this girl who was so different?" but he couldn't understand because his immaturity was quite big in that department too . . .'[26]

Two days after the announcement of her engagement, Diana moved into Buckingham Palace, symbolically cutting herself off from normal life for ever. Buckingham Palace, to an outsider, is not a welcoming place. A huge forecourt with railings and, at the gates, police boxes and security ramps, separate it from the public. It is the official royal headquarters in London, the office of the

'Family Firm'. Its vast grey bulk is intimidating. Inside a maze of corridors runs round a central courtyard, dark and redolent of the past, with busts on pedestals and paintings lining the walls. The Palace is quite unlike anywhere else in ordinary experience: there are courtiers, uniformed footmen and the sense that it is a great hive centring on the distant and unseen figure of the Queen. It is the physical expression of the British monarchy, formal, formidably organized, founded on dignity and deference.

Diana, 'nineteen going on fifteen' as one royal servant described her, felt swallowed up by it, its walls isolating her from her 'girls' at Coleherne Court, even her own family. She was allotted her own suite of rooms on the Chamber (former Nursery) Floor overlooking the Mall. The rooms, which had previously been occupied by the royal governess and nanny, Miss Peebles and then the famous Mabel Anderson, were smaller than the usual palace rooms. She had a sitting room, bedroom and bathroom and the use of the old nursery kitchen. She spent her days there sewing, reading and watching television, particularly her favourite soap, *Crossroads*, and waiting for Prince Charles to come home to his apartment down the corridor. She had been given her own aide in the Prince of Wales's office on the ground floor. Oliver Everett, formerly the Prince's assistant private secretary, had returned to his diplomatic career with a post in the Madrid embassy, but had been recalled at the Prince's special request in February 1981 to work with Diana. Lady Susan Hussey was assigned to keep her company and 'show her the ropes'. Diana shared the office with the Prince's people, including his principal private secretary, the Hon. Edward Adeane, who had succeeded David Checketts.

Edward Adeane was a courtier born and bred: great-grandson of the famous Lord Stamfordham who had been private secretary to Queen Victoria and George V, and son of Lord Adeane, private secretary to George VI and to the Queen. Witty and erudite, he had a sense of humour and independence of mind which made him unusual for a courtier, and he was later to resign when he felt that the Prince of Wales would not take his advice. He was kind to Diana, although somewhat baffled by her, uneducated but

Park House, where Lady Diana Spencer was born on 1 July 1961, her family home for fourteen years.

Diana's father, Johnnie, Viscount Althorp, with his bride-to-be, the Hon. Frances Roche, in 1954.

Diana's paternal grandmother, Lady Cynthia Hamilton (1892–1972). Diana inherited both her beauty and her empathy with the sick and suffering.

Sarah Jennings, 1st Duchess of Marlborough, one of the most formidably difficult and forceful women of her age, who bequeathed to the Spencers not only her wealth and possessions but her contrary temperament.

The Spencers at Park House, 1972. Edward John 'Johnnie' Althorp, later 8th Earl Spencer, with his four children, after their mother Frances left. From left: Sarah, Charles, Jane and Diana.

Diana as a child outside Park House, displaying the long legs,
alluring smile and the capacity to look natural while posing,
which were her lifelong characteristics.

Nine-year-old Diana goes to board at Riddlesworth Hall: 'If you love me, you won't leave me here,' she told her father fiercely on arrival at the school.

A pensive Lady Diana Spencer at the wedding of her eldest sister, Lady Sarah, to Neil McCorquodale in May 1980, just over a year before her own wedding to Prince Charles.

The 8th Earl Spencer and his second wife, Raine, in front of Althorp.

Lady Diana Spencer surrounded by press photographers outside her flat in Coleherne Court shortly before the announcement of her engagement to Prince Charles – the beginning of the constant attention that would bedevil her brief life.

'That dress': a buxom, newly engaged Lady Diana Spencer with Prince Charles and Princess Grace of Monaco at a gala at the London Guildhall.

'We're all delighted': Charles and Diana posing with the Queen after the Privy Council granted the couple permission to marry.

The two women in Charles's life: Camilla Parker Bowles and Lady Diana Spencer at Ludlow racecourse.

Prince Charles with another close woman friend – Lady Tryon, known as 'Kanga', at the christening of her son, Anthony.

Prince Charles and Lady Diana Spencer attending a final rehearsal at
St Paul's forty-eight hours before the ceremony. Diana later claimed
to have 'absolutely collapsed', sobbing because of the 'Camilla thing
rearing its head the whole way through our engagement', but one of
her bridesmaids remembered the occasion differently. 'She and Charles
were really in love … cuddling on the sofa … during rehearsals they
had their arms linked and were skipping down the aisles.'

The balcony kiss: the beginning of the nation's
obsession with the 'fairy-tale' marriage.

Wifely tenderness: Diana adjusts
her husband's tie on arrival at
RAF Lossiemouth, Scotland, from
their honeymoon aboard *Britannia*.

Charles and Diana on their Balmoral
honeymoon. Diana, tanned and newly
glamorous, drapes a possessive arm
round her husband's shoulders.

charming teenagers not having been part of his life hitherto. Diana teased him and, despite her objection to his cigar-smoking, later recorded her affection for him. 'Edward Adeane,' she said, was wonderful – 'we got on so well. Very much the bachelor and I was always trying to find him the ideal woman but I didn't succeed at all. He said: "I know some nice ladies who might be ladies-in-waiting. Will you come and see them and meet them?" So I said "Yes" to them all, even though I didn't really know them . . .' 'What I can remember,' she added, 'is that I didn't want to do anything at all on my own. I was too frightened. So I stuck with whatever Charles did.'[27]

Yet despite the stated willingness of people to help her, no one really knew what to do with her, the first Princess of Wales since before the First World War. The root of the problem was that no one had thought of a real role for her beyond the fact that she was to be the wife of the Prince of Wales. People went about their appointed business in the Palace while Diana floundered, not knowing what to do with herself. She was frequently alone, as Charles's official duties took him on tour to Australia and New Zealand and all over the country. 'What amazed me was that there was nobody in the family who was going to take her under their wing and tell her what to do or instruct her,' said a member of the household. The fairy tale was proving unexpectedly dreary, lonely and intimidating.

Diana yearned for 'ordinary people' who would make her feel at home. One such person was the Prince's personal secretary, Michael Colborne, who was, as his title suggests, privy to the personal side of Charles's life. Colborne did his best to provide a simple common-sense approach in the office: his informal duty was 'to look after Lady Diana'. That had been the refrain since the first time Colborne had met her before the engagement on a dramatic day at Highgrove after the Prince's favourite horse, Allibar, had died under him while steeplechasing. The Prince, dreadfully upset, had had to go ahead with his official duties, taking a helicopter to Bristol for an appointment. 'Please look after her,' Charles had said before leaving. 'She was then just nineteen and quite chubby, nicely chubby,' Colborne recalled, '[but] I realized straight away very attractive. And the first thing she said to me was "Can I call you Michael?" And I said, "Well his Royal Highness does, yes." She said, "Will you call me Diana?" I said, "No, because you know, later on you're going to become the Princess and then we can't do it, so let's start from now. I just call you Ma'am and that's it . . . We got on very well and then from the engagement to the wedding she shared my office at the front of the Palace . . . she didn't like me going to lunch, always wanted me to stay . . . just to talk about things.'

Diana may have been 'Lady Diana' and born into the aristocracy but her haphazard upbringing and her education at cosy, undemanding schools had left her unprepared to face this upper-class manifestation of the British Establishment, with its disregard for other people's feelings. Despite the fact that her brother-in-law, Robert Fellowes, was the Queen's assistant private secretary, she was suspicious and resentful of the Palace courtiers – 'the household' as they were known – who were all older than she was and used to toeing an invisible social line. To her they were the 'grown-ups' who misunderstood her and wanted to bend her to their ways. 'Grown-up' was a word which she often used and not in a favourable sense: to be 'grown up' was to inhabit an oppressive, alien world. The 'grown-ups' unfortunately included most members of the household supporting the Royal Family and particularly those among them like Oliver Everett and Lady Susan Hussey who were deputed to guide her. Diana was classless in a way in which only people to whom class really means nothing can be. And she was rebellious, disliking being told what to do.

The innate coldness and distance of the members of the Royal Family when they were at Buckingham Palace, each with their own separate apartments, did not help to make her feel at home. 'What was amazing in the Palace,' a member of staff recalled, 'was that each household was a water-tight compartment. I couldn't understand how the Queen didn't know what the Duke [of Edinburgh] was doing and the Duke didn't know what the Queen was doing. Then they'd go somewhere and the Queen Mother would be on the other side of the street . . .'[28] The Queen, the one member of the family revered by Diana, was busy and remote. Diana would go to see her and even take her little presents of china figures: despite what many people have inferred the Queen was, according to a member of Diana's staff, 'very, very supportive'. Charles was fond but also always busy and he had little time to devote to his adoring young fiancée. Diana missed the life of giggling and spontaneous humour she had been used to in the past. 'I missed my girls so much I wanted to go back there and sit and giggle and borrow clothes and chat about silly things, just being in my safe shell again . . . I couldn't believe how cold everyone was [at Buckingham Palace].'[29]

She gave small lunches in her sitting room for her 'girls' from Coleherne Court, and for her mother and sister Jane. Mostly, however, she was alone, and for comfort she turned to the staff at Buckingham Palace, just as she had at Park House and at Althorp. Diana would spend evenings at the home of Colborne, dubbed 'Uncle Michael', and his wife Shirley. She also became friendly with several other members of the Palace staff. One of them was Mark Simpson (whose title was nursery footman although the nursery no longer existed) who had been deputed to look after her. Simpson was one of those Walter Mitty-like people, gay, fantastic and fantasizing, who are attracted to the romance of royalty like moths to a flame. Mark had started life as a nursery footman at the age of seventeen, looking after Prince Edward, taking him to school and accompanying him to the dentist. Good-looking, popular and ever helpful, he was a favourite for royal tours and holidays and on *Britannia*. Two days after her wedding, when she was on the first part of her honeymoon at Broadlands, Diana wrote a 'thank-you' letter to Simpson: 'I just wanted to thank you for all your kindness and patience you've showed towards me since I moved into B[uckingham] P[alace],' she wrote. 'My stay was made so much easier by your company as it got terribly lonely & we had so many laughs & for that I can't thank you enough.' Mark, it appears, had supplied her with secret bowls of cornflakes (later she said that the eating disorder of binging and vomiting first attacked her at this time and her yearning for bowls of cornflakes was probably a symptom of this). The letter was written in almost schoolgirl terms with an endearing fallibility as to spelling and the 'smiley face' illustration which she loved to use. 'The bad news is that I haven't eaten *any* cerial [sic] – sob. How am I going to cope without my bowls of cerial . . .'[30]

On her twentieth birthday, 1 July 1981, Diana gave a small party for six of her friends among the Palace staff with a chocolate cake specially made for her by one of the chefs. The guests included her dresser (lady's maid), Evelyn Dagley, Cyril Dickman, the fatherly Palace steward and most senior member of the staff, her policeman, the housemaid who looked after her rooms and the chef who cooked the cake. A year later she wrote to Mark Simpson: 'Of course I remembered last birthday – I drank too much Pimms and ate a mass of chocolate cake . . .'[31] 'In the afternoon,' Cyril Dickman remembered, 'she came wandering down to where my office was . . . and she gave the boys all a slice of cake. They never could get her to take it back up. But you know that was the sort of person she was.' 'In those days, that first six months before they were married, she used to go down to the kitchens an awful lot, because the Palace is a lonely place and if you're on your own . . . She didn't have anything in common really with a lot of them, the Family were all working – they had all their engagements . . .' said another member of staff. 'She did a lot of this, particularly at Sandringham and Balmoral, she just wandered around everywhere. Nowhere was safe, the pantry and the kitchen . . . I think she just wanted to talk to people . . . At Sandringham she often appeared after tea and she went through and saw the pantry boys and had a chat with them and then she had tea with Mervyn [the chef]. She'd just wander in . . .'[32]

'It seemed funny to us,' Stephen Barry commented, 'she just wasn't adjusting to being royal.' Some people disapproved of Diana's familiarity with the staff. A senior member of the Queen Mother's household disliked the way that one of the Palace staff in particular would feed her with malicious gossip about the household. On one occasion at Sandringham he put her firmly in her place: 'She was sitting in the pantry, swinging her legs. And she looked at me and said, "You don't approve of me being here, do you?" He replied, "No, Your Royal Highness, I don't. Not at all. This is servants' quarters, you should be in the saloon learning your craft." And I turned on my heel, and walked out,' he recalled.[33]

Of all Diana's family, Frances Shand Kydd was the one who gave her the fullest support. While her father, still partially estranged after the Raine row, turned up once or twice, he was still suffering the effects of his stroke and a member of staff described him as 'charming, but not always on the ball, always delightful but not going to be a forceful view because he just wasn't at that stage of his existence'. Frances, however, was 'very, very sharp, very on the ball . . . always around asking questions'. But while Johnnie Spencer was a welcome figure with the family, Frances had been *persona non grata* since her 'bolting days', and her defensive attitudes undoubtedly affected her daughter. 'From February to July she [Frances] was in and out all the time and I found her such an attractive woman – beautiful blue eyes like Diana's – then she sort of disappeared,' recalled one official. In the run-up to the wedding, Frances occupied herself with taking Diana shopping for her trousseau. She pressed royal aides to tell her how much her daughter would be given in clothes allowance, only to be gently rebuffed with the assurance that it would be what was necessary. It was Frances who recommended that Diana use her interior designer, the South African-born Dudley Poplak, for the redecoration of Highgrove where Charles had had the rooms painted white, leaving Diana a clean slate.

Part of Diana's problem lay in her basic insecurity coupled with a determination to be her own person. Insecurity made her suspicious of people like Lady Susan Hussey and Oliver Everett, who had been in the Prince's life before her arrival and whose loyalty would inevitably be to him. Susan Hussey was, as one courtier described her, 'a female Mountbatten' to the Prince: 'Sue Hussey is totally and utterly devoted to the Prince and is probably the closest person to him . . . in a way because of her proximity to the Queen and how long she'd been there, she knew him absolutely backwards and he could relax totally with her . . . she has remained one of his best friends.' Lady Susan 'had huge loyalty to him, she wanted Diana to prove to be a success so therefore she gave all her support to her . . . she couldn't have been more helpful, friendly, courteous . . .'[34] Outwardly Diana got on with Lady Susan but inwardly she was as suspicious of her as she was of anyone who had been close to the Prince. She would ask Colborne, 'What hold does that woman have on my husband?' Oliver Everett did his best to help her understand the role that was facing her, providing lists of biographies of previous consorts and, earlier that year, even suggesting she should learn some Welsh in advance of a Welsh visit. His suggestions were treated with scorn. She never read the books and her reaction to his idea about learning Welsh was 'You must be joking'. She did not like the implication that she was ignorant and she resented being told what to do. Had she taken his advice to read about the lives of previous Princesses of Wales she might have been more conscious of what was expected of her. She might also have been aware of the suffering of Queen Alexandra, wife of Edward VII, at his repeated infidelities and particularly at his long-term relationship with Alice Keppel, great-grandmother and role model to Camilla Parker Bowles.

Diana found the intense, unceasing media spotlight focused on her difficult. Every step she took beyond the Palace was watched and recorded, making her nervous and afraid of getting anything wrong. The outstanding example of this was the episode of 'the dress', when Diana wore a strapless black dress to a gala at the London Guildhall on 9 March. Unwittingly she had broken a long-standing royal rule that the family never wear black except for mourning, as Prince Charles discouragingly informed her. The décolleté showed too much soon-to-be-royal flesh. 'I remember my first [royal] engagement so well,' Diana said as she relived the memory for Andrew Morton. '*So* excited. Black dress from the Emanuels [Elizabeth and David, designers of the wedding dress] and I thought it was OK because girls my age wore this dress. I hadn't appreciated that I was now seen as a royal lady . . . Black to me was the smartest colour you could possibly have at the age of

19. It was a real grown-up dress. I was quite big-chested then and they all got frightfully excited . . . It was a horrendous occasion. I didn't know whether to go out of the door first. I didn't know whether your handbag should be in your left hand or your right. I was terrified really – at the time everything was all over the place.'[35] When Diana confessed her feelings to Princess Grace of Monaco, whom she greatly admired, Grace replied: 'Don't worry, it gets worse!' On one occasion in a car with the Queen's press secretary, Michael Shea, she broke down in tears on seeing a huge picture poster of herself. 'I can't take this any more,' she sobbed.

From that time, her weight plummeted. According to her later account this is when she began to suffer from the eating disorder bulimia, gorging herself on bowls of cereal and custard and then vomiting. Later she said that it was first prompted by a chance remark by Prince Charles at the time of the engagement, when he put his arm round her waist and joked, 'Oh, a bit chubby here, aren't we?' Diana, like all bulimia sufferers, could not live with the image of herself as 'chubby': she felt she could control her life by forcing her body to lose weight. No one seems to have noticed what she was doing except Carolyn Bartholomew, who recorded: 'She went to live at Buckingham Palace and then the tears started. This little thing got so thin. I was so worried about her. She wasn't happy, she was suddenly plunged into all this pressure and it was a nightmare for her. She was dizzy with it, bombarded from all sides. It was a whirlwind and she was ashen, she was grey . . .'[36]

The happiness of her relationship with Charles was punctuated by her increasing fears over Camilla, concerns which he failed to understand. As he saw it, he had promised himself to Diana and that was it. Where other men might have tried to dissemble their feelings, he could not. 'Prince Charles always wore his heart on his sleeve,' said a friend. He was too honest for his own good, too emotional to realize the consequence of what he was saying, as the many indiscreet outpourings in letters to friends quoted by his biographer Dimbleby showed. Diana hero-worshipped him: 'Charles is very deep,' she told Robert Runcie, Archbishop of Canterbury, when they met that spring for premarital instruction.

The more she worshipped, the more jealous and possessive she became. The rows were always about Camilla. The evening before Charles left for a prolonged tour of Australia and New Zealand, Camilla telephoned when Charles and Diana were talking in the library together. On realizing it was Camilla, Diana magnanimously left the room to let them talk. When she saw him off at the airport the next day, she was in tears, later confessing that they were prompted by Camilla's telephone call rather than Charles's imminent departure. On another occasion Diana, who was given to eavesdropping, heard Charles in his bath talking to Camilla on the telephone: 'Whatever happens I will always love you,' he said. Friends say that was typical of the way he spoke to his women friends but to Diana it was a confirmation of what she suspected. 'We had a filthy row,' she said. Ascot week in June, just two weeks before the wedding, was another difficult moment: for a nineteen-year-old girl the pressures of being treated by the public and the media as if she were a film star were taking their toll. 'Diana was going through a terribly difficult time of adjustment and was feeling very claustrophobic,' one observer said. During tea at the back of the royal box at the races she was practically in tears and had to be escorted home early.[37] And during that week Charles expressed his worries to an old friend, one of his mother's ladies-in-waiting: 'She's so much younger than me, do you think that matters?' he asked. As she commented later:

It was not like talking to someone who was just about to get married and was thrilled to bits and longing for his life with her. And I – if it had been anyone else – I think I would have said, 'Look for heaven's sake' . . . I mean if it had been one of my children and they weren't quite sure – I would have said to them, 'Well, if you're not sure, don't do it.' But you couldn't say it to him really because everything was planned. Mugs being made with their faces and all these kind of things. You can't suddenly abandon something like that with ease. And I don't think he actually wanted to – I think he felt that he wanted it to be right but I could tell there were doubts and it was very sad . . .[38]

By June, Diana's distress and her jealousy of Camilla – what Charles referred to as her 'other side' – had affected him. The jolly, happy teenager who had enchanted them all at Balmoral six months earlier had metamorphosed into an emotionally demanding young woman. Coming as he did from a family not given to introspection over the effect of their behaviour on others, Charles was simply surprised, never imagining that his own behaviour or the royal surroundings to which he had become so accustomed could have had anything to do with it. Only in March, shortly after the engagement, he had written to friends, 'I do believe I am very lucky that someone as special as Diana seems to love me so much. I am already discovering how nice it is to have someone around to share things with.' Significantly, he added: 'Other people's happiness and enthusiasm at the whole thing is also a most "encouraging" element and it makes me so proud that so many people have such admiration and affection for Diana.'[39]

Neither Spencers nor Windsors had doubts about the marriage. The Duke of Edinburgh had expressed his delight to a friend three weeks before the engagement was announced: 'Isn't it wonderful that they're going to get married? We're delighted.' And they were, the friend confirmed, adding, 'It all seemed so perfect . . . They were so anxious for him to get married that they didn't look beneath the surface. They knew she came from a broken home but they thought a family atmosphere would be the answer . . .'[40] If Ruth Fermoy harboured doubts, as she later told Dimbleby, she was too much of a courtier to express them, beyond warning Diana in what must have been the understatement of the year: 'Darling, you must understand that their sense of humour and their lifestyle are different and I don't think it will suit you.' But according to Johnnie's cousin Robert Spencer, 'I remember what an amazing thrill [it was] for us that the Prince had chosen our Diana, and everybody thought at the time, with no reason not to, that she was young enough to be totally moulded into conforming as the future Queen.'[41] Only the perspicacious Princess Margaret foresaw the breakers ahead, the rock on which the marriage would founder. To a friend who said how delighted they must be with the wedding, she replied: 'We're extremely relieved but she [Camilla Parker Bowles] has no intention of giving him up.'[42]

The biggest explosion came over her discovery of a bracelet from Charles destined for Camilla with the initials GF (for 'Girl Friday') engraved on it. It was on Michael Colborne's desk among a heap of trinkets intended as farewell presents for various former girlfriends, including Susan George. Colborne was called out of the office and Diana went in, saw the parcel, opened it and rushed out. 'What have you done to Lady Diana?' the Prince's private secretary, Edward Adeane, asked Colborne as he came into the office. 'She rushed out in tears and disappeared.' Colborne saw her later 'pretty red-eyed'. When she accosted Charles about it he told her bluntly that it was indeed for Camilla and that he was going to give it to her at a farewell lunch on 27 July, two days before the wedding. At polo at Tidworth barracks, the Wiltshire headquarters of the 13/18 Hussars, on 25 July Diana was seen to be distraught, unable to bear the thought of that farewell lunch. With reason she doubted that it would really mean farewell. Sententiously, Dimbleby underlined the couple's noble acceptance of fate: 'His [Charles's] feelings for Camilla Parker Bowles had not changed but they had both accepted that their intimacy could no longer be maintained . . .'[43] If his feelings for Camilla and hers for him were unchanged, then one might justifiably wonder how he could contemplate marrying a twenty-year-old girl who adored him. The 1980s were not the 1890s: the Alice Keppel/Edward VII relationship had required a complaisant Queen Alexandra, a role which Diana would not be prepared to play.

On the day Charles presented the famous bracelet to his lover, Diana lunched with her sisters, Jane and Sarah. When she told them she couldn't go through with the marriage, their pragmatic response that it was too late to draw back – 'Don't worry, Duch, your face is on the tea towels so it's too late to chicken out now' – cheered her and made her laugh. Despite her adoration for Charles, Diana had had doubts over her ability to cope with the consequences of the marriage. Her close friend Carolyn told James Whitaker that not only was Diana worried about the age gap between her and Charles but she had realized that she had not had a single weekend away with Charles unless they were at Bolehyde Manor or Camilla was otherwise present. While Charles was away in Australia, she had gone to her father in tears, confessing her doubts about the marriage.[44] At the wedding rehearsal in St Paul's forty-eight hours before the ceremony, Diana said, she broke down, sobbing: 'Absolutely collapsed . . . because of all sorts of things. The Camilla thing rearing its head the whole way through our engagement and I was desperately trying to be mature about the situation but I didn't have the foundations to do it and I couldn't talk to anyone about it.'[45] If she did truly collapse, she did it in private. Eleven-year-old Sarah Jane Gaselee, one of her bridesmaids who was there, recalled: 'I don't think she was stressed by it or anything; it didn't appear that way. What I do remember is that she and Charles were really in love as far as I could see, at that age. I saw them cuddling on the sofa and during the rehearsals they had their arms linked and were skipping down the aisles. It was all really happy, or so I thought.'[46]

But that night, at the Queen's ball at Buckingham Palace, two guests found Diana in tears: Charles had danced only once with her and the remainder of the evening with Camilla, and gone off with her.[47] The story that Charles spent the night with Camilla at Buckingham Palace after the ball as Diana slept in Clarence House is, however, untrue. Diana was not at Clarence House on the night of the ball, but in her apartment in Buckingham Palace, and she and Charles left the ball at the same time. Camilla was at the ball with her husband and in any case it is highly unlikely that the Prince would have taken such a risk at that juncture. The two of them may have spent some time alone together earlier in the evening but the 'spending the night' story, told to James Whitaker, allegedly by Barry (who, however, denied it in his own book), was also categorically denied by Michael Colborne: 'It didn't happen, that's for certain. It couldn't have happened without a lot of people knowing . . .' Later, Andrew Parker Bowles told Nigel Dempster the story was absolutely untrue. Nor was Charles with Camilla on the eve of the wedding: with Diana he hosted a party

6. The Beginning of the 'Fairy Tale'

'The essential basis of that tragedy was that she was in love with him when she married him . . .' (Victor Edelstein, couturier)

Diana became an international media star on the day of her wedding, 29 July 1981. In terms of worldwide television, it was the greatest royal event ever staged: three-quarters of a billion people watched as 'Lady Di' became 'Princess Di' and from that moment on she was never to be out of the limelight, becoming an icon of the status of Marilyn Monroe or Jackie Kennedy. The beauty she had become was almost unrecognizable from the shy, chubby girl of engagement day only five months previously. Slim, almost fragile looking, she was radiant in her dress of ivory silk with its huge train, the magnificent Spencer tiara holding her billowing tulle veil. The moment when the passionate bride kissed her not so passionate groom on the lips on the balcony of Buckingham Palace in full view of the watching millions etched itself on the public consciousness as the remembered image of the 'fairy tale' which the Archbishop of Canterbury, presiding at the wedding, had pronounced it to be. Inextricably – and dangerously – the private and public faces of monarchy were seen as intertwined. Prompted by the romance of the 'princely marriage', polls showed the popularity of the monarchy as higher than it had been even at the time of the Queen's Coronation and her Silver Jubilee. It was the apogee of the twentieth-century monarchy. Dangerously too for Diana, the world became involved in what they saw as 'Our Story', when the fairy-tale princess and her dashing prince became *their* property.

Charles and Diana were carried away by the euphoria of the cheering crowds lining the streets, frenetically waving flags and shouting 'I love you'. The sun shone and all doubts and unhappiness seemed forgotten. Despite her sickness the previous evening, Diana had been reassured by Charles's present of the ring. In the run-up to the wedding there had been one of the not infrequent outbreaks of Spencer trouble which had resulted in Barbara Cartland, who was, after all, the bride's step-grandmother, staying away, while Diana had banned both Camilla and Lady Tryon from the guest list for the wedding breakfast. At St Paul's Cathedral, Diana had to concentrate on getting her sick father up the long aisle without mishap. One of the officiating clergy (Dean Webster) told friends how touching it was to see the way she practically carried him, walking painfully slowly, up the aisle. There before the altar, Charles stood waiting for her: 'I remember being so in love with my husband that I couldn't take my eyes off him,' Diana recalled. 'I just absolutely thought I was the luckiest girl in the world.'[1] 'You look beautiful,' he whispered to her. 'Beautiful for you,' she replied.

The feelings of jealousy of Camilla which had haunted her throughout her engagement melted away. Charles was her husband, the 'other woman' just a face in the crowd. As she made her way down the aisle, she spotted Camilla in pale grey with a pillbox hat, her son Tom (Charles's godson) standing on a chair beside her. The image remained with her but at the time, she said, she thought, 'Well, there you are, that's it, let's hope that's over with . . .'[2] As if to emphasize, however, how much the Parker Bowles family was part of the royal circle and inescapably, therefore, of her own future, Camilla's husband Andrew rode beside the Queen's carriage in his role as Commander of the 1st and 2nd divisions of the Sovereign's Escort both to and from St Paul's, and then accompanied Charles and Diana as they drove away from Buckingham Palace en route to the first stage of their honeymoon at Broadlands.

Despite the delirium surrounding her, Diana was alert enough not only to keep a watchful eye on her ailing father but even to notice that one of her bridesmaids, Catherine Cameron, aged only five, who had ridden back from the ceremony in a horse-drawn carriage, had suffered an allergic reaction to the horse and arrived at Buckingham Palace with streaming eyes and swollen face. A shot taken by Patrick Lichfield shows her concern for the little girl as soon as they arrive, bending down to comfort her while the Queen extends a comforting hand. 'I noticed that she was extremely quick to comfort the child,' Lichfield remembered. 'She had a lot of other things to think about: she had to be on the balcony, do the waving, she had to go and do the group photographs again and again and again, you know, so the whole thing was ahead of her, and yet she found time to make this gesture, which was in itself touching . . .'[3] That night she took the time to telephone the people who had helped her, including make-up artist Barbara Daly. 'I thought how remarkable that was,' Daly remembered. 'I can't imagine many people doing that after a day like that. There are many beautiful people in the world, but Diana had that extra thing, which is really a very genuine warmth because she had a very loving and compassionate heart.'[4]

There was a happy family atmosphere about the whole occasion at the Palace epitomized by Lichfield's informal shot of an exhausted Diana collapsed on the floor in a heap of ivory silk and taffeta, surrounded by her giggling bridesmaids, her quizzically smiling husband and two grinning brothers-in-law. At the going away, as the open carriage trailing tin cans and balloons attached by Edward and Andrew pulled away from the portico, the Queen started running behind it waving as everyone threw confetti. 'It felt just like a family wedding,' recalled Mountbatten's granddaughter, India Hicks, one of the bridesmaids, 'until they pulled outside the gates and it changed . . .'[5]

Diana and Charles spent the first two days of their honeymoon at Mountbatten's country home, Broadlands, now the property of Norton and Penny Romsey and the scene of Charles's courtship of Camilla just under ten years earlier. They slept in the same bed the Queen had used on her honeymoon with Prince Philip in November 1947. They then (to the indignation of the Spanish, whose royal family had consequently boycotted the wedding) flew to Gibraltar to join the royal yacht *Britannia*. Honeymooning on a yacht with a crew of two hundred was not a romantic experience. As Charles's official biographer put it, 'even an intimate dinner by candlelight was hardly a private affair, accompanied as it was by the camaraderie of senior officers at the table and a band of Royal Marines playing a romantic medley in the background'.[6] Diana's hopes of romantic bliss had been dashed by the time they left Broadlands: 'Second night, out come the van der Post novels [sic] he hadn't read. Seven of them – they came on our honeymoon. We read them and we had to analyse them over lunch everyday,' she later recalled.[7] A lady-in-waiting at Balmoral discussed the horrors of honeymoons in her day with Diana, who replied, 'Well, I bet your husband didn't read a book by an old boy called Jung the whole time.'[8]

Nor was there any hint of romance in the bridegroom's correspondence: 'All I can say is that marriage is very jolly and it's extremely nice being together in *Britannia*,' he wrote on the second day of their cruise. 'Diana dashes about chatting up all the sailors and the cooks in the galley etc. While I remain hermit-like on the verandah deck, sunk with pure joy into one of Laurens van der Post's books . . .'[9] It sounded as if he drew more 'pure joy' from van der Post's books than from the company of his young bride. He might have been an indulgent father observing the antics of a newly acquired puppy. Moreover, the shadow of Camilla, whom Diana thought she had left behind, hung over the *Britannia* honeymoon. 'She was on the telephone every day,' a friend said. 'And on *Britannia*. I know that's true because the poor girl was so upset that she told lots of people afterwards when she came back . . .'[10] Diana was devastated when Charles opened his wallet one day and two photographs of Camilla fell out. A few days later, as they were about to receive the Egyptian President, Anwar Sadat, and his wife for a banquet on board, Diana noticed that Charles was wearing cufflinks engraved with entwined 'Cs', a present from Camilla. Charles himself admitted that they were and was unable to understand why he shouldn't have worn them on his honeymoon. Years later Diana told friends in crude terms that their physical relationship on board *Britannia* had not been a success.[11] Poor

Diana, for all her youth and beauty, was sexually inexperienced, unable to compete on that level with the women Charles had known before. However honestly he tried, the image of Camilla was hard to erase and the two experiences did not compare.

Not once in his authorized version of the marriage did Dimbleby indicate that Prince Charles loved Diana. In his biography of the Prince, written after the Waleses' separation, he followed the official line which was to demote Diana's importance in Charles's life and to emphasize her difficult behaviour. Yet after Diana's death, Charles was to tell several intimate friends, 'There was a time when we were very much in love.'[12] As a royal relation recalls, 'When he talks about her sometimes, he will say, "You know we did love each other very much." Suddenly out of the blue, "You know there was a time when we did love each other very much." So there was something.'[13] All her life Diana herself always maintained that Charles was in love with her when they married and, so it seems, for a relatively brief time and in a limited way, he was. An eyewitness who was at Balmoral every holiday said that for the first few years 'when they used to arrive at picnics and things hand in hand they really looked devoted'.

Dimbleby's account of the couple's honeymoon, both on *Britannia* and through September at Craigowan Lodge on the Balmoral estate, is limited to biased descriptions of her state of mind. It was, in the Dimbleby version, Diana's failure to understand her husband that cast shadows over the relationship: 'For the Prince it [their stay at Balmoral] was a blissful interlude at his favourite home, complete with his books, his fishing rod, and his friends. He assumed that Diana would share his happiness but . . . she was quite unable to surrender herself to his good humour. So far from being the focus of her husband's attention, he seemed to go out of his way to avoid the moments of intimacy that she craved. Instead – or so it appeared to her – he seemed either to prefer his own company or to have others about him as well as her.'[14] Van der Post also featured at Balmoral: Charles's idea of bliss was to read the sage's books out loud to Diana as they sat on a hilltop. The familiar surroundings brought back to her images of

Camilla who had so often been in attendance at Birkhall. She dreamed of her at night, constantly suspecting Charles of ringing her up to ask her advice about his marriage. It was an obsession: as Dimbleby put it, 'Her insecurity about his feelings for her were fed by the canker of jealousy.' Yet both sides, writing with hindsight, exaggerated the misery of that time: at an informal photo call on the banks of the River Dee, the couple looked fond and Diana radiant. She was already transformed from the mousy girl of a few months previously: her hair was coloured blonde and with bare brown legs and tanned complexion she looked for the first time not just beautiful but glamorous. Sarah McCorquodale told James Whitaker, with whom she was constantly in touch, that Diana had far preferred the time at Balmoral to the days on *Britannia*, that Charles had been sweet to her, leaving loving notes and trinkets under her pillow, 'things which she found enchanting'.[15]

Yet, again with hindsight, that Deeside photo call said it all. While Diana, gazing seductively at the press, her legs adopting a ballet position, draped a possessive arm round his shoulders, Charles looked stiff, nervous and worried, the dead salmon lying as a trophy at his feet. In fact at Balmoral as at Buckingham Palace, Diana was finding it difficult to adapt to life in the Royal Family. She felt hemmed in and isolated, incapable of reaching beyond the invisible barrier which now separated her from the rest of the world. 'All the guests at Balmoral coming to stay just stared at me the whole time, treated me like glass,' she recalled, '[but] as far as I was concerned I was Diana.'[16] She herself had none of the deference which most people felt in the presence of royalty, or even of gratitude that she had been made a member of the exclusive circle. She thought, almost certainly correctly, that her in-laws and their friends and staff were looking at her critically. She thought they were old-fashioned and stuffy, they regarded her as 'a silly girl'. She clung to her sense of herself as 'Diana' which was battered by her perennial feelings of inadequacy; her behaviour, her sulks and bouts of tears, her leaving the table early at dinner or on occasions even refusing to come down, were interpreted as rudeness. The family operated by their own rules and traditions; her refusal to follow or even to try to understand them mystified her in-laws, utterly unused to being confronted by such behaviour. Her upbringing had not taught her to behave 'properly', as her resentment at her husband for always offering a drink to the Queen and the Queen Mother before turning to her showed. Even in ordinary families mother and grandmother would come before wife in such circumstances. 'But I had to be told that that was normal because I always thought it was the wife first,' she complained.[17] A royal relation commented, 'At Balmoral on their honeymoon she started saying that she wouldn't come down to dinner and him being asked by the Queen to go upstairs and persuade her, and then coming down red-faced and saying "I can't". Can you imagine any of us with our mother-in-law, can you imagine anybody, whether they were staying with their mother-in-law in a hovel somewhere, who would actually start to not do what their mother-in-law wanted on their honeymoon?'[18] Diana's defiant behaviour might have been allowed by her indulgent father at Park House: anywhere else, however, it would have been considered unacceptable and at Balmoral in the presence of the Queen it was outrageous.

Unsurprisingly, therefore, her relations with her royal in-laws were not easy. Although she revered the Queen, the aura which surrounded her mother-in-law, coupled with her innate shyness and reserve, precluded intimacy. Diana had once said that she saw her role as building bridges between her husband and his parents. Charles was in awe of his mother and intimidated by his father: it soon became obvious to Diana that no such role was envisaged for her either by her husband or her in-laws. The Duke of Edinburgh, always sympathetic to a pretty young girl, did his best to jolly her along, whirling her into dinner when she hung back overcome with shyness. Prince Andrew she had known and liked since childhood, Prince Edward she simply ignored. Princess Anne, the strongest character of the younger royals, had little time for Diana. Of the older generation, the Queen Mother remained an enigma to Diana herself, although those who knew her well detected she did not like her; that Diana's grandmother, Ruth Fermoy, later joined the ranks of those who denigrated her could be taken as an accurate reflection of her friend and employer's views. Only Princess Margaret was to become Diana's real friend and champion within the family. In her youth she, like Diana, had been the media star of the Royal Family, glamorous, idolized and criticized: no stranger to defiant behaviour herself, she empathized with Diana, seeing in her a reflection of her own rebellious self. Yet a relation denied that the Royal Family was 'cliquey': 'When you're staying there, it's not that they're all very cliquey together, and it's not all in-jokes which you can't join in on . . . they're not really touchy-feely, close-knit – it's not the in-joke that's going on from last night, it's not at all them and us. In a funny sort of way they're quite distant with each other. It doesn't make it too difficult for a stranger coming in, because you're not coming up against a family that is so strongly knit together that you are the object of attention, that you're on the outside and they've all got their in-names and their in-this and you don't know what they're talking about. But,' she added, 'if you don't like the great outdoors, if you don't like getting wet, putting on your gumboots, I can see that it's not the easiest, and I think that in the lead-up to this whole thing, she must have given the impression that she did like the great outdoors . . .'[19]

Part Scottish herself through her grandmother Ruth, Diana always denied disliking Scotland: she loved visiting her mother on the Isle of Seil. 'I was rather surprised that she took so violently against that sort of [Balmoral] life,' said a member of the court, 'because she was really quite keen when she came up for that weekend at Birkhall. They were out on the hills all the time and she appeared to be perfectly happy with it. I think it was the sort of relentlessness of it.'[20] What Diana hated was the regimented life of Balmoral, the emphasis on outdoor activities whatever the weather, the focusing on shooting and stalking and fishing (all sports which she detested) as the *raison d'être* of life there. Despite being on holiday, the Royal Family adhered rigidly to the forms of previous years: women guests would be expected to change their clothes four times a day, from something to wear down to breakfast into sporting clothes for lunch and out with the guns, back to change for tea and then into a long dress for dinner. Courtiers would be in attendance and, to a young girl like Diana, the whole place was oppressive and deadly dull.

It was becoming obvious to perceptive observers that the couple were basically incompatible. Both were psychologically needy, each seeking comfort, devotion and reassurance which the other could not provide (and, in Charles's case, had already found in Camilla). Charles was old for his age, Diana young for hers. Despite his essential kindness, Charles was too spoiled and self-centred to begin to understand Diana, while for her part she was too insecure and blinkered to understand the man he was, or to make allowances for him. The pattern of his life had been set for years and he was not about to change it for anyone. Frustrated, Diana began to play the tricks which she had played on her father to get what she wanted: sulks, tears, withdrawal, utter self-absorption. Perplexed and worried, Charles did what he could to placate her, inviting her flatmates up to stay and summoning 'Uncle Michael' from London to spend the day with her. 'I was summoned to Scotland, rung up on the Saturday night to catch the night sleeper on the Sunday and I spent probably the worst day of my life. I was having my breakfast in the kitchen and then he [Charles] came in and said he was going stalking with Lord Romsey . . . and then the Princess came in and we disappeared into the front room of Craigowan and didn't get out of there until four o'clock. There was a big white clock there and I think it went the slowest it's ever been in its life. At some stage I think it was going backwards. We had tears, we had temper, we had everything that day . . .'[21] Asked what the Prince's particular sin that day had been, the source replied that 'he'd started that attitude of his "You find your enjoyment, I've got mine" – and she didn't like the killing thing, to go stalking up a hill was about the last thing she wanted to do'.[22] Laurens van der Post, whose works had cast a shadow over her honeymoon, was recruited to analyse Diana, the result being mutual incomprehension. 'Laurens didn't understand me,' Diana later recalled. 'Everybody saw I was getting thinner and I was being sicker and sicker.

Basically they thought I could adapt to being Princess of Wales overnight . . .'[23] She was sent down to London to see analysts and psychiatrists and given a Valium prescription in a vain attempt to calm her. Vain because there could be no effective cure for her unhappiness, which was caused by basic insecurity and the tortured fears of unrequited love. The shadow of Camilla had lain over the relationship from the start. According to Dimbleby, Charles's friends with whom he had 'agonized' before ending the relationship with Camilla, considered that Diana had 'already reached the point of obsession'.

Media interest in Diana remained intense to a degree which no one had foreseen. Unworthy and inadequate as she felt herself, Diana somehow managed to cope with being the focus of this huge attention from public and media. On their first public engagement, a three-day tour of Wales in October, the world's press turned up in force, Japanese and American television crews descending on Welsh villages and towns none of them had ever heard of before. Diana was feeling 'ghastly', as one of her staff described it: on the second day of the tour she received confirmation of her pregnancy. She felt sick and apprehensive of people's expectations of her. 'I cried a lot in the car, saying I couldn't get out, couldn't cope with the crowds . . . He [Charles] said, "You've just got to get out and do it" . . . He tried his hardest and he did really well in that department, got me out and once I was out, I was able to do my bit.'[24] She did it superlatively, kneeling to talk to the children, bending down to speak to the elderly in their wheelchairs, exuding sympathy and compassion. 'She was just remarkable,' said a newly appointed member of her staff. 'We set off with no idea what we were really meant to be doing. She immediately saw how to deal with people. She would bend down to children, she got down on her haunches. Talking to very elderly men and holding their hand while they were sitting out in the cold. Probably completely tongue-tied, totally overwhelmed at actually meeting the Prince and Princess of Wales – but she would just talk. It was just that ability to know how to talk to people which was there from day one. She knew instinctively how to react to people, just ordinary people ... And she had been told that she should make a speech in Welsh, standing up.' Despite her shyness, Diana, who had been coached in the language by an elderly peer, managed it, no easy task for a twenty-year-old.

'This was her first walkabout as such,' remembered Dickie Arbiter, who was, at the time, one of the royal correspondents accompanying the tour, 'and she did it as if she had done it all her life, trying to please everybody, switching from one side of the road to the other, because all people were doing was "We want Di, we want Di, we want Di". And that's something he [Charles] had to get used to ... the trouble was that he was playing the supporting role, not the starring role. That started almost immediately with the first visit they did ...'[25] 'People wanted to see her, not him, and he couldn't stomach it,' said an aide. 'I was with Prince Charles and nobody came to us,' said a former police protection officer on the tour; 'everybody wanted her and that was the start of it really. I think she started thinking and people started looking at her as a divine something ...'[26] Diana was not yet the glamorous being she later became; she was not well dressed and her hair had returned to mouse, yet no one who saw her operating on that first tour could doubt the enormous rapport she had with the crowds. It was a new way of being royal although nobody realized it at the time. Nor did anyone in the Royal Family, not even Prince Charles who had been very supportive and protective of her during the Welsh tour, appreciate what an achievement it had been for the twenty-year-old girl with no training for the role. 'She was amazed,' said one of her staff, 'that after those few days in Wales nobody said anything, that the Queen didn't pick up the telephone and say "Well done". It was the lack of recognition that she got – and the same from Prince Charles – if he had come to her and said well done or a little bit more ... But again, he had done it all his life: he didn't realize what it would have been like for a relatively shy twenty-year-old.'[27]

Pregnancy increased Diana's malaise, her sickness and her instability. When they returned to London at the end of October, they had no home of their own, just a relatively cramped apartment

on an upper floor of Buckingham Palace: bedroom, sitting room,
study, bathroom and two dressing rooms. Diana's dressing room
was the only room which was exclusively hers. 'There was no
thought,' an aide said, 'as to where she could see her girlfriends,
or where she might be able to make a cup of coffee. You know,
those silly little things. If she wanted to have a cup of coffee or tea
or boil an egg, she had to summon a footman.'[28] Charles was used
to it; he had been born and brought up in the Palace. Nonetheless,
as one of Diana's aides said, 'It's extraordinary that a man of
thirty-two was still living in Mummy's home and it made it very
isolating for her . . . if you walk across the courtyard from the gate
to the Privy Purse door, the world and his wife are looking at you.
And for her friends who were aged nineteen, twenty, it's quite
intimidating. And then you have to be escorted upstairs by a
footman . . .'[29] 'One or two of Diana's girlfriends were quite
worried about her loneliness,' another courtier recalled. 'In the
early days when she was pregnant with William, I know she rang
one up and said, "Can I come round? I'm so terribly lonely . . ."'[30]

The imbalance between her empty life and Charles's busy one
became more marked. He had a programme of official duties, she
had none. 'One thing she couldn't accept was this wonderful word
called Duty,' a member of Charles's staff said. 'I sat with her one
day and she was talking about it and I said, "If you get that diary
for next year out, you could write it up: Trooping the Colour,
Remembrance Day Service, do a couple of royal tours, you'll go
to Balmoral, you'll go to Sandringham, you'll be shooting . . . you
could virtually fill half of that up anyway, and you've got to keep
on doing it. And unfortunately, your husband, it's his duty. He
lives in awe of his mother so you'll never change him."'[31] Diana,
besotted with Charles, still failed to comprehend why he could
not spend more time with her. Worse still was that no one seemed
to take her seriously. 'She was disregarded and that was what
probably hurt more than anything else,' said one of her staff.
Another recalled that she used to complain 'that there was no
equality in the marriage and that the Prince of Wales never for one
second considered her to be an equal which was an impossible

situation for her'.[32] This royal attitude is common to all the senior members of the family, who never consider other people, their lives, their feelings or opinions. Many of the courtiers share the same view, hard for outsiders to comprehend. For Diana, deter-mined to cling to her sense of self, it was baffling and frustrating to a degree. As one of Diana's staff remarked to Dimbleby, no one had approached her predicament with imagination: 'I don't think they had really thought about her role . . .'

It was not until September, three months after the wedding, that ladies-in-waiting were appointed to her, an indication of the strange lack of foresight and consideration where she was concerned. The ladies-in-waiting included Lavinia Baring, Hazel West and Anne Beckwith Smith. Anne Beckwith Smith was ten years older than Diana but she had been at West Heath and knew Diana's sisters, so there was common ground. Much of their time was taken up with the deluge of presents and correspondence generated by the wedding and then by the announcement of Diana's pregnancy. One 'wonderful' woman who had taken early retirement from Downing Street was there to cope. 'She was just marvellous, she wrote wonderful letters to children and grown-ups, and she kept a record. I think we had something like 28,000 letters, presents and cards, just for William. Every little old lady was knitting beautiful things, a layette and things like that. We always put the things she might like or something that was special aside.'[33]

Away from the gloom of Buckingham Palace, Christmas at Windsor was a rare period of peace and happiness for Charles and Diana. Christmas sees the Royal Family at their jolliest, with silly jokes and clowning, something which Charles greatly enjoys, and an exchange of the most commonplace and utilitarian presents which amazed Diana. Charles wrote to a friend: 'We've had such a lovely Christmas – the two of us. It has been extraordinarily happy and cosy [one of the Prince's highest accolades] being able to share it together . . . Next year will, I feel sure, be even nicer, with a small one to join in as well . . .'[34] Sandringham in January, however, was a different matter. Diana had always disliked going there, even as a child. The proximity of her beloved Park House,

Next month, Charles took Diana off to the Brabournes' house, Windermere, on Eleuthera in the Bahamas, staying with their son Norton and his wife Penny for what he described as 'a second honeymoon'. This time the tabloids excelled themselves: James Whitaker of the *Star* and Harry Arnold of the *Sun* supervised intrusive photographs of Diana, five months pregnant and wearing a bikini, from a nearby beach. 'CAREFREE DI THREW ROYAL CAUTION TO THE WINDS TO WEAR HER REVEALING OUTFIT' ran the *Sun*'s headline. The Queen was outraged, denouncing the tabloids' 'unprecedented . . . breach of privacy'. Just how carefree Diana was is open to question; the Romseys intimated to Dimbleby that she objected when Charles wanted to read or paint and openly expressed her boredom with his conversation. They were also probably among the 'tiny circle of his most trusted friends' with whom Charles discussed Diana's misery and who urged him to tell her to 'pull herself together' and stop indulging in self-pity. Charles apparently insisted that he was to blame and that it was too much to expect anyone to be married to the heir to the throne. While this may well have been true, he would have to have been very obtuse not to realize that the core of his wife's despair was her suspicion that he did not really love her.

Tabloid pressure on Diana increased: media expert Roy Greenslade called the bikini photographs the great turning point in the relationship with the press: 'Here was an intense interest, sexual interest really, in this woman. The press – editors and reporters – were in love with Diana . . . she looked terrific, she sold magazine covers, no one could get enough of her.'[37] Pressure intensified until finally, on 21 June, she gave birth to William Arthur Philip Louis. 'William had to be induced,' she told Morton,[38] 'because I couldn't handle the press pressure any longer, it was becoming unbearable. It was as if everybody was monitoring every day for me . . .' For Diana, guarding her privacy had become an obsession; but courtiers regarded the birth of a son to the Prince and Princess of Wales as an important royal event to be shared with the public, as all births, deaths and marriages have traditionally been. Diana had what was known in her office as a 'foot stamp'

7. 'Di-mania'

'In Australia . . . one was aware of little tensions. He [Charles] couldn't understand that people wanted to see her' (a member of Diana's staff on her Australian tour, March 1983)

Diana now had a new baby and a new London home: Apartments 8 and 9 in Kensington Palace, the dark, redbrick, seventeenth-century collection of buildings in Kensington Gardens which had harboured members of the Royal Family for more than three hundred years. Queen Mary (wife of William III) and Queen Anne had died there: Queen Victoria was born and brought up there before her accession as Queen. George VI, Edward VIII and his brothers used to refer to it as the 'aunt-heap', an allusion to the number of elderly royal relations who lived there. In modern terms, you could call it a royal condominium. The apartments, however, bear no relation to modern flats: they are attached houses, comprising several floors with state rooms as well as domestic offices. When Charles and Diana moved in, Princess Margaret occupied Apartment 10 where she lived in considerable splendour attended by numerous staff. Other royal neighbours were the eighty-one-year-old (born 25 December 1901) Princess Alice, Duchess of Gloucester, with her son and daughter-in-law, Prince Richard, Duke of Gloucester, and his wife, Birgitte, and Prince and Princess Michael of Kent. The Duke and Duchess of Kent lived nearby at Wren House, Palace Green, while Diana's sister Jane and brother-in-law Robert Fellowes lived down the drive in the Old Barracks. All of them were grace-and-favour tenants of the Queen. There had been a suggestion that Charles and Diana should occupy the far more splendid Spencer House overlooking Green Park, left to the younger Spencers under the terms of their father's will, but the costs of restoration had ruled that out. Perhaps, too, it had been considered unsuitable for the Prince of Wales to live in a house belonging to his wife's family.

Although living in a palace sounds very splendid, there were certain physical drawbacks to 'KP', as it was always known. Behind the splendid south-facing façade is a warren of courtyards and gardens surrounded by blocks of apartments. In fact the Waleses' apartment was far from suitable to the needs of the heir to the throne and his family. 'It was a small apartment,' said one of the staff who worked there. 'It needed to be bigger really. They had a sitting room and a study each, then a drawing room, then a dining room and that was it really as far as reception rooms went. Not a lot of corridor space . . . so it wasn't very comfortable. They needed a second reception room downstairs so that upstairs would be private, but the way it was it was all in together. They should have moved initially to somewhere bigger . . . They were far too important to be in such a small apartment. I think the apartment contributed to certain tensions . . . they were on top of one another as regards what they were supposed to be doing . . .'[1]

Patrick Jephson, who joined the Princess's staff in January 1988, serving first as equerry to the Princess and then as her private secretary, was surprised to find the apartment smaller and gloomier than he had expected. Despite the wide lawns and trees of the surrounding Kensington Gardens, the Waleses' apartment was dark and viewless, tucked away in the heart of the palace complex. There was virtually no privacy: 'Everybody could hear everybody else,' Jephson wrote. 'If you needed to get away from someone there was just not enough space.'[2] Most of the time the house was deathly quiet: the Prince and Princess were usually out and the staff retreated to their places behind the scenes. Outside the sun might be shining, the birds singing and children playing, but inside the apartment there was an historic silence and not enough light. 'If you sent the staff home, closed the curtains and forgot to turn on *all* the lights, no amount of TV channels, loud music or ringing telephones could keep the darkness at bay,' Jephson recalled.[3] For

Diana, despite its convenience in the heart of London, 'KP' was to be less a home than a prison.

She had cooperated over the decoration with Dudley Poplak, who was recommended by her mother and who had also been working with her on the redecoration of Highgrove. The decoration was a mixture of grand and contemporary: the seventeenth-century entrance hall, with its impressive staircase and baroque plaster ceiling (destroyed by a bomb during the Second World War, and subsequently restored), was carpeted in green and grey patterned with the Prince of Wales feathers, a theme emphasized throughout the house. On the first floor the reception rooms, the drawing and dining rooms were furnished either with wedding presents or furniture and paintings, and a tapestry from the Royal Collections, including a Veronese, *The Mystic Marriage of St Catherine*.

Diana and Charles had studies on the same floor. Diana's sitting room was feminine in dusty pink and grey-blue, with a pink sofa and, in a window alcove beside her desk, her school tuck box, stencilled D. Spencer, in which she kept her most private possessions. The room was a grown-up version of a teenager's room, with soft toys and cushions with slogans like 'Good girls go to heaven – bad girls go everywhere', and children's school paintings on the walls. Every surface was crammed with photographs, enamel boxes, porcelain figurines. It was cheerful, girlish and very cluttered, smelling deliciously of her favourite flowers, lilies, potpourri and scented candles.

Charles's more masculine room housed a box-kennel for his cherished yellow Labrador, Harvey, and on his desk a photograph of himself with his father, the Duke of Edinburgh, and the wry, or perhaps even defiant, inscription in Charles's handwriting: 'I was not born to follow in my father's footsteps.' In the master bedroom, the 7-foot 6-inch oak bed from his apartment at Buckingham Palace presented the poignant, even somewhat pathetic spectacle of the couple's toy animals ranged upon it: Charles's worn teddy, which he took everywhere with him and was tucked up in the bed at night by his valet, and Diana's 'family' from Park House, overflowing from the bed to shelves. It would be unkind to put too much emphasis on this attachment to childhood toys but it is hard to imagine such a collection featuring in the bedroom of, say, a Wall Street banker and his socialite wife.

Highgrove had been decorated by Diana and Poplak far more to her taste than Charles's. A royal relation described Diana and Poplak's schemes as 'terrible, like a sort of Trust House Forte idea of a modern princess's drawing room . . . three new magazines on this low table and the day's newspapers on that, I mean awful'.[4] It was to Highgrove (Kensington Palace was not yet ready) that Charles and Diana had returned after their Balmoral honeymoon. According to Stephen Barry, Charles had not seen the house since before the wedding: now the Princess, 'very excited, led him round, showing him every room. "Are you pleased?" she kept asking him. You could tell from his expression that he was. "He likes it," she said to me triumphantly. "And it's my dream house now."'[5] Yet Diana came to hate Highgrove, which became more Charles's house than hers; where he spent days hunting in the winter, playing polo in the summer and mixing with his horsey friends, while Bolehyde Manor, the Parker Bowleses' house, was in menacing proximity. Immediately after the separation, Charles, whose taste was more discriminating than Diana's, substituted his own style and that of his chosen decorator, Robert Kime, for hers. Although it had been their first shared home, Diana used to say that it was never her 'cup of tea'. For Charles it had always been his ideal house; he had chosen it himself instead of Chevening, the splendid eighteenth-century house in Kent which had been allotted as his official residence. His excuse to the then Prime Minister, Margaret Thatcher, for abandoning Chevening was that it was too far away from his properties in the Duchy of Cornwall. The real reason, however, was that Highgrove was in the heart of 'horse country' and convenient for the Prince's two favourite sporting activities, polo and hunting. It was also conveniently close to the home of Andrew and Camilla Parker Bowles. At Highgrove Charles could fulfil his cherished dream of creating a splendid garden which he had begun with the expert advice of a circle of grand gardening ladies including Molly, Marchioness of Salisbury, and Rosemary Verey.

'Horsey' people were anathema to Diana, who was spiralling into deep post-natal depression after the birth of William. She was twenty-one that July but no one – not even her family – thought to give her a twenty-first birthday party. A new friend came to lunch, Sarah Ferguson, whom Diana had met at the Cowdray Park polo two years before when Charles first made his advances and who was soon to become very much a part of Diana's life when she married Prince Andrew four years later. Charles, however, did arrange a candlelit picnic dinner at the Queen's House at Kew for their first wedding anniversary. At Balmoral that autumn, she became sicker and thinner, the scenes of screaming, crying and throwing things more frequent. Charles worried but he did not understand post-natal depression. No one in the Royal Family recognized either that or her bulimia.

Bulimia nervosa, as it is called, is an eating disorder where people have a cycle of binge eating and purging by vomiting; they can have a binge–purge cycle which occurs at least twice a week for three months or more. Its cause is not fully understood but it may develop owing to a combination of emotional, physical and social triggers. It can be caused by low self-esteem, which certainly characterized Diana, or mood problems, especially depression, from which she was suffering after the birth of William. Finally, it can be due to a specific emotionally upsetting event such as abusive family relationships. Later, the doctor who treated Diana attributed her bulimia directly to her problems with Charles and it became noticeably worse in surroundings with unhappy memories or in difficult situations, such as family gatherings at Sandringham and Balmoral. The general feeling in the royal circle was that Diana was 'an extremely tiresome girl', 'basically a bad character ... [with] flaws in her character' and that they had 'no patience with all this about being sick'.[6] Diana in her desperate depression became, as even her own staff admitted, 'very unpredictable'. By her own account she began to mutilate herself in an attempt to focus Charles's attention on her: the 'cutting' cannot have been very severe as she was so often seen wearing low-cut, sleeveless evening dresses and no scars were ever evident. But, as a result of these episodes, in mid-October he took her down to London again for psychiatric treatment. The analysts, as is their wont, probed Diana's family background, blaming everything on her 'broken home', which was hardly helpful in the circumstances.[7] While the Prince ordered his friends to say nothing (despite writing letters in which he told of his difficulties with his wife), the public nature of some of Diana's erratic behaviour made it inevitable that the rumour machine would start up. The most glaring instance came at a major royal public occasion, the British Legion Festival of Remembrance at the Albert Hall on 13 November 1982, always attended by the senior members of the Royal Family.

That evening, before leaving, Charles and Diana had a major row which resulted in Diana's refusing to go. He left without her but she then had a change of heart and determined to go after all, despite her staff warning her that it was now too late and she would arrive at the Albert Hall after the Queen, an unpardonable breach of protocol. Diana paid no attention and turned up, causing a commotion as a seat had to be found for her, and there she sat, clearly continuing the row with Charles in public view. Anne Robinson, editing the *Sunday Mirror* that weekend, put James Whitaker on to the story – 'James, I want you to find out why Princess Diana is looking as awful as she is. She behaved awfully at the Albert Hall and she looks f------- awful. She's so thin. Go and find out.' Whitaker rang his main contact, Sarah McCorquodale, who confirmed that the family were very concerned over Diana's loss of weight. 'We think she could be anorexic . . .' Robinson ran the story, and the result was a major complaint from the Palace which cost her her job.

Among the media curiosity to know the truth of what was going on was at fever pitch. Nigel Dempster, probably the best connected of the gossip-columnist diarists to the circles in which Charles's friends moved, having at first rubbished the rival journalist's report, then appeared on US television to denounce Diana as a 'fiend' and a 'monster', claiming that she was 'very much ruling the roost' and that Charles was 'desperately unhappy'. He later asserted that he had the information 'straight from one of Prince Charles's staff'. With tongue firmly in cheek, Auberon Waugh headlined a piece 'GOSSIP COLUMNIST ATTACKS PRINCESS FAIRYTALE. NATION RISES IN ANGER'. Cracking the crystal through which an adoring public gazed at the fairy-tale couple was not welcomed. Just after the birth of Prince William, Victoria Glendinning, reviewing a selection of royal books, quoted Robert Lacey as saying, 'it is important to us that the magic does not die', adding, 'and that is why we hope the fairy story will end in the proper way and that the Princess of Wales and her Prince and their son will live happily ever after'. The trouble, however, as the acute Lacey pointed out, was that Charles got 'the woman "we" wanted'. As far as the press was concerned, however, though no one wanted to believe the reports of cracks in the marriage, the 'fairy tale', which was still the image the general public cherished, had turned into a soap opera which was more like the current American favourites *Dynasty* and *Dallas* in which skulduggery, infidelity and double-dealing were the norm.

'At the point at which there began to be more hard and fast evidence, her weeping in public, that kind of incident, cancelling going to places at the last minute, him turning up alone when she had been expected . . . the whispers became more insistent that it [the marriage] was indeed going down,' said a well-known media analyst. 'And the press loved this because it was a drama, and it was a drama in which . . . because of the nature of the Palace's press relations which is "never admit, never deny", you more or less could get away with anything . . . You could actually schedule a news story on Di which would be inevitably a story about some difficulty in the marriage – some hint at what's been happening this weekend, he's been at Highgrove or she's been at Highgrove and he hasn't or she hasn't . . . the royal rat pack began to feed off each other [as to] who could outdo the next one with a more outrageous claim . . .'[8]

Media comment only increased Diana's unhappiness and the

pressure on her. She devoured the news, almost living her life by proxy through the press. *The Times* and *Telegraph* were the papers officially delivered to her but copies of the tabloids found their way to her via the back stairs. Consciousness of growing criticism of her within royal circles and especially from Charles's friends, added to the hostile comment in some of the newspapers, drove her to despair. Ruth Fermoy, always reflecting court opinions, told Roy Strong in March 1982 that Diana 'had a lot to learn' about royal life,[9] opening herself further to Archbishop Runcie: 'Ruth was very distressed with Diana's behaviour,' the Archbishop recalled. 'She [Ruth] was totally and wholly a Charles person, because she'd seen him grow up, loved him like all the women of the court do, and regarded Diana as an actress, a schemer.'[10] Charles, while still sympathetic, remained baffled by Diana's illness. Out hunting in March 1983, he turned to two lady companions and asked them: 'Have you ever been very, very sick? I don't understand it and my mother doesn't either . . .'[11]

One might wonder why – considering Diana's family were worried about her weight loss and that Sarah and her mother had had first-hand experience of Sarah's eating disorder – none of her family came forward to help her. Frances Shand Kydd had been curiously absent from her daughter's life for two years following the wedding. Diana had been upset by Frances's disclosures about her marriage break-up to the author Gordon Honeycombe, and Frances had made some curious statements to the *Daily Mail*, putting a favourable spin on her absence from her daughter's life: 'I am a firm believer in maternal redundancy,' she said. 'When daughters marry they set up a new home and they don't want mother-in-law hanging around. They should be free to make their own decisions and maybe to make their own mistakes.' This begged the question: Frances was Diana's mother, not her mother-in-law, but her absence from her daughter's life was confirmed by one of the Waleses' officials: 'After the wedding, she sort of disappeared,' he said. Diana's sister Jane was in the awkward position of being married to the Queen's assistant private secretary, which involved having to tread carefully where the

Waleses were concerned; she was a level-headed woman who was not much moved by Diana's more dramatic performances. She went round to check on Diana and found marks on her chest. Sarah, who was closer to Diana, had her own married life on a farm in Lincolnshire and, in any case, often found it wiser to keep her distance from Diana. Her brother Charles was away most of the time, at Eton and then Oxford. Johnnie Spencer, according to an entry in the visitors' book, had been one of the first visitors to the new apartment at Kensington Palace, but the sales of Althorp treasures which had begun shortly after Johnnie's recovery from illness were a further source of controversy between Raine and his children. News of the sales had led to much criticism in the press. According to *The Times* in December 1982 the Spencers had sold £2 million worth of art which they claimed was to pay the costs of refurbishing Althorp, but in September of that year they had bought three houses in Bognor Regis, which cast some doubt on their claim.

Yet, as with all depressive illnesses, there were periods of light among the clouds: in September, Diana had been well enough to attend the funeral of Princess Grace of Monaco who had died of injuries sustained in a car crash. Diana had greatly admired Grace, feeling a sense of empathy with her as another outsider who had married into a ruling family, and whose marriage also had not turned out the fairy tale it had initially been thought to be. 'I remember meeting Princess Grace and how wonderful and serene she was,' Diana recalled of the evening she had worn '*that* dress', 'but there was troubled water under her, I saw that.'[12] Charles's initial reaction when told she had wanted to go to the funeral in Monaco had been negative: it would be the first time she officially represented the Royal Family on a solo engagement. Diana, however, had been determined to go and on her own initiative written to the Queen about it and obtained her agreement. One of Diana's staff who accompanied her to Monaco later told a television programme, 'She was absolutely brilliant. She came into her own. And on the aircraft back she burst into tears with exhaustion. She asked "Will Charles be there to meet us?" We looked at her big eyes looking out of the window in expectation. She said, "There's one police car." That meant Charles wasn't coming.' Another remembered, 'She rang up and asked me "Have you seen the papers?" I said, "You were absolutely brilliant, Ma'am." She said, "Thanks for saying that because nobody at Balmoral has mentioned it." '[13] 'It was always important to Diana to feel appreciated from an early age,' her brother Charles said in a television interview after her death; 'she was childlike, wanting approval – "Am I doing OK?"'

The couple's joint tour of Australia in March 1983, accompanied by William, and New Zealand, was a pivotal moment in the marriage. Outwardly it was a glorious success but behind the scenes people travelling on the tour noticed 'little tensions' between them. It was the beginning of worldwide 'Di-mania'. Instead of seven photographers being there, there were seventy. Before there was one from each paper and a couple of freelances. Now they were coming from France, Germany, America and Japan. One hundred thousand people turned out to see them in Brisbane. 'The police are concerned about an element of hysteria that has become evident among the huge crowds that have turned out to see the Royal couple in the New South Wales cities of Sydney, Newcastle and Maitland over the past 48 hours,' a newspaper reported. A security officer told the reporter: 'We haven't seen this in royal tours here before. It is more akin to Beatlemania.' The adulation of the crowds at first terrified and then empowered Diana. This was something she could do, and do well. It was a part she was born to play.

It was the first time a hint was seen of Prince Charles's jealousy of Diana's huge appeal to the crowds, which was to be an increasingly divisive factor in the couple's relationship. Although he concealed it nobly and even joked about it, it was nonetheless humiliating for a man who since childhood had been the centre of attention wherever he went, to be upstaged by his wife, a novice on royal occasions. It was not pleasant to hear the crowds groaning, 'Oh, we've got old Big Ears', when they saw he was going to be on their side of the walkabout, or to hear the hysterical screams for

'Lady Di'. The scale of the adulation of his wife worried him. 'How can anyone, let alone a twenty-one-year-old, be expected to come out of all this obsessed and crazed attention unscathed?' he wrote to a friend.[14] Diana, according to a letter seen by Dimbleby, wrote that her black moods had vanished and that she felt ashamed of the way she had been behaving in the past. Now, she said, she only thought of Charles and the job. Alone together with William at the sheep station where they left him with his nanny, Charles wrote to Hugh and Emilie van Cutsem, '. . . we were extremely happy there whenever we were allowed to escape. The great joy is that we were totally alone together . . .'[15] At the same time he pondered glumly on the nature of the public's reaction to them, which was unlike anything he had ever experienced before. 'Maybe the wedding, because it was so well done and because it made such a wonderful, almost Hollywood-style film, has distorted people's view of things? Whatever the case it frightens me and I know for a fact that it petrifies Diana.'[16] Petrified at times, maybe, but also excited by the scale of the public's approval of her: Diana had discovered her great gift for satisfying people's expectations, communicating with them, lifting their spirits. Her rapport with ordinary people in public and in private was to be an enormous source of strength and comfort to her. There was no doubt about her media status: a Spanish magazine covered the tour under the headline 'THE FRONT PAGE GIRL', while *Tatler* dubbed her 'Number one, indisputable brand leader'. Their subsequent seventeen-day tour of Canada was also a huge media success, particularly for Diana: one newspaper described how journalists lavished particular attention on Diana, 'gorging themselves on her fresh good looks and her fetching ways'. Another paper, the *Ottawa Citizen*, referred to Charles as an 'also-ran'.

'I think they were happy, they had William out there, a sort of family enclave,' a member of staff recalled. 'But one was aware of little tensions. He couldn't understand that people wanted to see her. He couldn't understand that they wanted to see a beautiful woman rather than a man in a suit. And that was really sad, actually. It was so unnecessary because together they were absolute dynamite. But one was just aware of a sort of petulance in him and she, I think, found it very difficult, knowing how to cope with that. And she was quite emotional at that time, there were tears . . . she didn't understand and it was all very stressful . . .'[17] Things, however, were to go from bad to worse, and Charles's resentment at his wife's popularity began to poison their relationship. His puzzlement at people's reaction to her was palpable, as he once said to a friend: 'Why do they love her so much? All she ever did was to say "yes" to me . . .'[18]

Consciousness that she was a real success boosted Diana's still fragile confidence. While she had confessed to the wife of a Nova Scotia editor that 'the wolf-pack-like British tabloid press' still upset her – 'When they write something horrible I get a horrible feeling right here,' she said, pointing to her chest, 'and I don't want to go outside' – she told the Premier of Newfoundland that she felt she was doing her job as Princess of Wales 'better now than I previously did'. Like many others before him, Premier Peckford was struck by 'her really soft spot for people who are sick and disabled,' he said. 'She almost cried when she was told that little boy who had presented her with a bouquet was blind.' Worldwide adulation for Diana continued to grow: one British magazine dubbed her 'Royal Superstar': according to a recent American poll she was 'the most popular woman in the world'. *Paris-Match* said that she was more popular in France than even Brigitte Bardot, while the editor of *Ladies Home Journal* proclaimed, 'without a doubt she is the greatest media personality of the decade. One comes along every ten years – Jackie, Liz Taylor and now Diana.' Excessive press attention was by now inevitable: pictures of Diana sold newspapers and magazines. Popular women's magazines such as *Woman* and *Woman's Own* reported sales increased by up to forty thousand in weeks when Diana featured on the cover. One editor said that his sales dropped by 15 per cent when she was not on the cover. 'She's the one that's news, the one they want to see. We often think, for heaven's sake we've had her on for the last seven months, let's try someone else. It doesn't work.'

Between the two tours the couple had travelled on 30 April via private jet, lent them by Armand Hammer, from Los Angeles to the Bahamas to spend ten days at the Romseys' villa. Long-lens photographs published in a Spanish magazine showed Charles and Diana on a beach – happy and playful with each other, walking hand in hand: on one occasion the Prince hefted her over his shoulder to dump her in the water. 'The Prince, away from protocol, reveals himself as truly in love with Diana' the caption ran. Back in England for their second wedding anniversary, the couple publicly demonstrated their affection: 'They looked more like they were on honeymoon,' said a spectator.

But there was a downside to this public success and apparent happiness – the private difficulties. Prince Charles's friends lined up to denigrate Diana. While they were not aware, or did not recognize, that the marriage still had a chance, they seemed to think they should encourage the Prince to regret it. Charles's complaining letters had their effect. None of them, however, appeared to realize that, in encouraging Charles to feel that his marriage was hopeless, they were setting him on a course which might endanger the monarchy. It now seems incredible that these people, in order to curry favour or to maintain their influence with the Prince, should have actually attempted to undermine his marriage. One might ask oneself what they were trying to achieve.

Leaked stories began to appear, bolstering Dempster's claim that Diana was a 'fiend' and a 'monster'. Diana, according to the stories, was responsible for an exodus of staff and a dog. The first to go was Stephen Barry, the much indulged valet, who was intuitive enough to recognize that his reign and influence over Charles would end with the Prince's marriage. Most of the staff believed that she did 'winkle' Barry out of his position: 'he was keeping the Prince way back in the Dark Ages,' said one, 'she wanted to drift him into the present. Stephen . . . one of his great claims to fame was that he kept the Prince of Wales in the top worst dressed list for years and kept himself in the best . . .' On the honeymoon at Craigowan, Barry was completely insouciant as far as his duties were concerned. 'There's Stephen, Sunday morning, whacking great gin and tonic, radio under one arm, all the papers under the

other. "Darling, I'm just off to do a little heavy pressing . . ."
Three hours later he's snoring his head off,' one member of staff
remembered.[19] Diana was no fool where domestic staff were concerned and Barry himself recognized that his happy years of getting
away with everything with the indulgence of the Prince of Wales
would soon be over. He jumped before he was pushed.

Alan Fisher, whom Charles and Diana had met at Althorp where
he was acting as extra butler when they were staying there for a
big party, also left. It was rumoured that he did not like Diana, but
it was also said that, having worked in the past for people like the
Windsors and Bing Crosby, he did not like the way things were
done at Highgrove and Kensington Palace. The unkindest accusation concerned Harvey, the Prince's beloved yellow Labrador,
who had been bred by the Queen and accompanied Charles everywhere. The rumour ran that Diana had banished Harvey as she
had some of Charles's friends. In fact, Harvey was old and incon-
tinent, his hind legs dragged behind him and he was no longer
capable of getting up the stairs. He was given to the Prince's
comptroller, Colonel Creasy, to look after.

The saddest departure was that of Oliver Everett, who had acted
as the Princess's private secretary and aide from before her wedding.
Charming, highly educated and a skilful polo player, Everett had
given up a promising diplomatic career to answer the Prince's call
'to look after Diana'. At first they had got on well, joking and
chatting in the light-hearted manner which Diana enjoyed in her
relations with her staff. Suddenly, in a way which was, sadly, to
become characteristic of her, she turned against him for some
perceived although totally minor offence. She demanded that
Charles tell him to go, and go he did at the end of 1983. It was
evident that the Royal Family and household thought he had been
badly treated, since he was subsequently given the desirable post
of royal librarian at Windsor.

The resignations of Edward Adeane and Michael Colborne were
both unfairly attributed to Diana. Adeane, a top libel lawyer with
a first-class brain and a dry wit, managed to get on with Diana
although as personalities they were worlds apart. He was shocked

when, working on the preparations for the Australian tour, he discovered that the future Queen of England did not know the name of the capital of Australia.[20] Adeane was seriously taken aback when, after the birth of William, he was told to give up his early morning meeting with Charles because Diana insisted that William's father should spend some time in the nursery with his son. That was not at all how things had been in Adeane's father's time.

Yet it was the Prince, not the Princess, who prompted Adeane's departure. Adeane appreciated the conscientious way Diana dealt with her paperwork, in contrast to the confusion of her husband's handling of his office affairs. The Prince, said a former member of his staff, 'was a muddler and liked it like that so that he could blame other people, throw up his hands and say "Oh, the office!"' Edward Adeane, who had been brought up in the tradition of his father, the Queen's private secretary, had become increasingly annoyed with the confusion, the Prince's habit of taking the advice of the last person he had seen, of refusing to listen to Adeane's and taking private initiatives of which his private secretary was unaware until it was too late to stop him. The last straw for the private secretary was the Prince's notorious speech on 30 May 1984 given at Hampton Court Palace at a dinner in honour of the 150th anniversary of the Royal Institute of British Architects, when he compared the new design for the wing of the National Gallery in Trafalgar Square to 'a monstrous carbuncle on the face of a much-loved and elegant friend', and launched an attack on modern architecture and architects. Edward Adeane had vehemently opposed the Prince's plan for his speech: it was not only insulting to his hosts, the architectural profession, but pre-empted the judgement of the public inquiry on the development which was then in progress. While he attempted to persuade the Prince against the speech even in the car going down to Hampton Court, he did not know that Charles had already leaked the text to *The Times* and the *Guardian* for publication the next day.[21] Adeane resigned six months later after yet another row.

Michael Colborne's resignation was partly prompted, it was

rumoured, by the snobbery of the household, who could not envisage a grammar school boy with the title of Comptroller of the Prince's Household. Whatever the truth of that, a root cause of Colborne's going was the increasing difficulty he experienced in treading the tightrope between Prince and Princess. 'I couldn't look after two,' he said. 'I mean, he wanted me to do one thing and she wanted me to do another so I thought the best thing was to get out while the going was good. And I resigned in the April [1984] but didn't get out till the December because they kept asking me to change my mind, to stay on and do this and that.' The last straw for Colborne, as it had been for Adeane, was the behaviour of the increasingly edgy and jealous Prince on the April trip to Canada which followed the couple's Australian tour in 1983. Colborne had spent the afternoon with Diana at her request while Charles went about his official business. When Charles returned, he flew into one of his towering, shouting rages, accusing Colborne of neglecting him for Diana. Outside the door, hearing everything that had gone on, was a sobbing Diana. The Prince took her in his arms, but the damage had been done. Diana was aware of the resentment eating away at her husband, but there was nothing she could do about it.

For Colborne, who had borne the brunt of the Prince's tirades many times before, this was a row too far. 'I get an inner gut feeling when things are going to change,' Colborne said. 'I had ten wonderful years.' Members of the Queen's household, aware that Colborne was one of the few people whom Diana listened to and trusted, attempted to dissuade him. The effect of the resignations of both Adeane and Colborne was to diminish the numbers of people who could genuinely be called impartial in the Prince's office.

Diana's unattainable desire to have her husband all to herself, and his early willingness to do anything to please her and to avoid the constant rows, did result in the distancing of some of Charles's closest friends. Nicholas Soames, who for years had been accustomed to speak to him on the telephone at least once a week, heard nothing from the Prince for two and a half years. It goes without saying that the Parker Bowleses' and the Tryons did not receive invitations, a point which Diana had made very clear by crossing them off the list for the wedding breakfast in 1981. The Romseys, Brabournes and Palmer-Tomkinsons also found themselves blacklisted: Charles had let drop during one of their rows that Norton Romsey had advised him not to marry Diana. According to a royal relation, Diana crossed every single woman of Charles's previous acquaintance off their mutual Christmas card list.

Camilla's family and Charles's close friends were very upset when he ceased to get in touch with them. Not only were they genuinely fond of him but they also basked in the glow which surrounds royal access. 'I think they were a little put out that they didn't see him and gone were the close contacts and everything else,' a neighbour said.[22] Charles's friends – and Camilla's – were the country house set, the owners of great houses like Bowood in Wiltshire, Chatsworth in Derbyshire, families with resonant names like Shelburne and Willoughby de Broke. Diana was offending a powerful network reaching from the country to the court and she would not easily be forgiven. In social terms, despite being Princess of Wales and a Spencer, she had no comparable network of her own. Stories of her possessiveness were bandied round by the exiles, no doubt giving rise to the 'fiend' and 'monster' accusations. The mantra was that Diana was a scheming girl who had set her cap at Charles and got him, that she was 'a really nasty person', or at best an unhappy one. She was 'impossible to live with – the reason why so many staff had left'. Her treatment of Prince Charles had been cruel and domineering from the start. One friend recalled when the couple came to have a drink during their engagement period: Diana had left her engagement ring in another room and peremptorily ordered Charles to go and fetch it. The visiting couple had initially applauded her firmness with the Prince: 'at the time I thought this was good news but later it turned out not to be at all . . .' Diana, they said, 'tortured' Prince Charles, saying, 'No one wants to see you, they all want to see me', and, 'You'll never be King, no one wants you to be King.' Charles's riposte, according to Diana, would be, 'They only come to see you because you're married to me.'[23] When Diana's uncle Lord Fermoy, of whom she was very fond, shot himself in August 1984 after a long struggle against depression, the tragedy strengthened comments about 'bad Fermoy blood': Frances was a bolter, her sister Mary a recluse and Fermoy himself a depressive. Diana was, therefore, 'tainted'. Much was made of Ruth Fermoy quoting a school report on Diana describing her as 'the most scheming little girl I have ever met'.

While this last may have carried an element of truth, and it could indeed be said that Diana's desire that Charles 'should give up everything' for her was totally unrealistic, considering that he had official duties and responsibilities as Prince of Wales and was a spoilt bachelor already set in his ways to boot, the evidence is that, although she undoubtedly treated him badly when in one of her moods, she still loved him far more than he ever loved her. 'Prince Charles was so self-centred that he couldn't handle the situation with Diana when she behaved erratically [but] she was besotted with him and always put him first,' a member of their staff said. 'The Princess was very much in love with him − romantically so and at the same time rather afraid of him.'[24] The irony of the situation was that she was terrified of losing Charles and, above all, of his going back to Camilla, but her tormented behaviour only succeeded in turning him away from her. At some point, probably in 1983, Charles and Camilla began to get in touch again. Diana believed that Camilla had never gone away and that she had always kept in touch.

The allegation that Diana 'dominated' Charles was described as nonsense by Andrew Neil, then editor of the *Sunday Times*, who, with Charles Douglas-Home, editor of *The Times* and Diana's first cousin, lunched with the couple at Kensington Palace in April 1984. 'It was clear the royal couple had very little in common,' wrote Neil. 'Charles roamed far and wide on the issues of the day . . . Diana played little part in the conversation . . . Charles made no attempt to involve her.'[25] 'The Princess would consult Prince Charles on everything and he liked that,' a member of staff said. 'She was very anxious to get everything right.'[26]

At this point there was still intimacy between them. On Valentine's Day 1984 Diana's second pregnancy was announced. As Diana recalled it:

then between William and Harry being born it is total darkness. I can't remember much, I've blotted it out, it was such pain. However, Harry appeared by a miracle. We were very, very close to each other the six weeks before Harry was born, the closest we've ever, ever been and ever will be. Then suddenly as Harry was born it just went bang, our marriage, the whole thing went down the drain. I knew Harry was going to be a boy because I saw the scan. Charles always wanted a girl. I knew Harry was a boy and I didn't tell him. Harry arrived, Harry had red hair, Harry was a boy. [His] first comment was 'Oh God, it's a boy', second comment, 'and he's even got red hair'. Something inside me closed off. By then I knew he had gone back to his lady . . .[27]

At fittings with her couturier, Jasper Conran, Diana would break down in tears, pleading pathetically, 'Please make me look sexy for my husband . . .'. She was only twenty-three and the couple had been married barely three years. Prince Henry Charles Albert David, always known as Harry, was born on 15 September 1984. There were to be no more children.

8. 'The Best Double Act in the World'

'How awful incompatibility is, and how dreadfully destructive it can be for the players in this extraordinary drama. It has all the ingredients of a Greek tragedy' (Prince Charles to a friend[1])

'I think she was happiest almost when they were expecting Harry and soon after,' a close aide said. 'Again, I don't believe Prince Charles was upset that it was another boy. I think that was a complete fallacy [which took root] in her life later on . . . He was delighted with Harry.'[2] Both Charles and Diana enjoyed being parents: Charles in his Buckingham Palace days used to love going up to the nursery when Andrew and Edward were young, playing with them and talking to them while they were being bathed. With Harry, as with William, he took his fatherly duties seriously, even to changing nappies. He cut down on his engagements to the extent that it was publicly noticed, so that he could be at home more with the children. Shortly after Harry's birth, Diana wrote describing William's reaction to his new brother: 'William has totally taken over his brother and Charles and I are hardly allowed near as he covers Harry in an endless supply of hugs and kisses.' They had been deluged with baby clothes by the public: 'The reaction to our small son's arrival has been totally overwhelming – having been sent millions of pink (!) clothes for the last nine months.'[3]

Harry had been christened on 21 December 1984 in St George's Chapel, Windsor. The godparents were Lady Sarah Armstrong-Jones, the painter Bryan Organ, Gerald Ward, Prince Andrew, Lady Vestey (a friend of both Charles and Diana) and Diana's former flatmate Carolyn Bartholomew. Princess Anne was the only one of Charles's siblings not to attend the christening; it was announced that she and her husband were unable to attend owing to 'a long-standing private engagement that had been fixed far in advance of the christening'. When it turned out that the long-standing engagement was nothing more crucial than shooting with Mark Phillips's father, the press mischievously intimated that Princess Anne had 'snubbed' Diana who had not invited her to be a godparent. The outstanding beauty of the three generations – Diana, her mother and her grandmother – was evident in the formal photographs of the occasion taken by Snowdon, but while Diana looked radiant and Ruth Fermoy serene, poor Frances Shand Kydd, unnerved by the presence of Raine and Johnnie, and aware that the Royal Family neither liked nor approved of her, looked tense, sad and isolated. Her husband, Peter Shand Kydd, was not, apparently, present, although Diana's brother and sisters were.

In theory, Diana now had what she had always wanted: a home and children, and a husband whom she loved. At Christmas she would attach loving notes to her presents to him: 'to my adorable, wonderful hubby with special love at Christmas . . .'. 'My boys' in particular were the centre of her world and her life revolved around them, more so as she became lonelier in her later years. She would stick notes on a door: 'I love William and Harry'. She organized children's parties for them when the chef, Mervyn Wycherley, baked cakes shaped as Thomas the Tank Engine or some other popular toy. 'Everything was done for the boys,' a member of staff recalled. 'She took a lot of trouble. One birthday party she organized a bouncy castle in the middle of the quadrangle at Kensington Palace and we hired bear suits and raided their birthday party . . . William was very smart, he could recognize people by their shoes.'[4] William was christened the Wombat and Harry was Harry Snail. She was strict with them, rationing their chocolate allowance and insisting that they pick things up after them.

Diana was a modern mother, absolutely devoted to her children and dedicated to putting them first and arranging her life round them. 'The thing that mattered most to her was her sons,' said Sam McKnight, her friend and hairdresser, who saw a good deal of her in the family setting at Kensington Palace. 'They were at the heart of her life and her absolute preoccupation was to give them as normal a life as possible. She saw her whole mission as being to prepare them for their future roles but she wanted that to be based on as normal a life as possible.'⁵ Diana is often depicted as a rebel but she was committed to the monarchy and to her sons' roles in its future. It was the monarchy as she saw it, popular and communicating with the people, doing good in a heartfelt rather than distant and dutiful way. She wanted 'her boys' to know how other people lived and insisted that they should go to ordinary little schools with other children; first, Mrs Jane Mynors' nursery school and then Wetherby School. Her protection officer, Ken Wharfe, who had guarded the boys before being transferred to Diana, if asked what he would remember best about the Princess said: 'I always say that it would be my memory of her influence over the children as a mother and her care of them, because it was one arena that she felt totally confident in. I suspect, right from the day they were born she knew "this is the way I want these children to grow up". They were still in a very privileged, fortunate position, they were not going to be re-housed in any local funded programme, but given that, she did everything she could to give them a normal upbringing.'⁶

'The days were always set around taking William and Harry to school and, wherever possible, being home to pick them up. Or at least be in the house when they got back . . . She'd arrive at school in the morning in a tracksuit, no make-up, drop the kid off, say "hello" to the other children . . . One of the other parents would say, "Oh, William's coming round to us tomorrow night." "Oh, that's fine," she'd say. So they would go off to his friend's.' She would invite them back and 'they'd all come back to the nursery at some point, throw jelly at each other and have a fight behind the garden . . . So there was this natural interchange of friends that was approved in its entirety by the princess because the prince chose to be elsewhere . . . And I think that the success of that is what we see in William and Harry . . . I'm absolutely certain that that is why a lot of their friends now are the friends they met at prep school, through Eton and so forth . . .

'The reality of her life was so much more than this image of somebody performing on the royal circuit, shaking hands and taking bunches of flowers. Here was somebody with this incredibly complex life, able to find time, with all these pressures, to take her children to school and be there for them. But also educate them in a way that was going to be of value to them in later life. For example there weren't any grand teas . . . butlers laying tables . . . neatly cut fingers of tomato sandwiches. They'd sit with their mother in front of the television with a bowl of beans on toast . . . or we'd go into the kitchen and just sit there and knock up something together. So the children would have this interaction with normal people. And so it was a great education to them, frowned upon, I might add, by the prince, I think, in those early stages. I don't think he'd like what he deemed familiarity. I think it was crucial to William and Harry for where they now find themselves.'[7]

Diana was obsessed with protecting them from the press, arranging things through her excellent press secretary, Vic Chapman, so that they were not overwhelmed and yet would become used to the odd photo opportunity. She was determined that they would never suffer what amounted to the press persecution she experienced.

'I do remember one day at school,' a friend said,

when William was in the school play. He was very little, probably three and a half – and he came out with his school friends, all dressed up in their little nativity outfits. And there was this huge bank of photographers all on ladders. They've even got big coats and woolly hats. They look like a rabble and they've all got these big cameras. It's terrifying, anyway, let alone if you're a little tiny boy. And, everyone was shouting out, 'William, William, William!' It must have been incredibly difficult for a child that age to understand why they were all calling for him. I asked her once, 'What do you do about that?' Because she was very, very aware of this and was very worried about this with him. And she said she had had to say to him, 'You're going to go to school today, there's going to be all of these people who want to take your picture, and if

you're a good boy and you let them take your picture, then I'll take you
to Thorpe Park next week.'[8]

Shortly after Harry's birth, Diana began to involve herself in
charity work, replacing Princess Margaret, at the Princess's own
suggestion, as president of Barnardo's, the children's charity. In
1984 with Barnardo's, Diana, still only twenty-three, embarked on
the course which, after motherhood, was to give her increasingly
difficult life meaning. Roger Singleton, the chief executive, was
amazed that so young a woman could have such rapport with
people of all ages at Barnardo's projects round the country.

Her capacity to make people feel good was really quite exceptional and
I've seen her sit in a group of young mums struggling to bring up a
handful of children, very often on their own, almost choking with
cigarette smoke. Perhaps some of them themselves were in the care of
public authorities when they were children. She would just sit and listen
to what their everyday lives were like. Very often she didn't say a great
deal in response although she would always answer questions about
herself and her own children. But after she'd gone . . . that group of
people would feel sheer exhilaration about the fact that they'd been able
to talk to a senior person in public life . . . She left them with the very
full impression that she understood what they were talking about and
she knew what it was like . . . That was a particular skill and I would say
that her biggest single contribution to Barnardo's was the difference she
was able to make by dint of those visits to people's lives. I can visit those
same projects five or ten years later and if some of the same people are
involved they will almost invariably bring out the photographs and say
'Do you remember?'[9]

Despite her young age, Diana was a professional in her private
life as well as professional duties. 'She took being mistress of the
house very seriously,' a member of staff said. 'And she would do
the menus for both [houses] in the menu book each week. She
knew what she had to do and she did it.'[10] Each day she would see
the butler and give him a list of what needed doing, who was

coming to lunch or tea, or what appointments she or the Prince might have. However much she might complain that she didn't understand what being the Princess of Wales entailed, she was very domesticated and her Althorp background had taught her how the household should be run.

Similarly, she was considerably more professional than her husband when it came to dealing with her public life. While Prince Charles's secretaries might compare getting him to work on a regular basis to 'nailing jelly to a wall', Diana, even in these first years, was direct and competent in her attitude to paperwork and to her staff. Her principal aide in her early years was Anne Beckwith Smith who acted as private-secretary cum lady-in-waiting. One observer paid tribute to Anne's importance in Diana's professional life. 'Anne would be the last person to say it, but she was an excellent source of support and guidance to someone who was new to the Royal Family, very much in the public gaze and having to cope with public embarrassments especially around the patently obvious fact that she was more popular than her husband . . . in the full glare of publicity with people drawing attention to it, it couldn't have been easy.'[11]

From the beginning, only a few months after the wedding, Beckwith Smith had been impressed by how Diana handled a first meeting, and subsequently by a thoughtful note from Balmoral welcoming her to the staff on her first morning at Buckingham Palace. No one, Diana intimated, knew what precisely they were going to do, but they would muddle through together. As she developed, Diana emphasized 'her team' which she named the 'A-team', after the American TV series. In future no one would be in any doubt as to which was the 'B-team'. 'She was efficient,' said a member of the team, 'she turned things round quickly, you sent her things and she turned them round. On the whole she was extremely conscientious professionally.' As she matured and the demands of her public life multiplied, she became even more so. Patrick Jephson, who became her private secretary in 1988, described her as 'quick and decisive', and she expected him to be the same.[12] 'This,' he added waspishly, 'was at least partly to draw a distinction between herself and the Prince, whose capacity to sit on paperwork was legendary.' Diana's *modus operandi* in opening the 'Bag', which contained all correspondence, memoranda and other paperwork from the joint office at St James's Palace forwarded to Kensington Palace, was described by Jephson:

She would snap the little plastic seal [of the large red plastic envelope], pull back the heavy zip and delve inside. Balancing the inner cardboard file on her lap, she quickly sorted the papers into piles. Fashion catalogues or designers' bills were dealt with first; then loose minutes from the secretaries about things like therapists' appointments or school events for the boys; the personal mail – some of it saved for private reading later; then real work – memos that required a decision, outline programmes, draft speeches, invitations, suggested letters . . .[13]

She would leave notes for members of staff in her round girlish handwriting, sometimes even notes for herself. She had a compulsive desire to communicate, to reach out to people, even if she hardly knew them, people like the manager of the shoe shop she patronized, Charles Jourdan, to whom she wrote a sympathetic letter when she heard he had lost his job. She also wrote to staff from her past life, like Mrs Pendrey, wife of the butler at Althorp; one such letter, written three months after William's birth, read poignantly: 'William has brought us such happiness and contentment & consequently I can't wait for masses more . . .'[14]

But, according to Diana, Charles no longer shared her bed after William was born and she never had 'masses more' children or the daughter she longed for. Whether he did 'go back to his lady' in 1983/4, as Diana alleged, or, as Jonathan Dimbleby affirmed in a statement passed by Charles, only in 1986, 'after the irretrievable breakdown of the marriage', Camilla remained present in Diana's mind and no doubt in Charles's mind also. Diana's continuing jealousy and neediness made Camilla all the more attractive in contrast. A mutual friend said of Camilla and her undoubted attraction: 'It's hard to describe. She's got laughing eyes, she's full of fun and she's rather motherly and I can see what it is – what Charles must love in her. At the time I remember thinking "Oh God, she's got something Diana hasn't got" which is a sort of warmth . . . I mean my children adore her. She's warm and motherly. At the same time she must have known what she was doing then. There's no question . . . She must have been just as jealous [of Diana, as Diana of her]. How must she have felt when she saw this young girl – I know she contrived it, she obviously manipulated it a bit, but how must she have felt when this beautiful young girl married him? It must have been awful . . . knowing he had to marry. How could she possibly have lived with that?'[15]

The answer is that, as Princess Margaret had foreseen, Camilla never gave up on Prince Charles. Although Jonathan Dimbleby asserted that, apart from 'a few telephone conversations during the four months of his engagement and only one after his marriage (when he rang to report that the Princess was pregnant with William) they had not talked to each other at all', Camilla was interested enough in the whole scenario form a close [telephonic] relationship with a powerful tabloid journalist which lasted from 1982 to 1992. 'I mean here was the unique example, surely unprecedented,' a well-informed observer commented, '. . . here was a woman who was as close as it is possible to be to the Prince of Wales, a man of supposed rectitude in his dealings with the press. And yet she is talking to the editor [sic] of the most popular paper in the country, and the most scurrilous, and the most intrusive and the one that's been most hostile to him . . .' Stuart Higgins told Sally Bedell Smith, an early and authoritative biographer of Diana:

I talked to her once a week for ten years . . . I talked to her about Diana and Charles. She guided me on things that were not true or things that were off the beam. Everything was behind closed doors, and I didn't write about her, although I spoke to her all the time during that period. I didn't sense that she and Charles were out of touch. I felt she was involved, but not necessarily in a romance or affair with Charles. I never sensed that she was out of contact, though I definitely believe there was a cessation in the relationship and that Charles put an effort into the marriage . . . Our relationship was two ways. We had some long conversations. She was really trying to gauge whether the press was on to her [and Charles] so it was a question of keeping her in touch, too.[16]

It was a curious relationship which illustrated the web of understanding and complicity in the circle around Charles. 'She was always trying to find out what he [Stuart Higgins] knew . . . why was she doing that? There were extraordinary things on the phone . . . he'd ring her and say "they say you're about to do this" and she'd half cup the phone, not properly cup it and say "Andrew, guess what they're saying about us now" . . . and even Stuart was utterly baffled by how incredibly open this whole thing was between her and Parker Bowles and – obviously – between her and Charles . . . He [Higgins] could run stories past her.'

While Camilla was the shadow over the marriage, another factor was driving the couple apart: the way in which Diana, through no fault of her own, outshone her husband in their public lives. It cannot be denied that Diana had a mischievous desire to annoy and an apparently endless capacity to do so. That past November she had even gone so far as to upstage the Queen in public at the State Opening of Parliament. It was typical of her to do it with a fashion statement – in this case an entirely new upswept style with a chignon – which made her look regal – and older. Her new style was widely criticized by admirers and enemies alike. *Daily Express* fashion editor Jackie Modlinger wailed, unfairly as it happened, 'They've made her into a right royal clone . . .' 'Is she still our Princess Di?' the newspaper asked. Diana's coiffure generated far greater column inches than the government's programme for the new session of Parliament: 'The entire popular press without exception abandoned the attempt to squeeze excitement out of the Government's legislative programme and devoted several columns each to the most radical and contentious item revealed there, Princess Diana's new hairstyle.' Diana had driven to the Palace of Westminster in a carriage with the Queen, who, as usual, gave no hint of her feelings, but Prince Philip was said to have been enraged that press coverage of the day both in photographs and comment had elevated the Princess's image to the detriment of the Queen's on what should have been a solemn state occasion. Once again the newspapers reflected the nation's possessive obsession with 'our Princess Di'. Not long afterwards, on 21 November, Diana chose to exhibit another new hairstyle, dubbed by the papers 'the Vera Lynn style of the 1940s', at the Remembrance Day Service to the dead of two world wars at the Cenotaph in Whitehall, when she shared a balcony with the Queen Mother, Princess Alice, the Duchess of Gloucester, Princess Anne and King Olaf of Norway.

The two important tours the couple undertook in 1985, for all their success, brought the problem into high relief. Their joint seventeen-day tour of Italy in April 1985 was one of those times, even though staff who accompanied them remembered it as a 'very happy' trip. At Milan, in a borrowed palace, one of the staff, engaged in moving round the furniture to give the huge room a more lived-in air, found the couple waltzing round him. Prince Charles had been hugely looking forward to this, his second visit to Italy, but once again he found himself taking a back seat to his wife and her wardrobe. 'They were both popular,' a member of staff recalled, 'but even then the Prince of Wales couldn't cope with his wife's popularity.'[17] The couple stayed with the renowned aesthete Sir Harold Acton at his magnificent villa, La Pietra, on the outskirts of Florence. Diana was fascinated by Sir Harold who, an observer said, 'made up to her in his mandarin way'. At the Uffizi Diana stood amazed in front of Rubens' huge masterpiece, *The Horrors of War* – 'Did one man really paint all that?' she asked Sir Harold. As Charles praised Brunelleschi's great dome standing majestically above the Duomo, the newspapers commented: 'the Church could have been in the Mile End Road for all anyone cared. What really mattered, the pictures which would be carried by virtually every TV station and newspaper in the Western world, was Princess Diana's latest outfit.' The Waleses' press secretary, Vic Chapman, briefed the four-hundred-strong press contingent each day with details of the Princess's wardrobe. In Rome, they had a private audience with Pope John Paul II, which awed Diana;

Charles had wanted to attend a private mass with the Pope but the Queen, with her customary caution, headed him off. They lunched with President Pertini and dined at the smartest club in Rome, the Circolo della Caccia.

To make things worse, the British press lectured Charles on his duty to Diana: 'Charles must – and does – look at his life long-term. And at the moment it is Diana who is important,' the *Mail on Sunday* representative in Rome declared. 'The Italian tour has seen a new phase in their relationship,' he wrote. 'Few in the Palace entourage now deny that the marriage did go through an awkward stage when the Princess was pregnant with Prince Harry . . . some reporters who follow the Princess around the world full-time believe his coolness has continued. At the start of their marriage, Prince Charles was constantly seen to be taking his wife by the hand or the elbow.

'It happens less these days but two small incidents summed up for me how Charles and Diana feel about each other now. The first happened at Florence Town Hall when the Prince gave a speech in Italian. He obviously found the moment a strain. As he finished the speech the Princess leaned over and said "Well done, darling". Her eyes shone and he smiled warmly back.

'The second came when the Prince stopped opposite a self-portrait of the artist Filippo Lippi. It obviously reminded him of someone. He put his arm around Diana's shoulder and whispered something in her ear. She burst into a fit of giggles.

'*Such intimate moments show a man and a woman deeply in love.*'

At times like these, when the Charles–Diana partnership was acclaimed as the best double act in the world, the general enthusiasm carried them through. Unfortunately, the enthusiasm was largely for Diana's beauty and the glamour of the fairy-tale romance in which everyone still wanted to believe and in which the vast majority of those who did not pick up the media's hints still did. From the Palace point of view, however, such headlines as 'PRINCE HAS SECOND BILLING TO TRIVIA' were deeply disappointing.

A new international tour was planned for the couple – their first joint visit to the United States preceded by yet another tour of

Australia. By this time rumours of the couple's marital difficulties were common currency in media circles. Tina Brown, the Oxford-educated British journalist who was then editing the American magazine *Vanity Fair*, wove them together in a piece published in advance of their US visit, which underlined their differences: 'Diana is a very young twenty-four, he is a very old thirty-six'; in taste in music (Diana was unfairly pictured as glued to her Walkman and pop music while Charles organized musical evenings with the Royal Philharmonic); their differences over friends – he bored with her Sloanes and Hooray Henrys, she with his intellectual gurus and horsey couples from Gloucestershire – which was true. Both, she claimed, had lost touch with reality but, she finished somewhat improbably, reality was still there if they looked for it. 'He's in just the kind of mood to fall in love with a nursery school teacher in flat shoes who's kind to guinea pigs and babies. If he looks hard enough, she's still there . . .' the piece ended. The fairy tale was not yet doomed; there could still be a happy ending.

Fortunately for Buckingham Palace a timely interview with the couple designed to counteract the marriage rumours was ready for transmission. With skill and considerable self-control Charles and Diana put across the image of a diverse but essentially united couple. Diana, who had been coached by Sir Richard Atten-borough, displayed confidence as she spoke of her role as 'support-ing my husband whenever I can . . . and, also most important, being a mother and wife'. Only the sly upwards look from under her eyelashes gave any clue that she might have been playing a part, tongue in cheek. Charles admitted to 'becoming more eccentric as I grow older', defending his interests in alternative medicine and his criticism of modern architecture on the grounds that he hoped occasionally to 'throw a rock into the pond and watch the ripples create a certain amount of discussion and hopefully to see whether something better can come out . . .' Tina Brown's views were largely condemned; even the *Sun* declared that 'Di and Charles are so very much in love'.

On tour in Australia and the United States that autumn, Charles and Diana kept up the façade of a relaxed, happy couple with consummate ease, even in the presence of Mary Robertson, Diana's old employer, who visited them at the British Embassy in Washington on 8 November after their arrival from Australia. She was immediately struck by the change in Diana, blossoming from 'a naïve, unaffected teenager into a stunning, poised, adult', and particularly by how 'chatty and outgoing she had become . . . no trace of shyness left'.[18] Charles and Diana, she recalled, 'seemed very amicable together, even joking mildly about wanting a girl "the next time"'.[19] At the banquet and ball given by President and Mrs Reagan for eighty select guests, Diana looked stunning in an eight-strand pearl choker and an off-the-shoulder black dress by Victor Edelstein, and her dance with John Travolta was the star turn of the evening. She shone in a crew-necked white lace and satin gown at the British Embassy dinner and in an off-the-shoulder silver embroidered sheath at the dinner at the National Gallery of Art. Smiling, radiant, slim but not skeletal, she looked the picture of health and happiness. Photographs of the same occasions showed a less than radiant Charles, although, as previously in Australia when he had danced with Diana who was wearing an astounding emerald necklace as a headband, he put on a good show of affection and harmony when he took to the floor with her at the White House.

He was still smarting with resentment at the treatment he had received from certain sections of the press and public in Australia where it had become all too obvious that Diana was the draw for the vast crowds. 'So infatuated was the throng at every walkabout,' Dimbleby wrote, 'that as they got out to "work" the crowd, an involuntary moan of disappointment would rise from that part of the crowd which turned out to be nearest to the Prince and furthest from the Princess. Even as they drove through the streets, the Prince could hear the cries of disappointment, "Oh no, she's on the wrong side."'[20] Worse, sections of the crowd held up placards caricaturing his sticking-out ears; it was agony for him to have to confront 'the fatuous remarks and insults made to me; rude things shouted out, gestures made, plastic masks waved about, woundingly unnecessary things written in the papers about me etc,' he told a friend.[21] Not surprisingly, it sapped his confidence and made him long to escape the ordeal.

The Prince was happier in surroundings where he was appreciated, like 'Bunny' Mellon's estate, Upperville in Virginia, where the hostess, one of America's *grandes dames*, was a renowned gardener who also owned a superb stud. He was more relaxed too when they reached Florida for a polo match, exchanging a suitably sweet kiss with Diana as she presented the trophies. The principal reason for the visit to Palm Beach was a fund-raising dinner for one of the Prince's young people's charities hosted by the social-climbing and deeply controversial octogenarian chairman of Occidental Petroleum, Armand Hammer. Hammer had been wooing the Prince since 1977 when he had opened an exhibition of Sir Winston Churchill's watercolours and Hammer gave him one of the paintings as a contribution to the Queen's Silver Jubilee Appeal, of which Charles was chairman. Since then Charles, who seemed to have no qualms about accepting largesse from millionaires like Hammer and John Latsis, the Greek shipping magnate, had frequently been the beneficiary of favours from Hammer, including use of the private jet that had flown him and Diana from Los Angeles to the Bahamas after their previous visit to Australia. To be fair to Charles, the shadowy rumours surrounding Hammer – of his being a KGB stooge helping money-laundering to finance Soviet espionage activities, of bribing middlemen to arrange his oil concession in Libya, and misappropriating Occidental funds for his own use – had not yet been brought into the open. In pursuit of funds for his favourite charities Charles was prepared to overlook their source. Since the money was not for him, it never seemed to occur to him that renting out himself – and his wife – was undignified and unworthy of his royal position. One Palm Beach resident had written to the Prince's new private secretary, Sir John Riddell: 'We would like His Royal Highness to know that many loyal Americans would be offended if they looked upon a scenario in which one saw the Heir to the British Throne in any way to be in the pocket of a man they regard as a friend and ally of the Soviet Union and who seems to betray the best interests of the United

States, and therefore, of Britain.' Another anti-Communist described Hammer as 'a Soviet-sympathising slicker of dubious character and integrity . . . [who] has used guile, gold and gall to rope in a lot of good, well-meaning people, including British royalty, to help him organise a testimonial to himself'.[22] Ignoring all advice, the Prince went ahead, flying down to Palm Beach with Diana in Hammer's jet and making a well-received speech at the dinner where he had the much-appreciated pleasure of dancing with Joan Collins whose wit did not distract him from her eye-catching cleavage.

Diana, it seems, had sharper antennae where people were con-cerned. According to Charles's biographer, Anthony Holden, she had vetoed his suggestion that Hammer should be invited to be a godfather to William, describing him as this 'rather reptilian old man'. On the occasion of the Florida dinner, apparently, she made her distaste for Hammer apparent, as she towered over him on the dance floor. 'The Princess's instinct for people was spot on until the later years when it deserted her,' a member of her staff said. 'She used to say to Charles "Why are we having these people to dinner?", i.e. she knew they had ulterior motives for sucking up like being invited to shoot at Sandringham. He never seemed to realize that if he wasn't the Prince of Wales, they wouldn't give him the time of day . . .'[23]

Diana's success on these tours, instead of gratifying her hus-band, had only resulted in increasing his jealousy of her. 'He didn't understand her appeal and resented it,' a member of the Waleses' staff said. 'He didn't understand that people don't get excited by a man in a suit.' 'There was no way anyone could compete with that, the beautiful clothes, and then she was tall, slim and getting educated about dress sense and it worked beautifully. It's a per-fect recipe, isn't it? It's a young woman becoming a woman, maturing, learning how to wear things, but always that freshness. I think that was her secret. She could be dressed in the most fantastic thing but she could walk up to someone, smile at them – no shyness – no one's going to resist that.' 'She had a great gift for people, perhaps too much so, she could go into a room and go directly to someone – people fell in love with her – men and women too.'[24]

One important person did appreciate Diana's public success – the Queen, to whom the prestige of the monarchy was always all-important. 'The Queen liked her success – the glamour she brought to the monarchy,' a member of staff said. 'Diana always said she had immediate access to the Queen and it helped.' Although the Queen took no positive action as far as the Waleses' marriage was concerned, whenever the subject was raised Diana described her as looking worried and twiddling her glasses in her hands. She was, of course, anxious that the marriage should work and indulged Diana. 'Diana could do what she liked,' a member of the Royal Family said. 'Absolutely what she liked. She realized quite early on that there was nobody, not even the Queen, who would stand in her way. Because they were worried about her. Mustn't upset Diana . . .'[25]

As *Time* magazine put it in its cover story for the US visit of Charles and Diana, their storybook marriage had become a night-time soap opera, 'Palace Dallas', behind the imperturbable Windsor front. 'The Princess, once known as Shy Di, has been transformed as "Dynasty Di"; and Prince Charles, once dubbed Action Man for his intrepid sky- and skin-diving, has become a hermetic, mystical crank.' But, the magazine concluded, 'if "The Windsors" is like a primetime serial, it is one that, before Lady Diana Spencer joined the cast, was having ratings problems . . . Then, like an inspired casting director, Charles picked an unlikely *ingénue* for the role of Princess: the girl next door. *Voilà!* She became the biggest star of all and made "The Windsors" the most watched show of all time.'[26] But if the Queen was alleged to have appreciated what Diana's success contributed to the monarchy (and it is hard to believe that anyone could have known the Queen's feelings on that subject), a powerful section of her courtiers took the view that Diana was upstaging not only Charles but their illustrious employer and took umbrage on her behalf.

'To be perfectly honest,' said a member of staff, 'you wouldn't know what the Queen felt. And I think anybody who says they do know is absolutely wrong because she would never say. What I think is the case is that a lot of her household were very jealous of Diana – and I'm talking about earlier rather than later. And they saw that as threatening their Queen. There is terrible rivalry between all the different [royal] households. It's very difficult to get it across to anybody who has never worked there that it's not like a company, you are not working for the monarchy or the Royal Family. You are working for your individual and that is the difference.' Between Charles's friends and some of the Queen's people, a venomous attitude towards Diana was developing. '[One of Diana's friends] happened to be at a dinner party with a member of the Queen's household and they were slating Diana and this person said, "I don't think you should be doing that", and reported it back to Diana and Diana reported it to the Queen. The Queen remonstrated with them.'[27]

Increasingly, however, the couple's different approach to their royal duties was becoming a debate as to the nature of a modern monarchy. Charles, heir to the throne from the age of three, regarded the attention of the populace as a God-given right to which he was by birth entitled, which he could ennoble by his humane interest and his genuine attempts to communicate with people, while inwardly bemoaning his lot. He worried about issues, was concerned about people and did his best, usually successfully, to communicate that concern. In his own view he was the human face of the monarchy whose ceremonial aspects his mother represented. Hitherto, the monarchy had been supposed to be popular without doing much about it, certainly not descending to crowd level. Diana changed all that. Her glamour, her ability to communicate, her genuine rapport with the elderly, the sick and the young, her empathy which enabled her to guide the hand of an old blind man to touch her face when he was in tears because he could not see her, the witty repartee which lightened her dialogue with officials, combined to present a vision of the role of a member of the Royal Family which was utterly new and, to royal officialdom, confusing and in some way challenging to royal dignity. Charles felt unfairly outshone; Diana, with some reason, felt that her efforts to enhance the couple's public image were unappreciated. She enjoyed being regarded as a superstar but behind the walls of Kensington Palace and Highgrove she wanted the Barbara Cartland cliché of loving wife and husband, with adorable children. Increasingly the public success made private harmony more difficult. Caught between the radiant public image of herself and her own insecurities and longing for love and appreciation, she made demands on Charles to which he could not and would not respond.

Diana still hoped for Charles's love and approbation. Much as she loved him, she showed little real understanding of the kind of man he was: bred into him was a horror of public exhibitionism or displays of emotion. Secretly she prepared a surprise for Charles; whether she thought it was something he would appreciate or whether she wanted to show him what a desirable woman she was, underlining what he was missing, is impossible to guess. Charles's thirty-seventh birthday was to be celebrated at a gala evening at the Royal Opera House, Covent Garden. At the end of the performance Diana slipped out of the royal box to change into a slinky, body-hugging, silver dress, to perform something she had been secretly rehearsing with the Royal Ballet star Wayne Sleep, a dance routine to Billy Joel's 'Uptown Girl'. To see the Princess of Wales cavorting in a sexy number on a public stage was a severe shock to Charles's sense of royal propriety: how Diana could ever have thought otherwise is a measure of the distance between them and between her way of thinking and the inbred royal mind. She received eight curtain calls and a standing ovation, then dropped a curtsey to her husband in the royal box. 'Look what you're missing' did indeed seem to be her message: it fell on deaf ears. Charles was horrified. He saw the episode not as a gesture of love towards him but as yet another example of Diana courting the public eye.

The stage was set for another downturn in their private relationship.

9. 'Charles has gone back to his Lady'

'You know about Camilla, don't you? . . . I don't know how to deal with it. It's there and I can't do anything about it . . .' (Diana to Ken Wharfe, 1986[1])

The couple's sex life was virtually non-existent by then. Diana was only twenty-four: the contrast between the adulation she received in public and the total lack of appreciation she found when she returned home was hard to take. When asked by Peter Settelen, her voice coach, who taped their sessions, 'There's virtually no sexual relations between the two of you? . . .' she replied, 'Well, there was. There was, there was. But it was odd, very odd. But it was there, it was there and then it fizzled out about seven years ago . . . Well, seven was Harry. It was eight . . .' Asked how she knew it was odd, she replied, 'Instinct told me. It was just so odd. I just don't know. There was never a requirement for it from [sic] his case. Sort of once every three weeks, and I kept thinking, and then I followed a pattern; he used to see his lady once every three weeks before we got married . . .'[2] It seems that sex never mattered very much to Diana, certainly not as much as expressions of love and appreciation. Her careful preservation of her virginity – 'keeping myself tidy' – hardly indicated a passionately sexual temperament. With the consciousness of Camilla in the background and her husband's infrequent sexual advances, she was probably, like many beautiful and inexperienced women, insecure about her own sexual attraction. She liked to flirt and was immensely successful at it: men of all ages would go weak at the knees when she fluttered her eyelashes at them, focusing on them with her amazing blue eyes. Her lavatorial sense of humour, fondness for coarse jokes and fascination with other people's sexual behaviour indicated a vicarious rather than a practical interest in sex.

The role of the Royalty and Diplomatic Protection Department officers in the life of the 'principal' they are entrusted to protect is a curious one. The men are SAS-trained in threat avoidance while driving, the use of a gun, fitness and awareness, regularly tested and expected to keep up with the latest intelligence. 'From '72 until recently the IRA was the biggest threat,' one said. 'You get the nutters, you always got the nutters, but your main intelligence was that the IRA said that members of the Royal Family, while working and representing the Royal Family, were a legitimate target.' From the moment Diana symbolically entered the Royal Family on the night she went to stay at Clarence House, she became used to the presence of policemen dedicated to her protection.

Her private protection officer became part of her life: with her when she walked in the park, with her when she went shopping; wearing black tie he shadowed her at evening events, played informally with the children at home. One of Diana's first protection officers, Graham Smith, who was on *Britannia* for the honeymoon, became a father figure to her; she visited him in hospital just before he died of cancer. Diana was absolutely open with her protection officers, almost to the point of embarrassing them. It was Graham Smith who warned one of his successors of the frankness he could expect. 'He said, "Look, Ken, whatever I say it's going to be confirmed by her because you'll be a part of it."' 'In a way,' Wharfe said, 'this was probably one of Diana's strengths but it was also a weakness. I'm not so certain it's a good idea to keep telling people everything.'[3] Naturally the 'principal' and the policeman would become close. In 1985 Diana, in her loneliness and longing for love, comfort and appreciation, became close, perhaps too close, to her protection officer Barry Mannakee. When asked about Mannakee, a member of staff recalled him as 'Really a very nice man, very down to earth . . . genuine . . . a nice person to have around. He came across as being someone you thought "if there was a crisis, I'd be glad to have him standing next to me".[4] There has been much gossip and rumour about Diana's relations with Barry Mannakee. Diana, in the tapes she made with Peter Settelen, recorded in 1992 but broadcast on NBC, one of the major US networks, after her death, in the autumn of 2004, admitted to a crush on him: 'I fell deeply in love with someone who worked in this environment. And he was the greatest fella I've ever had.' 'I was always walking around trying to see him . . . I just wore my heart on my sleeve and was only happy when he was around . . . I was like a little girl in front of him the whole time. Desperate for praise. Desperate.' She even half-joked about running away with him (although he had a wife and children). When asked by Settelen, 'What you're saying is that there had been sexual . . . ?' Diana replied 'No'.[5] A later lover, James Hewitt, claimed that she told him that a teddy bear on her bed had been given her by Mannakee, and that he had been her lover. Hewitt's testimony, given in his second book about his affair with Diana, cannot be corroborated but any sexual affair was denied to Mannakee's successor, Ken Wharfe, by the house staff who would have known of it had it happened. This may have been out of a loyal desire to protect Diana: the rumour in the Kensington Palace village alleged that Mannakee used to go and see Diana when Charles was not there, and that he really cared for her, comforting her and fulfilling her needs.

What had happened, or was witnessed on one occasion, was Mannakee in Diana's sitting room, jacket off, having a cup of tea, laughing and joking and giving her a cuddle before he left. That was his downfall. As Diana told Settelen, '. . . it all got so difficult. And people got so jealous. Bitchy in this house [Kensington Palace]. And eventually he had to go . . . it was all found out and he was chucked out.'[6] Word from the staff got to the chief protection officer, Colin Trimming, who worked principally for the Prince of Wales. Mannakee was removed from his post overnight and sacked from royal service a few months later. Not one of Diana's staff believed Mannakee had slept with the Princess: 'He was just stupid . . . familiar and arrogant' was the general opinion. Did Charles know of it? Trimming was very much the Prince's creature

and recipient of his favours; it seems likely that, if asked why
Mannakee had left so suddenly, he would have given 'overfamiliar-
ity' as the reason. Certainly Charles knew enough about Mannakee
to inform Diana when he was killed in a motorcycle accident two
years later. He told her when they were travelling together in the
back of a limousine en route to RAF Northolt to catch a plane to
the Cannes Film Festival. Diana thought he had done it with
deliberate cruelty. She fantasized about Mannakee, consulting
clairvoyants in an attempt to contact him, having disturbing dreams
about him, that 'he was very unhappy wherever he's gone to'. She
found out where he had been buried (he had been cremated and
his ashes scattered), and laid flowers for him. The dreams stopped.

The death of Mannakee has been resurrected as part of the
investigation into Diana's own death. Mannakee believed that he
was in danger: 'He thought that if ever anything happened
[between him and Diana], something would happen [to him]
and he was terrified.'[7] Diana, always a fan of conspiracy theories,
believed it too. She asked Andrew Morton to find out the truth.
In fact, it had been a simple, tragic road accident: Mannakee had
been riding pillion on a friend's motorcycle, when an inexperienced woman driver pulled out of a side road, turning right across
their path. Mannakee was thrown off, went through the car's rear
window and was killed instantly. It was not the type of 'accident'
which could have been set up beforehand.

If Charles had indeed known of his wife's affection for her
detective, there is little reason to suppose that he cared. In court
circles, where it was known, it would have been regarded as yet
another instance of Diana's 'not knowing how to behave'.

Into Diana's life at this critical point, eager to be her new best
friend, came 'Fergie' – Sarah Ferguson, the bouncing, cheerful and
loud daughter of Prince Charles's polo manager, Ronald Ferguson,
always known by Sarah as 'Dads'. Fergie muscled her way into
Diana's life: 'I met Fergie when Charles was getting near me,'
Diana told Morton, 'and she kept rearing her head for some reason,
and she seemed to know all about the royal set-up, things like that.

She just sort of encouraged it. I don't know, she just suddenly appeared and she sat in the front pew of our wedding – and everything like that. She came to lunch at Buckingham Palace and didn't seem daunted by it all. I wasn't quite sure how to take it . . .'[8] In royal life, as P G. Wodehouse put it, 'nothing propinks like propinquity'. Contrary to perceived opinion, the Royal Family do not have a wide group of friends and tend to marry within the closed circle of people they actually meet who have been provided for them. The Queen herself met Prince Philip through his uncle, Lord Mountbatten; Diana was in essence 'the girl next door'; Fergie's passport to the royal circle was her father and, once again, polo was the entrée, as it had been for a succession of Prince Charles's girlfriends, including Camilla Parker Bowles.

Fergie and Diana had indeed first met in polo surroundings – at the Cowdray Park tournament on the weekend when Diana, staying with the de Passes, had shared a hay bale with Prince Charles with such momentous results. Fergie, although with aristocratic connections, had not been born into a 'great family' like Diana and there was no stately home in the background, simply an agreeable Hampshire farm, Dummer Down. Like Diana, she was no intellectual and, as with Diana, her parents had separated, although later and under less painful circumstances than Diana's. Fergie had had a more down-to-earth upbringing than Diana, ponies, gymkhanas and all the usual middle-class country pursuits. She had attended Queen's secretarial college in South Kensington – the same institution attended by Camilla – graduating in 1977 with the perceptive report: 'Bright, bouncy redhead. She's a bit slapdash. But she has initiative and personality which she will use to her advantage when she gets older.'

Sarah Ferguson was a Sloane, living south of the Thames where she, like many other impecunious daughters of the middle class, shared a flat and commuted to a job north of the river. She had been doing a variety of jobs to make ends meet, although her finances were always precarious, her most recent job being ac-quisitions director for the Richard Burton gallery. She had been having a relationship with a racing driver, Paddy McNally, based in Verbier, and had longed to marry him while secretly realizing he had no real intention of marrying her. She had been hurt that, after being invited to Diana's wedding, she was not on the more select list for the wedding breakfast but nonetheless, in her own words, she 'stayed close to Diana, kept having lunch with her each week'.

It was Diana who provided her entrée into the royal circle. Ronald Ferguson's credentials as the Prince's polo manager would not have been enough in the snobbish ambiance of the court to qualify his daughter for official admittance into the inner circle. 'A polo manager is not considered a gentleman in the household,' said an observer; 'it's not the same level as the courtier.' 'Fergie's a good girl. She's got no harm in her. She's just vulgar. It's not her fault, that's the way she was born and brought up. That's the milieu. She was a chalet girl having an affair with her boss. She wanted to marry him, she was older than his children, he kicked her out. She cried on Diana's shoulder.' When Diana put in a request that Sarah should become one of her ladies-in-waiting, it was firmly turned down as 'most unsuitable'. 'Diana was furious,' a witness said. 'I think it was the first time she had been turned down . . . she told me the courtiers, the Men in Grey – not the Queen – "they dared to turn down my request", that sort of attitude. And I said, "She's not exactly suitable, is she?" But that wasn't the point . . . Diana decided she was going to show them. Diana promoted Fergie's marriage to Andrew from Day One.'⁹ She invited Fergie to dinner at Kensington Palace to meet Andrew when they hit it off straight away, given as they both were to boisterous behaviour and 'idiot jokes'.

Andrew was Diana's favourite among her younger in-laws; they had almost grown up together, and she was sorry for him after the failure of his romance with the American Koo Stark. (Koo had been popular with everyone, Diana included, and had seemed set to become engaged to Andrew when a newspaper turned up some hazy stills of a lesbian shower scene in a film made by Henry Herbert, and Koo went the way of many of Charles's hopefuls.)

The friendship quietly developed: Andrew invited Sarah to a New Year's house party at Sandringham and confessed his love. In February, after Fergie returned from a skiing holiday with Charles and Diana, Andrew proposed to her at Floors Castle, home of the Duke of Roxburghe. On 15 March the Queen gave her consent, four days later the engagement was announced and Fergie left 40 Lavender Terrace, Clapham, for ever. Press and public were ecstatic at this new royal romance – Fergie, it was agreed, was to be the 'breath of fresh air' the Royal Family needed.

Fergie was to refer to herself in her autobiography, *My Story*, as Diana's best friend. This was a distortion of the truth. Fergie had hauled herself into the royal circle through Diana and from then on the two girls were in competition for royal and public favour. It had begun that February at Verbier, where Diana was not at her best, feeling sick and longing to stay inside, while Fergie, an expert skier, shone on the slopes and made everybody laugh with her antics. According to Fergie it was on this occasion that Charles, provoked by Diana's moping, prodded her with the unkind question, 'Why can't you be more like Fergie', a phrase which was to become a refrain. But Fergie did inspire Diana to be happier, to enjoy her lot and have fun.

On the day of the wedding, 23 July 1986, *The Times* leader greeted Fergie as 'a level-headed and attractive young woman', which was somewhat wide of the mark. Attractive yes, level-headed never, as a prank on the evening of Andrew's stag night demonstrated. On 15 July, a week before the wedding, Andrew held his stag night attended by show-business celebrities like Elton John and David Frost. 'I desperately wanted to gate-crash,' Fergie wrote, but the house was impregnable with high walls and a squadron of guards. With Diana and a few friends they staged a hen night which involved wearing grey wigs, dressing up as policewomen and pretending to arrest a 'prostitute' at the gates of Buckingham Palace. They were put in a police van and driven down the Mall until one of the policemen recognized Diana: 'Oh my heavens, it's the Princess of Wales in drag!' he exclaimed. The girls went on to Annabel's, the fashionable nightclub in Berkeley Square, hoping to surprise Andrew there but, having inveigled themselves in, they found him gone. After stopping the traffic in Berkeley Square, they succeeded in tricking the policeman on the Palace gates and shut them in Andrew's face as his car approached. Fearing an ambush, he screeched into reverse. 'It was about then,' said Fergie, 'that I wondered if we had gone a bit too far.' Technically the impersonation of police officers is a criminal offence, as some Members of Parliament pointed out.

'The Princess was rather in awe of her [Fergie],' one of her staff said. 'Fergie had her own agenda and used to get Diana into trouble and then disappear.'[10] The idea of going to Annabel's dressed up as a policewoman would never have occurred to Diana. Nor would the equally silly incident of the two royal ladies poking the bottoms of friends at Ascot in 1987. 'If you see where the photograph was taken – where the press stand when they take photographs at Ascot, the Royal Enclosure, well it was right there, so it was done as a photo op.,' said Dickie Arbiter. 'The Princess used to say wistfully that Fergie's friends were much nicer – i.e. more fun – than hers were,' said a member of her staff. 'But when Diana cut her off, Fergie was desperate to get back in with her.'[11]

The advent of bouncing, jolly, sporty Fergie with her mane of red hair and Rubenesque charms, made Diana's life more difficult. At Sarah's wedding, which was so obviously a marriage of love, observers noted that Charles and Diana did not exchange a word during the ceremony. 'FABULOUS FERGIE' trumpeted one headline, while the 'First Lady of Fleet Street', Jean Rook, was less complimentary, calling her 'an unbrushed red setter struggling to get out of a hand-knitted potato sack'. 'They were always made out to be so close,' Arbiter said, 'but they weren't close at all. Diana always wanted to be number one. She felt she was number one in their [the Waleses'] joint office and she was going to be number one when it came to the in-laws.' As far as Diana was concerned, almost all Fergie's initiatives were detrimental to her.

'I wasn't quite sure how to take it,' Diana told Morton.

Suddenly everybody said: 'Oh, isn't she marvellous, a breath of fresh air, thank God she's more fun than Diana.' So Diana was listening and reading every line. I felt terribly insecure. I thought maybe I ought to be like Fergie and my husband said: 'I wish you would be like Fergie – all jolly. Why are you always so miserable? Why can't you be like Grannie [the Queen Mother] . . .' I made so many balls-ups trying to be like Fergie. I went to a pop concert, Spider concert, David Bowie, with David Waterhouse and David Linley [Princess Margaret's son by Lord Snowdon] . . . I went in leather trousers which I thought was the right thing to do, completely putting out of mind that I was the future Queen and future Queens don't wear leather like that in public. So I thought that was frightfully 'with it', frightfully pleased to act my own age. Slapped hands. The same summer at Ascot I put a brolly up somebody's backside. In my astrological chart Penny Thornton always said to me: 'Everything you will do this summer you will pay for.' I did, definitely. I learnt a lot.[12]

It was Fergie who introduced Diana to an array of therapists, astrologers, psychics and healers who were to feed the more unstable side of her personality over the following years.

Two months before the Yorks' wedding Charles and Diana had undertaken an official trip to Canada for Expo '86, followed by Japan. In March that year, perhaps after comparing the un-complicated happiness of his brother and fiancée with the tortured state of his own marriage, Charles had written to a friend: 'It's agony to know that someone is hating it all so much . . . It is like being trapped in a rather desperate cul-de-sac with no apparent means of exit . . . It seems so unfair on her . . .'[13] In Vancouver, Diana, once again prey to her eating disorder, fainted by his side, only to receive minimum sympathy. Diana, it appeared, thought that he was convinced she had done it on purpose to gain sym-pathy and to distract attention from himself. When Charles spoke from the heart of 'the soul of mankind' and 'the beauty and harmony' that lay deep therein like the reflection in a 'mirror-calm lake', the British press jeered, advising him to look at his own bald spot in a mirror. But when Charles had said, '. . . so often the beauty and harmony is obscured and ruffled by un-accountable storms', he was undoubtedly referring to his own private life.[14] Yet to their staff, the couple kept up appearances. Diana wrote a warm note after the tours to the butler who had looked after them, thanking him for his care. Referring to the Canada and Tokyo tours she said: 'Both . . . were particularly demanding and your day started and finished long after ours and along with the jetlag and endless time changes must have left you feeling totally exhausted. Your support and endurance are vital to us and somehow you managed to appear calm and always there with a smile on our return. Both of us wanted you to know how enormously we appreciated everything you did for us while we were in Canada and Japan . . .' Whatever her troubles, Diana endeavoured to keep a calm face in front of her household. The same could not be said for Prince Charles whose complaining letters to his friends left no doubt of his feelings. By November he was openly appealing to his friends for help: 'Frequently I feel nowadays that I'm in a kind of cage, pacing up and down in it and longing to be free. How awful incompatibility is, and how dreadfully destructive it can be for the players in this extraordinary drama. It has all the ingredients of a Greek tragedy . . . I fear I'm going to need every bit of help every now and then for which I feel rather ashamed . . .'[15]

Help was, of course, forthcoming. Charles's friends rallied to his side against 'that tiresome girl' who had tried to banish them. The Brabournes, the Romseys, the Palmer-Tomkinsons and Nicholas Soames reappeared in his life. Conveniently, the Parker Bowleses had moved from Bolehyde Manor to Middlewich House, which was even nearer to Highgrove. Now, even according to his official biographer, Charles once again began to talk to Camilla on the telephone, and they started to see each other at Highgrove. Con-veniently also, Andrew Parker Bowles had a new appointment which kept him in London during the week. It would be true, as Dimbleby wrote, that Camilla Parker Bowles helped Charles out of the depression and sense of hopelessness he felt in the face of what had by now become the tabloids' persecution of him: 'In

Camilla Parker Bowles, the Prince found the warmth, the understanding and the steadiness for which he had always longed and
had never been able to find with any other person . . .'[16] Unfortunately it would also be true that, while indulging in his affair, the
Prince did not treat Diana with any more consideration than he
had before, his nagging guilt turning him even more against her.

Diana, who had long suspected that her husband had 'gone back
to his Lady' if not physically but in his heart, had somehow received
definite knowledge of his rapprochement with Camilla. At the
Marivent Palace on Majorca, where she and Charles were guests
of the King and Queen of Spain, Don Juan Carlos and Doña Sofia,
Diana called in her new protection officer, Detective Ken Wharfe.
She was alone. 'Everyone's gone out, the Prince has gone out
painting. I don't want to go out,' she told Wharfe. 'I just thought
you ought to know one or two things.' 'Golly, such as?' Wharfe
asked. 'And she said, "Well, you know about Camilla, don't you?"
Which I did,' Wharfe commented, 'because my colleagues had
said . . . and I said, "Well, you know, Ma'am, I don't really want
to get involved with this, it's not really my remit." And she said,
"Well, it may not be, Ken, but I'm telling you because I might go
into, really, mood swings and then you'll know why. It's not
because of anybody else, it's because of her and I don't know how
to deal with it." So I said, "What do you mean, deal with it?"
And she said, "Well, I don't know how to deal with it. It's there
and I can't do anything about it. It's not as if it's just re-emerged,
Ken, this has actually been here ever since I've been married and
I accepted that it was a long-term friend and thought that it would
just fade away." I said, "Well, have you spoken to your husband
about it?" and she said, "Oh, he wouldn't listen, he doesn't listen,
it's just a waste of time . . ."'[17] Diana sulked and Charles flew off
early to Balmoral, the only place where he felt at peace and
protected from the press.

Later that year, in a tit-for-tat gesture, she began an affair with
James Hewitt, a cavalry officer whom she had first met that summer. Hewitt, in Wharfe's opinion, was 'a huge protest vote'
directed at Charles. Unfortunately for her, by the time Charles got

to know of it – and one can be sure that the police rumour mill would have made sure that he did – it was a source of relief rather than anger.

Born into a services family in Londonderry, Northern Ireland, in 1958, James Hewitt was educated at Millfield School and Sandhurst and then joined the Life Guards and attained the rank of major. Tall, with thick, reddish blond wavy hair and an athletic figure, Hewitt had good manners, a boyish charm and was attractive and attentive to women. He was also a good polo player and it was when playing for the army against Prince Charles, representing the navy, at the polo ground at Tidworth, Wiltshire, home of the 13/18 Hussars, in 1981 that he had first set eyes on Diana. She was in tears, crying, she later told Hewitt, because of her fear that Charles did not love her as she loved him. He had seen her again at Buckingham Palace on the day of the Yorks' wedding, when he was in charge of security. She was sitting on the stairs, barefoot, animated and natural, chatting to some members of staff, her knees scrunched up under her chin, her fingers playing with her bare toes. Hewitt was struck by her loveliness: he was soon to see her again and be introduced to her at a drinks party given by her lady-in-waiting, Hazel West, and her husband, Buckingham Palace comptroller Lieutenant Colonel George West, at their St James's Palace apartment. Hewitt had become known to the courtiers through his acquaintance with Sir Martin Gilliatt, the Queen Mother's private secretary, who occasionally invited him to drinks in his room at St James's Palace. He was surprised at the invitation as it was a small party and he would not normally have expected to have been invited. Asked whether Diana might have had a hand in it, he replied, 'Hazel more or less let that slip, I think. I got on quite well with Hazel and George but only in passing. They wouldn't normally have asked me to one of their cocktail parties.'[18]

In conversation at the Wests', Diana told him of her fear of horses since a childhood accident and that she would like to conquer her fear and take up riding again. Hewitt, as she must have known, was a staff captain in the Household Division with responsibilities for running the Household Division stables. A few days later she telephoned him and the lessons began from Knightsbridge Barracks, conveniently close to Kensington Palace: Diana was chaperoned by Hazel West, the only one of her ladies-in-waiting who could ride and also with whom she was on friendly, relaxed terms. Later, apparently, Diana told Hewitt that she had only started the riding lessons so that she could see him: there had been an immediate attraction between them from the start. Again, asked about this, Hewitt demurred: 'I can't see that anyone would find me attractive [but] if you analyse it she was very keen and she had a busy schedule and she managed to squeeze in seeing me and she remained frightened of horses and she didn't really enjoy it . . .'[19]

Hewitt was very much Diana's type – she had a weakness for men in uniform – and not being in any way intellectual was definitely unthreatening. According to his biographer, Anna Pasternak, Hewitt 'had learned to respect and cherish women physically' and had become an expert lover, beginning with a woman eight years his senior, a pupil at his mother's riding school. Perhaps Diana sensed this and, suffering from her sexual rejection by her husband, felt that Hewitt, kind and unthreatening, was what she needed. Within a few weeks she had fallen in love with Hewitt (as she was to admit in her 1995 *Panorama* interview – 'Yes, I adored him . . . Yes, I was in love with him') and he with her. It became a risky physical affair, beginning with meetings at Kensington Palace, and going on to snatched weekends at Highgrove and visits to his mother's house in Devon.

Diana was sexually inexperienced. Before her marriage, she told Hewitt, there had been a moment or moments of the 'quick fumble' nature, but, as he put it, she had been 'more of a virgin' than her contemporaries. There could have been no real sexual passion in her encounters with Charles, spoiled as he was by experienced older women like Kanga Tryon and in any case already deeply committed to Camilla Parker Bowles. According to Hewitt, after many conversations on the subject with Diana, he thought that Charles 'held a torch for Camilla and he fancied her and

he wanted to sleep with her . . . he obviously didn't want to sleep
with Diana and she needed that. You know the chemistry is not
there and you fall out of love, you don't fancy the person and
you probably feel a bit hemmed in. I think you just sort of reject
them.' At one stage she suggested to Hewitt – and to other friends
of hers – that Charles said he might be gay. 'That was his excuse
to her.'

Hewitt was subsequently ostracized by senior army people for
his temerity in having an affair with the wife of the heir to the
throne but, in fact, it is difficult to blame him for that. 'She was
utterly charming and natural and fresh and vivacious and rather
lovely,' he recalled. 'There was a certain chemistry straight away.
Unfortunate, but there we are.'[20] At first Diana managed to hide
her vulnerability. 'She hid that very well, actually, but I became
more and more a shoulder to lean on, and she then learned to
open up to me and express her concerns and her fears and her
worries and the fact that she was feeling worthless, and that sort of
thing,' Hewitt said. 'I mean very early on in the [officers' mess]
places where we met she would try and be happy, try and be
positive but there was an underlying unhappiness which one had
to address . . . and then you talk it through and make it better.'[21]

Eventually the subject of bulimia came up. Hewitt had never
heard of it and when Diana confessed she had this problem – 'I'd
have liked to have seen the look on my face at the time . . . I think
I was pretty revolted by it,' he said. 'But I didn't really discuss it
in depth with her and she said, "Actually, when I'm with you I
don't have it", so there was no need. I mean, she explained the
whole thing and I learned to cope with it. It was a shock and she
explained that when she was unhappy she would go to the fridge
and gorge herself and then be sick and then do it again . . .' During
the periods they spent together, it did not happen – 'I spent
twenty-four/forty-eight hours with her actually side by side so I
would have known, I believe that. But then in the intervening
days it would happen again when she was back in Kensington
Palace, so it was horrid. And you could feel it in her body. You
could feel the effects of it . . . the flesh wasn't firm, the skin didn't

fit the flesh . . .'[22] As the bulimia became less frequent her body shape improved, as did her breath, which had held the telltale symptoms.

Subsequently, although the affair became known to inner circles via the Royal Protection Squad officers, no attempt whatsoever was made to stop it. Early in the relationship, Charles and Diana had come to some accommodation, comparing diaries to avoid the risk of one being caught by the other, or, at the very least, to avoid meeting each other. Diana 'told me that they had a diary conference every week so she knew where he was and he knew where she was'.[23] According to Hewitt, it was Diana who initiated the physical affair. 'Strange as it may seem,' he wrote, 'I had no real option.' Diana was emotionally and physically fragile, racked by bulimia and painfully thin. 'She was a woman deeply damaged by rejection,' he said. 'Whether it was true or not, she saw herself as being wholly alone in a hostile world . . .'[24] At the Palace, she told Hewitt, the only person who could really help her was the Queen. 'Things were so bad at one stage that she did summon up courage to make an appointment to explain the whole situation. Diana said she met with a very concerned response. The Queen promised she would do what she could to take some pressure off her and later newspaper editors were asked not to subject her to too much scrutiny. But when it came to the issue of her marriage to Charles, the Queen said there was nothing she could do. It would be wrong to intervene.'[25] As Diana was to put it later, when she asked the Queen what to do, the Queen replied, 'I don't know what you should do. Charles is hopeless.'[26]

The misery caused by her failing marriage continued to gnaw at her self-esteem. There were moments of happiness when she was with Hewitt. 'She'd come down and stay [at Hewitt's mother's house in Devon] and she'd arrive with laughter and smiles and love and then on a Sunday evening she would be a bit gloomy but very little other than fun and laughter and enjoyment in the intervening time,' Hewitt recalled of their weekends together.[27] Over the period from the summer of 1986 until just before Hewitt left for a tour of duty with the army in Germany, their relationship restored Diana to a measure of health and happiness. 'He was good for her,' a close aide of Diana's at the time said; 'he made her happy.'[28]

10. A Dying Marriage

'What have the newspapers ever done for me?' (Diana resents press persecution, 1987)

'By 1987 it [Kensington Palace] was the backdrop to a dying marriage and its walls had heard many angry words . . .' Diana's new equerry, Patrick Jephson, recalled in his memoirs. He had been recruited to replace Richard Aylard, who from then on was seconded to work for Charles. For the moment Diana's contingent – the 'A-team' – worked in an office at St James's Palace with Charles's in relative amity, having moved that spring from Buckingham Palace. In insider shorthand this was 'BP' (Buckingham Palace), 'SJP' (St James's Palace), and, of course, the base, 'KP' (Kensington Palace). The move was, in effect, a signal that Charles intended to secure his independence from his mother's establishment, a move which was to result in increasingly crossed signals between the two.

Jephson soon realized that the princely marriage was in freefall and that the chief preoccupation of the couple's staff was to conceal this from the public, for the sake both of the monarchy and of the young princes. The most dangerous moments from their point of view were the joint overseas tours – when British and foreign press assembled to probe the state of the royal marriage. Diana had commissioned a portrait by the photographer Terence Donovan which presented a new, more resolute image: with short, glossy hair, bare-necked above an off-the-shoulder evening dress, her expression sad and wary but with a determined set to her mouth. The picture was taken on the eve of the first joint tour of the new year, a visit by Charles and Diana to Portugal in February 1987, to commemorate the Valentine's Day wedding six hundred years before, of an English girl, Philippa of Lancaster, daughter of John of Gaunt, to the King of Portugal, João I. While the press focused on the fact that the couple occupied separate bedroom suites in the beautiful eighteenth-century palace of Queluz just outside Lisbon, the serious purpose of the visit, to concentrate on Anglo-Portuguese trade, seemed to be forgotten. Diana, in playful mood and almost certainly inspired by a desire to upstage and annoy Prince Charles, ostentatiously flirted with the President of Portugal: 'Are you cold?' President Soares asked her, looking at her off-the-shoulder evening dress. 'No, but if I were, would you take off your jacket to keep me warm?' Diana riposted. As they sat down she spotted his white braces beneath his dinner jacket, reached out, put her hand inside his jacket and twanged them. 'You're a social-ist,' she said, 'shouldn't you be wearing red braces?' At the ballet on another evening, Diana playfully asked Soares, 'What colour are you wearing tonight?' Soares opened his jacket and Diana tweaked his braces again. The Prince, touring Lisbon in stormy, sunless spring weather, was reported as looking 'somewhat dour'.

Public playfulness was Diana's way of teasing Charles. It was one of the few weapons left to her, something she could get away with without arousing an explosive fit of anger. Various people have testified to her fear of Charles, Jephson among them: 'I learned that, among other feelings he stirred in her, many of them still warm and affectionate, the Princess also felt fear. Except when she was roused with her own formidable brand of indignation, she would go to great lengths to avoid needlessly provoking the Prince. When she felt herself to be on the receiving end of his anger, before her characteristic defiance set in, I often saw a look of trepidation cross her face, as if she were once again a small girl in trouble with the grown-ups . . .'[1]

On a joint skiing trip to Klosters later, Diana was inspired by the presence of Fergie to clown around for the photographers. While the press clicked away, the royal brothers, according to reports, 'looked faintly disapproving' and Prince Charles snapped, 'Come on, come on'. Even the *Daily Mail* thought Diana's behaviour 'undignified'. Without Charles, Diana enjoyed the

après-ski life, with a party of young men, most of whom she had
met with Fergie, including Philip Dunne and David Waterhouse.
At home, Waterhouse became one of Diana's bridge set (a game
Charles did not play). She had begun to replace her old school
friends with a more sophisticated circle: Julia Samuel, Catherine
Soames (at the time still married to Nicholas Soames; they were
divorced in 1990) and Kate Menzies. Diana was now compart-
mentalizing her life in a way which was to become characteristic
of her. Asked whether she kept his existence from her friends,
Hewitt replied, 'They must have known a wee bit because we
went to the opera together, but that was only once. But she did
keep me separate from them . . .'[2] Hewitt was not part of Diana's
London group although still very much on the scene: they spent
weekends in Devon with his family, escorted by Ken Wharfe, and,
on some occasions, at Highgrove 'chaperoned' by Diana's most
faithful friend, Carolyn Bartholomew, and her husband William.
Diana was by now aware that when her husband was alone at
Highgrove, Camilla came over, often acting as hostess. According
to Hewitt, this was one aspect of her new life which upset her
dreadfully – that Camilla would come and 'be the lady of the house
when she was not there'.

   Charles's rejection of her both personally and sexually in favour
of Camilla made it inevitable that Diana should seek consolation
and companionship with other men. She played safe, keeping
friendships within her own class. The men were, to quote Ken
Wharfe, 'invariably good-looking, public school–educated, and
from landed families . . . They played bridge tolerably and enjoyed
going with her to the cinema or to dine . . . at the trendiest
restaurants, but small talk, the ability to chat endlessly for hours
about almost nothing at all, seemed to be their speciality. They
also had to know how to please the Princess which meant sharing
her liking for risqué jokes and playing adult games like Twister.'[3]
Diana's flirtations with men like Philip Dunne, nicknamed Super-
man for his resemblance to Clark Kent, and David Waterhouse
excited the tabloids to the extent that the notorious paparazzo
Jason Fraser stationed himself outside the South Kensington mews

house belonging to Kate Menzies, one of Diana's 'safe' houses, where she had been spending the evening with Waterhouse, and succeeded in photographing Diana coming out. (Ken Wharfe grabbed him and forced him to hand over the film.) The fact that Waterhouse was mentioned by Dimbleby as 'a frequent visitor to Kensington Palace, arriving to spend long hours with his dog' indicates that he was the closest of the men friends. With these men and girlfriends like Julia Samuel, Catherine Soames and Kate Menzies, Diana had a group to sustain her in her new, more separate life. And then for sex, romance and the satisfaction of her need for adoration, there was Hewitt. His presence and unselfish support were still important in bolstering her self-confidence.

Meanwhile, Fergie and Diana were no longer the close friends they once had appeared to be. Diana was not amused when the American press pointed to Fergie as her rival not only for the affections of the Royal Family but in the fashion stakes as well. That summer *Vanity Fair* had stated that Fergie had lost 28 pounds and ordered twenty Yves Saint Laurent outfits, outshining Diana, who remained loyal to British designers. At Ascot in June, sections of the press declared, 'Sarah wins by a head in the fashion stakes'. As if to rub it in, the cover of the *Sunday Times Magazine* of 19 July featured Fergie with the caption 'Move over Diana' and inside an article contrasting the two women distinctly to Sarah's advantage, with Diana labelled 'Beauty and Duty' and Fergie 'Freedom and Fun'. That year the papers had been full of Fabulous Fergie, learning to fly, appearing with twenty-three model aeroplanes pinned to her hair, clowning around boisterously at the televised *It's a Royal Knockout* programme. Charles, perspicaciously, had forbidden Diana to take part in this undignified affair. On the visit to Portugal, apparently, Diana had taxed the press with being more interested in Fergie than in her. On tour with Andrew in Canada in July, Fergie had been a roaring success, particularly when pictured in a Davy Crockett hat and paddling a canoe. Recently, too, the newspapers had taken to criticizing Diana for her disco excursions, her pop concerts, her dancing all night with Philip Dunne at the Worcester wedding ball and her choice of companions such as nightclub owner Peter Stringfellow and pop stars like Elton John and Boy George. Diana can hardly be criticized for preferring fun to serious dinners with her husband's friends and mentors.

On a more serious side, Fergie was more popular with the Royal Family than Diana was, particularly with the 'Top Lady' as Diana sometimes called her – the Queen. 'The Queen loved Fergie,' said a courtier, 'who took part in everything – maybe wearing bright pink pants but loving it.'[4] Fergie fitted in perfectly with the family's cherished outdoor life. Unlike Diana she was an expert rider and loved horses. She learned to carriage drive, Prince Philip's favourite sport now he could no longer play polo. At Buckingham Palace, while Andrew was away five nights a week on naval duty, Fergie would be invited to dinner by the Queen. However, where the Palace servants had loved and cherished Diana, Fergie shocked their higher echelons with her very unroyal ways: drinking in the pub behind the Royal Mews, and holding indecorous parties with the Palace footmen where she and her father would pass round extremely risqué presents. She would burst into dinner parties, shouting 'Curtsey, curtsey, curtsey' to the other women, as a triumphant joke. When warned by her godmother that she would have to change her ways to fit in with the court, she shrugged her shoulders and replied, 'Oh, I'll just be myself'. Unfortunately for both Sarah and the family this would turn out to be only too true, but for the moment Sarah's vivacity carried all before her.

'I got terribly jealous and she got jealous of me,' Diana confided. 'She kept saying to me, "You mustn't worry, Duch, everything is going to be fine, let me do this, let me do that." I couldn't understand it, she was actually enjoying being where she was [at Balmoral and Sandringham] whereas I was fighting to survive. I couldn't understand how she could find it so easy. I thought she would be like me and put her head down and be shy. No, a different kettle of fish altogether and she wooed everybody in this family and did it so well. She left me looking like dirt . . . up in Scotland she used to do everything that I never did. So I thought,

"This can't last, the energy of this creature is unbelievable." Meanwhile everybody [was] looking at me – "It's a pity Diana has gone so introverted and quiet, she was so busy and trying to sort herself out . . ." '[5]

By now Charles had mentally and physically withdrawn himself from Diana. It had become increasingly difficult for him to bear her presence. Always a loner, he sought solitude as a relief from marital disharmony – a four-day visit to the Kalahari Desert with Laurens van der Post in March was followed by three days living the life of a crofter in the Outer Hebrides, earning himself cruel jibes in the popular press: 'A Loon Again – the potty Prince's strange quest for inner satisfaction'. An outburst of renewed speculation on the state of the royal marriage came in October that year when it dawned on media commentators how many days the couple had spent apart. After their joint visit to Spain/Majorca earlier in the year, Charles had gone to Italy on a painting holiday while Diana had returned to England. It was noted that they had spent their sixth wedding anniversary apart – he in Cornwall, she in Tidworth. After the usual Balmoral holiday, they had been in London together on 16 September to accompany Harry to his first school, after which Charles had returned to Scotland, allegedly to oversee the Balmoral estate. They were not seen together again until 21 October when they made a brief – six-hour – visit to Wales to offer condolence to flood victims in the Carmarthen area. They hardly exchanged a word then Charles flew back to Scotland, leaving Diana to return home alone. For anyone used to the Prince's habits, this preference for the peace and quiet of Birkhall was nothing very surprising. Always set in his ways, he was not about to change them for his son's schooldays or to accommodate his wife. 'The Prince had always spent that period of the year in Scotland and didn't see why he shouldn't go on doing so,' said an aide. 'For example, when Diana insisted that they return to London for the beginning of the school term, Charles's reaction was to ask why they could not join the local school for the time being.'[6]

Earlier that year, in January 1987, William's much-loved nanny of four and a half years, Barbara Barnes, left 'by mutual agreement'.

Observers thought that Diana was jealous of her son's affection for
Barbara. The final split seems to have come when Barnes was
invited over to Mustique by her former employers, Lord and Lady
Glenconner. No objection was raised at the time but when Barbara
returned she was given the cold shoulder by Diana – rumour had
it that Diana thought her nanny 'shouldn't go to a place like that
with people like that', in other words it was 'above her station'.
Receiving no answer when she asked, 'What have I done wrong?',
Barnes left, finding herself no longer able to stand the atmosphere.
William, however, remained loyal, asking her to his eighteenth
and twenty-first birthday parties.

The contrast between pictures of Charles painting and relaxing
on his own on Deeside, while Diana did the school run in London,
was enough to precipitate a wave of hostile headlines with the
tabloids showing a savagery they had not displayed before: '33
days apart', 'Charles and Diana are not speaking', 'Patch up your
marriage, Di'. Reports that Charles had been seen with Kanga
Tryon (which turned out to be the work of a notorious Fleet
Street hoaxer, Rocky Ryan) caused frenzy. It was the end of the
press honeymoon. The *Sun*, enraged by a reported remark of
Diana's, 'What have the newspapers ever done for me?', turned
viciously on their former darling: 'The *Sun* can answer Her Loveliness in one word – EVERYTHING! The newspapers have made
her one of the most famous women in the world. They have given
her an aura of glamour and romance. Without them the entire
Windsor family would soon become as dull and commonplace as
the rulers of Denmark and Sweden. Were that to happen, people
might begin to ask what is the point in having royals at all.
Including lovely Princess Di.'

The rumours brought newspapermen to track Charles down in
his retreat; they had, in his words, 'unleashed a positive hurricane
of self-righteous, pontificating, censorious claptrap in the newspapers . . . and . . . led to car loads of beastly photographers etc.,
careering about Balmoral and following me up the track to Loch
Muick . . .'[7] In the same letter he expressed a fellow feeling for

Diana who, back at Kensington Palace, was pursued by paparazzi on motorbikes.

One well-known psychologist diagnosed the popular press as suffering from a double delusion: first that it saw itself as the creator of the royal couple and found it difficult when its creation began to behave in a way which the press had not planned or envisaged; second that it could destroy them if it wished. 'It seems to be done out of spite,' he commented. Alan Rusbridger, in 'A nasty twist to the fairytale', gave an account of the press pack trying to prime members of the public to ask awkward questions on royal visits, a technique which apparently failed. The Waleses' marriage diffi-culties even featured on chat shows in Britain and the US. Mean-while, the general public went on hoping that the apparent rift was not terminal and were not prepared to believe the rumours, while, in the face of the deluge, Buckingham Palace stonewalled, knowing the truth but wishing to conceal it for as long as possible.

As her marriage unravelled, Diana continued her charitable activities, particularly those supporting the young, the elderly and the suffering with whom she had a unique rapport, specifically the children's charity Barnardo's, of which she had become President in 1984, Help the Aged and the AIDS Foundation.

'She was completely brilliant in the way she related to every-body,' a Chair of Barnardo's recalled of the period of the charity's relaunch four years later in 1988. 'She created so much happiness. People forget, you know. The magic of her was tangible . . . I've never experienced it before . . . quite late on when she was quite experienced we had a huge conference in Birmingham – a huge meeting for all the Barnardo's volunteers, you know all the ladies in print dresses who work in the shops and raise money. It was an enormous occasion and she came. People wouldn't come through to lunch because she was coming in the afternoon and they'd got themselves an aisle seat and they literally wanted to touch the hem of her dress. And when she did come I was walking beside her as we went into this room and she was really very experienced by then but as we came in the atmosphere was so extraordinary that

even she stopped and said, "Oh, my goodness!" She was reeling.
And then afterwards she walked around talking to the people who
were there and as I was behind her I saw their reaction. She would
chat to them for a bit and then she would move on and as she
moved on they were literally weak at the knees. They sort of
crumpled and clutched each other. There was that thing about
her magic . . . it was a phenomenon, a real phenomenon. And
everybody she met just fell under that spell, women as well as men.
Men were just floored by her when she said goodbye, got into her
car and gave them that look underneath her eyelashes with those
wonderful eyes – and most of the top-flight Barnardo's were men
and I was there to sort of catch them as their knees buckled.'

Her appeal ranged from rebellious teenagers to Hollywood stars.
'Her relating to children was not just the cuddly ones who were
crawling over her as she was getting down to eye level and talking
to them and they said things like "Are you a real princess?" Also
the hairy ones with the Mohican hairdos and the rest of it, she was
brilliant to them too. We had a big AIDS conference and after
she had done her thing about AIDS which was phenomenal really,
she spent some time walking around the people who were there.
And there were some really grumpy, bolshie teenagers sitting
around the floor, they never moved when she came by. She just
looked down and said, "Are you all right down there?" And it
was perfect. It made them feel slightly idiotic but didn't put them
down really.'

At a Barnardo's event, the Champion Children lunch for those
who had won prizes for being brave or doing exceptional things,
Sylvester Stallone had put pressure on Barnardo's to be allowed to
come and to sit next to the Princess. 'In the end, he didn't sit next
to her; they had a child, a very ill child, sitting between Diana and
Stallone, and never for one moment did she make that child feel
left out. She flirted brilliantly with Stallone with the child. I
remember her saying to him, "Tracy and I have decided we would
like to ask you whether you are married at this moment?" It was so
clever. Then at one moment Sylvester Stallone got up and started
to walk out and she said, "Oh, got a better invitation then?"

'I never realized until after she died that she went on with those relationships with quite a lot of people who were suffering some kind of hardship, and she went on and wrote to them and things like that. I never knew that. Clearly it was a very, very important thing for her emotionally to have that relationship with people as she was giving them happiness . . . I mean it actually made her feel a good person, which she needed to feel, I think. And you knew when she got into her car and was whisked away that her fun for the day was over really. You felt that . . . Going back to Kensington Palace where there was nobody to talk to her, ask her if she had had a nice time . . .'[8]

Most of the charities noticed the change from shy young woman to confident individual overcoming her inhibitions about public speaking and taking on some surprisingly radical causes. They saw a connection with the public that bypassed the Establishment and, to some extent, the media. Diana, alone of the Royal Family, seemed to understand that this rapport with the public was something to which a modern monarchy should aspire. It was no longer enough just to turn up and smile; people needed to feel that she really cared about them.

Despite her personal problems Diana had now become established in the public mind as 'caring Di'. Her most high-profile moment had come in 1987 at the opening of the first UK AIDS ward. Professor Mike Adler, the doctor in charge of the ward, had written to Buckingham Palace asking if a member of the Royal Family would open the ward, apparently expressing a preference for Prince Charles. This was at a time when AIDS was regarded as 'the Gay Plague' exclusively connected to homosexuality in men: the Palace, clearly nervous about unfortunate connotations, preferred to send Diana rather than the heir to the throne. 'On the day she was very nervous and we were very nervous. We had been crawled over for weeks by the media and the Palace. But the moment she started meeting the patients she did relax and then there was that very famous photo of her shaking hands with a patient who had AIDS and that was wired all over the world. It made a tremendous impact.'[9] Baroness Jay, a founder director of the National AIDS Trust, recalled, 'There was the huge fuss about her not wearing gloves, and the fact that she didn't and that the world's media took it up was the moment we realized the power she had to influence public perceptions and she wasn't even at the height of her power then . . .'[10]

'The following day the pictures were all over every paper,' said the photographer Arthur Edwards. 'Diana with these AIDS patients. She chatted to them, joked with them . . . made them feel good. This was her magic. People were amazed to realize this wasn't a disease you ran away from; it was perfectly safe. And she was going against all the old guard at Buckingham Palace. I believe she single-handedly took the stigma out of AIDS.'[11] 'There was a lot of negative sniping in the background from the traditional courtier class,' said Dickie Arbiter, former Palace press spokesman then press secretary to the Prince and Princess of Wales, 'who just thought this was not what royals do.'[12] Princess Anne, the Princess Royal, made a speech a year later (26 January 1988) describing AIDS as 'an own goal by the human race' which implicitly raised questions of guilt. Establishment disapproval only spurred Diana on, an additional factor in the empathy she felt towards the sufferers. She was drawn to the vulnerable, the weak and the unrecognized. It touched a personal chord with her, linking with the rejection and marginalization which she felt she was suffering. And as a result of the impact she had made with the AIDS photograph, people started to be interested in what she was doing, rather than what she was wearing.

Perhaps Diana's biggest public contribution in the AIDS field was her visit to the Harlem Hospital Center in New York in February 1989. In the view of the head of the paediatric unit at the hospital dealing with children with AIDS, Diana's involvement in the issue transformed the perception of AIDS in the United States. 'She had this very magical way with the kids and they were immediately attracted to her. Then she did what I realized only in retrospect was so important: she had her picture taken with a child with AIDS. And of course that picture went around the world . . . the really extraordinary thing that happened is that people began calling, saying: "I didn't realise about these kids with AIDS until Princess Diana visited Harlem Hospital . . ." Suddenly we had a whole group of willing foster parents who wanted kids with AIDS . . . and at the end of two years for all of New York City, there was a surplus of foster parents wanting kids with AIDS . . . I know in my heart that Princess Diana is the one who made this possible.'[13] She was accused by her enemies of using these sick children as a photo opportunity. Photographer Tim Graham defended her: 'She definitely understood the power of images, but it wasn't just for the camera. The photographers would be in the room for two minutes to do the picture, and then we would all leave, but I know she would stay and talk to the other patients and pick up the other kids.'[14] Her friend Marguerite Littman said: 'She was somebody that people admired – and that's an understatement – who embraced and helped people who had AIDS. She made it OK, just as simple as that . . . she didn't need the publicity, not like a movie star doing it. There was no reason for her taking up something that the royal family wouldn't embrace . . . they certainly didn't encourage her. So it seems to me that she did it out of compassion . . .'[15] What is more, Diana made sure that she kept in touch with some of the children later. One particular child, Shamir, was known throughout the AIDS centre for his foul language, most of it sex-related. 'Shamir comes out of his room and runs up to Princess Diana and jumps up into her arms and begins to whisper into her ear . . . We will never know what he said, but she began to chuckle and sat him down and chatted with him. He went into a foster home in Brooklyn and she wrote to him a couple of times until he died.'[16]

People were beginning to see her as more than just a clothes horse but Diana herself was certainly aware of the power of the image. As she realized the power she could wield in aid of the causes she believed in, she was becoming aware of the aura she projected which gave her that power. She had begun to fight back against her rejection by Charles, besotted as he was by an older and far less physically attractive woman. 'She first started to become glamorous when her marriage began to go wrong,' said Victor

Edelstein.[17] She jogged, exercised, swam fierce lengths in the Palace pool, and played tennis at the smart Vanderbilt Club in Shepherd's Bush. In July she played doubles against a pair which included Steffi Graf. Tim Graham published a volume of photographs he had taken of Diana over the past eight years, comparing her shyness in 1980 to the confident smiling Princess of 1988. 'Princess Diana can make the act of strapping a child into a car seat seem glamorous,' he wrote. 'Whatever she does, she has total charm. That did not happen eight years ago when I first photographed her. Then she modestly looked at her feet all the time. Now the moment she steps out of a car the eyes come up and the smile is already starting.' She was photographed, wildly popular at Wembley, presenting the FA Cup to the winners. Dressed in khaki cover alls and pink trainers, she attended a day's training with the 13/18 Royal Hussars on Salisbury Plain. She fired a 76mm gun and drove a tracked armoured reconnaissance vehicle before eating a field lunch of steak and kidney pie.

Meanwhile, Charles pursued his own causes with passion: he turned green with a vengeance, surrounding himself with environmental advisers including Jonathon Porritt and his new aide, Richard Aylard, formerly Diana's equerry, who had studied zoology at university before becoming a naval officer. Unfortunately for the Prince he was ahead of his time on green issues and received little sympathy, not least from government ministers in the business of retaining jobs in the mining industries, or global companies to whom environmental concerns clashed with the demands for profit. Mrs Thatcher was enraged by his interest in housing and the inner cities and particularly by his Disraelian depiction of Britain as divided between the haves and have-nots. Undeterred by the unwillingness of ministers to listen to him, Charles launched his own crusades. In a powerful speech at Mansion House in December 1987 he accused property developers and their consultants of being more destructive of Britain's cities than the Luftwaffe, with particular reference to plans for the redevelopment of Paternoster Square round St Paul's Cathedral. He compared the sensitive post-war reconstruction of European cities with the 'Rape of Britain' which had occurred in Bristol, Birmingham, Newcastle and other cities. Addressing an audience largely composed of architects and planners, he said: 'In the space of a mere 15 years, in the 60's and 70's, and in spite of elaborate rules supposedly designed to protect that great view [St Paul's], your predecessors as architects and developers of the City of London wrecked the London skyline and desecrated the dome of St Paul's . . . Can you imagine the French building those same towers round Notre Dame? The Italians walling in St Mark's in Venice?'

The *Sunday Times* rightly praised Prince Charles for his seriousness and the effort he made to carve out a role for himself in his country's life from which he was virtually excluded as long as his mother remained on the throne, in other words, for as long as she lived. Unfortunately for him, he did not enjoy the ceremonial role his position demanded and the public expected. While carrying out engagements with grace and charm, he inwardly seethed, confiding to his diary and to his friends a picture of a being eternally put-upon, self-pitying and resentful. His innate pessimism undermined enjoyment of everything, even the birth of his children. After visiting Prince Harry in hospital he recalled: 'I looked down on him and I thought, "Poor little thing, what have I brought this poor child into the world for?" '[18]

There was a disconnection between Charles's concern for the environment and the private pleasures he enjoyed – as shown, for instance, in his passion for his gas-guzzling Aston Martin. 'One day a new, rich, racing-green Bentley was delivered to Highgrove; en route it had been given a silver coach line down the side. Charles walked out of the door to inspect it: "Mmm . . . that was meant to be my racing colours . . . Take it away." £10,000 later the car returns as the Prince wanted it. One day, after a day's hunting with the Belvoir, the Prince and his policeman were returning home; driving down the lane after heavy rain they found a large pool of water and on the far side cars which had been following the hunt and two men on a tractor. Halfway across, water came pouring in and they realized that the other cars hadn't driven through the water – they had been stuck in the water and been towed out by the tractor.' The tractor men approached in delighted anticipation. '"Hello, look who we've got here . . ."' The Bentley was towed out in a sodden state, all its electrics blown, and sent back to the manufacturers with instructions to provide another one the next day because the Prince had an engagement. There were only two similar models available – one in Scotland and one in Germany. The one in Scotland was duly driven down to the Bentley plant where it was refitted to the Prince's specifications. People worked all hours and drove through the night to get it to Highgrove on time. At eight o'clock the next morning, it was there ready and waiting. The Prince walked out of the door and took one look at it: "It's black. I hate black." Turns round and walks back inside. "Oh well, we'll take the Vauxhall . . ."'[19]

Charles's failure to realize or to accept that his private behaviour impinged on his public duty was becoming more serious by the day. If Diana could be accused of failing to understand the concept of duty – which was in fact no longer true of her since, despite her personal unhappiness, her duties as Princess of Wales still came first – how much more was it true of Prince Charles who simply failed to make the connection between his desire for Camilla and his increasing aversion to his wife, the mother of the future King, and his public duty as heir to the throne. He was becoming ever more like his great-uncle David, whose example Mountbatten had held up as a warning to him never to follow. Charles may have looked more like his father and his 'honorary grandfather' but in character – even in some of his physical mannerisms – he was more like his great-uncle, even in his habit of fiddling with his cufflinks and adjusting his tie, famously characteristic of Edward VIII. He was like him, too, in his self-pity and apparent resentment of the 'stunts' which being Prince of Wales demanded; like him in regarding his father as an ogre; like him, above all, in putting his desire for 'the woman I love' beyond considerations of the future of the monarchy and people's expectations of it.

Yet it is hard not to feel some sympathy for the Prince, cast from that year on as the villain in the royal soap opera. Penny Junor, author of a biography of Charles published in June 1987,

19

The Prince and Princess of Wales wave from Caernarvon Castle on their first
public engagement, a three-day tour of Wales in October 1981.

Diana riding with the Queen at Sandringham and looking back at the photographer. In fact, Diana had loathed horses ever since a childhood accident.

30 May 1982: a heavily pregnant Diana with the Queen watching polo at the Guards Polo Club, Windsor. Prince William was to be born on 21 June.

4 August 1982: Diana holds the newly christened Prince William Arthur Philip Louis. Prince Charles, the Duke of Edinburgh, the Queen and the Queen Mother look on. With barely a year to become used to being the Princess of Wales, Diana is now the mother of the future King.

Diana looking gaunt less than five months after William's birth. She is at the Guildhall to raise funds for Birthright, one of her many charities.

Australia, March 1983: the beginning of 'Di-mania' is very much in evidence
on the royal couple's official tour of Australia and New Zealand. The trip also
marked the beginning of tensions between Charles and Diana.

The Prince and Princess of Wales leaving hospital with Henry Charles
Albert David – Prince Harry – born on 15 September 1984. Both Diana and
Charles claimed that they would like to have had a daughter but by now their
relationship was such that there were to be no more children.

June 1985: an apparently spontaneous moment of affection – Charles kisses
Diana after she presents him with a prize at a polo match in Cirencester.

The 'surprise' Diana prepared for Charles's thirty-seventh birthday:
performing with Wayne Sleep at Covent Garden.

July 1986. 'Happy families': Diana
and Charles pose with William
and Harry at Highgrove.

June 1985: an angry row between Diana and Charles at
a Windsor polo match.

1985: watching a polo match at Smith's Lawn with police bodyguard Barry Mannakee. Diana, in her loneliness, became close to Mannakee, who was removed from his post and sacked from royal service a few months later.

May 1987: Charles and Diana arrive at the Cannes Film Festival. Charles has just told her that Barry Mannakee had been killed in a motorcycle crash.

1987. 'The Merry Wives of Windsor': the Duchess of York and Diana at the Derby, Epsom.

Charles and Diana at the Saudi Experience, London, 1986. The strained relationship between the couple is all too evident.

August 1989: Diana and James Hewitt at the Inter Regimental Polo Championship, Tidworth, Wiltshire.

for which she had been granted an interview with the Prince, claimed on BBC Radio 4 that Charles 'had lost confidence' and despaired at being 'outshone by his wife', that he was 'a sad character' with 'the loneliest position on earth' who 'did not have the support he should have from a wife', concluding that 'he married the wrong person'. Under the caption headline 'She's a winner of a wife, so why do they keep on trying to wound her?', columnist Lynda Lee-Potter riposted that Charles was lucky to get her, and so was the nation. Critics derided Diana's lack of intellect, Lee-Potter observed, but she certainly had the qualities her role required: an abundance of charm, intuition, a sense of duty, humour and common sense. To those who criticized Diana's glamour she claimed that 'to watch her crouch down next to anybody old, sick or young is not to see somebody with no more thought than the latest hemline . . .' Diana, in her charity role, was interpreting royalty as the people wanted it, connecting the Royal Family to the people in a personal way which hitherto had been the Queen Mother's secret of success. While Diana's charity activities such as Barnardo's and Help the Aged received the widest publicity, Charles's causes – the environment, public housing, modern architecture among others – were not the type to engage the interest of the tabloid press who labelled him 'loony' or 'the potty prince'. Unfortunately for Diana, on every public occasion they shared she did indeed outshine him. When the couple visited Enniskillen in Northern Ireland in the wake of the IRA bombing outrage in November, it was Diana who drew the photographers, not Charles.

In 1987 the monarchy took a sharp downturn in popularity, for which observers blamed the erosion of previous respect resulting from the antics of the younger royals: specifically the rumbustious *It's a Royal Knockout*, in which Andrew, Fergie, Edward and even Anne took part. Edward did not help the image of the monarchy by storming out of a post-show press conference, offended by the reporters' lack of enthusiasm. Fergie's and Diana's pranks with their umbrellas at Royal Ascot had also made a poor impression. Cracks began to show in the smoothly functioning edifice which the Queen had maintained with such devotion since her Coronation in 1953 as the media became increasingly confident of their licence to probe, knowing that, however outrageous their allegations, the reaction at the Palace would be 'No comment'. And it was, above all, the state of the royal marriage which was to shake that edifice to its foundations, as Palace officials were only too aware. They knew that the rumours were true but had no alternative but to maintain their silence.

The *Sunday Times* editorialized:

The Royal Family has become so used to being treated like a soap opera by large sections of the media that some of its members are beginning to act as if they are in one. This past week alone saw Prince Edward play the touchy, misunderstood youth, ready to rage against cynical journalists who did not share his passions. Prince Charles had a walk-on part as the bad-tempered husband who scolds his wife for sitting on the bonnet of his precious sports car . . . the carefree Princess Diana was meanwhile wandering round Royal Ascot playfully jabbing anybody in sight with her brolly; and the Duchess of York was at her jolly-hockey-sticks best (or worst) cheering on her team against other royal sports in a television charity fundraiser [*It's a Royal Knockout*].

While praising Prince Charles for his seriousness, the newspaper warned:

. . . there is something deeply unhealthy about the public's currently grotesque public appetite for all things royal, the lengths to which sections of the media will go to feed it and the extent to which the younger royals will go to accommodate it. If the Royal Family increasingly feels obliged to go down this road, then it is choosing a path which will eventually undermine our monarchy to its foundations. The present intense public fascination with the Royal Family cannot be sustained without doing it great harm . . .

Praising the Queen for providing the ideal role model, the *Sunday Times* pointed out that, as a result, the monarchy had enjoyed unprecedented popularity in post-war Britain and that 'unlike the 19th century there is no republican movement to worry about . . .'[20] But a poll later that year was to show a 10 per cent drop in the public popularity of the monarchy during 1987.

Given the particular qualities of both Charles and Diana and what they had to offer the people, it was a tragedy that they were increasingly driven apart. The strains in the relationship were clearly taking a physical toll on Diana: attending a Memorial Service alone for the victims of the King's Cross Underground Station fire, on 5 December 1987, she appeared rake-thin in her black coat. Four days later with Prince Charles at an awards ceremony held at the Victoria & Albert Museum, the director Roy Strong recorded her appearance in his diary: 'She is very, very thin and was in a little navy-blue suit, very tall, with all freshness sunk beneath an abundance of unnecessary make-up and hair lacquered to bounce.'[21]

Within the shell of their marriage Charles and Diana had almost no shared interests beyond their children. Music could have been one of them: despite the popular conception of 'Disco Di' bopping along to pop music on her Walkman, Diana loved classical music – particularly Verdi's Requiem which she would listen to over and over again. Although not as gifted as her grandmother Ruth, she had learned piano at school and was a fluent player even without music. She adored ballet and had once cherished an ambition to be a dancer; she loved opera – Verdi and Rossini – but not Wagner, which Charles loved. 'If she was criticized for not going to the opera with the Prince of Wales then she could be forgiven because it was invariably rather heavy stuff. All this business about the Pop Princess is not strictly true . . . I mean, yes, she loved pop music but she loved classical music too. She was perceived as a pop princess, she was perceived as a fashion icon but she would wear British designer dresses because it was good for British fashion, she had to be dressed as one would expect a royal princess and a beautiful one at that to be dressed.'[22]

When it came to the children, this was an area in which Charles, with his responsibilities, could not compete with Diana. William

had entered Wetherby School that year, and at his first school
sports day both parents had competed in their respective parents'
races. Diana, toned by jogging and swimming, won the mothers'
race and the publicity photographs, while Charles, despite his
morning exercises and zeal for physical fitness, trailed unsuccess-
fully in the fathers' event and, perhaps fortunately, was not pictured in the press. Diana was not remotely interested in his great
causes, nor in his private passion for his Highgrove garden. On his
side Charles, increasingly resentful of her popularity, never now
praised her for her efforts on public engagements and was more
likely to direct snide remarks such as 'Not that dress again', which
undermined her confidence.

Diana's disillusionment with the sham in which she was forced
to take part nearly caused her to refuse to participate in the next
joint tour – to Berlin on 1 November for the city's 750th anniversary celebrations – designed by the Palace to put on a good show
and stifle the rumours. 'The world's most glamorous couple' act
was at its superlative best. 'The Prince and Princess of Wales arrived
in West Berlin . . . smiling and apparently at ease,' *The Times*
reported. However, the popular German tabloid *Bild am Sonntag*
warned, 'everybody will be watching how their marriage
stands . . .' Charles and Diana were on their best behaviour; he
referred to her as 'one of the most glamorous colonels in the
British Army' (she was Colonel-in-Chief of the Royal Hampshire
Regiment) and whispered to his wife during the speech of welcome, causing her to giggle. 'Happiness in Berlin' the *Daily Mail*
cheered, noting that at one point, after they had got into their
limousine to leave an event, Prince Charles slid an arm round
Diana's waist. 'Triumph of the Tender Tour' headed one report
from Hanover: 'Germany bade farewell to the Prince and Princess
of Wales yesterday, after a week during which the Royal couple
showed their tenderness and affection for one another . . .
Unostentatiously, but with obvious sincerity, the Prince showed
devotion to his wife; he presented her with a piece of chocolate as
soon as he was out of sight of the press, murmuring: "For you."'
Only Diana was aware that, far from being a demonstration of

affection, it was yet another cruel put-down, a reference to her bulimia which only she would have understood.

Charles's jealousy of Diana's success with the public, and the lack of recognition he extended to her, was one of the principal causes of the failure of the marriage, fuelling a resentment in Diana which was to manifest itself in the most spectacular and destructive way possible within a few years.

11. Diana Fights Back

'He [Charles] makes my life real torture . . . but the distancing will be because . . . I go out and do my bit in the way I know and leave him behind' (Diana to James Gilbey[1])

In January 1988 Charles and Diana flew to Australia to take part in Australia's bicentennial celebrations in Sydney: on the surface it was happy and successful but, as before, Charles felt upstaged by Diana. In Sydney on the first day Diana surprised everyone by singing the words of Australia's national anthem 'Advance, Australia Fair'; Charles did not know the words. Almost two million onlookers 'were captivated by Diana', chanting 'We love Di!': as she and Prince Charles walked through a Guard of Honour at the Sydney Opera House, one man yelled, 'Three cheers for Diana!' and a thunderous roar erupted. Yet at a ball in Melbourne the following day, the couple jived energetically to Glenn Miller's 'In the Mood'. 'THEY'RE IN THE MOOD FOR LOVE . . . AND JIVING TOO' ran one headline. 'Seldom has so much happiness radiated from the couple so recently at the centre of hurtful marriage rumours,' the report went. Seeing the photographs back in London, a jealous James Hewitt was surprised that Diana could act so happily and affectionately with Charles, about whom at times she had expressed herself in vitriolic terms. But in Melbourne Diana once again eclipsed Charles, putting on a polished performance of Rachmaninov at the piano without sheet music, following Charles's reluctant attempt to play the cello, and effortlessly stealing his photo opportunity.

In March of that year they were in Charles's favourite skiing resort, Klosters, with Fergie, Patty Palmer-Tomkinson, her husband Charles, and a friend, former equerry to the Queen, Major

Hugh Lindsay. Lindsay was a favourite of all the members of the Royal Family, not least because he had the courage and frankness to tell the younger ones off if he felt it necessary. 'Why are you all so bloody rude to the servants?' he was heard to explode one day at Balmoral.[2] Perhaps because of this outspokenness, he was, Diana claimed, closer to her and to Fergie than he was to Charles. On the afternoon of 10 March, at the chalet they were sharing, Diana was in bed with a severe cold when Fergie returned, pale and shaken. She was four months pregnant and had had a skiing accident, ending up upside down in a ditch. That afternoon an avalanche swept down on Charles and his party as they were skiing off piste with their guide, Bruno Sprecher. Charles, Charles Palmer-Tomkinson and Sprecher escaped but Patty Palmer-Tomkinson was buried by the snow and Hugh Lindsay was killed. He had been married eight months earlier and his wife Sarah was six months pregnant. Diana proudly told Andrew Morton that she had taken charge: packing Lindsay's belongings, retrieving his body from hospital and consoling Sarah at Highgrove on their return. What she did not tell Morton, however, is that when she first heard of the accident, she was convinced it was Charles who had been killed, having been told by one of her therapists that he would 'die of suffocation in a foreign country'. 'She went to see all sorts of weird and wonderful people who tell fortunes,' Hewitt said, 'and one of them said an accident would befall Charles and that very nearly came true when Hugh Lindsay died in that skiing accident. She rang me from there and said, "It nearly happened" . . .'[3]

The accident was a body blow to Charles who felt it deeply. He was not helped by the British tabloid press which chose to blame him: 'ACCUSED. Official: Charles did cause the killer avalanche' the *Sun* headline blared a week later. The official report, however, blamed no one: as no one member of the party had a specific leadership role, it said, 'it was the task of each single member to assess the dangers and carry the responsibility for himself'.

That summer, Diana, her marriage in disarray, could no longer turn to her mother for comfort. Frances Shand Kydd had made several attempts to help the couple the previous year at Highgrove, without success, but now her own marriage was over. Peter Shand Kydd left her for another woman and in June they were divorced. She was devastated by a second failure and humiliated at being abandoned by the husband for whom she had given up so much. Asked why the marriage failed, a relation said laconically, 'They were both drinking a lot.' For four years Frances sank into depression, unable to help Diana any more than she was able to help herself. They had had an up-and-down, volatile relationship and frequently quarrelled over the telephone. Now, besieged by the press on the Isle of Seil, longing for her husband to return to her, she refused Diana's invitations to come to Kensington Palace.

Diana's bulimia had grown worse as the strains in her marriage intensified. Under pressure from Carolyn Bartholomew, she had begun treatment for it with Dr Maurice Lipsedge, who had treated her sister Sarah. The affair with Hewitt had helped restore her confidence but at every turn something connected with Charles would upset her, causing a fresh outbreak.

Diana's twenty-seventh birthday had been greeted with united praise from the press for her 'star quality', as 'the feminine ideal' and 'the best thing to happen to the royals'. She had realized, as she told Morton, that her antics at Ascot the previous year, her appearing in tight leather trousers and dancing till the small hours with men who were not her husband was not how the public wanted their princess to appear, and that such behaviour only gave ammunition to her enemies in her husband's camp. This frivolous image had been replaced in the public mind by her charitable activities and her virtues as a mother. The existence of James Hewitt was, amazingly, still a tightly kept secret. Yet, whatever she may have said to James Hewitt in private – and by his account it was vituperative – she was still anxious to win Charles's approbation. As Hewitt said, 'She still tried to make him love her and she cared.' For their seventh wedding anniversary that July she had made a video of herself dancing to a song from her favourite musical, *Phantom of the Opera*, 'All I Ask of You'. It was both a tease and a plea. The tragedy was that she was still in love with Charles, and secretly longed to win him back.

The Queen celebrated Charles's fortieth birthday on 14 November 1988 with a ball at Buckingham Palace. 'Although by then they were living virtually separate lives in private, Charles encouraged Diana to invite some friends of her own so that she would be more at ease,' Hewitt wrote. 'I had never met Diana on a formal occasion like this before and for the first time I experienced the incredible aura that just radiated from her, overpowering and almost eclipsing the presence of Charles and his parents. She had told me that one of her "crimes" was that she got more attention than he did, most notably when they were on a visit to Australia . . .'[4] As always in conspicuously royal surroundings, worshipped as a public figure but inwardly devastated by the presence of her husband's lover and his accommodating friends, and faced by the utter sham of her marriage, Diana was emotionally paralysed. Clive James had been introduced to her the previous year at Cannes, when she had shone: 'She came up like the sun,' he said, 'came up giggling.' Now, at Buckingham Palace, he noticed the difference in her: 'the lights in her face were dimmed down to about three-quarter strength . . . She was still there physically, but her soul had gone AWOL . . .'[5]

Only just over a week earlier, with Charles on an official visit to Paris, the couple had staged their most recent triumphant joint tour. Diana had arrived in a red and black Chanel outfit by Lagerfeld which she had chosen herself from a video sent to her at Kensington Palace. But on this occasion Charles had been allowed to shine, delivering speeches on the political future of Europe in fluent French, which, Diana admitted, she understood but couldn't speak. His Savile Row tailoring was much admired. *France-Soir* stated, 'They have conquered Paris – he with his charm and politics, she with her smile and Chanel suit.' Diana had specially requested in advance a visit to the Institut Pasteur to meet Professor Luc Montagnier, one of the pioneers who had isolated the AIDS virus in 1983. 'She was generally well informed on the topic,' he said, adding, 'It is very important that those in the public eye are seen to be involving themselves in supporting the campaign against AIDS and efforts on behalf of AIDS patients.' Diana, he said, would be seeing 'some very sick people' at the Institut. At a banquet given by the Minister of Culture, Jack Lang, at the Château de Chambord, Charles sat next to Princess Caroline of Monaco, once touted as his bride (they had been famously bored with each other and the press photograph of them sitting next to each other at Chambord suggested that things had not changed). After the cabaret and fan dance by the French star Zizi Jeanmaire, Diana chose to put on another of her dance exhibitions, shimmying provocatively in front of her husband. What he thought of this display was not recorded; it was yet another example of Diana's misjudging a situation where Charles was concerned. At the Arc de Triomphe ceremony to remember the dead of two world wars, Charles, wearing the uniform of the colonel of the Welsh Guards, with ribbons, sash and sword, eclipsed a demure Diana in veiled hat and long black coat. 'Prince Charles set the seal on his triumphant debut as the royal Statesman of Europe . . . yesterday,' an English newspaper reported. 'It was the final honour for a Prince, whose trip had been accorded virtual State Visit priority, and who enhanced his growing reputation as a statesman with speeches on architecture and European unity. In many ways Charles outshone his wife . . .'

The visit had to some extent been overshadowed by the serialization in the *Sunday Times* of Anthony Holden's biography of the Prince, its publication timed to coincide with Charles's fortieth birthday. Phrases such as 'Their marriage has reached a stage of mutual and cold indifference' and '[Diana] has a husband who no longer understands her – nor even, it seems, much likes her'[6] had stunned the nation, triggering ferocious denunciations from people who still did not wish to believe the fairty tale had really ended, and from others who feared the effect such a failure would have on the standing of the monarchy. In Paris, observers noted that, at one event at the Musée d'Orsay, Diana, visibly irritated, repeatedly jabbed at Charles with her knee, and at the Arc de Triomphe parade spoke to him continually without receiving an answer. Nevertheless, the magazine added, on numerous occasions the couple exchanged complicit glances and Charles never failed to translate for Diana when people addressed her. Although Holden was absolutely correct, only a relatively small circle knew the truth.

Dr Lipsedge's treatment of Diana for her bulimia had helped her enormously. Within six months, he predicted, she would be a different person if only she could manage to keep her food down. He also attributed her bulimia to her problems with her husband. Charles, instead of understanding her illness, was revolted by it. At times, according to Morton, he would watch her eat and then say sarcastically, 'Is that going to reappear later? What a waste.' Lipsedge's treatment calmed her; from vomiting regularly four times a day, it was reduced to once every three weeks, usually triggered by visits to Balmoral and Sandringham, or to Highgrove which she now regarded as hostile territory. Regaining her courage, she decided to confront Camilla, whom she regarded, perhaps even more than she did Charles, as the cause of her misery. The occasion was to be the fortieth birthday party for Camilla's sister, Annabel Elliot, hosted by their mutual friend Lady Annabel Goldsmith at her beautiful house on Ham Common, Richmond. It represented a gathering of the Highgrove Set – all the people whom Diana despised and dreaded – and originally the plan had been to invite only Charles and not Diana. When Lady Annabel heard of this she vetoed it; if they were going to use her house, she insisted, Diana must be invited. Incredibly, none of Camilla's and Annabel's friends appears to have expected Diana to go – including Charles. A party which included Camilla was his territory and, undoubtedly in his view, Diana should have had the sense to realize it. In the car on the way down he needled her, repeatedly asking her why she wanted to go.

After dinner Diana noticed that Charles was absent – as was Camilla. Determined to confront them, she called on her detective, Ken Wharfe, who was sitting in the kitchen, for support. She found them in the children's play area in the basement, deep in conversation. Despite Diana's pleas, Wharfe, determined not to be a party to any scene between the three, made his excuses and left. We only have Diana's account of what happened next. According to her there was another man present and she sat down and joined in the conversation, whereupon he said, 'I think we should go upstairs now.' As they stood up Diana said, 'Camilla, I'd love to have a word with you if it's possible . . .' After the men had left, Camilla and Diana sat down again, Diana saying to Camilla: 'I would just like you to know that I know exactly what is going on between you and Charles; I wasn't born yesterday.' Someone came down to see what was going on and Diana, before leaving, said: 'I'm sorry I'm in the way, I obviously am in the way and it must be hell for both of you but I do know what is going on. Don't treat me like an idiot.' In another version Diana told Camilla to 'leave my husband alone'. According to Ken Wharfe, who was accompanying the couple back to Kensington Palace, the return journey was 'chilly and tense' with Diana repeating to her silent husband, over and over again, 'How could you have done this to me? It was so humiliating. How could you?'[7] Apology or explanation came there none. Crying alone that night at Kensington Palace, Diana considered her marriage was over. That would not deter her from trying to win her husband back. Over frequent lunches in the following year with two friends Diana, 'half-joking, half-serious', would plan how to bring him back to her and, above all, into her bed: 'she wanted to have another baby, she was desperate to have another baby . . . she continued to love him.'[8]

Whatever she felt in private, Diana remained meticulous in her public duties. She was fanatically punctual. 'She was very good at her homework,' Patrick Jephson recalled, 'and usually swotted up the main points of the programme before she left the Palace . . . Once on duty she hardly ever coasted. She took a professional pride in giving her public full value, which was one reason why they were ready to wait for her in vast numbers in any weather for even a fleeting glimpse of her.'[9] As the helicopter's rotor blades wound slowly to a stop, she would undo her seat belt, stooping by the door, waiting for it to be slid open, poised like an athlete before the starting gun. Sometimes, between engagements, she would ease her tension by comfort-eating sweets, devouring a whole fruit and nut chocolate bar at a sitting. Otherwise she would escape the solemn atmosphere of official functions by making coarse jokes to her entourage and shrieking with laughter. 'The theme of sex was a standard feature of her joke repertoire,' Jephson reported. 'She seemed immune to the embarrassment it might cause others. Careful never to exceed the bounds of good taste while in the public eye, her reticence was thrown to the winds as soon as she felt she was in relatively safe surroundings . . . The desire to shock outweighed any possible pleasure she might have gained from the humour of what she said.' Occasionally she would refer to her in-laws with nicknames. Charles was 'The Boy Wonder' or 'The Great White Hope', Prince Philip 'Stavros' and her in-laws generally 'The Germans'.[10]

Jephson, before he accompanied the Princess on his first 'away day' with her, had been expecting 'an essentially shallow person . . . a sort of royal super-Sloane'. Instead what he found was a polished and confident performance from a professional celebrity: 'Every gesture, every glance and every word – at least in public – had been consciously planned. Sometimes the planning had taken only a split second, but that simply showed how quickly she thought and how sharp were her public-pleasing instincts . . . Behind the good looks and expensive grooming there was much more than the bimbo caricature to which her critics . . . would have liked to limit her. That first day I saw, from her effect on the people she met, that she had a powerful, even hypnotic, charisma.' Her 'quicksilver one-liners', he said, played a key part in the impression she left. Her spontaneity cut through the self-conscious small talk of British social nervousness. She reacted instinctively against pomposity. With an audience of drug addicts, mental patients or battered wives, she would listen to a 'turgid briefing' from an earnest therapist before leaning forward with a smile and perfect timing to whisper loudly, 'Does he always go on like this?' She had made contact and everybody laughed. It was a technique which gave her public that feeling of intimate knowledge which is the secret ingredient of devotion. Yet even her wittiest remark contained a nugget of sympathy, understanding or concern. 'She may have been short of O levels, but she never dropped a public clanger, never mocked disability or disfiguration.'[11]

From first-hand experience gained by accompanying Diana on hundreds of her engagements, Jephson concluded that 'much of the Princess's compassion was very definitely the genuine article':

As I watched her at a dying child's bedside, holding the girl's newly cold hand and comforting the stricken parents, she seemed to share their grief. Not self-consciously like a stranger, not distantly like a counsellor . . . Instead it just seemed that a tranquillity gathered round her. Into this stillness the weeping mother and heartbroken father poured out their sorrow and there, somehow, it was safe. The young woman with the smart suit and soulful eyes had no answers for them, but they were left feeling that somewhere inside she knew at least part of what they were feeling.[12]

Diana, Jephson said, did indeed share some of what they were feeling; yet it had none of the clear grief and suffering of bereavement but came from something dark and complex within her, the product of years of stunted emotional growth. 'The compassion she showed others was not drawn from some deep supply within her. Rather it was a reflection of the attention she herself craved. Once we had returned her to the lonely privacy of her palace, I sensed she had little left over for herself . . . As for the cumulative, corrosive effect of all this on her own sense of self-worth, I was to discover that it could be severe,' he added. 'Even at the outset I could see that receiving credit for virtues she did not possess could not satisfy the hunger for recognition that burned within the Princess of Wales.'[13]

Diana's lack of self-esteem born of a feeling of rejection since the day her mother left was at the root of her complex personality. The golden girl, shining, witty, affectionate, had a dark, self-destructive side which caused the self-mutilation, the bulimia, the mood swings, the difficulty in sustaining relationships. Diana found it hard to believe people loved her for herself and therefore easily came to distrust their motives, turning against them and cutting them out of her life. There may have been a hint of manic depression to the mood swings and she was taking Prozac for her bulimia. 'She had terrible mood swings, for instance when she had the binge of eat eat eat and then she would throw up and after that she was on a high. Laughing and a bit too much for her normal self,' said a close friend.[14] The friend, accustomed to seeing the symptoms in another member of her family, suggested they consult a doctor who she knew would be discreet. After talking to Diana, however, his verdict was that she seemed all right. The only cure for her suffering would have been the love and approbation of the Prince of Wales which she so passionately desired, something which would always be denied her. His was the final rejection; the way in which he consistently denigrated her reduced her to despair: 'My husband made me feel so inadequate in every possible way that each time I came up for air he pushed me down again . . .'[15] 'She was not a mad woman, she was a wounded woman,' a friend of hers said.[16] Another friend, Rosa Monckton, called her 'a wounded animal': increasingly her dark, wounded side would drive her to acts of self-destruction, paranoia and apparent cruelty. Deep within her, her always fragile psyche splintered under the pressure, divided between her instinct for the good and her reactive, cruel side.

'Diana had such a conflict of personalities within one character,' Rosa Monckton wrote. 'She was complicated on the one hand and simple and naïve on the other. These two coexisted, sometimes awkwardly, and made her life more difficult than it should have been. Her dark side was that of a wounded, trapped animal, and her bright side was that of a luminous being . . . But as a wounded animal she could be terrifying . . . it was born of some basic desire to hurt those whom she felt had betrayed her . . .'[17]

Yet she was very far from the whining, self-pitying individual she has been portrayed as being in tapes and books which she, in her worst victim mode, inspired. (In this she compared favourably with her husband who in reality had so little about which to complain.) 'The truth is,' Jephson said, 'that what amazed me every day was how gutsy she was, how positive she was. And the proof of that always for me was no matter how dark things were – and we had some dreadful days – if you were able to give her a humorous lead she was far happier and far more ready to see the lighter side in the darkest situation. The pity was that Diana, out of a sense of low self-esteem and an irresistible wish to be a victim, instead of being what she actually was – rather stoical – when there was an option for victimhood, she would select it. And she would select friends and advisers who fed that wish . . . This rather tragic picture that was presented was not the whole person at all. The tragedy was that the whole person wasn't given the chance to flower.'[18]

Faced with the reality of her unfaithful and unloving husband, Diana tried to solve her problems, mental, psychological and physical, by consulting a series of astrologers, therapists, masseurs, psychics and tarot card readers, some of them at the suggestion of Mara Berni, a close friend and owner of the San Lorenzo restaurant in Knightsbridge, introduced to her by Fergie. While many of the people round her scoffed and disapproved, Diana was embarking on a spiritual journey which calmed her and gave her strength to face her daily life. She believed in astrology in so far as she sought the answers from them that she wanted to hear. The first astrologer was Penny Thornton, referred to her by Fergie, whom she initially consulted in 1986. In February 1989, possibly after the Goldsmith party episode, she went to another, Debbie Frank. She was pathetically credulous as she thrashed about for a solution to her problems.

From December 1988 she also consulted Stephen Twigg, a 'mind–body' therapist who specialized in deep massage, diet consultation and new age advice. At his suggestion she tried vitamin supplements, detoxifying processes and the Hay Diet. She used aromatherapy, hypnotherapy and acupuncture in her search for physical relaxation and inner calm. Diana was, as her biographer Sally Bedell Smith, wrote, 'vulnerable and gullible . . . she leaned on her therapists as she did [on] her friends and lovers',[19] calling them at all hours of the day or night. Oonagh Shanley-Toffolo, who first visited her in September 1989, encouraged her to a more spiritual outlook with meditation and prayer. Oonagh Toffolo's first impression was of a shy and retiring person. who emanated sadness and vulnerability.

Meanwhile, changes were taking place in Diana's principal private relationship – with James Hewitt. Poor Hewitt, who had given of his best in support of a needy Diana, sometimes, as Anna Pasternak recounted, to the bounds of his physical capabilities, was, as far as Diana was concerned, expendable. She lavished presents on him – one of her foibles was to dress the men she liked, and therefore Hewitt, whom, she later said, she had 'dressed from head to toe'. Her loyalty to him, however, was finite, as he was soon to find out. In May he and Diana – but not Prince Charles – attended a ball at Althorp in honour of Raine's sixtieth birthday (which actually fell in September). Diana led him to the pool pavilion that night and they made love there. Hewitt, however, committed the cardinal sin in her eyes of leaving her to follow his career. He was posted to Germany with his regiment that autumn and, despite all Diana's tearful protests and accusations of desertion, determined to go.

On 16 September 1989 her beloved brother Charles married Victoria Lockwood. Diana attended the wedding at St Mary's, Great Brington, and the subsequent reception at Althorp. Relations between the Spencer children and their stepmother had gone from bad to worse since their father had recovered from his illness, grateful for his life to Raine and now entirely in her hands. The sales of silver, furniture, archives and manuscript music, drawings and paintings which then took place – to avoid publicity – to dealers at below market-value prices, had attracted increasing criticism. In April 1987 *Harpers & Queen* launched a devastating attack on the Spencer sales, with a detailed listing of the objects which had disappeared. Many items were sold via a London dealer against his charges for the 'restoration' of Althorp's interior, 'restoration' which incurred the withering scorn of arbiters of taste. Bright gilding abounded; the beautiful wooden floor of the great Long Gallery was close carpeted, the set of chairs from the Spencer House Great Room was broken up, six going to the dealer in payment for his restoration work which involved the remaining

white and gold eighteenth-century chairs with green brocade seats
being transformed with glittering gilt and upholstering in mango-
coloured stamped velvet. Two solid gold ice pails made for the 1st
Duke of Marlborough were sold, again via a dealer, for £1 million.
The money, it was argued by Lord and Lady Spencer, was to be
spent on the restoration of Althorp, and indeed some of it was: in
many of the rooms double-glazing was installed to keep out the
Northamptonshire draughts, while close carpeting made the bedrooms more comfortable if less authentic. The handsome stable
block, restored by Johnnie's father Jack and intended to house a
family museum, now housed The Shop, a 'place of unmatched
tawdriness' according to the critics. Some people surmised that the
sales were subconscious revenge by Johnnie on his fierce, unloving
father, Jack Spencer, who had expended all passion and love on
the preservation of Althorp and its treasures. Raine simply had a
strong, unsentimental business drive: the house was to be profitable
and made over in her own image (a garish portrait of herself hung
in pride of place at the head of the main staircase). Three villas
were bought at Bognor – 'Tradewinds', 'Hacienda' and 'Water's
Edge House' – and a five-storey house in Mayfair.

Diana expressed the children's fury when she attacked Raine at
Charles's wedding: 'I took it upon myself to air everyone's griev-
ances in my family. I stuck up for Mummy and my mother said
that was the first time in 22 years anyone had ever stuck up for
her. I said everything I possibly could . . . I was so angry. I said: I
hate you so much, if only you knew how much we all hated you
for what you've done, you've ruined the house, you spend Daddy's
money and what for?'[20] According to one account she also physically attacked Raine, giving her a sharp shove in the back so that
she fell down some stairs on to a landing.

That summer, at Julia Samuel's thirtieth birthday party, she had
met a man whom she had known in her first days in London,
when they had had a long talk about their unsatisfactory love lives
– he with a failed romance, she with her failing marriage. James
Gilbey, charming and popular, who worked as a dealer in expensive

cars, was the son of a family who had founded their fortunes on Gilbey's gin. He was the nephew of England's most distinguished Catholic cleric, Monsignor Alfred Gilbey, a highly sophisticated and social man whose home was the Travellers' Club on Pall Mall. They began to meet in London, at Mara Berni's or at Gilbey's flat nearby in Lennox Gardens, Knightsbridge. Once they spent a secret weekend at a rented farmhouse near Blakenham in Norfolk.

From the famous 'Squidgygate' tapes recorded on New Year's Eve 1989 and released two years later, it seems that the relationship had become serious in the autumn of 1989 after the departure of Hewitt for Germany. Gilbey was clearly besotted with Diana who, although six years younger than he was, was clearly calling the tune. The passion seemed to have been all on his side – 'Squidgy . . . love you, love you, love you . . .' he moaned at one point, and there were strong erotic undertones to their conversation. The two of them were planning a brief, secret rendezvous in London the next night, Diana on the excuse of needing acupuncture and back treatment. The tapes were, above all, revealing of Diana's state of mind at the time and of her relationships then both with her husband and the royal in-laws.

Christmas at Sandringham that year seems to have been unusually frigid. Diana's unhappiness over the family Christmas was manifest. In answer to Gilbey's query, 'And so, darling, what other lows today?' she replied, 'So that was it, I was very bad at lunch. And I nearly started blubbing. I just felt really sad and empty, and I thought, Bloody hell, after all I've done for this fucking family . . .' The Queen Mother puzzled her: 'His grand-mother is always looking at me with a strange look in her eyes. It's not hatred. It's sort of interest and pity mixed in one. I am not quite sure. I don't understand it. Every time I look up she's looking at me and then looks away and smiles . . . It's affection, affection – it's definitely affection . . . It's not hostile anyway . . .' In this Diana's instinct, in which she placed so much faith, had led her astray. Charles's beloved grandmother had no affection for Diana, whom she had been heard to declare a 'liar'. Not only did Queen Elizabeth have the high standards of behaviour befitting the granddaughter of a clergyman, which she was, but her loyalty to Prince Charles was absolute. She was capable of 'ostriching', closing her eyes to his behaviour in terms of his adultery with Camilla; indeed, she continued to invite the Parker Bowleses to stay when Charles was there just as if nothing had happened. Her eldest grandson's happiness had always been one of her priorities since he was a lonely little boy. He was suffering because of his marriage to Diana, therefore it was Diana's fault. The state of the marriage was taboo in Queen Elizabeth's presence; privately she would have attributed the difficulties to Diana's 'unreasonable behaviour'. The Queen Mother was cool and clever in a way which Diana could never hope to emulate. Diana very much wanted to believe Queen Elizabeth, the matriarch of the Royal Family and revered by every-one, felt 'affection' towards her. It was indicative of her compre-hensive failure to understand how the Royal Family worked which caused her so much pain.

Increasingly Diana saw herself as a 'victim' and a rebel. Talking about her relationship with Charles she said: 'It's just so difficult, so complicated. He makes my life real, real torture, I've decided. But the distancing will be because I go out and – I hate the word – conquer the world. I don't mean that. I mean I'll go out and do my bit in the way I know how and I leave him behind. That's what I see happening.' By now, on the eve of 1990, after just under ten years of marriage to the Prince of Wales, Diana already saw her role; how she could 'leave him behind'. She reported a conversation she had with the Bishop of Norwich which illustrated both her resentment of and rebelliousness towards what she saw as 'the Establishment'. The unfortunate bishop tried a line which he thought would be an easy introduction but which Diana saw as patronizing. This is the conversation as recorded on the Squidgy-gate tapes, with Diana as the main character, the conqueror, the Bishop as the vanquished and James Gilbey the supporting chorus:

DIANA . . . He said: 'I want you to tell me how you talk to people who are ill and dying. How do you cope?'

JG He wanted to learn. He was so hopeless at it himself.

DIANA . . . I said: 'I'm just myself.'

JG They can't get to grips that, underneath there is such a beautiful person in you . . . They can't think that it isn't cluttered up by this idea of untold riches.

DIANA I know. He kept wittering on about how one must never think how good one is at one's job. There's always something you can learn round the next corner. I said: 'Well, if people know me, they know I'm not like that.'

JG Yes. Absolutely right. So did you give him a hard time?

DIANA I did, actually, in the end. I said: 'I know this sounds crazy, but I've lived before.' He said: 'How do you know?' I said: 'Because I'm a wise old thing.'

JG Oh, darling Squidge, did you? Very brave thing to say, actually . . .

DIANA It was, wasn't it?

JG Very. Full marks. Ninety-nine out of 100.

DIANA I said: 'Also I'm aware that people I have loved and have died and are in the spirit world look after me.' He looked horrified. I thought, 'If he's the bishop HE should say that sort of thing' . . .

DIANA . . . with that bishop. I said: 'I understand people's suffering, people's pain, more than you will ever know', and he said: 'That's obvious by what you're doing for the AIDS.' I said: 'It's not only people with AIDS, it's anyone who suffers. I can smell them a mile away.'

After this exchange, the flummoxed bishop turned the conversation to children's toys. Triumphant Diana, she told Gilbey, thought, 'Ah! Defeated you.'

Diana was not being unfair when she described Charles as making her life 'absolute torture'. His jealousy and resentment of her had led him to treat her with what amounted to emotional cruelty. Aware as he was of her vulnerability, he could not refrain from constant pinpricks to her already low self-esteem, putting her down in public in the most humiliating way. Patrick Jephson witnessed an incident on the royal couple's tour of the Gulf States earlier that year, in March 1989. The royal host was offering his visitors coffee:

The royal host and his senior guest [the Prince of Wales] were sticking manfully to their scripts . . . Plainly uncomfortable, the Princess was not joining in either, nor was she invited to by the Prince or her host.

She seemed to have created an invisible barrier round herself, as if to say that she was apart from the polite charade going on around her. To me she looked excluded and vulnerable. To the host as well, presumably, because eventually he leaned across the Prince to ask her politely what she was going to do during her visit. Under the unexpected attention she visibly brightened, perhaps thinking – as I was – of the serious programme we had arranged: visits to a day centre for mentally handicapped children, a clinic for immigrant women and a girls' business studies class.

The Prince also turned towards her, looking as if he were seeing her for the first time, ruefully indulgent, patronising. There was an expectant hush. Before she could reply, he said with studied innocence, 'Shopping, isn't it, darling?'

The words dropped into the marble stillness like bricks into plate glass. The Princess coloured, mumbled something inaudible and lapsed into silence. There was an awkward pause, broken by the Prince pointedly resuming his conversation with a host whose aquiline features now registered a politer version of the disbelief I felt.

When we were outside again I cornered John Riddell [former private secretary to the Prince and Princess of Wales]. 'Did I see what I thought I saw in there?' I asked him.

He looked at me pityingly. 'Oh yes, Patrick. Indeed you did. That is the world we have to live in.'[21]

It was a world in which Diana would find it increasingly hard to live.

physical need for each other. Camilla's role in Charles's life as principal comforter and soul mate was clearly revealed: 'You're a clever old thing. An awfully good brain lurking there, isn't there,' she told him. 'Your great achievement is to love me,' Charles said. 'Oh darling, easier than falling off a chair,' Camilla replied. 'You suffer all those indignities and tortures and calumnies,' he responded. 'I'd suffer anything for you. That's love. It's the strength of love,' she told him. Fortunately for Diana's peace of mind, the contents of the tape were not revealed until January 1993 when the full extent of the conspiracy of Charles's friends to provide rendezvous for the lovers came to light. A web of deception surrounded the affair, from people whom she had thought of as mutual friends, who provided safe houses where Charles and Camilla could spend the night, to loyal Highgrove staff who had no alternative but to cover up for the Prince both to ingratiate themselves with their principal employer and to spare her pain. Long before the eventual separation, the Waleses' staff had divided into two camps. Most of them did not enjoy being used in the deception of Diana, even to the extent of the butler being asked to wrap a sapphire and diamond brooch as a present to Camilla from Charles, while the Prince's gift to Diana was a paltry souvenir straw hat decorated with fruit, acquired during a trip to Cornwall.

Unlike many unfaithful husbands who are kinder to their wives as a result of their adultery, Charles by now seemed almost to hate his wife. And despite her declarations of love for Charles, Diana's screaming scenes only succeeded in alienating him further. While their disharmony was concealed from outsiders, the un- happy relationship created tensions within the family. At Balmoral later that summer, with problems in both the Wales and the York marriages, the atmosphere was noticeably difficult. The Queen, unusually, expressed her frustration at Prince Charles, his arm in a sling, who had chosen to take the van Cutsems' choice of doctor rather than hers. It was a celebration of Princess Margaret's sixtieth birthday but the atmosphere was far from cordial – there were endless evening picnics at which Prince Charles appeared 'in a very cross mood'. Colin Glenconner 'did some silly things with napkins to amuse Fergie and Di, when they all did a number and everybody laughed except Prince Charles'. Asked if he found it amusing he said icily, clearly referring to his wife and sister-in-law, 'Little things please little minds.'[3]

At Balmoral, Fergie and Diana appeared as allies once again but, as Diana's secretary Patrick Jephson pointed out, 'running through it all was her mistrust of Fergie'.[4] In her Squidgygate conversation with James Gilbey on New Year's Eve 1989, Diana had referred cautiously to Fergie: 'The redhead is being actually quite supportive . . .' Gilbey had warned her that Sarah was not to be trusted, that she had her own agenda and was trying to hang on to Diana's coat-tails. Her former popularity with the public had disappeared, after the Australia visit when she had been severely criticized for leaving the baby Beatrice behind for six weeks. She was slated for her weight, her dress, her penchant for free holidays, and she was becoming increasingly unpopular at court. 'I just worry that she's desperately trying to get back in. She's trying to tag on . . . She knows that your PR is so good, she's trying to tag on to that.' Charles, Diana told Gilbey, had been trying to help Fergie, calling on a Royal Family favourite, the broadcaster Sir Jimmy Savile, to advise her on improving her image. Diana, more cautious and instinctive than Sarah, watched 'the redhead's' head-long rush towards destruction with more than a little Schaden-freude. Always sensitive of her public image, she was well aware that Fergie's infatuation with an American, which she made little effort to conceal, and her open defiance of the Queen's senior courtiers, including her cousin and particular *bête noire*, Sir Robert Fellowes, was not the way to proceed. Fergie, as has often been said, was indeed the 'yellow canary' used by miners to test for dangerous gases underground.

There is little evidence that Sarah listened to Savile's advice any more than she did to anyone else's. By August 1990 her marriage was in trouble. Sarah was evidently bored with her husband whose frequent absences on naval duty left her at a loose end. Sarah told a friend that in 1988 Andrew had spent only forty-two nights at home out of a year. Once the Yorks' controversial home,

Sunninghill Park, dubbed Southyork for its *Dallas*-like ostentation, was finished in the summer of 1990, she was not prepared to live as a naval wife in married quarters or even in a rented house near Andrew's base, and when he was at home she found his preferred way of relaxation boring. Andrew liked to watch videos and play golf and, when the couple entertained, Sarah found his behaviour embarrassingly boorish. At dinner parties he was served first and gobbled down his food regardless of the other guests, and he had a fondness for telling loud and unfunny naval jokes. To the Queen's household it appeared that he had no control over his wife's behaviour, while to Sarah it seemed that he was not prepared to stand up for her when she was lectured by his mother's courtiers. Andrew, sadly, still loved his wife but, as Sarah's father had told his mistress, she had been in love with the Royal Family rather than her husband. Now both 'love affairs' were cooling from Sarah's point of view.

The man with whom Sarah had fallen in love was the handsome Texan Steve Wyatt, whom she had met in Houston at the home of his mother, the glamorous Saks heiress, Lynn Sakowitz Wyatt. Wyatt's stepfather, Oscar, one of the richest and toughest men in Texas, could offer Sarah all the luxury that a huge ranch and a fleet of private planes could provide. Sarah had flown to New York in the Wyatts' plane and stayed at their expense at the Plaza Athénée. Her affair with Wyatt continued when he was transferred to London; she was photographed with him and her daughters at the Wyatts' villa on Cap Ferrat (formerly the home of Somerset Maugham) and again, according to Sarah, at a weekend house party in Gloucestershire. Later that summer the extent to which Sarah had become involved with Wyatt was blatantly revealed. Declining an invitation to dinner with Lord McAlpine and his wife, she instead, at Wyatt's instigation, gave a dinner in her second-floor Buckingham Palace apartment to Ramzi Sultan, an Iraqi oil dealer, whose country was about to invade Kuwait and who was therefore very much *persona non grata* to the British government. Blithely unaware of the faux pas she had committed, Sarah took both Ramzi and Wyatt, uninvited, to join the

McAlpines later that night, making no secret of her attraction to Wyatt. With a complete lack of propriety, she obtained an invitation for Wyatt to the Christmas ball held that year by the Queen to celebrate the ninetieth, sixtieth and thirtieth birthdays respectively of the Queen Mother, Princess Margaret and Prince Andrew. Just over a year later Wyatt, warned off by his socially astute mother, returned to the United States, leaving behind on the top of a wardrobe in his former flat holiday snaps of himself with Fergie and her children to be found by a window cleaner and passed to the newspapers. (Sarah herself claimed that the flat had been searched and found to be 'clean', implying that the photographs had been placed there at the instigation of the *Daily Mail*.) By then Fergie had linked up with another Texan, John Bryan, in a liaison which was to prove her downfall.

Yet Diana, lacking in self-confidence and always aware that her affair with James Hewitt, even though temporarily in abeyance, could destroy her reputation, still kept up her competition with Fergie for public esteem. 'No matter what misfortunes publicly befell her sister-in-law,' Jephson wrote, 'the Princess would still torture herself with the thought that she might yet become a real rival rather than just a useful counterpart to her own good fortune.'[5] Sometimes she appeared to be in direct competition with her sister-in-law, as when she reacted to a newspaper report of 'caring Fergie'; she would complain to Jephson, 'Patrick! We seem to be reading rather a lot about the red-haired lady . . .'[6], whereupon a charitable counterstrike would be arranged. But if some of these charity duties were thus cynically motivated, Diana's actual performances were undertaken in a genuine spirit. Often her charitable forays took place when she was bored, cooped up in Balmoral, longing for an outlet and not totally unaware of the good publicity to be earned by being seen to visit a hospice while her in-laws were known to be slaughtering game. The less the Royal Family seemed to appreciate her, the more Diana felt the need to be wanted by the public, to receive from their response the unconditional love and understanding which she so badly needed. Yet Diana's responses, according to Jephson, who accompanied her on numberless public occasions and charitable duties, were not feigned. 'The impression I had formed on that first outing . . . – that she genuinely cared – was not untrue. It was the instinctive reaction of any sensitive adult, heightened by a strong maternal instinct and a personal acquaintance with pain . . . Not even the best actress could sustain such a convincing show of compassion for so long; nor would those on the receiving end be so easily fooled.'[7]

The Queen's courtiers, although wary of the future, still, unlike the principals themselves, hoped that somehow the Waleses' marriage would survive in some form. Sir William Heseltine, the Queen's private secretary, who retired that year, was relieved by Diana's assurance: 'Don't worry, I'll stick it out.'[8] Two tours that year, to the Far East and to Hungary, sent the spurious message to the world that all was well. Jephson described them as 'the last grand gestures of togetherness' which produced some misleadingly optimistic comments about how well they seemed to be getting on. Photo opportunities featured the couple gazing romantically across the River Danube, and enjoying themselves on the upper deck of a river boat, looking for all the world as if they were on holiday together. You had to be very close to the action, said Jephson, who accompanied them, to perceive the guerrilla warfare being waged below the surface. Point scoring against Charles was a game which Diana played with consummate skill: she was photographed holding hands with the Hungarian President's wife during the arrival ceremony (it was the story with all the papers at home, she later told Morton) and posing with romantic Magyar horsemen. Patrick Jephson, who was to leave her five years later in a mood of some disillusionment, described the delicate balance between sincerity and ulterior motive in her actions. There was no doubt, he wrote, that her underlying intention was 'to attract attention, to signal an independence from her marriage, and to exert by guile and gamesmanship the strength she felt unable to express openly. Foreign tours, no less than home engagements, were vehicles for a subliminal message: I am not a dumb clothes-horse, a junior player in a marriage that frustrates me: I am a figure in my own right, and none too scrupulous.'[9]

In private, Diana was playing a dangerous game. Hewitt returned from Germany before Christmas before being ordered to the Gulf War in January and they resumed their passionate affair. Prince Charles was aware of it, as he was also of the relationship with James Gilbey, probably through Superintendent Colin Trimming, head of the Waleses' protection squad, who reported everything back to his boss. Sometime around the end of the year Diana – possibly from Gilbey, who had been confronted with the tape by the *Sun* – learned that that newspaper had a copy of the recording. The owner, Rupert Murdoch, and Andrew Knight, chairman of News International, proprietors of the *Sun* and the *News of the World*, decided that the material was too controversial to publish and the tape was put into a safe where it would remain for two and a half years. The *News of the World* also had a story alleging Diana's affair with James Hewitt from Hewitt's batman, Lance Corporal Malcolm Leete, which they proposed to publish. Knight also sat on this story; the fact that he didn't believe it showed how skilful – or lucky – Diana had been in covering up the affair.

Diana was still in love with Hewitt after he flew out to serve with his regiment in the Gulf, where war had been going on since the previous August. She was obsessed with war news and wrote Hewitt a series of passionate letters, often as frequently as four times a day, expressing her longing and loneliness, putting her every thought down on paper. She said that she was 'finally trying to understand herself'. She told him that she could not stand the deception in her marriage any longer and that she had given Charles an ultimatum that 'something had to be done' about it. Moreover – an indication of the direction her thoughts were tending towards – she wrote that she felt frantic that 'the truth about Charles and Camilla ... had not become public knowledge'.[10] Some people, like Max Hastings, did know, but out of loyalty to the monarch and perhaps for fear of finding themselves in court (like Penny Junor, who was sued by Andrew and Camilla

Parker Bowles for misidentifying Camilla) kept their knowledge
to themselves. Diana determined to find a way to get the story
into the public domain, just as she was determined that Hewitt
should remain in the shadows.

But on that front, things were becoming difficult. The *Daily
Mail* now not only had a copy of the Squidgygate tapes, but their
chief royal reporter, Richard Kay, had made friends with the naïve
Hewitt in the Gulf, even to the extent of lending him his satellite
telephone to make calls – which he did, to his mother and to
Diana, their numbers registering on the telephone.[11] The previous
year Diana had made friends with the paper's editor, David English,
who was later to become her chief media mentor. Yet it was Nigel
Dempster who in February 1991 first publicly named Hewitt as a
friend of Diana's. 'Nigel Dempster outed him,' said a fellow
reporter. 'And I believe that Andrew Parker Bowles was the source,
and it was designed, I think, to take the heat off the Parker Bowleses
at that time.' Then, in the following month, Hewitt was exposed
in the *News of the World* by his estranged girlfriend, Emma Stew-
ardson, who revealed that Diana had been sending letters and
expensive presents to the Gulf (where Richard Kay had noted the
quality of the hampers of food which Hewitt enjoyed). No one,
however, went so far as actually to claim they were lovers. For
Diana, however, the hints were enough; as so often in her relationships, she became suspicious that he was using her, that he was
becoming 'too serious', that he was more in love with her position
than he was with her. This was unfair: James Hewitt was genuinely
in love with her and the relationship was almost as dangerous for
him and his career as it was for her. She had given him hope for
the future in her letters, talking of her belief that in July 'her life
would change'. 'Her determination to be free was so strong,'
Hewitt later recalled, 'that I had formed a real hope that some time
in the future we could be together.'[12] In fact the *News of the World*
revelations had sealed his fate. After a couple of meetings on his
return from the Gulf, Diana told him on the telephone that it
would be better if they 'cooled it'. The cut-off came in the usual
manner: when he telephoned the Palace, his call was not put

through. He was sent to Germany: when he returned to England, despite his being conveniently stationed at Knightsbridge Barracks, less than a mile from Kensington Palace, his dream was over. According to Ken Wharfe, with whom Diana discussed her relations with Hewitt, she had explained to him that she had to resolve the many problems in her life and could not do so while conducting an adulterous affair. Typically, when Hewitt accepted his dismissal with good grace, she was slightly irritated, having expected at the very least protestations of undying love.

With Hewitt out of the way, Diana concentrated on her war with Charles. Yet another joint trip, this time to Brazil that spring when, once again, the couple put up a good show in public, inspired optimism in the press. The *Sunday Mirror* described them as presenting 'a united front to the world . . . their closeness sent a shiver of excitement around the massed ranks of media men and women'. Yet only the previous December, Diana had told James Hewitt that there were times when she could not bear to be in the same room as Charles. And on the trip to Brazil, despite attempts to put on a show, Charles's jealousy of Diana manifested itself in dismissive comments, not just in private but in front of the British Ambassador to Brazil and the recently appointed Brazilian Ambassador in London, Paulo Tarso Flecha de Lima and his wife Lucia, soon to become one of Diana's greatest and most trusted friends. Onlookers observed that there was great tension: 'They were on speaking terms, but it was very tense. It was not a normal conversation between husband and wife. He would talk to her, she would answer. But he was already very dismissive of her. On the plane she was reading some papers, remarking to the Ambassadress, "This is my homework about Brazil." Charles chipped in, "Oh, she doesn't know a thing about Brazil." '[13] Public put-downs by the heir to the throne in front of high-ranking officials fuelled Diana's desire to escape from the sham her marriage had become.

According to Hewitt, Diana had planned an 'escape' in July, as her thirtieth birthday and the tenth anniversary of her marriage came up, determined that this period would be a watershed in her life. What kind of watershed it was to be he did not specify, but it seems probable that Diana envisaged a dramatic breakaway (with the inevitable exposure of Camilla), not divorce, but a separate court and acknowledgement of her position as mother of the future King. Again according to Hewitt, the timing she had worked out had been thwarted by the fact that the Yorks' marriage was also on the rocks. Sarah had been on the telephone to Diana wondering what to do. Lesley Player, Ronald Ferguson's mistress (whom at one time he had shared with Steve Wyatt), said that Sarah and Diana had a pact to leave their husbands at the same time. If such a pact existed, Diana was too canny to go ahead with it. Hewitt implied that pressure had been put on her by Buckingham Palace: 'There was no way the Palace was going to let both royal couples announce they were splitting up at the same time,' he wrote. 'Diana had been informed in no uncertain terms that the effect on the Royal Family would be disastrous.'[14]

Nevertheless, Diana forged ahead with her pledge made to Gilbey in the Squidgygate tapes when she had boasted: 'I'm going to go out and conquer the world, I'm going to leave him [Charles] behind . . .' 'Diana was obsessed with Charles,' a close friend said. 'And I think all the wrong steps she took in life were because of him . . . either to hurt him or to show off to him.' 'She was a very, very special person. She had a wonderful side to her – bright, courageous and unique. But she also had a very dark side to her personality, a very destructive side.'[15] This friend saw Diana's collaboration in Andrew Morton's *Diana: Her True Story* as 'the first move in her self-destruction'. Diana herself explained her decision as being a psychological necessity: 'It's because my life being as complicated as it is the only way for me to survive is to let people know what I have been going through.'[16] Her confidante thought there might be an element of vengeance on Charles and Camilla in her motivation. Morton himself was puzzled by her willingness to open her heart to a virtual stranger. 'If it was a way of getting at her husband, it's a remarkably reckless and foolhardy exercise,' he said. 'If it's a way of changing her life then the simplest way would be to speak to the Queen and Prince Charles.'[17] There was, he said, no deliberate decision to do a book with him; it just happened gradually. Diana knew Morton as a prominent member of the royal media pack. He was tall, good-looking, genial and university educated. They had met and chatted together on occasion, and he was also in contact with Dr James Colthurst, an old friend of Diana's who was to act as go-between for Morton and Diana. Morton, through Colthurst, had done Diana some favours, including advising her on the safest way to dispense with her hairdresser, Richard Dalton, without his going to the newspapers to sell his story. Morton advised her to write him an honest letter, buy him a good present and send him on his way. The strategy worked. Morton also kept her happy by writing sympathetic pieces about her in the papers.

'I think she wanted people to know what life was really like for her. I used the phrase "the prisoner in the Palace" and all that kind of thing. She felt constrained by the environment in which she worked. She felt there was no out, she felt disempowered both as a woman and as a human being. She felt trapped, not just in her marriage but by the system. And she felt, essentially, that when somebody comes along and is able to do something for her and make her look good – I mean I was writing pretty pro pieces and there was the Dalton episode, little things like that meant a lot because when you don't have any control over your life, then to have control through another agent – i.e. myself – was tremendously liberating.'[18]

Colthurst arrived at Kensington Palace armed with a tape recorder and a list of prompt questions one morning in May 1991. Neither he nor Morton was prepared for the deluge of words, which Diana delivered – thirty thousand in that one session. 'The first tape was just like – I can't emphasise it strongly enough – just like the desperate confessional, wanting to get everything out, it was ten years of her betrayal and unhappiness, depression and ridicule . . . And it just came flowing out in a huge torrent . . .' 'Did she really think it through? The answer is No. Because I and Mike [Michael O'Mara, Morton's publisher] and James had to do a lot of thinking it through for her. So, for example, the idea of bringing friends in, keeping her in the background, wasn't her idea, it was our idea.'[19] Added to that was a strain of aristocratic recklessness inherited from her Spencer forebears and, perhaps even more, from her mother, Frances, 'the bolter', which impelled her to go ahead regardless of the consequences. Morton also thought there might be an element of getting her retaliation in first, of putting Charles's adultery with Camilla in the public domain before her affair with James Hewitt was exposed. Diana wanted to expose the sham of her marriage and her role in the Royal Family, to expose the behaviour of Charles and Camilla and her own helplessness in the face of their betrayal.

Another reason for the involvement of Diana's friends was the dawning realization that Diana's version of events was not always strictly the truth. In *Diana: Her True Story*, Diana was recounting the reality of her life as she saw it in 1991–2 (towards the end of her life, Diana would frequently say that what she thought in 1991 was not how she saw things in 1996), a reality dominated by Charles and Camilla, her illness, the predictions of her astrologers and the constriction of the royal circle. Perhaps the most poignant testimony of all was that of Carolyn Bartholomew, who had known Diana since her school days and watched anxiously from the sidelines the deterioration in her health and happiness. 'She's not happy now, but once she was . . .' Carolyn told Morton. Diana's friends felt duty bound to help her by exposing the living lie she was enduring.

But if Diana felt threatened and constricted by 'the system', royal officials, even before the bombshell of the Morton book burst in June 1992, were wary of Diana as an unknown quantity. Buckingham Palace tended to regard the chaotic office of the Prince of Wales at St James's Palace as something of a joke. 'One of the reasons Buckingham Palace runs on smooth lines by and large is that people decades ago learned what the Queen wanted and how to do it and a way to get on with it,' one of Diana's aides said. 'I think from Buckingham Palace, St James's seemed a bit of a madhouse, and the maddest component was this strange, very tall, very blonde, very articulate, very charming, very powerful,

very regal person' – Diana.[20] Until 1990 the charming Sir John
Riddell had been private secretary and treasurer to the Prince and
Princess of Wales. Aristocratic, with the required background of
Eton, the Rifle Brigade and the City, Riddell's presence had
ensured that relations with Buckingham Palace, where Diana's
brother-in-law, Robert Fellowes, had now become principal
private secretary, with the Marlborough-educated, Foreign
Office-trained Robin Janvrin as his deputy, ran on an even keel.
Even he, however, would treat the Princess's representatives, Anne
Beckwith Smith and Patrick Jephson, as very much the junior
branch of the operation, summing up a meeting with kindly con-
descension: 'And meantime Her Royal Highness will continue to
do very little, but do it very well . . .' 'The Prince had had an
organization before Diana came along and it was never really
expected that she would make much of an impression on it, and
when, rather irritatingly, she became more and more of a figure
in her own right, the machinery didn't really exist to accommodate
her in anything other than a purely decorative role. And as she
became more productive in carrying out royal engagements, this
was viewed with amused tolerance,' an aide to the Princess
recalled.[21]

   Riddell withdrew gladly from the Waleses' fray to the City,
replaced briefly by Sir Christopher Airey and then, in what
amounted to a palace coup, by Airey's deputy, Commander
Richard Aylard, the grammar school–educated former naval officer
who had read zoology at Reading University and acted as Diana's
equerry from 1985 to 1988. Diana had regarded him as a turncoat
when he left her to become assistant private secretary and
comptroller to the Waleses' joint office. Later, she began to regard
him as an enemy when in 1991 he became private secretary and
treasurer to the Prince. In the background, the Prince's party at
court regarded Diana as 'a mystery and a threat and somebody
to be demeaned, mocked or briefed against, or constrained and
restrained in some way. They used to talk very patronisingly about
"putting her in a box where she couldn't do too much harm" . . .'[22]
While the Queen's principal aides, Robert Fellowes and Robin

Janvrin, 'tried very hard to remain even-handed, to keep the Queen above the fray . . . people in the Prince's camp – and they were outside St James's as much as inside . . . liked to think they could invoke the authority of the Crown against Diana, which I thought was the height of arrogance and double standards, especially since the Crown herself chose to remain pretty much aloof.'[23]

The British Establishment, from courtiers down to aristocrats and their hangers-on in the country, can be a formidable and isolating force; small wonder, therefore, that Diana felt trapped and alone in what she felt to be her fight for survival. Beyond that she could not rely on her family: she had argued too much with her mother and grandmother. Frances, far away in the west of Scotland, had made her own life there where she ran a newsagent's and gift shop and was popular with the villagers as a crusader for local good causes. In the evenings, however, she could be incoherent. 'I can't speak to my mother after 5.30,' Diana complained, as she sought advice and comfort from mother figures Lady Annabel Goldsmith and Ambassadress Flecha de Lima. Frances Shand Kydd was still a remarkably attractive woman and loved by her grandchildren, who nicknamed her 'Supergran', but, as far as Diana was concerned, the relationship was volatile rather than supportive. 'I would say that, like the rest of her [Diana's] family, when the chips were really down, I'm afraid they weren't able, or perhaps willing, to give Diana the support she needed. She and her mother fought too much, there was far too much water under the bridge going way back . . .'[24] According to Andrew Morton, Diana felt 'constantly disappointed by her father'. 'She would say, "He arrives at six'o'clock", pointing to the entry in the visitors' book, "departs at 6.08." She adored him, loved him desperately . . . I remember he once rang from Japan saying, "I'm going to buy you a really lavish present." And she said to him, "I don't want that, I just want for you to be here with me." '[25] He was by now infirm and totally dependent on the devotion of Raine; moreover in September 1991 another Spencer family row broke out over the extent of Johnnie and Raine's sales of Althorp's contents. Nor was there support from her brother and sisters.

Charles, whom she adored, was involved in his own life and had problems in his marriage: Jane, mindful of her husband's career at Buckingham Palace, was in a very difficult position, while Sarah, in the words of a mutual friend, 'found it better to keep a safe distance between herself and Diana'.

So Diana was obliged to rely on the support of her friends and of her allies in the media. It was there that the war against Charles was publicly fought out. Sadly, the theme emphasized by Diana and the press was of Charles's failings as a father compared with her maternal devotion. A trip with the children to Thorpe Park brought headlines critical of Charles from her favourite *Daily Mail*. Under the headline 'CHARLES THE ABSENT ROYAL FATHER' the newspaper asked, 'Why do we not see from him the demonstrations of warmth, affection or closeness Diana frequently displays towards her sons in public?' Later Diana took William and Harry on a skiing holiday to Lech in Austria. Once again, Charles did not accompany them; once again his absence was noted by the press. In June media outrage stormed round Charles when William was hit on the head by a golf ball at his private preparatory boarding school, Ludgrove, sustaining a depressed fracture of his forehead. Both Charles and Diana accompanied William from Ludgrove to the Great Ormond Street Hospital for Sick Children in London for surgery. It was in no way to be a risky operation: Charles therefore decided to carry out a long-standing engagement to entertain British and European officials to a performance of *Tosca* and to travel to Yorkshire overnight to fulfil another official engagement. Diana spent the night in a bedside vigil at the hospital. Over the following days the press was in full cry, contrasting Charles's lack of caring with Diana's maternal devotion. 'WHAT KIND OF DAD ARE YOU?' the *Sun* shouted, while the *Daily Express* branded the Prince 'A PHANTOM FATHER', and another newspaper featured 'THE EXHAUSTED FACE OF A LOVING MOTHER'. Charles very much resented the mileage Diana extracted from the incident, accusing her of exaggerating the seriousness of William's injury for her own ends. Yet Diana did indeed feel bitter at the lack of support from Charles, expressing her feelings privately to friends.

The truth was that neither could bear the presence of the other and it must be asked whether it was not really better for the children for their parents to be apart. They were naturally aware of the fierce rows that took place: William used to listen at the door, taking in every word. Later, in her *Panorama* interview, Diana recalled her elder son pushing Kleenex tissues under the bathroom door as she sat sobbing on the other side. On one occasion Harry attacked his father, beating on his legs with his fists and shouting, 'I hate you, I hate you, you make Mummy cry . . .'

Diana continued her campaign in the press. The large-circulation popular press headed by the *Daily Mail*, the middle/upper-class tabloid, was on her side, thanks principally to its editor, David English, and royal reporter Richard Kay, deputed by English to be their contact with the Princess. Other well-known journalists were sympathetic: Anthony Holden, distinguished journalist and biographer; Andrew Morton, then a freelance who, while working with Diana on her life story, published favourable articles in the influential *Sunday Times*. In the tabloid press, James Whitaker and Harry Arnold tended to take the Princess's side, while Nigel Dempster of the *Mail* and Ross Benson of the *Express*, both of whom had contacts within Charles's circle, often stood out for the Prince.

Diana's thirtieth birthday on 1 July 1991 and her tenth wedding anniversary on the 29th, the two occasions which she had originally intended to use to make some sort of statement about her marriage, represented the next round. Now that she was engaged on the Morton book, Diana had shelved any plans for dramatic statements, but she did not intend to let the occasion pass without a demonstration. On 28 June a story, probably inspired by David English, was headlined in the *Mail* to the effect that Diana planned to spend her birthday apart from her husband.[26] She would be in London, lunching at the Savoy and hosting a party for her close friends, while Charles remained at Highgrove. 'That was PR straight from Diana,' Nigel Dempster told Sally Bedell Smith. Two days later he received a telephone call from one of Charles's friends, 'a well-bred lady's voice' putting the case for Charles: 'Charles has offered her anything for her birthday – lunch, dinner, a ball, but she has refused because she wants to be a martyr.' Dempster produced a front-page story for the *Mail*: under the headline 'CHARLES AND DIANA: CAUSE FOR CONCERN' he revealed that Diana had thwarted Charles's plans for her birthday and that there was 'a growing coolness in the marriage'.[27] After this furore, the couple spent their tenth wedding anniversary dining quietly at Highgrove; an article in the *Sunday Times* apparently celebrating this rapprochement, written by Morton, was headed 'Truce'. Far from representing any real reconciliation, however, the article, Morton admitted, was written specifically to prevent any momentum building up in the press over the unhappy marriage, to maintain his own reputation for inside knowledge of the royal scene but not so much as to allow his colleagues to 'cotton on so much that they would then start to follow the trail'. 'I wrote it quite deliberately to put them off the scent,' he said; 'the pieces I was writing were designed for her. You've got to bear in mind that for her, that the whole object for me was to get that book out unscathed . . . The game plan was that kind of balancing act, to show sophisticated observers . . . that I knew what I was talking about but at the same time not to let them get in on it.'[28] Morton, anxious for verification of the main story, indicated to Diana that he needed evidence of the Charles/Camilla relationship: in August she found notes from Camilla to Charles (how she did so has not been disclosed), which she found deeply upsetting, and showed them to Morton.

Meanwhile, according to Sarah Ferguson's account, 1991 was the year that she and Diana first put words to the unspeakable idea that they had been discussing for some time: that one or both of them might leave the Royal Family. They burned the phone wires into the night trading secrets and jokes that no one else would understand. Sarah even sent Diana a tape of the film *The Great Escape*. Sarah had been marked down as out of control for some time by the Queen's courtiers and her officials, dubbed by Sarah and Diana 'the grey men', principally 'Mr Z' (by whom she almost certainly meant Robert Fellowes, who also happened to be a cousin). The Ramzi Sultan affair had alerted them to Sarah's relationship with Steve Wyatt. These 'new American friends', she was told, 'were not the right sort of people' she should be mixing with. Sarah was in debt, her extravagance funded by unlimited credit at 'the Queen's bank', Coutts & Co. The miles she travelled on freebie holidays far exceeded those expended on official duties. In 1990 she had dropped to last in the royal engagements list, with ten fewer than the ninety-year-old Queen Mother. Sarah Ferguson was likeable, jolly and amusing but, in the famous words of one of the Queen's senior courtiers, she 'was never cut out to be a royal princess'.[29] 'Diana wasn't as bad,' said a royal official. 'But [for] Fergie who already had a life, it's like catching a wild animal and caging them up – they want to get out.'[30]

At Balmoral late that summer both girls behaved like rebellious teenagers. In her book, Sarah recalled how one night after dinner, she and Diana slipped out of the back door, commandeered a quad bike and drove it at speed down the golf course, damaging the greens. And to compound their bad behaviour they were foolish enough to stop at the lodge occupied by Robert Fellowes and his family and ring the bell, although it was almost midnight. They then 'liberated' the Queen Mother's stately Daimler limousine and, with Diana at the wheel wearing the chauffeur's cap and Sarah in the back imitating the Queen Mother's royal wave, did wheel spins on the gravel drive surrounding the castle. Diana, Princess of Wales, was thirty years old, Sarah, Duchess of York, thirty-two – two spoiled princesses who had absorbed the adulation and cosseting to their every whim which membership of the Royal Family involved, but failed to understand the true implications of their position. 'The thing that was hard on Diana – and Sarah Ferguson,' one of the Queen Mother's ladies said, 'was that they were both totally uneducated. They had no idea of what the constitutional monarchy was, either of them. They thought it was a mixture of Hollywood and William Hickey, they really did, they thought it was endless freebies and romantic princes riding about and everybody cheering. I don't think they had a clue.'[31]

Typical of the 'me' generation, they were neither prepared to compromise on what they saw as personal fulfilment nor to consider fully the implications of what they were about to do. Between them they would be responsible for the greatest crisis of the British monarchy since Edward VIII had abdicated to marry 'the woman I love'.

13. The Volcano Erupts

'. . . you got this flavour of intense unhappiness, real movement, almost as if the people at the Palace could see this volcano about to explode and just being petrified what to do about it. And in fact Diana wrote to someone before the book came out, "I can feel this volcano is going to explode but I can cope . . ."' (Andrew Morton[1])

While the royal household struggled to keep the lid on the swirling currents surrounding the Wales and York marriages, no one dared warn the Queen of what might happen. The year 1992 would mark the fortieth anniversary of her accession to the throne: the Queen in her Christmas broadcast message to her people, unaware that her family was crumbling around her, chose to emphasize the family theme as she affirmed her determination to serve as their monarch in the years to come: 'With your prayers and your help, and the love and support of my family, I shall try and help you in the years to come . . .'

The first shock to the family came in the first month of the year. On 15 January the *Mail* published the photographs of Steve Wyatt and Sarah on holiday with the children which a window cleaner and odd-job man had found on top of the wardrobe in Wyatt's vacant flat. This time the naïve, long-suffering Prince Andrew, in his father-in-law's words, 'hit the roof'. 'They were only holiday snaps,' Ronald Ferguson told Lesley Player, 'but they show that Texan fellow in a basket chair with his arm around her [Sarah] – and the one that really annoyed Andrew was little Beatrice with no clothes on being cuddled by him . . .'[2] Six days after the publication, Andrew and Sarah agreed to separate and travelled down to Sandringham to tell the Queen of their decision. According to Sarah, the Queen asked them to reconsider and no announcement was made for the time being. According to Sarah's autobiography she was determined to divorce Andrew in order to escape 'the Firm' in which 'grey man Z' (Robert Fellowes) had been joined by a new press secretary, 'grey man X' (Charles Anson). Without mentioning the developments in her private life which had led her to the decision, she blamed the grey men and their bully-boy tactics. They were determined to oust her and to protect Diana, she said. She did not mention Wyatt, who had left for the United States that month, apparently vowing eternal love, nor did she mention his replacement, another Texan, John Bryan.

Sarah was apparently expecting Diana to follow suit in bolting from the family but it soon became evident that she had no intention of doing so – yet. Perhaps in order to distance herself from the rumours surrounding Sarah, she appears to have been behind the lead in the *Daily Mail* on 18 March when a front-page 'exclusive' by Richard Kay and Andrew Morton declared that 'the Palace is preparing to announce the separation of the Duke and Duchess of York'. The story precipitated the Palace into action: the following day they did indeed issue a statement that lawyers acting for the Duchess of York had initiated discussions about a formal separation, accompanied by the pious hope that the media would spare the Duke and Duchess and their children 'any intrusion'. Their hope that the story could be kept quiet until after the General Election campaign then in progress had vanished. Sarah immediately suspected Diana since both Richard Kay and Andrew Morton were close to her and therefore the story must have been prompted by her, possibly to deflect any speculation about her own situation in the run-up to the publication in June of Andrew Morton's book. A representative of a public relations firm was summoned to Sunninghill Park. He arrived to find only Andrew there: Sarah was upstairs with John Bryan who had now taken over her affairs. They later appeared downstairs together in a state of high excitement. Sarah attacked the man for the bad publicity she had had to endure and indicated that John Bryan would be a more effective adviser. Tempers flared and the Yorks, with another guest, left the room (although it later transpired that they had been listening at the door). There was a scene during which champagne flutes were smashed. Witnesses commented that Andrew seemed to be frightened of Sarah and now hated Diana, his former friend, on his brother's account.

Diana was intent on her own survival and had no intention of becoming embroiled in her sister-in-law's self-induced troubles. She distanced herself from Sarah and carried on her own public relations campaign. In February she travelled with Charles on a visit to India which was to feature the famous 'Princess alone' photograph of a pensive Diana seated in front of the Taj Mahal, romantic monument to the enduring love of the Mogul Emperor Shah Jehan for his dead wife, Mumtaz Mahal. The impact of the picture showed Diana's phenomenal public relations skills. In itself, the location of the shot was absolutely normal; it was taken from the only spot to which the authorities would allow media access. Charles himself had sat on the same bench on his visit twelve years before, when he had given a hostage to fortune by saying, 'One day I would like to bring my wife here.' At the time, Charles himself was at a meeting for business leaders in Bangalore – the separation of itineraries was normal practice on intercontinental visits such as this. 'The trouble with these visits,' said Dickie Arbiter, the couple's press secretary who accompanied them, '[is that] they only last for four days, five at the most, and everybody wants a piece of the action. They are only two people and they can only do so much so they have to split and do what was required of them.'[3] The media, aware of Charles's previous pledge, put their own interpretation on the picture, following the precise line Diana intended. Famously, she followed it up with the cruel 'kiss that never was' at a polo match when, as Charles bent towards her to kiss her for a much awaited photo opportunity, she swiftly averted her head at the last moment, so that he was pictured pecking ineptly at her neck. 'Oh, Come On You Can Do Better Than That, Charles!' the *Mirror* admonished.

Such well-publicized images of a marriage in trouble caused consternation at the Palace, where the top officials had already picked up rumours of the Morton book and were desperate to shore up the marriage of the heir to the throne. It was only to get worse. On 29 March, Johnnie Spencer died suddenly of a heart attack in the Humana Hospital Wellington in north London where he had been recovering from mild pneumonia. His death was quite unexpected: Diana, who had visited him with William on 25 March, had left the following day for a family skiing holiday with Charles in Lech. None of the family was with Johnnie when he died, not even Raine who had felt able to go down to Althorp to supervise funding events. Diana, distraught in Lech, prepared to fly home without Charles. On this occasion of her private grief she could not bear the thought of yet another 'happy families' act for the media. Charles, his private secretary Richard Aylard and Dickie Arbiter tried to persuade her to go with her husband for the sake of the public image of the Prince and of their marriage. It took a telephone call from the Queen to persuade her to make a joint journey back to England. Even then the couple's private estrangement was such that, on arrival at Kensington Palace, Charles departed immediately for Highgrove, leaving Diana alone to grieve for her adored father. On 1 April she drove down to Althorp for the funeral at the family church of St Mary the Virgin, Great Brington. Charles flew over by helicopter to join her in the car for the church, maintaining the fiction of a supportive husband. Immediately after lunch, he flew back to London. Following her father's coffin out of the church with Raine, Diana's instinctive sympathy caused her to take the first step towards ending the feud with her stepmother. 'She did a very moving thing at Johnnie's funeral, Diana,' a relation who attended said. 'Raine was on that side and Diana was on this side, and when they left their seats she went over to Raine and held her hand and walked down the church with her. I was very impressed with that because I thought it showed a desire to reconcile everything, and in front of the whole congregation doing that . . . so that it was evident to every-body what she had done. And I thought that was very tender . . . bringing Raine in and not isolating her.'[4] Frances Shand Kydd

did not attend, although she was present – making herself as
inconspicuous as possible – at the London memorial service on
19 May.

By then Diana was standing on the edge of the abyss – the
pre-publication serialization of the Morton book which would
precipitate her isolation from the Royal Family. For some time
she had hugged the secret triumphantly as she looked forward to
putting her case to her public, exposing Charles and Camilla and
revealing the sham of her 'fairy-tale' marriage. But, with less than
a month to go, she began to be apprehensive of the consequences
of what she had done. 'I was with them going to Expo '92 in
Seville,' said one of her close aides. 'She said, "You don't know
what I've done." She was scared, really scared.[5] I think she was
just beginning to realize . . .' To David Puttnam, former film
producer and future Labour peer, she confided, 'I've done something which I may really live to regret . . .' Sitting next to Puttnam
at a dinner meeting of powerful media executives called the Thirty
Club at Claridge's in March, she confessed that she was terrified
of the consequences. Puttnam was then governor of the National
AIDS Trust of which she became President. 'Before, she was
talking about wanting to do something unusual, big,' Puttnam
recalled, 'so I arranged for her to address all the media owners,
Rupert Murdoch, Conrad Black . . . at the Thirty Club . . . she
was absolutely terrified, so I coached her through it, we worked
out what she would do, we even set it up so that there were some
interviews by very, very young interviewers. And she was brilliant,
and she knew she was brilliant. The speech about the incidence of
AIDS in women was a really "grown up" thing to do.' It may be
that seeing the media power ranked in front of her brought home
to her for the first time what she was getting herself into. At dinner,
to Puttnam's surprise, she 'suddenly started confiding in me how
unhappy things were in her marriage. She said "Neither of us has
been perfect, but I've done a really stupid thing. I have allowed a
book to be written. I felt it was a good idea, a way of clearing the
air, but now I think it was a very stupid thing that will cause all
kinds of terrible trouble", adding, "I would like to reel the movie

back. It is the daftest thing I have ever done.'[6] On the day the serialization of the Morton book came out, she rang the Waleses' press secretary Dickie Arbiter in a panic: 'What do I do?' 'You don't do anything,' Arbiter replied. 'Why didn't you tell me when I first asked you four months ago what help you had given the Morton book? You swore you hadn't given any.' And on that day, Diana still repeated, 'I haven't given any help.'[7]

By now thoroughly apprehensive, Diana was given an opportunity to demonstrate both her courage in the face of private anxiety and her value as an ambassador of the Royal Family and the British nation with an official visit to Egypt on 10 May. Ironically, as her private secretary Patrick Jephson noted, while the Princess flew out on her official tour in an aircraft paid for by the British taxpayer, the plane was diverted to land the Prince (on his eighth holiday of the year) and a party of friends in Turkey. In yet another example of the Prince's poor PR, when Diana flew back to London the same plane was forced to double back to Turkey again since the Prince's plans had not dovetailed with the Princess's official schedule. Despite a sobbing fit on the plane, possibly induced by apprehension over the Morton book but also perhaps because of the presence of the Prince and his friends off on their holiday, underlining the separateness of their ways, she heroically pulled herself together before the arrival at Cairo. 'No matter how close she came to the edge of bottling out,' Jephson wrote, 'she always produced the last-minute effort of will that could turn imminent disaster into serene triumph.' Immaculately groomed, she played her part in the arrival ceremony with 'consummate professionalism, poise and devotion to duty'. 'I wondered,' Jephson added, 'if her opponents really understood the bloody-minded determination of the woman they were seeking to banish into the backwaters of royal life.'[8] Not only was Diana a huge success with her hosts, President Hosni Mubarak and his wife, but she won the admiration of the travelling press pack, alert for any sign of weakness. A report in the *Sunday Times* congratulated Diana on her courage. 'It is a mark of her confidence that even after the recent publicity about her marriage she is prepared to walk into a room of tabloid hacks. The transformation in Diana is quite incredible. Diana will never be a great intellectual but she is a very shrewd sharp woman with amazing strength of character.'[9]

Yet even she had underestimated the bombshell effect of the public revelations of the reality of a marriage – which the majority had firmly believed, or wished to believe, was still the fairy tale of that July day in 1981 – when they were published in the *Sunday Times* beginning on 7 June 1992. The book told of Diana's psychological problems, the bulimia, self-mutilation and depression – including the Sandringham suicide attempt that never was. Charles's infidelity with Camilla and his unkindness to Diana were similarly revealed. The nation as a whole was shocked and angry. There was disillusionment with the Royal Family, and hence the monarchy, which had been building over the antics of Sarah and Diana; with *It's a Royal Knockout*; with the Yorks selling pictures of themselves with their babies to *Hello!*; with Princess Anne's divorce from Mark Phillips in 1992, accompanied by the rumours of her affair with one of her policemen. Middle England, brought up to regard the Royal Family as role models, 'ourselves behaving better', was shaken to the core. The heir to the throne came out worst of all: a cynical adulterer who mistreated his virgin bride and selfishly ignored his children. This last was a recent theme of Diana's which she had been putting across in the press: James Gilbey quoted her as saying. 'She thinks he is a bad father, a selfish father; the children have to tie in with whatever he's doing.'

The representation of Diana as a victim struggling to free herself from the crushing weight of an ultra-traditional family and an adulterous, uncaring husband won her widespread sympathy from the public at large, as she had intended. The trouble about the book from the Royal Family's point of view was that its essential presentation of Diana as a virgin sacrifice offered up on the altar of the dynasty was near enough to the truth to be believable. At first, however, it was dismissed as a journalistic fabrication. Diana's repeated denials of collaboration to her brother-in-law, Robert Fellowes, who assured the chairman of the Press Complaints Commission, Lord McGregor, that she had not been involved, led to his statement condemning the press for 'dabbling their fingers in the stuff of other people's souls'. Her friends who had collaborated in the Morton book were accused of betraying Diana by revealing her secrets. A photo opportunity was arranged at the request of Carolyn's husband, William Bartholomew, who was determined that Diana should be seen publicly supporting his wife.[10] A cousin of the Queen remembered being told by a photographer that Diana herself had telephoned him telling him to be at the Bartholomews' Fulham house at a precise time.[11] Diana's evident approval of what Carolyn had done and the use of photographs from the Spencer family album gave Morton's revelations authenticity. One of the contributors, Angela Serota, a friend of Andrew Knight, executive director of News International, told Knight that Diana had indeed authorized her friends to cooperate with Morton.[12] When the Bartholomew photographs appeared, McGregor, who had received Robert Fellowes' assurances, rang him in Paris, where he was with the Queen, to berate him for deceiving him. Fellowes, who had asked Diana several times if she had been involved and received direct denials from her, had believed her. He was fond of his sister-in-law, whom he had known since childhood, and, being an upright man of Christian principles, had thought it inconceivable that she could have lied to him. He apologized to Lord McGregor and the Press Complaints Commission for misleading them and offered his resignation to the Queen who refused it. The affair greatly damaged Diana's future relations with her sister and brother-in-law, whom she had lied to and betrayed, making him look ridiculous to his own official circle. She continued to deny that she herself had been responsible for the book or that she had spoken to the author. No one believed her on the first count, although her undoubted responsibility for the second was not to be publicly revealed until Morton published extracts from the tapes after her death.

While Diana had succeeded in her aim of revealing the sham of her marriage and gaining the sympathy of the wider public, the British Establishment and the upper echelons of British society were outraged at what they saw as a betrayal of the Queen and the monarchy on her part. It was the first self-destructive step towards the final parting of the ways. Diana never wanted a divorce; in her heart she still loved Charles to the point of obsession and saw him as her husband. She still hoped that she could have it all: remaining in the Royal Family, keeping her children and her title as Princess of Wales, while keeping a separate court. 'Diana would never have got out,' Dickie Arbiter affirmed. But, although at a private meeting with Charles the day after the serialization began they agreed to separate on the grounds of incompatibility, Diana continued to feel a passionate resentment over her treatment, refusing to play an accommodating Queen Alexandra to Charles and Camilla's Edward VII and Mrs Keppel. Like Sarah Ferguson, she was a child of a modern generation which was not prepared to accept the upper-class conventional marriage in which fidelity and romance did not play a part. But, unlike Sarah Ferguson, who for selfish reasons turned her back on a husband who loved and supported her through all her infidelities and antics, Diana had every reason to complain as the loving, inexperienced bride who had been used and abused by an uncaring, selfish husband incapable of giving her the love she craved, nor even the normal married life she had dreamed of. Moreover, as she saw it – and who is to say she was wrong? – he was backed up by a powerful social set and ultimately by the Palace, who had tried to silence and sideline her.

Jonathan Dimbleby wrote of the aftermath of the serialization:

After the publication of the first instalment of the Morton book, a handful of the Prince's closest friends, including the Romseys and van Cutsems, felt compelled to tell both the Queen and Prince Philip how stoical they thought the Prince had been through the long trauma of the marriage. Perhaps nudged by this intervention but certainly shocked by the media blitzkrieg surrounding the publication of the book, both the Queen and the Duke, who had been at pains not to take sides, rallied to the Prince; in particular, the Duke wrote a long and sympathetic letter to him in which he praised what he saw as his son's saint-like fortitude. It was in this atmosphere that the Queen and Prince discussed for the first time whether he should seek a separation from the Princess.[13]

The Prince went on to consult Lord Goodman, lawyer and adviser to the powerful, as to his position, but took no further steps.

As Charles's authorized biographer, Dimbleby is well informed and reliable on the Prince's side of the story, although no official biographer can be entirely impartial. What he did not say, however, is that despite their initial shock at the effect of the book in battering down the wall of confidentiality traditionally surrounding the family, and at Diana's deviousness in first encouraging it and then concealing its progress, the Queen and Prince Philip were not at heart totally unsympathetic to Diana. The Prince's first reaction was anger at his daughter-in-law for bringing the situation and its accompanying scandal into the open. With the Morton book, she had 'destroyed everything', he wrote to her. Yet the Queen and Prince Philip disapproved of Charles's adultery with Camilla which, far more than any unreasonable behaviour of Diana's, had brought scandal on the monarchy. Indeed, at Easter the following year, a courtier was amazed when Charles, who was sitting beside her, exploded in fury at his father: 'You should have seen the letter he wrote me . . . !'[14] 'What Charles has done is very wrong,' Prince Philip wrote in a compassionate letter to his daughter-in-law. Both the Queen and Prince Philip were – and are – strong in their religious feelings and convictions; divorce was abhorrent to them and they hoped above all that it need not come to that, both for the sake of the young princes and the monarchy – 'the image of a family on the throne', as Walter Bagehot had put it. It was the Prince's party at the Palace and in society who undermined Diana by implying or saying publicly, as one certainly did, that Diana was mad – 'that bad Fermoy blood'. The general Palace view – but not in the Queen's office – was detestation of Diana for her revelation of family secrets and sympathy for 'the poor Prince'. The fact that the basis of her story was the truth counted for nothing in the face of her breach of the rules.

Yet, despite everything, the royal show rumbled on: the traditional celebration of the Queen's official birthday, Trooping the Colour, went ahead with Diana as part of the family party standing on Buckingham Palace balcony for the RAF fly-past as if nothing had happened. Fergie, however, was nowhere to be seen. As the second instalment of the Morton serialization hit the news-stands on 14 June, the family were at Windsor for the racing at Ascot. The following day the Queen and Prince Philip had a meeting with Charles and Diana, during which the subject of divorce was mentioned but rejected. The Queen was led to believe that Diana would stand by Charles and suggested a six-month cooling-off period. Once again Diana was asked if she had collaborated on the book and once again she denied it, in tears. Prince Philip, by her later account, was 'angry, raging and unpleasant'[15] and later cold-shouldered her in the royal box.[16] On the opening day, as the Queen and the rest of her family drove in open carriages down the course, the disgraced Sarah took her two daughters to wave at their grandmother from the rails. The Queen waved back but inwardly she no doubt despaired at yet another manifestation of what the press now liked to call her 'dysfunctional' family. Guests at lunch at the Castle noted that the Queen seemed to be 'in a pretty bad temper' and when she did talk to her guests she was less than her usual gracious self. In the royal box after lunch, again, no one dared speak to her.

At the end of June Diana gave yet another demonstration of the crowd-pleasing qualities which made her such a valuable royal asset. On a visit to Belfast (security had been breached by the leaking of her visit the night before), she paid a spectacularly successful visit to the Republican heartland, the Falls Road, the dominion of the IRA. An estimated twenty thousand people came to 'shout for Diana'. The Morton revelations had evidently made their impact and there was no doubting where the popular sympathies lay. As the *Daily Mirror* front page put it under a banner headline 'WE WANT DI!', frontline Belfast had 'a message for the Royals'. Even the normally anti-monarchist Dublin press reported sympathetically on the Princess. It was a timely reminder of her popular appeal, and her enemies responded accordingly. On the same day as the papers published ecstatic reports of her success in Northern Ireland, others carried stories that could only have been planted by her enemies, clearly suggesting that the Princess suffered from mental instability.[17]

At the end of July both Charles and Diana attended a dinner to celebrate the Queen's fortieth anniversary on the throne and in August, after a brief, unsatisfactory 'family holiday' on millionaire John Latsis's yacht, they flew up to Balmoral for the annual family holiday. They were all there when, on 20 August, the *Daily Mirror* published the notorious 'toe-sucking' pictures featuring Sarah and her 'financial adviser' John Bryan on holiday in the South of France with the two little princesses. Nothing was said when Andrew, forewarned by Sarah, went down to face the younger members of the family at the breakfast table littered with newspapers blaring headlines and explicit photographs. Sarah herself went to face a furious Queen at 9.30. One can only imagine the conversation. While the scandal raged in the press, at Balmoral it was as if nothing had happened. Sarah remained for a further three days, sitting in her usual place beside Andrew. A young member of the family said to a relation, 'You won't believe it – nobody said a word. There was Fergie sitting next to Andrew and the topless pictures all over the papers . . .'[18]

Four days after the publication of the 'toe-sucking' pictures of Sarah and John Bryan, it was Diana's turn for embarrassment. The *Sun* published the Squidgygate tapes of the conversations between Diana and James Gilbey on New Year's Eve 1989 under the heading 'MY LIFE IS TORTURE', which not only underlined the deep rift between herself and Charles but her difficulties with the Royal Family in general and, more damagingly, her close relationship with Gilbey. The terms in which she had spoken of the family's ingratitude and lack of appreciation of her dutiful public efforts – 'after all I've done for this f . . . family' – were difficult for the Palace to come to terms with. The *Sun* then alleged that Diana and Hewitt had had a 'physical relationship' with no evidence beyond analysis of their 'body language' in photographs of them together. Diana suspected a conspiracy to destroy her but there was none beyond the destructive effect of the relentless tabloid circulation war. In these circumstances and after the publication of the Morton book which, however much she may have regretted it, still represented her 'manifesto', her protest against the sham of her marriage, it was hardly surprising that she dug in her heels over the projected joint tour of South Korea.

'As the Prince's staff contemplated the nightmarish task of explaining to the Korean authorities that the Princess would not after all be accompanying her husband on the first royal visit to their country,' Dimbleby's official account ran,

Peter Westmacott, the deputy private secretary to the royal couple, was obliged to do the Korean 'recce' as if he were organising a joint visit – which, from his conversation with the Princess, he was convinced would not in fact take place. At Balmoral, the Prince tried to persuade the Princess to change her mind. Even the Queen intervened to advise her daughter-in-law that she ought to go. Finally the Prince told her bluntly that she would have to come up with an explanation of her own for staying behind. At this, the Princess finally relented, saying meekly that as the Queen had asked her to go she would after all accompany him.[19]

The resulting tour, as Diana knew it would be, was a public relations disaster. The glum faces of the couple only served to indicate the depths to which the marriage had sunk. There could no longer be any pretence that the situation was salvageable. On the aeroplane returning from Korea, the Prince wrote one of his gloomy, self-pitying letters, recounting his despair that Diana could not be 'a friend' to him and how he had been battling the temptation to cancel his engagements: 'I feel so unsuited to the ghastly business of human intrigue and general nastiness . . . I don't know what will happen from *now* on but I *dread* it.'[20]

In contrast, Diana's subsequent solo visit to Paris on 13 November represented in Jephson's eyes her 'apogee'. Greeted with the welcoming message 'COURAGE PRINCESSE!', Diana went through the perfectly orchestrated schedule at the peak of her beauty and professionalism, charming President Mitterrand, the French public and the press alike. For Jephson that moment represented Diana at her best. Strengthened by her stand over the Morton book, she had not yet encountered the pitfalls which awaited her bid for independence. 'To my eyes,' Morton wrote, 'knowing what she had already endured and what lay ahead in the immediate future, there was something heroic in her.'

For Diana the endgame of the first phase was near. The final confrontation of the year came in a quarrel over one of Charles's annual November shooting weekends at Sandringham, planned for the 20th and timed to coincide with an exeat from Ludgrove so that William and Harry could join them. In a last act of defiance, Diana decided not to go and, moreover, to inform Charles that she would be taking the children to see their grandmother, the Queen, at Windsor, or, if she could not stay there, to Highgrove. The Prince metaphorically stamped his foot and threatened her with his authority – he could not be defied in the eyes of his friends. Diana held her ground. His intemperate attitude gave her the excuse she needed to write a defiant letter which, paraphrased, said, more or less: 'Given the way things are between us I'm not sure I want to subject myself to the company of your friends and I certainly don't want to subject the boys to the company of your friends given that we both know who might be there . . .'[21]

According to Dimbleby, it had 'become the custom for the royal couple to invite some sixteen friends to stay for three days of relaxation, shooting, and walking'.[22] In practice, the 'friends' were all Charles's, not Diana's, and by now they had almost no friends in common. Charles's friends, Diana well knew, would include the inner circle who provided safe houses for his rendezvous with Camilla. As Diana complained to Jephson, 'They're all *his* friends. I'm going to be completely outnumbered.'[23] And as a friend said, 'She'd been put through this Sandringham ordeal over and over again . . . it was a real little love-in for the Prince's buddies and his whole household was mobilized to make it an extraordinary expression of his regal position. It was a [Michael] Fawcett production in overdrive, playing King in the Queen's house . . .'[24] Diana's position, while absolutely understandable as regards her own presence in the house, was less tenable when it came to preventing the boys from seeing their father. Unfortunately, they were her principal weapon and in her rage and distress she was not above using them as pawns in the war with her husband.

Charles's patience finally snapped. He would not be defied like this in front of his friends, or, as Dimbleby judiciously put it: 'Unable to see any future in a relationship conducted on these terms, he decided he had no choice but to ask his wife for a legal separation.'²⁵ On 25 November he and Diana met privately at Kensington Palace and agreed to put the matter in the hands of their lawyers. Discussions continued for some weeks over the matters to be agreed, principally arrangements over the children, secondly a financial settlement for her upkeep, and lastly and most controversially, Diana's future role as a working member of the Royal Family, described, according to Jephson who took part in the negotiations as 'a semi-detached member of the Royal Family'.

'It was at about this time,' Jephson commented with distaste, 'that the phrase "loose cannon" became popular.'²⁶ The Queen herself, he said, was taking great trouble to remain neutral, but the Prince's advisers (he did not name them but hinted that they were not his legal ones) seemed determined to thwart Diana's ambitions to become an independent royal operator, attempting to restrict her use of the Queen's Flight and the royal train, and downgrading the protocol accorded to her when on official visits. In the end, since the Queen declined to come down on the Prince's side, Diana got almost everything she wanted in the final negotiations except for the financial settlement which was not agreed until the divorce was finalized in 1996. The only stipulation made by the Queen was that Diana should not represent her abroad. Significantly, in an attempt to promote fairness and bipartisanship between the households and staff of all the Palaces, the Lord Chamberlain circulated a letter impressing on everybody the necessity of understanding for both sides. Whether it actually made any difference to the attitudes in the opposing camps is doubtful but it was useful in emphasizing the neutrality of the Crown (that is, the Queen) in the disputes between the Waleses.

On 9 December in the House of Commons, the Prime Minister, John Major, read out the prepared statement issued by Buckingham Palace:

It is announced from Buckingham Palace that, with regret, the Prince and Princess of Wales have decided to separate. Their Royal Highnesses have no plans to divorce and their constitutional positions are unaffected. This decision has been reached amicably and they will both continue to participate fully in the upbringing of their children.

Their Royal Highnesses will continue to carry out full and separate programmes of public engagements and will, from time to time, attend family occasions and national events together.

While the first statement was received by Members of Parliament in respectful silence, the Prime Minister's following words to the effect that 'there was no reason why the Princess of Wales should not be crowned Queen Consort in due course . . .' produced a collective gasp. The idea that the Princess of Wales, living apart from her husband and at daggers drawn with him, could still be crowned Queen Consort struck most people as absurd. The idea that the Prince of Wales's succession was assured as Head of the Church of England, even if constitutionally correct, also required some swallowing. The Archbishop of Canterbury, when officially consulted before the statement, said that for the separation to be widely accepted two important provisos should be met: 'both parents would have to be seen to maintain close bonds with their children; and extra-marital love affairs that might be brought to public attention would need to be avoided'.[27] It would soon become obvious that the Archbishop's second proviso was very far from being met.

Symbolically, on Friday 20 November, the start of the fateful Sandringham weekend, Windsor Castle caught fire. The images of flames shooting from the great castle on the hill, home of the British monarchy for almost a thousand years, seized the imagination of people around the world. Not only did it represent the bonfire which had finally consumed the Waleses' marriage, but with it perished the 'family' image which had been so carefully cultivated.

14. The First Step Towards the Abyss

'She was lost without him' (a friend's comment on Diana after the separation)

At Kensington Palace after the separation was agreed there was a lightening of the atmosphere and a sense of solidarity between the house and office staff which had not been there before. They were all on the Princess's team now: a party was held, Diana played the piano and everyone sang and danced: '. . . we glowed with the sudden feeling that the grown-ups had gone out for the evening and would not be back for hours . . . if they were going to come back at all,'[1] Jephson recalled. Yet, when James Hewitt telephoned to congratulate her on having successfully made 'the Great Escape', she sounded 'very flat and down'. At both their residences, the separation was symbolized by the removal of the Prince's personal possessions (including his lavatory) from Kensington Palace and Diana's from Highgrove: the couple's respective interior designers, Robert Kime and Dudley Poplak, were instructed to wipe out all traces of their common life together.

An immediate consequence of the separation of the two households was the division of the staff. Some were offered the choice of which household they chose to remain with, some were not. At Kensington Palace the charming, loyal and discreet head butler, Harold Brown, remained with the Princess; the Highgrove butler, Paul Burrell, was assigned to Kensington Palace against his wishes. With his wife, Maria, and two sons, Burrell was happy in his cottage on the Highgrove estate and was extremely unwilling to be transferred to the Princess's service. 'He was blubbing and bad-mouthing her,' said a fellow member of staff. In fact, Diana hardly needed two butlers at Kensington Palace but Burrell had been a favoured footman to the Queen at Buckingham Palace while his wife had worked for the Duke of Edinburgh and they were therefore entitled to consideration. The Prince, it was alleged, did not want to keep Burrell on at Highgrove since he (Burrell) was only too aware of what was going on in the Prince's private life. Burrell became devoted to, even obsessed with, Diana and later succeeded in manoeuvring Harold Brown out of her good graces. At the Prince of Wales's side, his valet, Michael Fawcett, now became the most powerful figure on his domestic staff. Both Burrell and Fawcett were to become notorious in the years up to and following Diana's death. Mervyn Wycherley, the Waleses' chef, who had been transferred from the royal household on their marriage, remained with her. 'Muscular, flamboyant and extremely witty,' Wharfe wrote, 'Mervyn was devoted to the Princess and she was fond of him in return. Much more than the man who prepared her food . . . he became a close friend whose loyalty to her was unquestioned. There were some, however,' he added mysteriously, 'who wanted to break their intimacy, seeing it as a threat to their own positions.'[2] Both Burrell with Diana and Fawcett with Charles were jealous of their respective closeness to their employers and undermined anybody who posed any kind of threat to their positions.

At first it seemed as if Diana had won hands down. She had got all she wanted – access to the children and a subsidized, independent life of her own. *Vanity Fair* called it 'DI'S PALACE COUP' in a headline of February 1993. On 13 January the publication of the Camillagate tapes had cut what remained of the moral high ground from beneath Charles's feet. The mutual passion of the couple (and Charles's silly language) served to underline the fact that the Morton representation of Diana as the betrayed wife was the truth. Tabloid newspapers speculated that the tapes could cost the adulterous Prince the throne. Much sanctimonious nonsense was written but the central fact that the Prince of Wales had betrayed his wife, the mother of his children, over a long period of time and, with the connivance of a circle of aristocratic friends, had deceived Diana, brought his popularity to an all-time low. In contrast Diana, the innocent victim of the deception, was resoundingly vindicated. Times — and the press — had changed since Charles's great-grandfather, Edward VII, enjoyed with impunity regular winter holidays with Camilla's great-grandmother, Mrs Keppel, at Biarritz or on luxurious shooting weekends at the country estates of his aristocratic or plutocratic friends.

Yet Diana felt bereft without Charles, the focus of her life over the past eleven years. However hostile, however undermining he might have been to her at times, she was unused to living alone without a male prop in her life. The future seemed very uncertain even if materially luxurious, and her life was in limbo without the predictable form she had enjoyed (or, rather, resented) within the unchanging pattern of the Royal Family. From now on she would have to operate exclusively at the dictate of her own instincts (not always a wise motive for action) with the guiding hand of Patrick Jephson. She began to gather round her a band of loyal friends and advisers. Carolyn Bartholomew was still a friend, as was Laura Greig (now Lonsdale). Sadly, some of her circle — Julia Samuel, Kate Menzies and Catherine Soames — would not survive the nature of Diana's friendships, when she would abruptly and definitively cut off contact for some perceived disloyalty or misdemeanour. The most long-lasting of these younger friends was Rosa Monckton, born the Hon. Rosamond Monckton, daughter of Viscount Monckton of Brenchley, and wife of journalist the Hon. Dominic Lawson, the son of a former Chancellor of the Exchequer and at that time editor of the prestigious *Spectator* magazine. Rosa Monckton, a clever, ambitious woman, became head of Tiffany & Co. She had her ups and downs with Diana, who sometimes suspected her of using her to further her own purposes, but the two women always made up. At Diana's instigation, Rosa's stillborn child was buried in the garden at Kensington Palace, and she became godmother to the Lawsons' daughter, Domenica. A major row took place when Diana attended the christening party for Domenica only to find herself photographed at the event by *Hello!* magazine. Diana took her role as godmother seriously and would look after Domenica herself when needed.

With Rosa, the two women close to Diana for the remainder of her life were glamorous mother figures, Lady Annabel Goldsmith and the Brazilian Ambassadress, Lucia Flecha de Lima. Another older woman, Elsa, Lady Bowker, was the recipient of many confidences about her love life. Lady Annabel, a daughter of the 8th Marquess of Londonderry, had formerly been married to Mark Birley, founder of the smartest of London nightclubs which he named after her. Glamorous, popular and sociable, Lady Annabel had two sons and a daughter by Birley, and subsequently two more sons and a daughter by the fabulously rich Sir James Goldsmith, international financier and celebrated gambler. Annabel Elliot, Camilla Parker Bowles's sister, was a particular friend of Annabel's and it was at her birthday party at the Goldsmith house, Ormeley Lodge, on Ham Common, that Diana's face-to-face interview with Camilla had taken place. The Camilla connection was, in a perverse way, an attraction for Diana, as was later the marriage of Annabel's beautiful daughter Jemima to Imran Khan, when the Pakistani connection became important to her.

Annabel was a contemporary of Diana's mother, Frances, and had known her well. Her own children ranged from Rupert Birley, born in 1955, to the youngest, Zac Goldsmith, born in 1980, and with nephews, nieces and stepchildren the Goldsmith house supplied a wonderful family atmosphere which attracted Diana. Ben Goldsmith was only just over two years older than William, and Diana would bring the children with her to marathon Sunday lunches at Ormeley. Or she would come alone to relax and be herself – witty, funny and charming. 'Oh, she could be funny,' an observer said. 'She'd walk in on Sunday lunch, sweep in, rush in, kiss all the staff, come running in and sit down, and she'd have us all in stitches, and sometimes she would bring the boys and they would go off and play tennis, and sometimes she'd send William down because she said William was like a caged lion [at Kensington Palace].'[3]

The Brazilian Ambassadress, Lucia Flecha de Lima, was even closer to Diana: the embassy on Mount Street was a refuge for her and she often spent weekends there. The Ambassador, Paulo Tarso, and his wife and children were almost a second family to her. Beautiful, chic, forthright and outgoing, Lucia was a loyal and candid friend. Only once did they fall out when Lucia told Diana off over something she had done and Diana got on her royal high horse. With Lucia, Annabel and the other older women she liked and trusted, such as Marguerite Littman and Pamela Harlech, Diana never showed her darker side; she was always funny, charming, light-hearted, although there were times when she did reveal to Lucia her misery over her marriage and her anger about what she saw as Charles's unkindness. Diana confided copies of Prince Philip's letters to Lucia for safe keeping; Rosa Monckton, apparently, helped draft her replies.

The letters were written over the months following the publication of the Morton book, with which, Prince Philip had told Diana, she had destroyed everything. Diana was furious at his criticism but in fact Prince Philip's letters were a heartfelt attempt to put things right. Appealing to her sense of duty, he told her how, when he (referring to himself as 'Pa' and the Queen as 'Ma') and the Queen had married, they had thought that they would have a few years ahead of them to live their own life but then, when the Queen's father died, the Queen had had to renounce her own family life and he had to give up his own career for the sake of the family. He wanted Charles and Diana to stay together but living separate lives while continuing with their duties. He said that Charles's behaviour with Camilla was really wrong – he even, apparently, expressed surprise that Charles could prefer someone of Camilla's looks and age to Diana. Touchingly, he wrote how 'Ma and I' were very worried about the situation.[4] 'Contrary to what people say, she [Diana] got on very well with Prince Philip,' a friend said. 'She really did. He was nice to her. He said to her once – she thought he was going to tell her off – he tapped her on the shoulder one day and he said, "Now look here, young lady, if you ever think of having an affair for God's sake keep it in the family, where you can keep it quiet." And she was rather taken aback!!' 'And the other thing he said to her when she was in trouble and had started [the divorce proceedings], he

said, "Now if you're a bad girl, you are going to lose your title."
And she said "No, Pa, no I can't, because I've already got one",
which was quite funny and he laughed.'⁵ 'The Queen and Prince
Philip were never at loggerheads with Diana as people made out,'
a courtier said. Diana continued to take the boys to tea with their
grandmother, although it was a cause of sadness to her that the
two of them were not on the same wavelength when it came to
conversation. Indeed, one courtier described the Queen as 'frigid'
when Diana and the boys came to tea, but it was not so much
frigidity as shyness and a certain awkwardness. It was also partly
generational: the Queen's view of bringing up children and Diana's
could hardly have been more different. Once at Balmoral, when
William was small, his nanny was on holiday and Diana naturally
looked after him, the Queen's reaction was one of surprise: 'I
don't understand why Diana has to do this; there are millions of
housemaids around.' Princess Margaret, who had liked Diana from
the beginning and tried to help her with the details of her public
role, sympathized with her in her marital troubles which she herself
had experienced, remaining friendly with Diana even after the
Morton affair, telling Prince Charles, whom she adored, 'I'm not
going to give her up. I like her and she's my friend.' And when
Diana sent her a Hermès scarf as a birthday present in August 1993,
Princess Margaret's letter of thanks began 'Darling Diana'. The
Snowdon children, David Linley and Sarah Armstrong-Jones, both
adored Diana.

By this time, Diana had become involved in another affair: with
Oliver Hoare, a handsome Old Etonian dealer in Islamic art,
married to a French heiress, Diane de Waldner. Hoare was charming and universally popular. He and his wife were friends of Prince
Charles and, ironically, Hoare had come into Diana's life as a result
of his efforts to mediate between her and the Prince in 1991. 'He
is the most charming man,' a friend said. 'He is really fascinating
. . . I think Diana picked him because he was one of Charles's
good friends. His interests are Charles's interests. He loves art, he
loves literature, very much like Charles, you know.'⁶ 'Oliver Hoare
was divine, and charming,' a friend said, 'but what was appalling

was that he was a great friend of Prince Charles's, they used to go on holiday together with Derek Hill, the painter and Charles's friend and artistic mentor, going to Italy and looking at Islamic stuff. I'm very fond of Oliver but he's always been badly behaved. His behaviour was absolutely atrocious. And poor old Prince Charles didn't know it was going on until afterwards.'[7]

Diana had first met Oliver Hoare with his wife during Ascot week at Windsor in the mid-eighties. Diane Hoare's parents, Baron Geoffroi de Waldner and his wife Louise, were friends of the Queen Mother. Rich, Anglophile and, like Queen Elizabeth, racing enthusiasts, they fitted perfectly into the Ascot racing scene. Louise de Waldner owned a chateau in the South of France where Charles often went to paint and, later, to rendezvous with Camilla. Oliver, glamorous though penniless, had a cosmopolitan background. He was only distantly related to the rich English banking family of the same name. His mother, Irina, was a Czech émigrée, his father, Reginald, an English civil servant who had managed to send their son to Eton and then to the Sorbonne. Beyond his Etonian charm and manners, Hoare had an exotic, bohemian background: at one point in his life he had become a part of Rudolph Nureyev's uninhibited circle before rejoining the Establishment as head of the Islamic department at Christie's London auction house. He had a wide circle of friends, including David Sulzberger of the *New York Times* dynasty who became his business partner, and whom he had met in Tehran where he had learned Arabic and Persian and begun to collect Middle Eastern art and antiquities. He had in fact begun his career there as a protégé of a beautiful, influential older woman, Harmoush Bowler, a princess of the Hajar dynasty. 'She was a very rich Iranian lady of great style and elegance,' said a friend, 'and Oliver was somebody she discovered. She taught him all about the Orient and the arts and everything like that. He went on with it but she was the first to interest him in it. I remember him sitting at her feet playing the guitar . . .' 'She was very generous. And so Oliver really made himself. Oliver was self-made and very beautiful.'[8]

Hoare married the striking and intelligent Diane de Waldner in

1976, but subsequently had a four-year affair with Ayesha Gul, a fascinating Turkish woman, married to the controversial tycoon Asil Nadir. Oliver Hoare, with his thick dark hair, mobile, attractively lined features and articulate charm, appealed to both sexes. Although quite unlike the men Diana had previously been attracted to, she was drawn to Hoare from the first, while his interest in ballet gave them a bond in common. Oliver and Diane became friends of the couple, as they also were of Andrew and Camilla Parker Bowles. Diana found him fascinating not only for his physical attractions but his status as a friend of Charles's which would give their relationship added piquancy, as did the fact that the Hoares were friends of Camilla. On the other side of the coin, Hoare's Turkish contacts provided him with safe houses, and even a yacht, where he could carry on his romance with Diana.[9]

As with James Hewitt, secretive Diana managed to keep knowledge of her relationship with Oliver Hoare from the newspapers. Even the frequency with which she called Hoare – as often as twenty times a day, beginning in September 1992 – remained a secret for another two years.[10] She called him in his car, and apparently made a string of anonymous calls to his home as many as twenty times a week, some as late as midnight. She would wait until Hoare answered and then hang up. The couple met at the homes of Diana's friends the Flecha de Limas and another of her mother figures, Elsa, Lady Bowker. On other occasions, Diana would smuggle him into Kensington Palace – either in the boot of her green Rover with blacked-out windows or driven in by Paul Burrell under a blanket. These cloak-and-dagger operations were a waste of time: Kensington Palace being the heavily guarded small village that it is, there was no question of keeping his visits secret. According to one of Princess Margaret's staff: 'this business where Burrell kept saying he used to sneak people into the Palace was an absolute joke, because one, the policeman on the gate knew exactly what he was doing bringing people in under the blanket and then he [Burrell] would drive into Princess Margaret's courtyard which hasn't got security cameras but everyone knows what's going on because as you go into the courtyard there's an old drain and every time a car hits it it goes, clonk, clonk, clonk. So sometimes Princess Margaret would go and see who it was for herself . . . And she [Diana] would park outside Princess Margaret's offices and then this chap would run in and of course all the staff upstairs would see him. It was no secret at all . . .'[11] 'She'd drive in sometimes and Princess Margaret would say, "Whose is that car?" knowing full well whose it was. "Go and find out who it is." And I'd have to go over and tap the window and she'd open it very gingerly and I'd say, "Why don't you go away?" . . . And then I'd have to tell a downright lie to Princess Margaret. I'd say the driver doesn't know where he's going but I've told him to go off round the corner . . . but she knew I was telling lies . . .' 'And then the next time I saw her [Diana] I'd say, "Look, you're far better off bringing people right to your front door . . . because nobody would bat an eyelid . . ."'[12] Ken Wharfe, Diana's protection officer, told the same story. 'An old uniformed police sergeant said to me, "Got a bit of a security problem, sir . . . The Princess came in the other night, sir . . . a man got out of the boot, sir." I said, "Who was that?" "Well, I think it was Mr Hoare, sir." The cloak-and-dagger act, both witnesses said, was Burrell's idea: 'Burrell actually said, "The best way to get him in is in the boot of a car." And stupidly she did it. I said, "Look, Ma'am, this is not a good idea. If you think you're going to get away with it, you're not."'[13] Wharfe and Hoare, according to the former, heartily disliked each other, so Wharfe greatly enjoyed an incident in 1993 when the smoke alarm shrilled through the apartments at Kensington Palace at 3.30 a.m. In the hallway of Diana's apartment he found a 'dishevelled' Hoare puffing on a cigar. Diana, who hated the smell of smoke, had obviously told him to smoke in the hallway, forgetting that this would set the alarms off.[14]

'Next morning,' Wharfe wrote, 'I tried to make a joke of the incident. Diana, however, clearly did not want to talk about it. So when I suggested that she had been playing cards, perhaps strip poker, she flushed scarlet and went back to her room.' 'No doubt,' he went on, 'I had overstepped the mark, but by this time she was already in danger of losing all sense of perspective. She knew this, yet she was not prepared to admit it, and I realized that, where I was concerned, it could only be a matter of time before there was a parting of the ways . . .'[15]

According to Ken Wharfe, who was in a position to monitor the comings and goings of Diana's men, Diana, as she confessed to him, 'absolutely adored' Oliver Hoare to the point of obsession. Her love for him – which was reciprocated ('He loved her very much,' a close friend said), her romantic hopes for a future together which could never be realized, and the difficulties she always experienced in sustaining a relationship – formed the background to her life over the next three years. 'I think Hoare was instrumental in a lot that changed the course of the Princess's life,' said Wharfe.[16]

In the year after the separation, Diana came to realize clearly that, rather than the freedom she had hoped for, she was more constrained than she had ever been. The Palace, in the form of Robert Fellowes, his deputy Robin Janvrin and press secretary Charles Anson, were not inimical to her and were always willing to help if possible. Her 'team', comprising her private secretary Patrick Jephson and the popular Australian Geoff Crawford, seconded to be her press secretary, were utterly loyal. John Major and the members of his government were sympathetic. But beyond them were 'the friends of Charles' looking for every false step she might make and resentful of her popularity. To combat them, and to maintain her all-important position in the heart of the British people, Diana had recourse to the weapon which she wielded with consummate skill – the press. And as allies in the continuing war against Charles, Diana enlisted powerful individuals, media figures, editors, pundits and opinion makers, who fell easy victim to her beauty, wit and alluring charm.

Complementing the stream of therapists, psychics and their like whom Diana continued to favour in her unending quest to understand herself and find peace of mind, a number of influential men from the media came to lunch at Kensington Palace to dispense their wisdom and guide her in her public career. David

Puttnam, Jacob Rothschild, Peter Palumbo, Paul Johnson, Clive James, Gordon Reece, Max Hastings, Piers Morgan and Auberon Waugh were among the figures whose advice she sought and usually, characteristically, ignored.

One recalled: 'The two things I particularly stressed to her were, one, have absolutely nothing to do with the media under any circumstances – and she was very shocked at this – and I said, "You think that you can manipulate them but in fact that is not how it works. They will end by manipulating you and by distressing you and by destroying you as they always do. And there is no absolute defence against them because we live in a country where the media are on top now ... The best possible defence against them for somebody in your position is to have nothing to do with them. Never speak to them under any circumstances. That will minimize the danger and damage they can do to you. She agreed ... but of course she didn't because she thought she could [manipulate them], so they got her.

'The second thing I said was "No sex". I said, "That is absolutely fatal. You'll have to do without it and be very virginal and so on, and, if you don't like it – hard cheese." That made her laugh and she said, "Oh, you're so right, absolutely", and the next thing you knew she was in bed with x ...'[17]

The *Telegraph* editor, Max Hastings, not known for his susceptibility to women, found himself unable to resist invitations to Kensington Palace, his low opinion of the Prince of Wales making him more open to the Princess. Diana had wangled an introduction to him through her friends Peter and Hayat Palumbo and had charmed him as thoroughly as she did most men, as he wrote in his diary: 'I was obliged to acknowledge ... that like others of my kind, I found myself unable to keep my distance ... Diana ... had become a masterly media lobbyist. Selected journalists and editors were regularly invited to see her. Most of us deluded ourselves that we were offering her advice. I am not aware of any instance in which she acted upon any of the sage words that were offered. But of course, she charmed us brilliantly.'[18]

Anthony Holden, writing in *Vanity Fair*, detected a master plan to establish Diana in her own right: 'Diana's staff is discreetly orchestrating a rapid move to centre stage, an upgrading from minor to major player in a drama whose plot gets thicker every time',[19] citing as an example Diana's stunningly successful solo visit to Paris the previous November when she had been feted by President Mitterrand as if she were a Head of State and not a mere 'semi-detached member of the Royal Family'. Diana wanted a role as ambassador-at-large, and courted John Major and sympathetic ministers like the Foreign Secretary, Douglas Hurd (and subsequently his successor, Malcolm Rifkind). As Foreign Secretary and therefore in a position to authorize and assist her foreign excursions, Hurd was a particular target. At a European summit in Edinburgh just two days after the announcement of her separation, Hurd described Diana in his memoirs as 'bestowing that special mixture of beauty and charm which melted men's bones. Presidents, prime ministers and foreign ministers as they dined could make no sense of what was happening in our Royal Family,' he wrote, 'but were content to bask for an hour or two in an extraordinary radiance.'[20] Hurd wrote that there was never any question of her having a formal appointment as a roving ambassador but that the good causes with which she was associated wanted her help overseas and she was keen to provide it. 'She looked to me for support in just one matter important to her . . . her overseas work. I was glad, or more accurately, enchanted, to give it.'[21]

In March, Diana toured Nepal to view British aid projects in the official company of the minister concerned, Lynda Chalker. While Prince Charles, attended by a much reduced press pack, was pictured glumly trying his hand at peasant farming in Mexico, the Princess, against the more colourful background of Kathmandu, attracted a good deal of media attention, much of which focused on the non-playing of the national anthem when she arrived, interpreted as a Palace downgrading of Diana, which it was not. This was a simple working visit, not a state occasion, and the absence of the anthem had passed without notice on similar visits to Egypt, Pakistan and Hungary before the separation. While Douglas Hurd was at pains to stress that at no time did the Palace seek to downgrade Diana or cut her contact with the Foreign Office, St James's Palace, the Prince's office, was a different matter altogether. At a party held in St James's around the time of Diana's Nepal visit, ostensibly concerning historic buildings in Prague, a guest was 'absolutely appalled that all that had happened at this party was people trashing Diana; they never talked about historic buildings in Prague at all'.[22]

As with Nepal, Diana's tour of Zimbabwe in July was a resounding success. Diana had taken care not only to keep the Queen informed of her plans but also Princess Anne, who had made charitable visits to Africa her particular territory. Nor did she seek to meet Heads of State as of right; she had no need to. A beaming Robert Mugabe told the press: 'She brings a little light into your life . . . naturally you feel elated, you feel good!'[23] The presence and cooperation of the top management of Diana's three charities relevant to her tour – the Red Cross, Help the Aged and the Leprosy Mission – gave the visit a serious, humanitarian aspect. On a visit to a hospice for children orphaned by AIDS, Diana wept: none of the children was over five years old and none was expected to reach the age of six.[24] Comments by the more respected correspondents on the tour emphasized the need for Diana's work to be taken seriously. Robert Hardman, then court correspondent for the *Daily Telegraph*, a newspaper usually expected to take the 'traditional', sceptical, view of Diana wrote approvingly: 'The latest tour has been a public relations triumph not just for her favourite charities but for the Princess herself. Africa, until now the undisputed realm of the Princess Royal [Anne], has a new champion . . .' He also delivered a warning on behalf of his more sophisticated and cynical readers: 'Visits are vital if the Princess is to maintain her world profile and thus continue the work she sees as her mission. But she will need to use them sparingly and vary the diet. Too much of what cynics call the Mother Teresa routine could lead to compassion indigestion by the media . . .'[25]

Yet Diana was sincere in her compassion, despite the 'Mother Teresa' moments. From Harare she flew out to the Red Cross

Mazerera feeding centre in the bush. Diana stood by a huge iron cooking pot doling out food to tiny children who had trekked seven miles on foot for their only meal of the day. It made a great photo opportunity – one British newspaper ran the headline 'DINNER LADY' – DIANA SERVES UP ROYAL TREAT FOR HUNGRY CHILDREN' – but, Ken Wharfe recalled, she was close to tears as she recounted her experiences of the day, knowing that she was going back to her comfortable life while the children were returning to poverty, drought and hunger. 'Those who believe that Diana's work was nothing more than a series of photo-opportunities in glamorous locations around the world,' he wrote, 'should have seen this drained, exhausted woman sitting in the back of the helicopter that day and heard her speak of the heart-breaking scenes she had just witnessed.'[26]

At home, Diana concentrated on women's issues to which she could relate. Determined to be seen as a professional, she employed a voice coach, Peter Settelen, to teach her voice techniques to improve her public speaking. She visited the Chiswick Family Refuge for women victims of domestic violence in April 1993, following it up with several visits and attendance at a high-profile conference on domestic violence at the Queen Elizabeth II Conference Centre. A visit to Great Ormond Street Hospital, where she learned more about a subject close to her – eating disorders in young women – led to her speech in Kensington Town Hall in April 1993 which was widely publicized and brought eating disorders to the top of the public agenda. Diana was delighted with the speech, not only because Settelen had taught her how to express emotion in public speaking (too much so in the view of Diana's aides) but because she had come close to expressing her personal experience and suffering. As patron of the charity Turning Point, she spoke at a conference in June 1993 about the need for support of mentally ill women. The conference was chaired by Libby Purves who said, 'The [Princess] is one of us, a wife, a mother, a daughter who has known problems in her own life and who has courageously used these experiences to comfort other people.' It did not escape the general public that no other member of the Royal Family would have addressed personal issues in such a way.

On the world, or rather the European, stage, Diana's march towards acceptance as a major figure continued. In company with the Crown Prince of Luxembourg she attended a British trade fair; in Brussels as patron of Help the Aged she attended events and discussed provision for the elderly with the EU Commissioner for Social Affairs, took tea with Queen Fabiola and attended a reception at the British Ambassador's residence. In London, at the invitation of Conrad Black, she was a guest at the Hollingsworth dinner at Spencer House, which her family still owned, among a crowd of all the top people in the British and American media, and in Cambridge she laid the foundation stone of the new Queen's Building at Emmanuel College at the invitation of Lord St John of Fawsley. 'All over the system which operated the interfaces between royalty and government,' Jephson summed up her achievements for the year, 'the simple reality was dawning that the Princess of Wales remained a major player, certainly in media terms.'

One of her last public engagements of 1993 served as a reminder of the quasi-royal status she had maintained through her own efforts that year. With the Queen's approval she headed the Remembrance Day service in Enniskillen, Northern Ireland. The ceremony was given additional poignancy by the memory of the same service in the same place six years before when eleven people had been blown up by an IRA bomb. The square still bore the scars of that terrible day, as did many of the people standing there. Diana, slim, elegant and solemn, stood at the head of the mourners and soldiers, prime target of a terrorist attack had there been another one. During the two minutes' silence, a pair of swans flew directly overhead, silhouetted against the clear winter sky. 'Did you see the birds?' she asked Jephson. 'It was so moving. I couldn't help feeling they meant something.' 'You mean the spirit of the dead?' he asked. 'Yes. Something like that. Or peace.'[27]

But underneath the smoothly regal exterior, the conflicting currents of her private life were pushing her towards yet another self-destructive, contradictory decision. Another door closed on her former life with the death that summer of Ruth Fermoy. Lady Fermoy had been deeply upset by the Morton book and the separation, ashamed in front of her fellow courtiers that her own granddaughter should have been responsible for going public with the details of her unhappy marriage. Even before the Morton bombshell, Diana had regarded her grandmother as siding with her enemies, telling Morton that on the Queen Mother's ninetieth birthday (4 August 1990) the atmosphere had been 'grim and stilted'. 'They are all anti-me,' she added. 'My grandmother has done a good hatchet job on me.'[28] There had been several angry exchanges between them in the past, and at one point, after Ruth had been particularly critical of her behaviour, Diana threw her grandmother out of the house. As Lady Fermoy was dying, Diana made two visits to her, so at least she was on terms with her when she did die. She flew to Lady Fermoy's funeral with her grandmother's old friend and employer, the Queen Mother, who undoubtedly shared her lady-in-waiting's view of Diana's behaviour. The previous month she had closed another old feud, with Raine, Countess Spencer, inviting her to lunch at Kensington Palace with her new husband, the Comte de Chambrun. The two women now got on famously and frequently lunched together over the following years. The reconciliation was part of Diana's campaign to clear her life of past unpleasantness wherever she could. An element in the reconciliation may also have been Diana's urge to spite her brother Charles after a recent row.

As part of her new life Diana had envisaged a country house as a bolt hole from the fortress of Kensington Palace, somewhere she could take the boys during holiday times and the weekends which they spent with her. In June her brother Charles had offered her the Garden House on the Althorp estate at a rent of £12,000 a year. Diana rushed down with Dudley Poplak to make plans for the house, highly excited at the prospect of a new home of her own. A fortnight later her hopes were dashed when her brother wrote withdrawing his offer on the grounds that the police and press interference caused by her presence on the estate would make family life impossible at Althorp, and suggesting she should rent a farmhouse outside the park if she wanted to. 'Diana used to say "At least my family never let me down",' said one of her staff. 'And then they did.' When the letter arrived she called the member of staff (it was not, as Paul Burrell later alleged, himself) upstairs and showed him the letter, dreadfully upset. She was devastated, then angry, writing her brother a letter in which she no doubt expressed her feelings as strongly as she could. When he telephoned she slammed down the receiver, and when Charles Spencer received her letter he returned it unopened, with the comment that he doubted whether reading it 'would help our relationship'.[29] Communication between them ceased for a few months, and it seems their relationship was never quite the same as it had been before the Garden House row. In the opinion of Ken Wharfe, who, as the Princess's protection officer, was in a position to know: 'Spencer couldn't have been more helpful. He offered her the house on the estate which was actually too small and I actually said it was too near the perimeter fence. He even offered her his house, the Pheasantry, within the grounds of his estate . . . [but] the local police were having heart attacks by the day and when they did present their security plans I said, "Well, maybe they have a case" . . .'[30] Significantly, in view of future developments, the episode strengthened her determination to get rid of her police protection. 'He [Spencer] has a point,' she told Ken Wharfe despondently. 'Why would anyone want the fuss that goes with me?'[31]

Another disagreement took place between Diana and two of her closest friends that spring. Known as 'the Leap of Lech' it was a reckless move even by Diana's impetuous standards. At the end of March 1993, Diana took her boys skiing in a party which included her friends Catherine Soames and Kate Menzies and their children. The reaction of the international paparazzi was a foretaste of the problem which was to dog Diana until the end. Diana was a cash cow to the photographers who competed fiercely with each other to get the best, that is, the closest and most dramatic, shot. Not content with a photo opportunity on the slopes, they crowded

round the Princess and her sons as they entered the Hotel Arlberg
where they were staying. Diana, unusually for her, began to panic,
screaming 'Go Away' at the paparazzi. Ken Wharfe stepped in
and pushed one particularly persistent man to the ground; there
followed a mêlée during which Wharfe was able to shepherd Diana
and the boys inside. Diana, Wharfe said, was on an emotional
see-saw throughout the holiday. 'Her feelings about Hoare had
unsettled her. She was falling out with everybody right, left and
centre, seemingly unable to help herself . . . She had always been
erratic but in the past she had invariably pulled herself back from
the brink.'[32] Not this time. In the small hours of the morning,
when all the hotel's outside doors were firmly locked, Diana
jumped from her first-floor balcony, a twenty-foot drop, into deep
snow and took off without informing any of her protection squad.

She returned at 5.30 in the morning. Immediate speculation was
that she had gone to meet Oliver Hoare, who was staying at Zurs,
but had she done that she would have had to take a taxi, and the
whole adventure would have been too risky even for risk-taking
Diana. A more likely hypothesis was that she was escaping from
her party in order to meet a journalist with whom she was on
close terms. Kate Menzies and Catherine Soames were in Diana's
confidence. They knew about James Hewitt and no doubt about
Oliver Hoare and they would have understood a romantic escap-
ade; but contact with a journalist, however honourable he might
be, was another matter altogether. Apparently they told Diana
exactly what they thought, which did not please her. Diana, like
her separated husband, did not take criticism well.

Underlying Diana's actions at this period was her media war
with her husband. Even holidays with the boys could be turned to
her advantage. Pictures showing her at Disneyland, Florida, or on
the beach with William and Harry would serve to underline in the
public mind what a good mother she was, the subtext being
comparison with her selfish, uncaring husband. Arriving at Disneyland in August 1993, Ken Wharfe noted that Diana's chief channel
to the media, Richard Kay, was booked to arrive the same day
as Diana, at the same hotel, and that the booking had been made

on the very day Diana had told Wharfe she would like to go to Florida. Unfortunately for the British press, although they had been mysteriously alerted to her movements, the Disney system of VIP security frustrated them: not one photograph appeared in the press. Moving on to the Menzies' house on the smart development of Lyford Cay in the Bahamas, Diana still appeared angry and upset by a telephone call from her lawyer which reminded her of the problems with her husband awaiting her back home. She made attempts to be photographed which, for security reasons, Wharfe frustrated. 'I'll do what I want,' she told him. 'I think it's so unfair that I can't do what I want. I just want to be normal . . .'[33]

On their return to England, Diana began to give Wharfe the cold shoulder, the inevitable preamble to dismissal. The atmosphere between them became so frosty that Wharfe decided to jump before he was pushed. It had been building up for some time: Wharfe's attempts to prevent her doing what she wanted, however unwise, and his readiness to criticize her when she was going wrong, had angered the Princess. Others speculated that the parting had come because Wharfe knew too much about her, having seen her in some very unroyal situations. Wharfe himself speculated that Oliver Hoare had had a hand in it, as the two men disliked each other and Wharfe had first-hand knowledge of their affair. Another member of the Waleses' staff, her chauffeur, Simon Solari, left at around the same time as Wharfe. Like Wharfe, he had become the subject of her suspicions since, as her driver, he knew a great deal about her movements and she began to wonder whether he could be trusted not to betray her. He therefore elected to change to working for the Prince as one of his valets. As such he too was to fall foul of Michael Fawcett.

Perhaps the last straw was Wharfe's attitude to the 'gym photos' affair when photographs of Diana working out at a gym – LA Fitness in west London – originally taken in May 1993, were published in the *Sunday Mirror* in November. The 'Peeping Tom' pictures caused an outcry against the *Mirror* for invading Diana's privacy and she took legal action against the newspaper. Wharfe suspected – and he was not alone – that Diana had colluded with

Bryce Taylor, the owner of the gym, to have the pictures taken to use against the *Mirror*. 'I remain convinced,' he wrote, 'that she had invented an elaborate sting to ensnare a newspaper and then milk the publicity – and the public's sympathy – for all they were worth.'[34] Wharfe knew Diana well enough by then to understand that such a devious plan was not beyond her. Yet, despite everything that had passed between them, the loyal detective appreciated Diana's unique qualities: 'She was a truly inspirational woman who had the ability to change things for the better. She knew how to lift people from the greyness of normality and make them feel truly special. She did the same with me.'[35]

Despite colluding in these invasions of privacy – as she undoubtedly did in manipulating the media to ensure the maximum publicity for herself – Diana was becoming increasingly resentful over her lack of a private life and the demands made on her by her public role. She felt that she could no longer bear the restrictions of having a protection officer always with her, aware of her every move, in power over her to the extent that either the media or her husband could reveal her private life and its secrets. In November, in the wake of the gym photos furore, she decided on a second headstrong, reckless step on the path to self-destruction. In a single speech on 3 December, delivered at the Dorchester at a meeting in aid of the Headway Foundation, she threw overboard all the good work she had done that year in establishing a role for herself. She intended, she said, to withdraw to a considerable extent from public life: 'I hope you can find it in your hearts to understand and to give me the time and space that has been lacking in recent years . . .' she said. 'When I started my public life twelve years ago, I understood that the media might be interested in what I did. I realized that their attention would inevitably focus on . . . our private lives. But I was not aware of how overwhelming that attention would become; nor the extent to which it would affect both my public duties and my personal life in a manner that's been hard to bear . . .'

While she emphasized that her decision had the backing of the Queen and Prince Philip (who had in fact, without success, attempted to prevent her from injecting so much drama into her decision) she conspicuously omitted mentioning Prince Charles, whose publicity campaign against her, she implied, had had much to do with her decision.

When she sat down, obviously upset, with her head down, biting her lip, tears sprang to her eyes. The main beneficiaries of Diana's high profile – the media and charity organizations – were bewildered. One pressman expressed their feelings when he asked rhetorically, 'Have we killed the goose that lays the golden eggs?' It did not take long for the tabloids to find the villain of the piece: 'CHARLES FORCED DIANA TO GO: SAD PRINCESS QUITS PUBLIC LIFE' was the *Sun*'s headline, its theme being that 'the campaign to downgrade' Diana and Charles's 'sophisticated propaganda machine' had driven her out. But, as usual with Diana, the motives for her dramatic decision were not quite so simple.

15. The Inconsequential Years

'If I can't believe what I've been told about her . . . then I can't believe any of it' (Jonathan Dimbleby[1])

As always with Diana there were many motives that had persuaded her to announce her withdrawal from public life. One was that she truly felt she needed 'time and space' for herself. Since the separation, she had carried on alone, trying to keep up with the public work so necessary for maintaining her profile, making an effort for her public, fighting her media war with her husband and seeking to manipulate her own publicity. In the white glare of the media spotlight she had become anxious that people close to her should remain loyal, should not reveal the darker corners of her life. She had become, to some extent, paranoid. It is easy to blame her for her publicity seeking; her determination to make a public drama of her withdrawal with the Headway speech had caused consternation to her aides and Buckingham Palace and there had been anxious conferences over the drafting of her speech in an effort to tone down its effect.

There is no doubt that Diana was under extreme pressure. The separation had left her lonely, abandoned, bitter, sad and uncertain of the future. 'I think she always had this issue within herself,' said the daughter of one of her closest friends, 'which was "I want to be the Princess of Wales, I want to be Charles's wife and I want to have a normal family life". Finally she didn't have any of that. She was no longer Charles's wife. It's very hard to find a role for yourself and she wanted to be loved, she was constantly seeking approval, constantly, there was not a minute off. And I think she felt she was rejected by her mother; her mother left, her husband left her and I don't think it's easy for a woman in her position to

Diana and William photographed with Dodi (left) and Mohamed Al Fayed at a polo match in 1988.

June 1989: Charles and Diana with William and Harry prepare for a cycling trip in Tresco during their holiday in the Scilly Isles.

Diana returns to her old school, Riddlesworth Hall, and walks in the grounds with pupils and her former headmistress. Ken Wharfe, her protection officer, can be glimpsed at the far left.

Diana and Charles at an Arab feast on their tour of the Gulf States in March 1989.

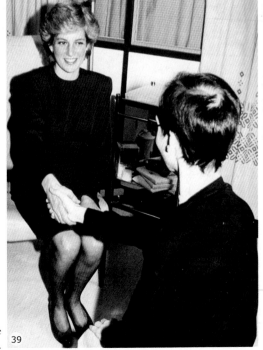

The notorious AIDS handshake that made headlines.

Will Carling (left) and Diana at Twickenham.

James Gilbey pictured post–'Squidgygate' revelations.

Charles and Diana walking at Highgrove, 1989.

1 July 1990: Diana collects Charles from Cirencester Hospital, his arm in a sling after a polo accident. She drove straight to Kensington Palace after he made it clear that Camilla would nurse him.

43

Diana and William share tender moment.

44

São Paulo, Brazil, April 1991: Diana visits a hostel for abandoned children, many of whom are HIV positive or suffering from AIDS.

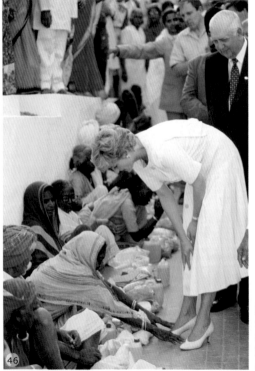

Hyderabad, India, February 1992: Diana visits Mianpur Old Age Welfare Centre and has her feet touched as a sign of respect.

Lech, Austria, 30 March 1992: Diana and Charles leave their skiing holiday after news of Earl Spencer's death. Diana could not bear the thought of yet another 'happy families' act for the media and it took a telephone call from the Queen to persuade her to make a joint journey back to England.

Public sympathy causes Diana to break down on a visit to Ashworth Hospice, Liverpool, in 1992, just as Andrew Morton's book, *Diana: Her True Story*, is serialized.

Oliver Hoare, 1994, pictured as the news breaks that Diana has been making anonymous telephone calls to his house.

Diana and her sisters, Sarah (left) and Jane (right), after a night out.

South Korea, November 1992. 'The Glums': Charles and Diana on their last official trip together, attending a presidential banquet in Seoul. Their separation would be announced one month later.

have so much pressure, to have so many eyes on you that analyse everything you do every single day. I would have gone bonkers myself.'[2]

In her quest for personal freedom, Diana took the step which was ultimately to have fatal implications: she dispensed with her right to police protection. If it momentarily gave her a feeling of liberation, it also left her open to persecution by the paparazzi who became increasingly merciless. Only a few months later, in May 1994, flying out to Malaga on a private holiday with friends, she found herself totally unprotected on arrival at the airport and things did not improve over the rest of the holiday when she was stalked with long-range lenses. One photographer succeeded in getting a 'topless' photograph of Diana sunbathing when she adjusted a strap. Eduardo Junco, proprietor of *Hola!*, the original model of *Hello!*, picked up news of the photographs and bought them to prevent their publication. In London photographs were taken of her panic-stricken dodging round parked cars outside the house of her therapist, Susie Orbach, and in other places where she could be expected to be found. All of this was a direct consequence of her dismissal of her protection officers, and the situation was to become worse.

And there was a personal reason. Asked why Diana had taken the decision when she did, a close friend said: 'Because at that moment she thought she'd be able to have a normal life with someone else . . . That was her explanation at the time.'[3] The 'someone else' was Oliver Hoare. The 'anonymous' telephone calls to Hoare's house had resumed in 1993. Naturally, Diane Hoare became angry and suspicious, as his chauffeur later told the newspapers. Around the time of Diana's speech, she threw her husband out and he retreated to a friend's flat in Pimlico. The move no doubt raised Diana's hopes of a happy ending. Her confidante Elsa Bowker, to whom Hoare had introduced her, told Diana's biographer that Diana wanted to marry Hoare and buy a house in Italy with him. Hoare had told Elsa Bowker that he thought Diana 'was radiant inside and he loved that'; he had, Bowker said, 'done a lot for her. He helped give her confidence but it was never enough. Diana had wonderful qualities of heart but she was terribly possessive. If she loved someone, he had to leave everything, including children. Her possessiveness frightened men. Everything became a drama.'[4] As Sally Bedell Smith told it, Oliver Hoare was confronted with the magnitude of Diana's insecurities one evening when his wife was away and he had to be with his sick daughter. Diana refused to believe that this was not an excuse to go and see his wife and, as he was driving her home, she jumped out of the car in a traffic jam in Sloane Square and disappeared. Hoare was so worried that he never got to see his daughter, instead spending three hours driving round London looking for Diana. He finally found her weeping in Kensington Gardens near the Palace.[5]

In January 1994, after a two-month separation. Hoare returned to his wife. Diana can no longer have been under the illusion that he would leave his wife and children. 'He is a very good father, a good person,' a mutual friend said. 'He always said he could never leave his family.'[6] The relationship continued nonetheless and was noted by the media: In December 1993 they had been seen sitting together in his car for an hour, Diana's head on his shoulder. They breakfasted together at 7 a.m. at the Chelsea Harbour Club where Diana was currently working out, and in March 1994 they were caught by a photographer driving into Kensington Palace after dinner with a friend. The theme was still favourable, rather than prurient. Diana, one newspaper reported, was tearfully pouring out her heart to her loyal friend.[7] More dangerously still, after Hoare returned to his wife in January the silent calls to his house had resumed. By now, after complaints from the Hoares the previous October, the police had equipped their telephone with a computerized code that could activate tracers. Over the next six days the police had tracked a dozen silent calls made between 8 a.m. and midnight originating from Kensington Palace and Diana's mobile telephone.[8] When, on police advice, Hoare challenged Diana by name, the calls stopped for a while but then started up again, traced to public telephone booths in Kensington and Notting Hill. Scotland Yard alerted the head of the Royalty and Diplomatic Protection Department; a message was conveyed from the Palace to Kensington Palace, intimating that a prosecution under nuisance call laws might be considered. The calls stopped but Diana's relationship with Oliver Hoare had continued.

Andrew Morton, who was preparing a follow-up book on Diana post-separation (*Diana: Her New Life*) for publication in 1994, asserted that the influence of Diana's astrologers could not be ruled out in the motivation of her decision and its timing. Diana believed that she would never be Queen but, equally, that Charles would never be King, his exit being either voluntary, abdication in favour of William, or involuntary, by accidental death. Recently, apparently, one of them had predicted that, owing to his unpopularity, Charles would have to resign as heir to the throne, leaving that position to William.[9] Another version of this continuing theme was that he would retreat to Italy with Camilla and fulfil himself by painting. Diana saw her eventual role in relation to the monarchy as Queen Mother, guiding the destinies of William, the future King.

'My boys' – or, as Gilbey had put it in the Squidgygate conversation of 1989, the 'lovebugs' – remained the unchanging focus of her life. Both were now boarding at their preparatory school, Ludgrove. When they were away, Diana was lonely at home by herself at Kensington Palace. She deeply missed her greatest friend, Lucia Flecha de Lima, and her family with whom she had been used to spend the weekends, when they left for a new post in Washington in November 1993. When the boys were at home for the prescribed weekends or part holidays, her life revolved around them. Diana has been pictured as an empty-headed woman with no idea beyond her personal benefit, but, perhaps because of her own experience of a hereditary position, and the importance of 'the heir', she understood very well the meaning of the hereditary monarchy and William's place in the scheme of things. Despite her own difficulties with her husband and his family, she was not about to deflect those problems on to her children. She was determined that they should be brought up in as 'normal' (one of her favourite words) a way as possible both at home and in the world outside. This went beyond expeditions to Thorpe Park and Disneyland, or shopping expeditions when they, unlike other members of the Royal Family, paid with their own money; she took them to share her own experiences of people much less fortunate than themselves. While some of the Royal Family – including the boys' father – disapproved of the ultra-democratic way in which they were brought up, Diana believed it was essential for them to see life beyond the royal enclave in a way which it had not been thought important for their father to experience.

William in particular learned to be at ease with the homeless; later, when Harry was old enough, she involved him too. Diana had already visited The Passage on her own in June 1989. On two subsequent occasions, inspired by her friend the Catholic Archbishop of Westminster, Cardinal Basil Hume, she took first William and then both boys to The Passage Day Centre and Night Centre attached to Westminster Cathedral. Diana and William arrived on 20 December 1993 unannounced; there were no press with her, nor did the people in The Passage know that she was coming. Sister Bridie Dowd, director of The Passage at the time, recalled how, when they walked into The Passage, a long area with people sitting at tables along the wall, the atmosphere was electric: 'They just moved to their feet right away. They were so taken with the fact that she was there.' Diana, shadowed by Sister Bridie, had difficulty moving among the people and talking to them because 'they wanted to hold on to her, because she had that great ability to listen to people and really to make you feel that she heard every word that you were saying and even what you weren't saying . . . She made you feel that she was listening with her eyes as well as her ears. Her eye contact was very very special . . .'[10]

Diana told Sister Bridie that she 'wanted William to be aware of the other side of life. She didn't want him to grow up cosseted. And she had talked to him about it and he had seen photographs and said he would like to visit. So that was his first visit to any centre for homeless people. It was before he went to Centrepoint. And that was a huge thing for him to do because going into The

Passage was very intimidating. There could be a hundred people in The Passage at any one time. People from all walks of life who for one reason or another had experienced difficulties, who had dropped out of society for whatever reason. Some who had been to university . . . two university lecturers, ex-priests, a very broad mix of people . . . Many of them were street homeless, others were homeless living in hostels . . . people who were insecurely housed, people who were lonely or people who had drink problems . . .'[11] 'There were people who have been in the army and when they left just weren't able to cope, two nurses who were not well enough in themselves to keep a job, people whose marriages haven't worked out, people who have been made redundant.' They would be made welcome, given a cup of tea, breakfast, lunch; there were washing facilities, showers and clothing stores, education classes and counselling. And William? 'He was very shy initially and stayed close to Mum for a while,' Sister Bridie said. 'But the people were very good and very sensitive to his needs and talked to him about football. Once he got talking to them he was absolutely fine. He was reserved. He was a child, but you could see the potential there.'[12] Later both William and Harry accompanied their mother to the Night Centre and played chess with the people there. Diana's vision of a popular monarchy was a potent one which was to survive her death, even in an attenuated form.

Diana was concerned for William who was sensitive and to some extent, like his father, a worrier. It was, after all, William on whom she leaned in her unhappy periods, who had listened at doors and heard things it would have been better for him not to have heard. Despite that, theirs was a very normal, not a neurotic relationship. Anybody who has listened to the Settelen tapes broadcast on NBC will have heard the boys jeering their mother good-humouredly when they thought she had gone too far – 'Isn't she *awful*!!' She was less concerned about Harry, a cheeky, cheerful boy who had inherited her optimistic temperament but none of her problems. Sensitive to the fact that the boys' future positions would be so very unequal, she was intent on involving them both

in their future role. William would be King but it was important
to them both that Harry should be there to support him.

In the background over the two years since the separation
were the long drawn-out divorce negotiations, pressed by Charles,
fended off at a meeting in October 1993 by Diana, who repeatedly
told friends that she did not want to divorce. Both sides man-
oeuvred to win over public opinion. Since the summer of 1992,
Charles's camp had planned a riposte to Andrew Morton's book
that would win back the high ground for the Prince. 'Prince
Charles wanted it as a justification after the Morton book,' one of
his close circle recalled.[13] This was to be a biography by the
broadcaster Jonathan Dimbleby, already seen by the Prince as a
sympathetic figure for his green views and the fact that he had
once worked at Windsor Home Farm. It was to be an authorized
book based on interviews with the Prince's friends and staff and
use of the Prince's correspondence and diaries. Officially, it was to
mark the twenty-fifth anniversary of Charles's investiture as Prince
of Wales. It had initially been intended as a television documentary:
'Well, the original concept when I was involved was a celebratory
documentary to mark his twenty-fifth anniversary,' recalled Dickie
Arbiter. 'Harmless sort of thing, jolly fine fellow, the organizations,
bland but big plug for the organizations rather than for the man,
because the organizations are the key . . . so we use that vehicle.
Then Aylard moved the goalposts. "The Prince has decided that
[it should include personal matters]" and I said, "I'm sure the
Prince hasn't decided that, I'm sure you've decided, but you do
realize it's going to be warts and all?" He said, "Oh, we'll do that."
And I said, "Richard, I really do mean WARTS AND ALL."
And he said, "Yes, go ahead." So I said, "Well, I'll do your bidding
because that's my job to lay on the facilities for the crew, but I
don't agree with it."'

The project was given a cautious welcome by the Palace who
may have hoped to monitor it – 'fact-checking' – but refused
cooperation by Diana's staff who, rightly as it turned out, foresaw
that a panegyric to the Prince could hardly fail to be unfavourable
to the Princess. The Prince and his camp cannot be blamed for

aiming to raise his public profile and to emphasize the good work he did, which was still often derided or ignored. The effect of the Morton book on his reputation had been devastating, and the efforts of his friends through the media had been largely unsuccessful. A tabloid editor said, 'Charles's friends, Romseys, van Cutsems, etc, were at it all the time, ringing me up, giving me stuff . . .'[14] Charles, it seems, could not win. Diana worked her magic even on Jonathan Dimbleby. Although she had refused an interview, exposure to her personality over lunch had its intended effect.

'The Princess,' Jephson wrote, 'put on a great performance in which regality and informality were mixed in proportions that would frustrate the most determined critic. She ate her lunch with obvious enthusiasm and laughingly sympathised with Dimbleby's Herculean task on the Prince's behalf. After she had departed in a cloud of fond farewells, I caught on Jonathan's face the dazed look familiar to me from so many others who had just received her dazzling best . . .'

Asked how the impression he had received compared with what he had been told, he seemed 'momentarily uncomfortable', replying: 'if I can't believe what I've been told about her . . . then I can't believe any of it'.[15]

The programme went out on 29 June 1994. Given the personal content, it seems unlikely that the Palace would have had any input beyond providing facilities. There was apprehension among the Queen's circle, and rightly so, as it turned out. 'He's on a hiding to nothing' was the general opinion, hoping that it might not be even worse. They were as yet unaware of just how personal the programme would turn out to be; those who were begged the Prince not to do it. One of his aides resigned. The main thrust of the programme, the public man, his charities and his views of the causes he believed in, came across as a sympathetic portrait of a good man with serious intentions. The programme was aimed at the young, the future King's constituency, showing the Prince, normally an indifferent television performer, at his best as an environmental crusader, speaking articulately, passionately and without notes. With pop star Phil Collins at a holiday camp organized by his successful inner-city youth help foundation, the Prince's Trust, he appeared at ease and in his element.

Unfortunately, the 'hook' of the programme for which it would always be remembered was his answer to Jonathan Dimbleby's direct question as to whether he had been faithful in his marriage. Charles replied that he had – until his marriage 'had irretrievably broken down'. He went further to describe Camilla Parker Bowles as a 'very dear friend' whom he would continue to see. Nothing could have been calculated to infuriate Diana more. It invited a response and, in due course, one would be forthcoming.

While the general public applauded the Prince for his honesty, people close to the Royal Family, and indeed the Waleses and Camilla, were unanimous in their condemnation. Charles had complained of the media's insensitivity to the feelings of his sons with their 'Charles v Di' stories but here he was on television watched by millions, first pictured relaxing with his sons and then confessing that he had been unfaithful to their mother. The royal establishment from top to bottom was shocked. Chief among Diana's crimes had been 'speaking to the media' but here was the heir to the throne publicly proclaiming his adultery and, not only that, his devotion to his mistress and his intention to carry on exactly as he had been doing in the past. The most charitable view was that he and Diana 'had been driven mad by the media'. 'That's what brought the house down . . . the advice had been "Look, don't talk about your marriage at all, let Jonathan ask you as many questions as he likes but you just say 'Look, my marriage, just like anybody else's, is entirely private'." [He should have said] "It's not your business and it's not the audience's business" and the whole of England would have stood up and said, "Good on you. Absolutely right." So what mileage was there in talking about it? It was a red rag to a bull . . .'[16] At Balmoral Charles asked a close friend, the Duchess of Westminster, what she thought about the interview. 'She was very outspoken and she said, "Well, actually, Sir, I didn't think it was very good" and he got into a frightful rage, didn't speak to her the whole weekend – he's very petty, Charles. He went straight to the private secretary [Aylard], blamed him, just flew at him, he screamed and shouted and yelled at him. I mean Charles is terribly spoiled . . .'[17]

Whatever the public approval rating may have been, in the words of the Palace aide the interview 'brought the house down' as far as the loyal household staff was concerned. It was indeed 'a red rag to a bull'. Several bulls, to be precise. Talking to the media had been the ultimate sin, inconceivable for a member of the Royal Family to do, and yet here was the heir to the throne admitting his adultery on television and pledging his loyalty to his mistress. Loyal servants were outraged. Charles's valet, Ken Stronach, 'the most loyal and discreet of all' according to colleagues, beside himself, went to a newspaper with damaging stories about Charles and Camilla. He repented and tried to withdraw; the newspaper went ahead anyway. The experience destroyed him. 'The general feeling was,' said his colleague, 'that having been made to sign things and lying down the line for their master, this has been [for them] the ultimate betrayal.'[18] Loyal staff, trained to absolute discretion following the example of the Queen and the Duke of Edinburgh, were dismayed, fearing that the monarchy was disintegrating. The reaction of a royal aide who went with a colleague to view the interview was: 'God Save the Queen, long may she reign over us.'

The other consequence of the programme, which in the end was to be more far-reaching in its effect, was Andrew Parker Bowles's decision to divorce Camilla. While he had been perfectly willing to countenance his wife's relationship with Prince Charles as long as it remained discreet – or, at least, not public knowledge – Charles's admission, coming as it did only just a year after the Camillagate tapes, had put their relationship beyond question, placing Parker Bowles in an impossible position. The day after the programme was broadcast, the Prince's private secretary, Richard Aylard, admitted in a press conference that the woman in question was Camilla. In January 1995 Andrew and Camilla Parker Bowles divorced.

Diana feigned indifference. On the evening the programme was shown, she fulfilled a long-standing engagement at the Serpentine

Gallery, photographed wearing a sexy, clinging black dress which showed off her tanned, toned legs. Her whole manner radiated confidence. 'She bounded out of the car in that wonderfully athletic way she had,' Peter Palumbo, who, as chairman of the gallery, was on hand to greet her, recalled.[19] The underlying message was, 'Look at me . . . look what you've thrown away and see how much I care.' The photograph appeared on all the front pages. The *Sun*'s take on it was: 'The Thrilla he left to woo Camilla', accompanied by an unflattering photograph of Camilla. While Diana was angry under the surface, she had a certain admiration for Charles's courage and honesty in revealing what he did, as, it appeared, did the general public. Her own riposte would have to wait until the notorious *Panorama* interview eighteen months later.

Beneath the radiance, Diana was concerned that her media image was slipping: the press knew that Diana manipulated her own publicity, tipping off favoured newspapers as to her whereabouts when she wanted them to be known. She had been hoist with her own petard in early June 1994 when she was photographed having a clandestine rendezvous with Richard Kay of the *Daily Mail* in his parked car. At the instance of his editor, David English, Kay had been assigned to Diana 'as a sympathetic ear' and had been working closely with her since 1993. Tall, lean, good-looking and transparently trustworthy, Kay had become genuinely friendly both with Diana and the Spencer family and had been acting as her media mouthpiece for some time. Jealous rival newspapers now had photographic evidence of her closeness to Kay, and a hypocritical howl of rage went up.

More trouble lay ahead. In March James Hewitt, at Diana's instigation, gave an interview to Anna Pasternak which was published in the *Daily Express*, giving an anodyne account of the relationship. Diana had asked him to talk to Andrew Morton but he had refused, finding in Pasternak what he thought to be a more sympathetic ear. As far as Diana was concerned, Hewitt said, 'It was a pre-emptive strike, but the rumours grew stronger than they were before.' Diana's strategy failed: where she had intended the public to swallow the story of an innocent friendship, Hewitt was roundly condemned for cashing in on their relationship. 'Diana was happy for it to go out,' Hewitt told Bedell Smith. 'But once it backfired, the support I got from her was non-existent . . .' Hewitt had already been ostracized in high-level quarters when knowledge of the affair became widespread. As an officer and a gentleman, it was thought, he should not have contemplated a physical affair with the wife of the heir to the throne. In March he had had to leave the army and his future seemed uncertain. Now Diana had cut him off for doing her bidding. He felt bitter and abandoned; the result would be Pasternak's Mills and Boon-ish version of the affair to be published in October 1994 as *Princess in Love*.

In mid-August 1994 Diana was holidaying with the Flecha de Limas on the fashionable island of Martha's Vineyard off the Massachusetts coast. Sally Bedell Smith, invited to join the party for lunch on the beach, noticed that Diana 'seemed strikingly subdued . . . preoccupied', moving her chair apart from the group to talk intently with her confidante and mentor, Lucia. Later she cut short her holiday and returned home. The reason was that she had learned that the Pasternak book about her affair with James Hewitt, based on the passionate letters she had written him in the Gulf, was to be published in the autumn. She was deeply upset at what she saw as this betrayal, although, had she been shrewd enough not to cut Hewitt, it might have been avoided.

August was not to be a good month in the media for Diana. Quite apart from the Hewitt rumours, the newspapers had picked up on the nuisance calls story with regard to Oliver Hoare: the public were amazed to read of Diana as a 'phone pest' which suggested that she was psychologically unstable. Diana asked Hoare to make a public statement; understandably, in consideration of his family, he refused. Women were understanding, considering that Diana, lonely and in need of reassurance, had wanted to hear Hoare's voice. Yet the fact that Hoare was married with children did show her in an unfavourable light. The scandal subsided but the negative publicity she had attracted and the revelation of her two affairs, which it implied, unnerved her.

Anna Pasternak's account of the Hewitt affair, which confirmed their physical relationship, was published on 3 October. However, Diana escaped lightly: after all, she had been abandoned by Charles for his lover and Hewitt was unmarried, so there was no 'marriage wrecker' shadow hanging over it. The ceiling fell in on Hewitt, who from then on became a tabloid hate figure. 'Love Rat and Cad' declared the *Sun* and it is by these epithets that he is apparently to be forever known. It was, after all, Diana who dumped Hewitt when it no longer suited her and she had found a new interest in Oliver Hoare. Hewitt had fallen genuinely in love with her and, if her later television confession is to be believed, she with him. He had given her confidence through some of her darkest days and she had emerged stronger with her confidence revived. Hewitt was naïve, gullible, the reverse of streetwise. He should have kept his mouth shut and never have allowed himself to be lured into cooperation with Pasternak but he did and paid for it. After that he was dead in the water while Diana sailed radiantly on.

At the time, however, she felt the betrayal deeply. In a letter dated 11 October 1994 to Chryssie Fitzgerald, the reflexologist who also carried out her colonic irrigation treatment, she described what had happened as 'THE toughest week yet I have had to face'; when she had come for her appointment she had been 'in a total state of shock and very distressed about Hewitt's so-called revelations'. She had been equally hurt, she wrote, on hearing what Sarah, Duchess of York, had said about her. The two women shared most of their therapists and psychics – Sarah to an almost excessive degree. Despite their rapprochement over the past two years, when they had made common ground over their troubles with the Royal Family, there was no real depth to their relationship and a considerable tinge of jealousy. Sarah, not infrequently and always unwisely, made her feelings about Diana known, sometimes to whoever answered the telephone at Kensington Palace. In this case she had obviously unburdened herself to Chryssie Fitzgerald. 'I never expected to hear on top of all that [the Hewitt revelations] about someone else's hatred for me & what accompanies those feelings,' Diana wrote. 'It hurt so [double underlined] much to hear from you, Chryssie, that Sarah found me a problem . . .' Chryssie and Diana appear to have parted company around that time, a frequent occurrence where Diana was concerned.

The great publishing event of the autumn was to be Jonathan Dimbleby's biography of the Prince, something to which Diana, with reason, had been looking forward with some apprehension. Dimbleby had done his estimable best to be fair; his remark to Jephson after his lunch with Diana was indicative of the kind of information he had been receiving about her from Charles's circle. It was, of course, the case for Charles, as opposed to Morton's case for Diana. Since Diana herself had first brought her depression, lack of self-confidence, bulimia and attempts at self-harm into the public domain with the Morton book, she could hardly complain about finding them reported in Dimbleby's biography. A quick glance at the index to the book would be enough to reinforce her fears: 'weight loss', volatile behaviour', 'jealousy of Camilla Parker Bowles', 'attempts to control the Prince's life', 'resentment of the Prince's interests', 'self-absorption', 'marriage breaks down irretrievably' . . .[20] This last, Dimbleby, forced to give a date by the Prince's television confession, attributed to 1986, illustrating this particularly with the Prince's failure to sympathize with Diana when she fainted in Canada on their official visit for Expo '86. 'The truth was that he had started to withdraw the support which for so long had drained his reserves of sympathy and compassion.' The truth was, rather, that Charles's failure to respond to her need for affection and his lack of understanding for her predicament (unlike his sympathetic reaction to her sister Sarah's anorexia) had been evident far earlier than the summer of 1986. Basically, the cause of Diana's affliction was not only post-natal depression after the birth of William but her early realization that Charles did not truly love her and that this marriage in which she had invested so much hope could never approximate to her romantic dreams. Charles's true love for Camilla Parker Bowles and his powerful sexual attraction to her above all other women had made those dreams impossible. Charles had abandoned Diana, not she him.

16. Towards a New World

'A friend . . . once asked her if she gambled. "Not with cards but with life . . ." [1]

Increasingly, as problems at home mounted, Diana had begun to see a new life for herself in the United States prompted, perhaps, by the refuge which the Flecha de Limas' embassy in Washington represented for her, as a home from home, just as the Mount Street embassy had been for her before they left. Jacqueline Kennedy Onassis's death from non-Hodgkin's lymphoma at the early age of sixty-four on 19 May 1994 had made worldwide news, her iconic status as American royalty confirmed by the solemn public manner of her passing. Mourning spectators and television cameras focused on her Fifth Avenue apartment, retailing pictures round the world. After JFK's assassination in 1963, Jackie, then as pressured by publicity and semi-royal status as Diana now was, had made her escape into the protection of Aristotle Onassis, whose vast wealth, private island and ocean-going yacht could provide her with the privacy she craved. When Jackie had returned to America permanently after Onassis's death, her friends had formed a praetorian guard around her and her quasi-royal status had won her respect and consideration from the paparazzi (with the notable exception of Ron Galella). If Jackie could do it, why couldn't she? Diana thought. Jackie still had her beauty, trailing clouds of glamour when she left America to marry Onassis in 1968 aged thirty-nine; when she returned for good in 1975 she was still beautiful but in her late forties and, to her fans, distant and mysterious. Diana was in her thirties, at the height of her radiant beauty and glamour. It was a delusion to think that she would ever have been left alone.

And there was even an Onassis figure on the horizon: billionaire

Teddy Forstmann, partner of Forstmann Little and chairman at the time of Gulfstream Aerospace, whom she had met through one of her particular mentors, Jacob Rothschild. Lord Rothschild, who was on the advisory board of Forstmann's company, had introduced her to Forstmann at an Independence Day dinner which he had given at Spencer House. Forstmann was charming with dark good looks and they had quickly become firm friends: later that summer they had met again and played tennis together when she was on holiday with Lucia Flecha de Lima and her family on Martha's Vineyard. 'He came over two or three times to see her,' a friend said. 'Friendly visits, I don't think they even held hands.' 'They didn't have an affair,' she went on, '[although] he was besotted by her . . . when she flicked those eyes [at him] . . . in a way Teddy would have been the ideal man for her, [but] Teddy is a very selfish man.' But, although Diana's thoughts were definitely tending in that direction, Forstmann's were not. He was level-headed enough not to want the disruption marriage to Diana would have caused in his life. 'She thought that way [i.e. marriage],' the friend said, 'but he didn't. There was a moment when she thought it would be a good idea for her because he had a private plane; she could come and go across the Atlantic to see her children. It was a problem for her to see her children but not to live in England. [But] I think in a way she knew that the only way out would be a non-Englishman with money.'[2] Patrick Jephson, who was with Diana on her second tour, was impressed with Forstmann: 'I think it was his common sense, delivered straight and with the confidence that only experience and pots of self-made money can bring, that was his greatest service to the Princess,' he wrote; '. . . what's more, he was kind to her.'[3]

In October she made a five-day visit to the United States which was an unqualified success. As opposed to the implacable hostility of the British Establishment and the hot and cold treatment given her by the British media, she was met with enthusiastic and uncritical appreciation. In New York the artist Nelson Shanks, who had painted what was generally considered to be the best portrait of Diana, gave a dinner for her at the National Arts Club in New

York where she was welcomed with a bear hug by one of her greatest admirers, Luciano Pavarotti. She stayed at the Carlyle Hotel (from then on her favourite hotel), where the manager, James Sherwin, made it a home from home for her, before flying by private jet, a Gulfstream IV provided by Forstmann, to Washington the next day to stay with the Flecha de Limas. Forstmann was her escort at a dinner given in her honour by the most influential woman in Washington, Katharine 'Kay' Graham, owner of the *Washington Post*.

Kay Graham had first met Diana when the Flecha de Limas brought her over to Graham's private beach on Martha's Vineyard. Later, Kay Graham recalled being immediately struck by Diana's 'natural, low-key charm'. 'We seemed to enjoy each other,' she wrote. 'From that point on we were able to have easy and candid conversations during long walks on the beach.' Diana came over to play tennis at Kay Graham's house. On the drive back to the Flecha de Limas, Diana talked 'lovingly' to Kay about her sons: 'I want them to grow up knowing there are poor people as well as palaces,' she said. 'If you spent time with her,' Kay Graham wrote, 'you felt Diana's extraordinary strength, as well as vulnerability and her somewhat mocking and ever-present sense of humour.' 'I asked her if she had ever thought of going to college now that she was alone,' she recalled. 'She found my question hard to believe, and commented with irony, "I've already had an education".' A friend of Graham's who met Diana on 'the Vineyard' once asked her if she gambled. 'Not with cards,' she answered, 'but with life.'[4]

On the Vineyard in August, Diana, just after she arrived, had heard that Elizabeth Glaser, with whom she had corresponded and who was a well-known AIDS patient, was on the island. Diana dropped everything to pay her a long private visit. In Washington that October, Diana was still searching for the right way to focus her energies. She had, she said, heaps of requests but she had to decide in which area she could do most good. 'Make sure it matters to you,' a fellow guest told her. 'Because if it doesn't you can't make it matter to others.'[5] Later she told Kay Graham that if she had to talk about a cause she would make sure that she went to

see the problem and learned about it first, saying that she was only
going to work in areas where she thought her presence could make
a difference.[6]

At a lunch given the next day in her honour by the British
Ambassador, Sir Robin Renwick, and his wife, Diana sat at a table
which included two major figures in American public life, the
President's wife, Hillary Clinton, and the hero of the Gulf War,
General Colin Powell, only recently retired as Chairman of the
Joint Chiefs of Staff. Diana and Colin Powell hit it off immediately:
then, after lunch, she retired for a private talk with Hillary Clinton
whom she had first met at the D-Day celebrations in June. The
two women had much in common: 'We talked of the challenges
of public life and the struggle to protect our children from the
scrutiny of the world,' Hillary recalled. 'She told me of her new
hopes and plans for using her position to focus attention on the
needs of suffering people. Although she seemed vulnerable and
unsure about the direction her life was taking, I sensed in her a
reservoir of resilience and determination that would help her take
charge of her own life and help others, despite great obstacles.'
Later in their relationship, Diana spoke with heartfelt feeling of
the 'disease' of not being loved.[7]

On her return to London Diana, still exhilarated by her experiences, wrote a note to Patrick Jephson, thanking him for his
'strength and support' and saying how 'thrilled' she was 'by the
new path we are treading'.[8] Jephson called it a delusion to think
that anything positive could come out of what had been not much
more than a happy social trip but at least, he added, it was a positive
delusion. After a year of more or less minor activity which had
included backing out of a suggested presence on the International
Committee of the Red Cross, Diana took up her charity work
again with enthusiasm. She visited two special hospitals for mental
patients, Carstairs in central Scotland and Broadmoor in southern
England, visiting Carstairs in the company of Jayne Zito, whose
fiancé had been killed by a schizophrenic mistakenly released into
the community. At Broadmoor, Diana attended – alone – a meeting of the patients' council which consisted of the patients them-

selves. 'I watched her take her seat in what was to be a private session of the council, surrounded by men who were thought to be a serious threat to the public,' Jephson wrote. 'As the door closed, I heard her voice and whatever she said raised an immediate warm laugh of greeting.'⁹ She ended the year visiting Paris in her role as President of Barnardo's, touring the community projects in the poorer parts of the city but ending on a regal note with a banquet in the Hall of Mirrors at the Palace of Versailles given in her honour where she charmed President Mitterrand. As she 'made a majestic exit', she was applauded by nine hundred guests: it was Diana 'going out to conquer the world'.

Meanwhile, Jonathan Dimbleby had published his biography of the Prince, serialized in the *Sunday Times* that autumn: Diana returned to find her husband and not herself the focus of publicity, very little of it favourable. Well written and authoritative though the book was, it was also, unsurprisingly, one-sided. Everything that had gone wrong in Charles's life was somebody else's fault, particularly inadequate parenting by a remote mother and a bullying father who had been 'unable or unwilling to proffer . . . the affection and appreciation' Charles had craved. Diana's neuroses were to blame for the failure of the marriage. Only Camilla emerged with any credit from the Prince's self-pitying account. As one reviewer put it, she was portrayed as a kind of virginal Mills and Boon heroine: 'Her warmth, her lack of ambition or guile, her good humour and her gentleness endeared her to the household . . .' Dimbleby wrote.

In mid-September, pre-publication, there had been 'a terrific explosion from the Queen' when it was discovered that the Prince had handed over to Dimbleby a drawerful of papers which included not just his childhood diaries but also State Papers, without bothering to check what was there. He was forced to take them back and go through them. Recently he had been staying with his grandmother at Birkhall. 'He'll only be coming here for one day,' the Queen said grimly. 'And he chose the day of the Ghillies' Ball when there wouldn't be time to talk,' a courtier recalled.¹⁰ The general opinion among the Royal Family and the household was that 'it was a great error to do this book at all. In fact washing your dirty linen in public for somebody in that position is a very stupid thing to do,' said a courtier. 'There's no doubt that their policy of never talking or giving interviews in the past has been a very good one.' 'Things have been rather difficult here,' a courtier told a member of the family from Buckingham Palace, 'but they've calmed down a bit, thank God.'[11] 'I remember having long conversations with him [Charles] about his children and how he mustn't do anything to hurt them. So what does he do? He does this book, the most hurting thing in the world.'[12] Whatever else he may have been trying to achieve by the book, publicly blaming his father and mother for his own shortcomings was unkind and hurtful, to say the least. Princess Anne and her brothers telephoned Charles objecting to his depiction of his parents: 'they rang and told him off and he sulked against them for weeks,' an aide recalled.[13] Publicly everyone blamed Richard Aylard, who was to be the scapegoat for the affair.

Monarchists who had condemned Diana over the Morton book were outraged by the Prince and the Dimbleby book. Even Charles Moore, a prominent media figure and stalwart monarchist, was prompted to say: 'When the Royal couple separated I wrote a column in this space [the *Spectator*] which criticised the Princess for indulging her "craving for private happiness" and ended "how do you know some will object that the Prince does not suffer from this same debilitating craving? I do not know but since he is the next King I do not think we should discuss the matter." Now he is forcing us all to discuss it, wrenching the conversation back, just when we hoped it might stop, to him and his woes.'[14]

Tensions were aroused by the Dimbleby episode between Buckingham Palace and St James's Palace. The Waleses' media war was irksome and embarrassing for Buckingham Palace. That Charles should let Diana take command of the press and in fact provoke her to it and then lose the moral high ground was a source of discomfort. 'I think that sense of frustration and anger and disappointment which undoubtedly radiated from the centre of the royal establishment is directed on the Prince,' said one of Charles's aides, 'and it's hard to argue against it sometimes.'[15] There was a distinct feeling that, as far as St James's Palace was concerned, things were out of control.

And it was true that Diana commanded the media heights. Margaret Thatcher's public relations guru, Gordon Reece, had introduced Diana to David English, editor of the *Daily Mail*. The parent company, Associated Press, then took what English described, apologetically, to representatives of the Prince as 'a commercial decision' to support Diana, who sold newspapers, as opposed to the Prince, who did not. The powerful Murdoch press, proprietors of *The Times*, *Sunday Times*, *Sun* and *News of the World*, was, for much the same reasons, inclined to favour Diana. 'Diana was quite friendly with Murdoch himself,' said an expert in the media field. 'They had a correspondence. They would see each other occasionally and they would write to each other. She wrote to him . . .'[16] Relations between Charles and Murdoch, who was not naturally a monarchist and hated inherited privilege, were non-existent. A meeting between them in the late eighties organized by ex-King Constantine of Greece had had the opposite effect to that intended. '. . . Murdoch went away thinking that the Prince was this sort of pinko commie leftie sort of weirdo – and I think those kind of words were used – and the Prince went away thinking he [Murdoch] was a kind of crypto-fascist megalomaniac, so that didn't work. So I think that News Corporation generally had an agenda and Diana was very, for them, commercially she was very powerful . . .'[17] The Telegraph Group, the most conservative and naturally pro-monarchist media organization, was then owned by the Canadian-born tycoon Conrad Black. 'Conrad Black and the Prince of Wales didn't get on,' said the aide. 'Max Hastings, when he was editor [of the *Daily Telegraph*] couldn't stand the Prince of Wales – it's all in his book – thought the Prince was unfit to be King, should stand aside for William . . . Express Newspapers were the only real group which were friendly with him [the Prince of Wales]. She [Diana] commanded the media, there's no doubt about it. Because a picture of Diana

sold papers . . .'[18] And, while the Prince dealt with the press
through his aides, Diana had deliberately set out personally to
charm the editors, from the broadsheets to the tabloids, influential
columnists like Auberon Waugh and Paul Johnson, and media
celebrities like Clive James.

Diana's seduction of one of the more ruthless tabloid editors,
brash thirty-year-old Piers Morgan of the *Daily Mirror*, which he
recorded after her death in his memoirs, provides an interesting
illustration of her methods. Meeting at a reception for the charity
Childline at the Savoy in January 1996, Diana asked Morgan
jokingly how all these editors claimed to know everything about
her when they hadn't even met her. ' "Now's your chance to
enlighten me, your royal highness," I replied. She eyed me up.
"Hmm . . . I don't have the time, I'm afraid . . ." Then she giggled.
"Or the inclination, come to that!" ' She moved on, leaving
Morgan agape. 'It was fascinating just watching her work the
room,' he wrote. 'Everyone, and I include myself in this, just
melted in her presence. She is radiant, sexy, and very direct – so
you get the feeling you're the only one she cares about for the few
seconds she's talking to you. It's a class act.'[19] On 8 May she invited
him to lunch at Kensington Palace. Morgan was as excited as a
schoolboy. 'Diana's the biggest star in the world and I am getting
a private audience . . . *Wow!*'[20] Morgan was even more excited
when William joined them for lunch. It was a frank conversation
and Morgan was allowed to ask Diana anything he liked, despite,
surprisingly, the presence of William, who, he noted in his
memoirs, 'is clearly in the loop on most of her bizarre world, and
in particular, the men who come into it from time to time'.[21] But
Morgan, despite the temporary intimacy, knew that Diana was
calling the shots. 'She knows she's got me over a barrel,' he wrote
later. 'If I want any more from her, I am going to have to play the
game by her rules.'[22]

At the opposite end of the press spectrum was Peter Stothard,
then editor of *The Times*. Their meeting had come in May 1994
when Diana had concerns about leaks on the subject of her expen-
diture, put at more than £3,000 a week, via her husband and his

friends. 'My husband said it at a dinner party last week,' she told him, 'where it got to Ross Benson and to Nigel Dempster . . .'[23] Diana's approach to the intellectual Stothard was not quite the same as her dealings with Piers Morgan. He found her extremely sophisticated 'about the media, her use of it and its use of her'. The interview was conducted on her terms, within strict but surprising lines. Flatteringly, inside those lines were 'the very aspects of her life which most people keep outside in discussion with media editors – her husband, his mistress, her in-laws, her own fragile sense of herself. Within minutes I felt I was talking to someone I knew. By the time she had toyed herself through her foie gras and lamb, I knew things about her that I did not know about my closest friends . . . The speed with which she ran through her list of subjects would not have disgraced a bank chairman anxious to catch the Ascot train.'[24] Lacking Diana's sophistication, it seems, Stothard quite failed to catch the story Diana had meant him to take in – how she had saved a tramp from drowning in the Serpentine. Although she dragged him to University College Hospital where she was to visit the rescued tramp, Stothard still failed to see the light until the story appeared in all the newspapers the next day, including his own – but without a briefing from him. Diana the Good Samaritan had been designed to counter Diana the Spendthrift.

As an estranged member of the Royal Family, Diana was in limbo. She relied ever more on her close friends, particularly Lucia Flecha de Lima, even though she was in Washington. Lucia was, according to Diana's butler, Paul Burrell, best friend, mother figure and counsellor rolled into one. Even now that the time difference between England and America made communication more difficult, their relationship continued to grow, becoming stronger as the years went by. In Washington, Lucia would set her alarm clock for 3 a.m. so that she could speak to Diana at the start of her day. 'If the princess needed advice or consolation, she rang Lucia,' Burrell wrote,[25] and Lucia was ready to answer whenever Diana needed her. 'I faxed an endless stream of messages across the Atlantic to her,' Burrell continued. Diana repeatedly told him how 'marvellous' Lucia was, that she could not cope without her, and that Lucia was 'like a mother to her'.[26] According to Burrell, who was best placed to know, Diana's 'surrogate family' now included first of all Lucia, then Lady Annabel Goldsmith, Rosa Monckton, Susie Kassem and Diana's doctor, Dr Mary Loveday. Richard Kay had by now transcended the role of media mouthpiece: he was a confidant – at least for what she needed him to hear – and helped her with her speech writing and correspondence. Sarah Ferguson was also close to Diana at that time. She was living apart from Andrew, although not yet divorced, with her daughters Beatrice and Eugenie at Romenda Lodge, Virginia Water. Diana frequently went down there to lunch, particularly at weekends, taking William and Harry, if they were at home, to see their cousins. Diana adored the York children and kept their childish paintings on her walls. At this time, the two women were constantly on the telephone to each other, gossiping, complaining about the treatment they were receiving from royal circles and the press, or discussing the latest words of wisdom from one of their gurus.

Outside this inner circle, Diana had a wider network of advisers – such as Clive James – who would lunch with her at Kensington Palace to offer her their expert wisdom when she asked for it. As with all her friendships, she compartmentalized these relationships. They came to Kensington Palace or lunched with her in restaurants *à deux*; only Diana knew what she had told each of them, and Diana was absolutely in control of the friendship. Apart from Raine de Chambrun, these counsellors were all men, intelligent, successful, who were nonetheless besotted with the Princess and protective towards her. Clive James, indeed, was an admirer of Charles yet he could not resist the lure of Diana. 'Even before I met her I had guessed she was a handful ... Clearly on a hair trigger, she was unstable at best, and when the squeeze was on she was a fruitcake on the rampage,' he recalled. 'But even while reaching this conclusion I was already smitten, and from then on everything I found out about her at first hand, even – especially, her failings and her follies, only made me love her more . . .'[27] James forgave her even when she lied to him, as when she denied having anything to do with the Morton book: '"I really had nothing to do with that Andrew Morton book," she said. "But after my friends talked to him, I had to stand by them." She looked me straight in the eye when she said this, so I could see how plausible she was when she was telling a whopper.'[28]

Another confidant and friend was David Puttnam. It was he who had arranged the Thirty Club dinner for her in 1994 to address and impress the media magnates, he who had – with Patrick Jephson – urged her to form a Princess of Wales Trust to fund her charitable giving. (She later rejected the idea – apparently on the advice of Colin Powell – since it would be seen as setting herself up in opposition to Charles's cherished Prince's Trust.) 'She drew you into her life in quite a definite way,' said one of her friends, 'the drawing-in involved deep confidences which she knew the person in question would never betray, as if it were a secret compact.'[29] She would talk about her personal life in what one friend described as 'sometimes . . . excruciating detail'. Diana was fascinated by the cinema, identifying with some of the stars, particularly Marilyn Monroe. 'She loved Marilyn Monroe, she really did,' said a friend. 'And I got hold of a fantastic biography, a documentary from America, and I don't know what made me do it, but before sending it to her I thought I'd have a look at it. And I looked at it and never sent it. And I never sent it because I thought this is not good stuff for Diana to be looking at. So the point here is that I was dealing with a sufficiently vulnerable person, that this ostensibly fascinating piece of material about someone she admired could actually have a different context . . . I think without doubt she [Diana] had suicidal tendencies. But people with whom I've had that conversation have said that in a sense she was too selfish for that, that's not the way she would have done anything – and then there were the children . . .'[30]

Extraordinarily, Diana would be the same age as Monroe when she died. (Charles, who of all people would have been aware of her recklessness and her bravery, is alleged to have said that she would either get herself killed or end up in a wheelchair.) Perhaps with hindsight (these conversations took place some eight years

17. Fall from Grace

'Events of the last few weeks . . . have enforced the perception of the Princess as a predatory figure preying on other women's men'[1]

Early in 1995, Diana drew up what her secretary called 'her own, very private manifesto'. She wanted her 'true worth to be recognised', the chance to use her 'healing interests and abilities', to 'address increasing world problems', 'to make a contribution on a world platform . . . and to deal with many countries'.[2] In essence she saw her priority as being 'survival against the forces who had so nearly suffocated her'. That year she was to make no fewer than ten overseas trips. Sadly, as Jephson revealed, these brilliantly successful trips, which did more good for the British image abroad than months of trade visits and business initiatives, were regarded with suspicion at Buckingham Palace and the Foreign Office. 'I think they're all scared of the Princess of Wales,' a member of the Royal Family said at the time.[3] Diana had cultivated a relationship with the Foreign Secretary, Douglas Hurd, who had regarded her with 'a kind of paternally concerned interest' but he left office that year to be replaced by Malcolm Rifkind. If not to the bureaucrats, 'the grey men' whom Diana so resented, Diana's beauty, charisma and fame made her welcome wherever she went in the world. 'While I fenced tensely with officials in Buckingham Palace and the Foreign Office about the precise definition of the Queen's stricture that the Princess should not represent her abroad,' Jephson wrote, 'Presidents, Kings and even – in the case of Japan – an Emperor let it be known that they expected the Princess of Wales to come to tea when she was in town.'[4]

Typically of Diana, she had called in the best advice before the Japanese tour – her friend Clive James, the Australian writer, wit, poet and broadcaster who had been among her legion of platonic admirers for the past few years. James presented a television show which featured Japanese wannabes doing the most outrageous stunts. He was also a serious student of the Japanese language and Japanese literature. Diana asked him what would be the best thing she could do there, apart from her hospital visits. James advised her to learn some Japanese phrases and sent her his Japanese teacher. Diana, in his words, 'flew to Japan, addressed a hundred and twenty-five million people in their own language, and made the most stunning impact'.[5] The published purpose of the visit was to enable Diana to acquaint herself with the work of various charitable centres for the old, the young and the disabled, and to formalize the link between Great Ormond Street Hospital for Sick Children, of which she was president, and Tokyo's National Children's Hospital. As Jephson put it, 'such innocent objectives nevertheless attracted scrutiny from those now convinced that the Princess of Wales was a dangerous guided missile, ready at a moment's notice to explode with devastating effects for British diplomacy and the prestige abroad of the British royal family'.[6] Diana was invited to tea at the Imperial Palace, the ultimate accolade for a visitor to Japan. She mischievously made the most of it. Already towering over the diminutive imperial couple, she chose the highest heels she could find. 'It's very important to wear really high heels,' she joked with Jephson. 'I'm already taller than the Emperor, but it won't do any harm to look just that bit taller!' Next day the eye-catching photographs of the meeting featured Diana, curtseying respectfully low, the main feature of the picture being the consequent exposure of 'a generous expanse of athletic royal thigh'.[7]

Diana followed this up with a highly successful fund-raising trip to Hong Kong under the auspices of entrepreneur David Tang and with the blessing of the Governor, Chris Patten. In one evening she raised a quarter of a million pounds for medical and youth charities in Hong Kong and China, notably for the work of the Leprosy Mission, a cause to which she was especially attached. She made fund-raising charity trips to Venice, Paris and New York and two more official visits – to Russia and Argentina. She carried out 127 public engagements as compared with only ten in 1994 following her 'time and space speech'. On one such trip, Diana's companions witnessed one of the odder manifestations of her compassionate impulses. While they were eating their dinner in first class, Diana was sitting apart listening to her Walkman. Suddenly she snatched off the Walkman, leapt to her feet and dashed into the compartment behind, to return with a yelling baby in her arms. Despite all her efforts to calm it, the baby continued to scream and there soon appeared its anxious and somewhat alarmed mother to whom Diana had no alternative but to relinquish the child.

But at the same time as her public exploits were winning her praise, the old, reckless, self-destructive Diana was at work. In February Oliver Hoare's chauffeur went to the *News of the World* with damning details of their affair. By now even Diana recognized there was no future in their relationship and, after the *News of the World* revelations, that it was positively dangerous for her to continue. She dumped Hoare, who wrote her a characteristically charming letter thanking her for all the happiness she had given him and returning her present of a pair of her father's cufflinks. Despite her resolutions as to her public career, in private she could not find happiness. The year 1995 was to be a particularly difficult and unstable year for her. She was lonely at Kensington Palace with both the boys away at boarding school. During one of her visits to the Chelsea Harbour gym in Fulham, she met England rugby hero Will Carling, whose dark, rugged good looks and sporting celebrity appealed to her. They met at the Harbour Club and at Kensington Palace; Carling confessed that his marriage was in trouble, Diana sympathized.

Diana led him on, while at the same time mocking him to the staff at Kensington Palace as 'my puppy dog'[8] (he always visited accompanied by his black Labrador). The same 'puppy' simile was used by Carling's former personal assistant, Hilary Ryan, in a *News of the World* report in August that Diana had been having 'secret trysts' with Carling at Kensington Palace. She told of furtive meetings, long, secretive phone calls, and the pet names they used for each other. No evidence was produced of any physical relationship, although it was rumoured that Carling had made some indiscreet – indeed ungentlemanly – remarks about Diana to fellow rugby players. Will Carling gave a newspaper interview confessing that his meetings with Diana had been a mistake, and that he regretted the distress he had caused his wife Julia. Julia Carling herself was no shrinking violet and experienced at dealing with the media. She told the same newspaper that she did not want her husband seeing Diana again, saying, 'She picked the wrong couple this time.' (Ever supportive, Prince William told Diana in front of Piers Morgan that at school he used a photograph of Julia Carling as a dart board.) The effect of Julia Carling's stand on Diana's public reputation was to tarnish her in a way that had not happened before. Following on the Hoare affair, and now this, the tabloids described her as a home wrecker. She became the butt of snide jokes. On the BBC's sports quiz *They Think It's All Over*, the England cricketer David Gower and the footballer Gary Lineker laughed heartily at jokes about Diana and men made by comedienne Jo Brand. It was no secret that Diana had asked Lineker to lunch and that his wife had absolutely forbidden it. Asked by presenter Nick Hancock if he had lunched with her, Lineker replied ungallantly, 'That woman's too much trouble.'[9] But Carling, it seems, could not keep away from Diana. The stories were repeated at the end of September when the Carlings split. In Diana's circle it was alleged that Diana had turned her back on her old friends Kate Menzies and Catherine Soames when they had criticized her over the Carling affair.[10]

On 20 August 1995, a vicious attack on Diana appeared in the *Mail on Sunday* under Nigel Dempster's byline: 'Is Diana the Mistress of Manipulation?' the headline asked. The subhead was even more damaging: 'Mental anguish behind fall of Diana the "saint"'. 'Events of the last few weeks, concerning Diana's so-called relationship with Will Carling, the recently married captain of the England rugby football team, have enforced the perception of the Princess as a predatory figure preying on other women's men,' the article announced. She was known as 'Zuleika' (after the *femme fatale* of Max Beerbohm's novel *Zuleika Dobson*) 'among those who wish to see her marginalized from mainstream British life'. She was like her mother, who was a bolter, and had failed to sustain a marriage, the newspaper asserted, adding a comment by 'an observer': 'The apple does not fall far from the tree.' Worst of all, the article asserted that Diana was suffering from a mental illness.

Rumours of mental instability had been circulated by Diana's enemies within St James's Palace. It was alleged at the time the Dimbleby book was being written that Diana had a psychological profile which was found to fit a well-recognized if controversial condition called Borderline Personality Disorder, or BPD for short. Eight symptoms characterizing BPD had been put forward at the time, most of which neatly fitted Diana's behaviour, all of which were quoted in the *Mail on Sunday* piece. This theory was allegedly considered unsuitable for inclusion in the Dimbleby biography; it was, to put it mildly, diagnosis from a distance and extremely damaging. Put otherwise, it was another manifestation of the continuing argument between partisans of the Prince and those of the Princess: was Diana disturbed before she married or did his behaviour with Camilla and the circumstances surrounding the couple drive her to bulimia and irrational behaviour? Diana was not unaware of the whispers in Charles's circle and from his defenders in Buckingham Palace that she was 'mentally unstable' as a result of 'bad blood' (a favourite in aristocratic circles, in which bloodlines were so important) deriving from the Fermoys – dating particularly from the suicide of her uncle Edmund in August 1984. In 1994, however, the BPD allegation had been considered too scandalous to make public. But for Diana's enemies it was too good to waste, hence its publication in Dempster's column. The allegations were repeated later that year on a television programme, but their first formal manifestation did not come out until the publication of the book by pro-Charles author Penny Junor, entitled *Charles: Victim or Villain?*, published in 1998, after Diana's death. According to Junor, it was several years before the Prince realized that Diana had a problem.

In fact, the theme of Junor's book went further: Diana had always been mad, bad and dangerous to know and this had been the case long before she knew the Prince. The father of one of Diana's Norfolk schoolfriends had gone so far as to make specific inquiries about where Diana would next be going to school. He was concerned about the effect his daughter's friendship with Diana would have on her. Junor's book also included what is rumoured to have been Ruth Fermoy's deathbed statement to Dimbleby, that she could have kicked herself for not having the courage to warn the Prince about Diana before they married, a statement that hardly fitted the facts as they were in 1980. The argument that the unfortunate Prince was dealing with what amounted to a madwoman was too basic to the case of Charles v Diana and it was never going to go unsubstantiated for long.

At the time the *Mail* article was published, Diana was suffering feelings of continuing insecurity and increasing paranoia. Alone in the claustrophobic atmosphere of Kensington Palace, she would imagine all sorts of things; among them was her conviction that she was being bugged: 'She had a wild and vivid imagination,' a former aide said. 'You know, talk of bugs – I have to say this was absolute nonsense because besides the private lines, the other lines there came through Buckingham Palace switchboard and if they wanted to listen in they could listen in without putting bugs on and she knew as well as anybody else that the majority of her calls went through Buckingham Palace because it was a safety valve. Because all sorts of peculiar people would telephone. So to avoid that, she would give the switchboard number and they would filter. They wouldn't put anybody through without talking to the principal first, saying I have so and so on the line . . .'[11] A senior ex-police officer also dismissed the idea that Diana was being bugged: 'Some people are very ready to believe that there is this undue interest, that their house is being bugged or their letters being opened or their phone is being tapped . . . but the reality is that it's terribly difficult to get permission to do any of those . . .

There are not the facilities to do instant tap at the drop of a hat. The permissions one has to get, the difficulty in getting it, the difficulty in actually technically doing it is quite considerable. That doesn't stop people believing that they are being tapped or followed or whatever. And it's usually the sign of someone who's quite paranoid . . .'[12]

But beyond actual bugging, Diana did have grounds for her suspicions in another way. 'It must have been very difficult for her,' a close friend said. 'She was spied on, I've no doubt about it. I think that after she withdrew her police bodyguards, I think the police continued to maintain an interest in her, they say because they needed to be sure she was safe but one wonders . . . there's a lot of prurient stuff went on, a lot of people took a great deal of pleasure in finding out who she was seeing and making sure it was leaked to the papers . . .'[13]

One day the well-informed *Daily Mail* told Jephson that the Princess did not trust the loyalty of even those close to her. 'I knew my employer well enough to recognise a career prospects review when I saw it,' Jephson wrote. That year others who had served Diana long and loyally were made redundant, namely head butler Harold Brown and the head chef, Mervyn Wycherley, surplus to requirements now that Diana's divorce was approaching. Brown's loyalty and discretion were recognized by Princess Margaret who hired him herself, ensuring he kept his apartment.

The beneficiary of all these redundancies was Paul Burrell, the former Palace footman, who had not wanted to leave his comfortable family cottage at Highgrove when the division of the Waleses' staff had taken place in 1992. 'He was on to a good thing down there,' said a former aide of Diana's. 'He liked the country, was used to the country, and it wasn't a case that Diana had asked for him, it was a case that the Prince didn't want him because he had shown whose camp he was in. And so you could hardly fire someone because they happened to be in someone else's camp; you find him another job and that's what he did.'

By 1995, however, Burrell had become to some extent Diana's

confidant, or at least confidential servant. Despite having a wife
and two children, Burrell was besotted with his employer, even to
the extent of adopting her mannerisms; nothing was too much in
order to please her. He spent long hours at Kensington Palace with
her, to the annoyance of his wife, who might have said, as Diana
was subsequently to say, that there were 'three of us' in the marriage. It was an emotional attachment: Diana became the centre of
his world. 'She got rid of all her dressers and staff and people like
that,' said David Griffin, Princess Margaret's chauffeur, who had
frequent conversations with Diana while waiting outside the Palace
for his employer. 'And then he [Burrell] started to take on a role,
like we used to call him Mrs Danvers [the sinister housekeeper in
Daphne du Maurier's *Rebecca*] and everywhere she used to go he'd
appear, and that sort of thing. Stupid things, like she used to ask
me "Can you give my car a going-over", which I did. He came
out one morning and said, "I'll do this from now on ... he
thought it was a great honour for me to do it ..."[14] Diana was as
popular with the Kensington Palace staff as her butler was not: no
doubt jealousy may have played a part but, used as they were to
serving the Royal Family, the relationship between the Princess
and her butler was a source of comment: 'We used to call them
"the Odd Couple" sometimes,' Griffin said. 'It wasn't done in a
detrimental way, but it seemed sort of strange ...'[15] Even Burrell
was not exempt from Diana's suspicion and, in some cases, understandably. On one occasion Griffin was passing her front door
when Diana came out. 'She slammed the door with such ferocity
that I thought "Oh!!" and I said, "Good morning, we're not in a
very happy mood today, are we?" "No, we're not," she said.
"Oh," I said, "what's happened?" And she said, "He'll have to
go." And I said, "Who's got to go?" She said, "He [Burrell] will",
and I said, "Who?" "I caught him going through my letters,"
she says.' Later, Diana seriously intended to sack him when she
discovered that he was running up huge telephone bills on her
account.

One piece of evidence illustrating Diana's state of mind in the
autumn of 1995, the famous 'letter' stating that her husband

planned to have her killed, was published by Paul Burrell and dated, he said, October 1996. The letter ran:

> I am sitting here at my desk today in October, longing for someone to hug me and encourage me to keep strong and hold my head high. This particular phase in my life is the most dangerous. My husband [not in the book but published later] is planning 'an accident' in my car, brake failure and serious head injury in order to make the path clear for Charles to marry.
>
> I have been battered, bruised and abused mentally by a system for 15 years now, but I feel no resentment, I carry no hatred. I am weary of the battles, but I will never surrender. I am strong inside and maybe that is a problem for my enemies.
>
> Thank you Charles, for putting me through such hell and for giving me the opportunity to learn from the cruel things you have done to me. I have gone forward fast and have cried more than anyone will ever know. The anguish nearly killed me, but my inner strength has never let me down, and my guides have taken such good care of me up there. Aren't I fortunate to have their wings to protect me . . .[16]

Friends of Diana say that the mood in which this statement was written was more indicative of her state of mind in the autumn of 1995 than 1996. It could also be pointed out that in October 1996, after their divorce had come through, there would have been no necessity – even if he had had the inclination – for Charles to have her killed so that he could remarry which, by October 1996, he was legally free to do. Colin Tebbutt, ex-Royalty and Diplomatic Protection Department, now running his own security firm, was asked by Diana in 1995 to drive for her and provide protection with a two-man back-up when she needed him. Tebbutt had concerns about the letter: '. . . because being in charge of transport and still being a great friend of the private secretary, Michael Gibbins . . . why wasn't it pointed out to me? Why didn't somebody say to the team who were driving the car . . . and I knew the man who supplied it and the car was always

under lock and key and always in a garage with an electrical
lock. Could nobody say to me, "Colin, the brakes are dodgy" or
"Somebody's going to make an attempt on her life"? Why didn't
Burrell tell the private secretary to tell the chauffeur or the security
team?'[17]

Other people who worked closely with the Princess did not
believe that, although the text was undoubtedly in Diana's hand,
it was addressed to Burrell in particular. 'Now, if she'd written
that to Paul, it would have been "Dearest Paul" and in that case it
would have been very much in his [Burrell's] interest to show that
letter, but the very fact we didn't see it [the superscription] and
the very fact that it wasn't even on the letter with not even a
signing off [signature]. I know for a fact that it was a memo to
herself and she would not bullet point it, she would just get it
down.'[18] Another aide confirmed, 'this alleged letter to Burrell,
yes she wrote it, the paper was genuine, the writing was genuine,
but she did write notes to herself'. Often the theme of these
memoranda would be the result of a conversation she had had
recently and wanted to jot down as a memo to herself. They
might, equally, be the result of some consultation with one of her
therapists or clairvoyants. The point is that the memo was an
expression of Diana's state of mind at the time and an illustration
of the forces driving her towards what would turn out to be the
greatest mistake of her life, the notorious *Panorama* interview. A
year later, the idea of writing a memo such as this would never
have crossed her mind. Yet, such had been the impact when
Burrell's book was serialized, and so seriously was it taken when
Burrell reproduced the text in his book, that Lord Stevens, the
retired head of the Metropolitan Police, went so far as to interview
Prince Charles about it for the purposes of his inquiry in 2005 into
the death of Diana.

The idea of giving a spectacular television interview had been
taking shape in Diana's mind throughout 1995, sparked by her
meetings with two media giants of American television, Oprah
Winfrey and Barbara Walters, both of whom she had invited to
lunch with her at Kensington Palace, while her friends Clive James

and David Frost had tried to lure her on to their shows as the ultimate celebrity guest.[19] In the end it was a rank outsider, Martin Bashir, who persuaded her to give what was to become perhaps the most notorious television interview of all time. Bashir, then a junior journalist on the BBC's *Panorama*, succeeded where the other luminaries failed and he did so by preying on Diana's fears for her security and safety. His original idea had been to do an investigative programme on the current fears about the activities of the Security Services in monitoring the lives of celebrities and the Royal Family which had been prevalent since the publication of the Squidgygate and Camillagate tapes in 1992 and 1993 respectively.[20] Andrew Morton, in his last book on Diana, published in 2004, was convinced that there would have been no interview had Bashir not tapped in to Diana's secret fears. According to Morton, Bashir first met Diana's brother, Charles, at Althorp in the summer of 1995 in order to discuss his suspicions of being bugged. Charles was suing the *Daily Express* for a series of articles alleging that he had helped to launder the proceeds of a multimillion-pound fraud carried out in New York by his close friend and best man at his first wedding, Darius Guppy. Spencer won £50,000 damages and an apology. At the same time he had taken out an injunction against his former head of security, James Waller, forbidding him from disclosing information about his private life and that of members of the Royal Family; this had followed the publication in March 1994 of a letter Charles had written to Diana in December 1993 warning her that her public appearances were damaging her popularity.

Allegedly through Spencer, Bashir secretly met Diana, whose insecurities he fed by convincing her that her apartment was being bugged. In order to advance his cause with Charles Spencer and Diana, according to Morton and, later, the *Mail on Sunday* (April 1996), Bashir had a set of forged bank statements made up by a graphic designer showing payments made to James Waller and a former business partner of Waller's, Robert Harper, from *Today*, the newspaper which had published Spencer's letter to Diana, and a Jersey-based company for unspecified services. Whatever the truth of the matter, something happened to persuade Diana to give the interview. The prime motive, according to this reading of the affair and the sentence of her October memo, written at the time of the negotiations with Bashir about the interview, about Prince Charles arranging her 'accidental death' and her references to 'my enemies', was fear for her own safety and a determination to make herself so popular as to be invulnerable. The interview was to be a pre-emptive strike. Diana's biographer, Sally Bedell Smith, attributes this paranoia to Bashir's warnings and it was at about the time of their meetings that Diana had insisted on having her apartment and her car swept for bugs. Bashir also apparently warned her not to trust Catherine Soames and Kate Menzies, although she had in fact already parted company with them, and, significantly, Julia Samuel, one of the most intelligent of her friends, whom she then dropped.[21]

Diana had previously consulted three of her media mentors, David Puttnam, Clive James and David Attenborough, about doing the Bashir interview. 'Because we had told her not to do it,' said one, 'in all three cases she gave us the impression that she'd listened to us and had decided not to do it and all three of us got quite a shock when she did.'[22] 'I mean, my argument was very simple, rather cynical in a way . . . whenever she used to bang on about the possibility of doing something like these interviews, was – you'd be mad to do it because once you've done it the weapon that it is ceases to exist, so you're handing over the one serious weapon that you have, and in a sense you're then just a victim of events, you have no control over events; whilst you haven't done it you are actually in control of events. So that was my position . . . and when I said that she always said, "You're absolutely right, of course you're right, I absolutely understand that." '[23] Clive James wrote in his remembrance of Diana after her death: 'I counselled her against it. I said if that happened the two camps thing would go nuclear, and continue until there was nothing left. She would be on the run forever and there would be nowhere to go . . . She seemed convinced, but of course she was pretending. She had already decided.'[24]

Several things moved Diana to take the fatal step of the *Panorama* interview: her longing to put her case to the people over the heads of her 'enemies' in the Establishment; her love of publicity on her own terms; her intrinsic belief in the rightness of her own instinct even over all the wise opinions she had been given by people who had only her interests at heart; her determination to counter allegations of Borderline Personality Disorder; and lastly, and, least attractively if understandably, the desire for vengeance. This was evident in her instructions to the BBC over when to release the news of the broadcast. On Diana's specific instruction[25] the BBC released their press announcement on 14 November, an unwelcome forty-seventh birthday surprise for Charles, on an official visit to Tokyo. Photographs taken at the time show him cutting a celebratory cake, his face expressing total dismay.[26] That morning Diana called the Palace to inform them of the interview which was to take place in six days' time. The Royal Family were, with justification as it turned out, appalled at what they regarded as the second betrayal after the Morton book. It was by now too late to do anything but wait and see.

The fifty-five-minute programme went out on 20 November. Dressed in black, wearing little jewellery, her eyes heavily ringed with kohl, Diana was in victim mode but nonetheless defiant, and seemingly oblivious to the significance of what she said in the context of the monarchy. Her words echoed the October 1995 letter as she spoke of her sufferings, her betrayal by her husband, the efforts of people to destroy her by painting her as mad, her bulimia; she admitted to her love affair with Hewitt, but with no one else. ('Yes, I adored him, yes, I was in love with him. But I was very let down.') Above all, the attack was directed at her husband, his mistress and their friends. They – 'her enemies' – had said she was 'unstable, sick and should be in a home of some sort in order to get better', and, when asked if Charles agreed with them, she said, quoting (without attribution) from a book by the former hostage Brian Keenan, 'there's no better way to dismantle a personality than to isolate it'. Asked what part Camilla Parker Bowles had played in the break-up of her marriage, she replied in the most memorable phrase of the evening, 'Well, there were three of us in this marriage, so it was a bit crowded.' She admitted to helping with the Morton book because she had wanted the true story of her unhappy marriage to be made public: 'I was at the end of my tether. I was desperate. I think I was so fed up with being seen as someone who was a basket-case, because I am a very strong person and I know that causes complications in the system that I live in.' The word 'strong' came in no fewer than four times. Some people 'in the Establishment that I married into, have decided that I'm a non-starter. Because I do things differently, because I don't go by a rule book, because I lead from the heart, not the head.' She, however, wanted to reign not officially but as a Queen of Hearts (a phrase borrowed from the works of her step-grandmother, Barbara Cartland) and to be an ambassador for Britain, giving affection and helping 'other people in distress'.

The key moment of the programme – the point at which Diana cut herself off from the monarchy and the Royal Family – came when she cast doubt on Charles's fitness to rule, and raised a further doubt as to whether he would succeed to the throne. 'It's a very demanding role, being Prince of Wales', she said, 'but it's an equally more demanding role being King. And because I know the character, I would think that the top job, as I call it, would bring enormous limitations to him, and I don't know whether he could adapt to that.' 'My wish,' she added with a sly dig, 'is that my husband finds peace of mind.' Speaking of herself in the third person, always a bad sign, she declared with an undertone of menace as well as defiance: 'She won't go quietly.'

It was a stunning – and to some a shocking – performance, watched by fifteen million people in Britain and millions more round the world. Diana's friends were horrified: 'Diana at her worst,' Rosa Monckton wrote. 'A brilliant suicide note,' said another. Camilla, watching with her family, apparently laughed at the theatricality of the 'Mad Cow', as she sometimes referred to Diana (possibly in reference to BSE) but its effect on her standing with the public would be even more drastic than the Morton book had been. Nicholas Soames loyally rushed on to the BBC's serious news programme *Newsnight* to declare that the interview showed 'the advanced stages of paranoia'.

The week before the broadcast, when it was too late for him to derail her plans, Diana finally told Patrick Jephson she had done the interview. He immediately rang the Queen's press secretary. Over the car phone Charles Anson was his usual laid-back self but there is no doubt that the news of what Diana intended to do caused consternation to the Queen and her staff. Diana refused to reveal the content of what she intended to say to anyone and the fact that it was to go out on *Panorama*, the BBC's flagship current affairs programme, only served to increase nervous suspicion. As it happened, even the chairman of the BBC, Sir Marmaduke Hussey, had been kept in the dark for the simple reason that he was married to one of the Queen's and Charles's favourite Women of the Bedchamber, Lady Susan Hussey. Had he been told of the project he would undoubtedly have moved heaven and earth to stop it. The director-general, John Birt, Hussey's chief executive, was in on the plan but did not inform his chairman, nor did he make any effort to stop it or even to tone down the content. The result was a serious rift between the Palace and the BBC. Nothing the Palace, Jephson or even Diana's lawyer, Lord Mishcon, could put forward succeeded in getting Diana either to reconsider or to reveal what she was going to say. After watching *Panorama*, the Palace, Jephson and the Princess's press secretary, Geoff Crawford, were in a state of shock. Crawford resigned immediately, although he accompanied the Princess on her tour of Argentina two days later. Jephson, his plans for Diana's rehabilitation and reintegration into the royal circle in ruins, determined to resign as soon as he decently could.

Diana remained resolutely convinced she had done the right thing. The night before, she had telephoned one of her mother figures: 'She rang me and said to me, "I've done the most wonderful interview, I've put everything right." I was slightly worried about it. She said, "You will watch it, won't you, and tell me in the morning?" I watched it, and it was so frightful I – literally – was thinking I'm never going to be able to stand up for her again because it's so frightful, the *Panorama* thing. She rang me. The telephone rang at eight o'clock in the morning – she was an early riser, like me – and I couldn't . . . I had to pretend to be on the other line because what was I going to say to her? Well, it was so frightful that I did, I told her that I wasn't mad about it and she was furious . . . I said it was a frightful mistake, and she didn't like that at all, she hated being criticized. But it was appalling, it was a total error of judgement.'[27] Diana's friend, who knew both Charles and Camilla well and was much liked in court circles, encapsulated the reaction of everyone who wished her well. In terms of a royal future, she had thrown herself off the edge of the cliff. The interview finished her friendship with Princess Margaret who was outraged by Diana's remarks about Charles and the succession and wrote her a stinging letter to tell her so, and Margaret's children, previously so friendly, avoided her. The interview was devastating for her sons; in her lack of consideration for their feelings and her public admission of adultery she had behaved no better than Charles. It was rumoured that William would not speak to her for several days.

In public relations terms, however, the interview was a popular success. Diana had appealed to her own followers, the converted: favourable results of newspaper polls helped convince her that she had done the right thing. Two days after the interview, buoyed up with confidence, she left for a pre-arranged charities trip to the Argentine, Britain's erstwhile enemy in the Falklands War. The democratic President, Carlos Menem, took Diana's visit as a signal that 'Argentina has gradually regained a position in the world which it had lost'. Faced with her return to London and normality – at least her form of it – realization of the possible consequences of what she had done had begun to dawn on Diana. Patrick Jephson commented sharply, 'she had taken the biggest possible injection of her favourite drug, and now she felt even worse'.[28]

While St James's Palace may have been happy to see Diana publicly imploding, Buckingham Palace was not. Jephson was still trying to put together the broken pieces of Diana's relationship with the Palace, presenting a blueprint for their future dealings.

He suggested that Diana's secretarial staff should move to offices in Buckingham Palace, and that the Queen's press office should deal with her public relations. He proposed removing her from dependence on Charles for her financial support, and that Buckingham Palace should provide domestic back-up for her apartment at Kensington Palace. Finally, her areas of work both abroad and at home, charitable and public, should be clearly defined and agreed. Both he and Diana attended a meeting at the Palace, when it became obvious that, while Jephson might have hoped to lure his thoroughbred into the safety of the Palace stable, the Queen's staff were not entirely willing to receive her, having been bruised once too often by Diana's initiatives, of which the *Panorama* interview had been just one too many. On 29 November, Jephson and Diana attended a meeting with the Queen's principal officials at the Palace, headed by her brother-in-law, Robert (Sir Robert since 1991) Fellowes. Given the guarded response his proposals received, Jephson soon realized they were doomed. 'Whatever goodwill there might have been at Buckingham Palace towards her as a person,' he recalled, '— and I had no doubt there was plenty, not least from Robert himself — the offence she had caused was too great. It was a classic case of "love the sinner hate the sin".'[29] Furthermore, the Prince's team were not willing to see the Princess transferred to the shelter of Buckingham Palace, as Jephson proposed. 'A move under the wing of the senior household, and hence to the centre of royal power, was hardly going to have the marginalising [of Diana] effect they undoubtedly hoped for,' Jephson commented.

Still unaware that events were moving on without her, Diana flew with Jephson by Concorde to New York to receive a humanitarian award from her old admirer Henry Kissinger on 12 December. It was an American occasion of the kind which always stimulated and empowered her in distinct contrast to the difficult atmosphere reigning at home. 'There were motorcades, Secret Service agents, adoring crowds and rooms full of rich, powerful and beautiful people to be charmed,' Jephson wrote of his last foreign trip with his employer. As a gesture of appreciation,

Diana appointed her old friend and supporter Liz Tilberis, formerly editor of *Vogue* in London, now New York editor of *Harper's* and suffering from what was to be terminal cancer, as her honorary lady-in-waiting. She returned to the Harlem Children's Hospital, scene of her moving visit six years earlier. As always, the welcome she received in America had its effect on her: Diana in New York, Jephson recalled, was a different person from his temperamental London employer.

She returned to the gloomy confines of Kensington Palace full of confidence to take on 'her enemies', the first of whom was to be Alexandra 'Tiggy' Legge-Bourke, employed by Charles to be his Girl Friday and to look after William and Harry. Diana had been jealous of Tiggy's closeness to her sons since her appointment, when a photograph of Charles kissing her on a skiing holiday had convinced her, quite groundlessly, that Charles and Tiggy were having an affair. Tiggy's visits to her private gynaecologist that year prompted Diana, disastrously, to conclude that she had had a termination and that the baby had been fathered by Charles. At the Christmas staff lunch on 14 December, she confronted the unfortunate young woman. '*So sorry* to hear about the baby,' she smiled. Tiggy was horror-struck, almost fainted, and had to be helped from the room by Charles's valet Michael Fawcett. Diana was triumphant but at St James's and Buckingham Palace, where Tiggy was universally liked, there was consternation and disgust. Tiggy instructed her lawyers; Sir Robert Fellowes telephoned Diana to find out precisely what her allegation implied when Diana gleefully repeated the allegation to him. Sir Robert investigated and found the whole affair groundless, as he informed Diana in a stern official letter rebutting what she had said. Her allegations were completely without foundation, he told her; Tiggy's relationship with the Prince had never been anything other than a professional one: 'on the date of the supposed abortion, she was at Highgrove with William and Harry. It is in your own best interests that you withdraw these allegations . . .' Attached was a private note to Diana: 'This letter is sent from one who really believes that you've got this whole thing dreadfully wrong, and that you *must* realise it – please.'[30] Later that month, lunching with friends at a favourite Italian restaurant in Chelsea, La Famiglia, before going down to Eton to meet Charles for the Christmas carol service, she was 'very pensive' and 'very nervous': 'she was very brittle and her mouth was much tighter, she was doing that whole lowering the head thing,' an observer said.[31] Diana, the goddess of New York, had metamorphosed into Diana, the Naughty Little Girl, about to meet the Grown-ups.

Diana had become obsessed with the unfortunate Tiggy. In the notorious 'Burrell letter' of October 1995 Diana had indicated that Charles was planning a car accident to remove her from the scene and enable him to marry not Camilla, but Tiggy. Diana's extreme possessiveness over her 'boys' had fuelled her anger, triggering her unreasonable and inexcusable behaviour.

The blow fell a week before she was due to take William and Harry to Sandringham for Christmas. A letter arrived from the Queen, addressed in her handwriting to 'Dearest Diana' and ending 'With love from Mama'. Its content, however, was stark: having consulted both the Prime Minister and the Archbishop of Canter-bury, the Queen had come to the conclusion that it would be in the best interests of the country to end the uncertainty and for Charles and Diana to take steps to divorce. Diana, according to her butler Burrell, to whom, he said, she showed the Queen's letter, sat down to reply, saying to her mother-in-law that she needed time to reflect. Time, however, was exactly what she was not going to be given; a letter from Charles arrived. Their marriage was beyond repair, he wrote, representing a 'national and personal tragedy'; since divorce was inevitable, it should be done quickly in order to resolve the 'sad and complicated situation'.[32] The 'fairy tale' was definitively over.

As a gesture of goodwill, the Queen still extended her invitation to Diana to spend Christmas at Sandringham. A royal invitation amounts to a royal command but Diana had gone too far to care. Discussing the Queen's letter with her butler, she had shown no interest in the constitutional issues of divorce. Enraged that the government and the Church had been consulted over her marriage, she had 'yelled', 'This is my marriage and it is no one else's business.' As for the Queen's reference to 'the interests of the country', her reaction was 'In the country's interests, is it? What about the interests of me? What about the interests of my boys?' To show her displeasure, she refused the Queen's invitation to Sandringham and spent Christmas instead at Althorp. It can hardly have been a very happy one: the marriages of both the younger Spencers were in trouble and both would end in divorce.

18. Out on a Limb

'She knew she had nowhere to go' (a member of Diana's circle)

By the end of 1995 Diana was in limbo. The past year had been the most confused and difficult of her life so far. Now, with the *Panorama* interview, she had cut herself off from the Royal Family, the real source of her power and celebrity. She may have been the prime architect of her own downfall, but she was not the only one. St James's Palace had long regarded her as the principal obstacle to the heir to the throne's popularity; his friends had queued up to denigrate her, the newspapers tracked her every movement and every public word. There were ample reasons for the paranoia which had haunted her through 1995 and would continue to do so as negotiations for her divorce progressed.

In January 1996 Patrick Jephson resigned. *Panorama*, which she had kept secret from him until it was too late to do anything about it, was the trigger which had convinced him that, after eight years' service, he must escape from his relationship with Diana. He had been fascinated, almost besotted, by her, as was every man close to her. Diana had joked and laughed with him, given him expensive presents – Hermès ties were a favourite for all her men friends – paid for expensive lunches. In return he had served her with utter devotion to the detriment of his private life. The secrecy with which the *Panorama* affair had been conducted had finally caused the scales to fall from his eyes. He determined to jump before he was pushed. Perhaps Diana, with her acute instincts, had sensed this; she initiated the process by cutting him out of her official confidence, replacing him as her speech writer with Richard Kay and, more recently, Martin Bashir, who acted in some cases almost as her private secretary. According to Jephson, she had begun to

send him venomous anonymous messages on his pager, as she had
to other members of her staff who had fallen into disfavour.[1] Diana
regarded his departure, which formally took effect on 22 January,
as a personal act of treachery. She had prepared a riposte with a
story in the *Mail* to be run the following day stating that he
had been sacked for professional incompetence. Jephson had been
tipped off about it and timed his resignation to forestall it.

Like almost all the people – men and women – who had been
cut out of Diana's life, after the initial bitterness Jephson remained
loyal to her: his subsequent memoir, *Shadows of a Princess*, published
four years later, although frank about her failings paid tribute to
her outstanding courage and charisma. 'You cannot just walk away
from the Princess of Wales,' he wrote.[2] There was bitterness on
Diana's side, too, at what she saw as a personal betrayal. She
telephoned friends who might have been prepared to employ him
and even fell out for a time with one of her mentors, David
Puttnam, whom she suspected of luring Jephson away from her.
Other people who had been sacked or driven out by her retained
a liking, loyalty and sympathy for her, understanding the impossibility of her life and not blaming her for it. Everyone denied that
she was mad, or had ever been so, blaming rather the people who
had failed to help her or understand her and, indeed, had driven
her to her present predicament.

Her butler, Paul Burrell, who now, since the departure of
Jephson, had become Diana's gatekeeper and the repository of her
secrets, had described Diana as 'heartbroken' in the week before
Christmas 1995.[3] She still loved Charles and did not want a divorce.
Now, with that interview, she had played into his hands. While
she might refuse the Queen's invitation to Christmas at Sandringham, she could not refuse her mother-in-law's demand that the
couple divorce for the sake of the country. In any case, the matter
was no longer in her hands: someone leaked the news of the
Queen's letter to the press. For once it was not Diana: it would
not have been in her interest to do so. The Palace resolutely denied
any responsibility; one can only surmise that it might have come
from St James's Palace or the Prince's circle, to pre-empt any

stalling on the issue on Diana's part. Diana had no alternative but to acquiesce, although digging in her heels all the way to get what she wanted in return for the sacrifice of her dream. On 14 February she sent Charles a Valentine's card, 'with love, Diana'.

The next day, 15 February 1996, she had a meeting with the Queen at Buckingham Palace, with notes taken by the Queen's deputy private secretary, Robin Janvrin. The only account of the interview which we have is that given by Paul Burrell, now privy to all the Princess's secrets and, indeed, her correspondence (whether authorized or not). At any rate, his account would have been Diana-inspired: this would have been how she recounted it to him. Diana made her position clear to the Queen: 'I do not want a divorce. I still love Charles. None of what happened is my fault,' she said.[4] She then unburdened herself: 'She unbottled years of suspicion and emotion before the Queen, and not for the first time,' Burrell wrote. She spoke of her enemies who were jealous of her popularity with the public. 'She knew she could talk to the Queen. Answers and solutions were rarely forthcoming, but Her Majesty always provided a sympathetic ear.'[5] The one subject on which the Princess and the Queen were in total agreement was the welfare of Princes William and Harry. The Queen assured Diana that she should not worry about the custody of her sons, always Diana's primary concern. 'Whatever may transpire in the future, nothing will change the fact that you are the mother of both William and Harry. My concern is only that those children have been the battleground of a marriage that has broken down,' the Queen said.[6] Diana expressed her hurt that she had received letters from both Her Majesty and the Prince of Wales at the same time urging divorce. The Queen said that although the exchange of letters had led nowhere, she remained of the opinion she had expressed at the time: 'The present situation is not doing anybody any good, either country, family or children.' The underlying message was that there could be no going back, and that the sooner the divorce was agreed, the better.[7]

Then came the question of Diana's future which would involve how she would be viewed by the Royal Family and the public.

This turned on the question of whether she would be entitled to keep the title 'Her Royal Highness' after the divorce. The Palace later insisted that dropping the title was Diana's idea, a statement she hotly contested but one that was probably true at the time. The Queen made her views clear when she said that she thought the title of Diana, Princess of Wales, would be more appropriate, and said it was a matter for discussion with Charles. Diana may have acted hastily in offering to give it up and then regretted it, not realizing, perhaps, the significance of the title to the Queen as implying membership of the Royal Family. Historically, the refusal of King George VI to grant Wallis Simpson the title of HRH on her marriage to his brother, the former Edward VIII, now Duke of Windsor, had caused an irreparable rift between them. The King's decision, made on the grounds that it was for him and him alone to decide who should and who should not be considered as a member of the Royal Family, overriding the common-law principle that a wife should take her husband's style or title, was controversial then and remains so today. At the time it was also privately considered undesirable that a twice-divorced woman of questionable reputation, who might divorce again, should go about the world as a member of the Royal Family calling herself 'Her Royal Highness'. (Who knows whether such thoughts had not lingered on into the 1990s?) The Queen had been eleven years old when her uncle had married Wallis, certainly old enough to remember the huge upset the abdication and its aftermath had caused her family. As she did in so much, she would have been conscious of precedent and of following her father's example. In her mind, a divorced wife of a Prince of Wales could no longer claim membership by marriage of the Royal Family, hence her statement, 'Speaking personally, I think that the title "Diana, Princess of Wales" would be more appropriate.'

Diana soon realized that she did not want to give up her title, telling her friends how 'hurt' she was by the proposal, and how humiliating it would be for her to curtsey to lesser royals. The public did not understand the royal way of thinking: to them, it appeared a petty and vindictive move against Diana which was to resonate with disastrous consequences at the time of her death. Diana was still the mother of the future King and it would probably have been more politic to have made her an exception, leaving her the HRH at least until she remarried.

On 28 February Charles and Diana had a private meeting at St James's Palace, during which, according to friends, she told him, 'Whatever happens, I will always love you.' Prince Charles's response is not recorded. No one else was present and subsequently, to the fury of both St James's and Buckingham Palaces, Diana jumped the gun with her own version of the meeting. Since Jephson's departure, Diana had appointed Jane Atkinson as her press adviser, and Michael Gibbins as her private secretary. Jane Atkinson was waiting in Diana's office with her lawyer, Anthony Julius of Mishcon de Reya, when Diana returned, determined to pre-empt the Prince with a press statement. She indicated that she had consented to a divorce, and that they both had agreed that she would continue to be consulted about all decisions concerning the children, that she would live at Kensington Palace but continue to keep her office at St James's Palace. Outraged at what they saw as a blatant breach of confidentiality (and a pre-emptive strike in the legal war) the Queen's officials issued their own statement pointing out that what Diana had represented as 'decisions' were merely 'requests' and that details about the divorce remained to be discussed before being settled. Further, Diana used Richard Kay to leak the accusation that the Queen and Prince Charles had pressured her into giving up the title HRH.

Once again, Diana's use of the media, 'going public' on private affairs, infuriated the Palace, and even the Queen. Charles Anson, the Queen's press secretary, came forward to make a statement denying Diana's claim that the Queen and Prince Charles had pressed her to give up her title. 'The decision to drop the title is the Princess's and the Princess's alone,' Anson said. 'It is wrong that the Queen or the Prince asked her. I am saying categorically that is not true. The Palace does not say something specific on a point like this unless we are absolutely sure of the facts.' Instead of keeping the Queen on side, Diana had, as she had with her defiant refusal of the Sandringham invitation, thrown down the gauntlet to her royal in-laws. Ill-tempered divorce discussions dragged on into July until Charles presented her with his final settlement offer. (Before this, at the end of June, Diana had made one last-ditch attempt to keep the HRH, leaking the story via Richard Kay that the Palace now insisted she keep the title as mother of the future King – which was quite untrue.)

Diana's resistance, and, no doubt, the unarguable fact that she had moral right on her side, paid off. Compared with the meagre settlement given to the Duchess of York for her divorce in May, Charles's offer – underwritten by the Queen, since he was forbidden by law to sell off Duchy of Cornwall assets to pay for it – was a generous one. Diana would receive a lump sum of £15 million, plus some £400,000 a year to run her office. Diana's title would be 'Diana, Princess of Wales' and she would be 'regarded as a member of the Royal Family', which made the withdrawal of the title HRH even more peculiar. She would be invited to state and national occasions when she would be treated as if she still had the title. Her public role would be 'for her to decide' although any working trips overseas – as distinct from private holidays – would require consultation with the Foreign Office and permission from the Queen (standard practice for members of the Royal Family). She would have access to royal flights and to the state apartments in St James's Palace for entertaining. She would also have the use of all the royal jewellery, eventually to be passed on to the wives of her sons. The couple would sign a confidentiality agreement, prohibiting them from discussing the terms of the divorce or any details of their lives together. On 15 July Diana and Charles filed their decree nisi, the document declaring that their marriage would be dissolved six weeks later, on 28 August. Two days after that, on 30 August 1996, an entry appeared in the *London Gazette* (the traditional place for such royal pronouncements): 'The Queen has been pleased by Letters Patent under the Great Seal of the Realm dated 21 August 1996 to declare that a former wife . . . of a son of a Sovereign of these Realms, of a son of a son of a Sovereign and of the eldest living son of the eldest son of the

Prince of Wales shall not be entitled to hold and enjoy the style, title or attribute of Royal Highness.' The language may have been archaic, but the meaning was stark: Diana was to be stripped of her title.

Yet nothing could compensate for the final end of the marriage by which Diana had set such store, the final end to her romantic dreams of a loving marriage with husband and children. Diana had fought, but ultimately she had lost, as much through her own impetuous misjudgement as through any Machiavellian manoeuvres by the Palace. Both the Queen and the Duke of Edinburgh had counselled her to live apart but in harmony with her husband. Recklessly, and against all advice, she had determined to follow her instinct down unwary paths, refusing to compromise. Perhaps she should have read about the life of Edward VII and Queen Alexandra sooner, but if she had it is unlikely that it would have made any difference. Alexandra had compromised and made her own life, increasingly isolated at Sandringham, but with the respect of her husband and the love of the public. As the daughter of the King of Denmark, she knew the royal rules and played by them. She was also fortunate in having a loving and close family to support her and to whom she could retreat in times of trouble. Diana had none of those advantages and paid the price of resistance to the rules; she was now alone, divorced, and had left the field clear for her rival, Camilla.

Three friends stood by her through thick and thin – Lucia Flecha de Lima, Annabel Goldsmith and Rosa Monckton. Only Rosa saw what Lucia called Diana's 'dark side'. At Ormeley Lodge, the Goldsmiths' house, where she was one of the family, observers saw only her charming and witty personality. 'She was so funny,' one said. 'She used to have us on the floor with laughter, some of the remarks she made . . .'[8] When she heard that Lucia's husband, Paulo Tarso, had had a stroke and was in hospital in Washington, Diana, without telling anyone, flew straight there to visit him. 'She couldn't see herself as other people saw her, how people were totally in awe of her. She would come into a room and people would stop,' said Flecha de Lima's daughter, Beatriz. 'When my father was in hospital and she flew to America . . . Again this is why we loved her so much, she had this kind of thing that was unbelievable, which was, my father is in the hospital, he had a stroke and she flew without anybody saying "Please come" . . . The next day she flew and she came to the hospital and the floor where my father was there was the Coca-Cola machine, with a slow queue of people just to take a glimpse of her, people would not leave the floor, they wanted to see her . . . and my father had to be woken up from time to time, people saying "Paulo, Paulo" and [he] would not respond. Then Princess Diana whispered "Paulo" and he woke up. Then there was this man screaming for the doctor, saying, "I'm hallucinating . . . I thought I saw Princess Diana." [9]

Diana's social friends received the same compassionate treatment in crises. When the husband of Pamela Harlech, whom Diana knew through her work for the English National Ballet, died, Diana went out of her way to ensure that his widow did not feel lonely, telephoning her, asking her to lunch. 'That was the nursing side of her,' Lady Harlech said. 'Diana was wonderful to me after Terence died,' said Diana Donovan, widow of the celebrated photographer who had been a great friend of Diana's. 'He died in late 1996 so in all that time she was quite a presence in my life, really an incredibly supportive presence for a young girl to be supporting an older woman. The first call I got on that Christmas Day of 1996 was from her. She was in the Caribbean . . .' [10]

'What people don't understand about Diana was the incredible pressure she was under. All the time,' said a friend. 'Incredible pressure from when she was nineteen . . .' [11] That pressure led her to seek release in 'fun' urban social circles which she now regarded as 'normal life'. These circles included the people whose names were to be found in the 'High Life' column written by Taki Theodoracopulos in the *Spectator*, people who on the whole were never going to give her the support or even respect she required. Diana desperately needed sympathy and understanding. She found both in a new friend who was part of the Goldsmith circle, Lady Cosima Somerset.

Cosima Somerset, then thought to be the daughter of Annabel
Goldsmith's brother, Alastair, 9th Marquess of Londonderry, met
Diana at lunch at Ormeley Lodge in January 1996. Cosima's
mother, the beautiful and much loved Nicolette, had killed herself
in August 1993 at the age of fifty-two. Cosima herself had separated
that month from her second husband, Lord John Somerset, a
younger son of the 11th Duke of Beaufort, and had recently left
their children, aged five and three, with their father at Badminton,
the stately home of the Somerset Dukes of Beaufort, in Gloucestershire. Cosima herself had been brought up as Lady Cosima Vane-
Tempest-Stewart at Wynyard, the English estate of the Marquesses
of Londonderry until it was sold by Alastair. Meeting Diana at a
lunch for only the three of them – Annabel, Diana and Cosima –
she had seen in Diana's eyes 'true empathy'. 'The parallel of our
experience was exact,' she recalled. In tears, Cosima told Diana
that she felt as if 'the umbilical cord between myself and my
children had been cut again . . . I was beginning to mourn what
had for decades been a great part of my life. I had formed a
deep bond with Badminton and everybody who belonged there.
Badminton had healed the pain of losing Wynyard, my father's
estate near Durham, where I spent my childhood . . . In Diana's
eyes I saw that she understood. All she said was, "Cosi, you will
get used to it." '[12] 'At a moment of great pain,' Cosima wrote, 'I
fell in love with this girl.'[13]

The two women became inseparable, constantly on the telephone to each other, sending each other videos. After a trip to
Lahore with Diana and Annabel Goldsmith in February, Cosima
wrote: 'What we had experienced was real intimacy and companionship, and from that moment I felt that she was my sister
and that we had both been adopted into Annabel's ever-growing
family.'[14] The day after they returned home to London, Diana
sent Cosima a scented candle in a clay pot with the note, 'I hope
this candle lights some of your darkest moments.' Cosima found
the gesture 'almost telepathic'; she lit Diana's candle every day
for six months. They met once a week for lunch at Kensington
Palace – 'almost like a mutual therapy session, full of silences and

outpourings'. 'We shared the experience of being separated from our husbands and uncertain about what the future held. We had both broken away from large, powerful families and therefore we had lost our protection. Both of us were considered "hysterical, unbalanced, paranoid, foolish".'[15] Both of them sought explanations for their painful, chaotic lives in the spiritual and the psychic, for some reason finding comfort in the idea that life is predestined.

In May that year the two of them spent a weekend at La Residencia in Majorca, gossiping, talking about everything – childhoods, children, marriages. On the drive down the mountains to the airport, Cosima gained an insight into the nightmare aspects of Diana's life. As they left the gates of La Residencia, driven by the hotel manager, they were immediately pursued by paparazzi in cars and on motorbikes. They careered down the winding road with the convoy in hot pursuit; as they hit a dual carriageway at speed, a motorbike drew alongside. The paparazzo on the pillion pointed his lens right up against the car window. 'I felt as if Diana had almost been assaulted,' Cosima said, 'but she remained ice cool. Her coolness was shocking to me, for I had been sure the car would crash.' All Diana said was, 'Welcome to my world . . .'[16] It was an eerie foretaste of things to come.

Although ostensibly in aid of Annabel's son-in-law Imran Khan's cancer hospital in Lahore, where the former Pakistan cricket star, now a politician, lived with his young wife, Annabel's daughter Jemima, there was another, more personal reason for Diana's visit to Pakistan. Diana had been in love since the previous autumn with a handsome Pakistani heart surgeon, Hasnat Khan, whom she had met while visiting the sick husband of her therapist friend and counsellor, Oonagh Shanley-Toffolo, at the Royal Brompton Hospital in west London. Diana had been treated by Oonagh, perhaps the most trusted of the long list of psychic helpers, since 1989, when they had met through Mara Berni, of San Lorenzo. Diana was at the hospital with Oonagh when her husband Joseph suffered a relapse after his triple bypass operation on 31 August. Hasnat Khan, assistant to the celebrated Professor Sir Magdi

Yacoub who had performed Joseph Toffolo's operation, came into the room and was introduced to Diana. While preoccupied with Toffolo's condition, he barely noticed Diana; she, however, was immediately struck by him. After he had left the room she apparently said to Oonagh, 'Isn't he drop-dead gorgeous?' She later told another of her therapists, Simone Simmons, that she was sure her meeting with him was 'karmic'.[17] For the remaining years of her life, her passion for Hasnat underlay various initiatives she would take, the visit to Pakistan with Annabel and Cosi being one of them.

The answer to her prayers was thirty-six years old, born into a rich middle-class family living in Jhelum, in the province of Lahore in Pakistan. He had studied medicine at the King Edward Hospital in Lahore, then moved to Sydney where his uncle, a distinguished heart surgeon, arranged a position for him at St Vincent's Hospital. In 1992, after the murder of his mentor, cardiac specialist Dr Victor Chang, Khan left Australia for England. Kind, honourable and compassionate, as well as being a dedicated professional, Hasnat seemed to personify to Diana everything she had ever looked for in a man and never found. She had become interested in Islam and Islamic philosophy – Sufism in particular – through Oliver Hoare but as early as the autumn of 1990, at the time of the Gulf War, she had attended at her own request a lecture on Islam given by the Cambridge professor Akbar Ahmed at the Royal Anthropological Institute. In the lecture Professor Ahmed had emphasized the importance of the family in Islam and afterwards Diana had asked him in private what she could do to help: 'How can I improve the understanding between Islam and the West? What role can I play?' The professor later thought that he had raised 'a tiny spark' of interest in Islam in Diana, that she might have been seeing it as a civilization where not only is there a position for women but where women are loved and respected and given the attention and care they deserve. In fact Diana had been planning an official visit to Pakistan that year which had had to be postponed. It finally took place in September 1991, when Diana had arranged to have a prior briefing by Professor Ahmed. Anxious to make a good

impression, Diana had asked his advice as to how she should dress
and what she should say if asked to speak. Ahmed advised her to
quote from the work of Sir Allama Mohammad Iqbal, Pakistan's
national poet, giving her a passage which would become relevant
to her own life later when she met Hasnat Khan: 'There are so
many people who wander about in jungles searching for something, but I will become the servant of that person who has got
love for humanity.'[18]

Diana arrived in Pakistan for her first visit on 22 September. She
was assigned a woman member of the new Cabinet to accompany
and guide her through her tour of healthcare and educational
institutions. Syeda Abida Hussain, a successful woman in her own
right, was unimpressed by Diana's romantic perception of Muslim
men. Diana, she said, appeared to be fascinated by the Pakistani
male image, the strong Muslim man whom she saw as being
protective towards women. It seemed to be all she wanted to talk
about.

Imran Khan, who was based in London where he enjoyed
considerable social and sexual success but whom she had not yet
met, seemed to Diana to combine the ideal qualities of East and
West: sophisticated but with the strong background of Muslim
culture. By the autumn of 1995, when Diana first encountered
Hasnat, she had met Imran at the centre of her social life, the
Goldsmith household. Imran had married the beautiful twenty-
one-year-old Goldsmith heiress Jemima in June and taken her to
live in Lahore with his family in the time-honoured Muslim tradition. Jemima (whose father was Jewish) had converted to Islam
and wore the shalwar kameez. Diana very much admired Jemima,
although she was university-educated and more than ten years
younger. Her family thought that Diana empathized with Jemima
Khan and visualized herself leading the same life.[19] In February
1996 Diana, Annabel and Cosima Somerset flew out to Lahore
in the Goldsmith private jet for a fund-raising dinner in aid of
Imran's cancer hospital. That was, at least, the ostensible motive.
Privately, Diana was determined to meet, and if possible win over,
Hasnat's family in Pakistan. In the event, fear of press publicity

prevented the meeting but Diana conscientiously fulfilled her charity obligations to Imran. A friend touring the hospital with her was worn out by Diana's determination not to disappoint: 'I thought we were never going to get out of that . . . hospital. She went into every room, she practically picked up every child. She went from room to room; now you don't have to do that to make your impression but she got herself right into the whole thing, sometimes with humour, sometimes with compassion, she was utterly, utterly dedicated . . . I was absolutely exhausted but she kept on going. I think we started at eight or nine in the morning and we didn't sit down to lunch until something like 3.30 . . .'[20] 'She made more for that hospital than anyone, the fund-raising dinner that night was amazing . . .'[21] Back in London, on 4 July, the day on which details of the proposed divorce settlement were published in the press, Diana attended a fund-raising dinner for Imran's hospital at the Dorchester Hotel. In a gesture which, to herself at least, symbolized her breakaway from the Royal Family, she wore the shalwar kameez designed for her by Rizwan Beyg in Lahore for her February visit. She was thinking, of course, of Hasnat: over the next thirteen months thoughts of him would dominate her actions. Immediately after the dinner, she drove herself up to Stratford-upon-Avon to visit his relations.

It was a secret affair, shared, apparently, with therapists Shanley-Toffolo and Simmons, but kept for some time even from Burrell. Diana made nightly visits to Khan at the Royal Brompton and nearly got herself into trouble when she was spotted by a cameraman in the car park, only escaping detection by spinning a story to Clive Goodman, the accompanying reporter from the *News of the World*. In a brunette wig and casual clothes – leggings and trainers – she and Khan would make nightly expeditions to Ronnie Scott's jazz club. Diana, in true Marie Antoinette fashion, thrilled to the unfamiliar experience of joining a queue to get in. Later, Burrell would pick Khan up at the KFC near the hospital and drive him into Kensington Palace, as they thought *inconnu* and under a blanket. They did not, however, escape the notice of Princess Margaret's eagle-eyed staff. 'Here comes Khan in MOA [the registration number of Diana's car]', the cry went up. Once inside, Khan would turn on the television and often watch a football match. Hasnat Khan broke every rule in Diana's book: he was overweight, smoked and ate junk food; nevertheless she was besotted with him. His medical skills fascinated her; she read Gray's *Anatomy of the Human Body* and watched surgical operations. Caught on camera by Sky News she was accused of phony ghoulishness. But despite tabloid sniffing, the affair remained secret for some time.

Shortly after the announcement of her filing for divorce on 15 July 1996, Diana let it be known that she was drastically curtailing her charity patronages, retaining only six: the homeless charity Centrepoint, the Leprosy Mission, the National AIDS Trust, the English National Ballet, Great Ormond Street Hospital for Sick Children and the Royal Marsden Hospital. Unfortunately she could not avoid injecting a sour note into the announcement which she ordered Jane Atkinson to put out: 'The move is entirely because of her loss of royal status . . . The loss in her standing will not be beneficial to those charities and her pulling power must be diminished. She can no longer give them the strong position they are entitled to.' Diana got a bad press over both her decision and her statement, which indeed could have been interpreted as a dig at her soon to be ex-in-laws. Nonetheless, since she was in theory retiring into private life, it was only natural that she should want to cut down on her public commitments and keep the causes which were particularly important to her – AIDS, lepers, the sick, the dying and the dispossessed. The English National Ballet she kept because of her love of ballet and belief in the company, something which she emphasized on the day her divorce was finalized by visiting the ballet school.

'On the day her marriage ended,' her driver-cum-security man Colin Tebbutt recalled, 'we were at the Ballet School round the back of the Albert Hall. I always remember at 10.26 we had the official Jaguar and at 10.28 we didn't have it any more (well, at least we had it to drive away). And there was an enormous amount of interest when we came out of that Ballet School . . . the Princess looked great, she was wearing her engagement ring and she flashed her engagement ring, and I thought she had great, great strength that day . . .'[22] 'She asked if she could come to rehearsal,' Pamela Harlech said. 'I think she just wanted to get out and I think she also wanted to be seen to be fine and having a good time, and she came to a rehearsal and that mews [Jay Mews] was absolutely stacked with press.'[23]

But for all her emotional intelligence and talk of wanting a 'normal' life, Diana was conservative enough at heart to resent no longer being the member of the Royal Family which the title Her Royal Highness had declared her to be. Always lacking in self-esteem, she seemed not to realize that her worldwide celebrity was such that she would always be 'Princess Diana' or 'Princess Di' to the public, that she had reached a different plane from merely being royal. In June she had made a three-day trip to Chicago to raise money for cancer charities where, according to her American biographer, she had attracted large, enthusiastic crowds that recalled the early days of 'Di-mania'.

And now Diana was reaching beyond her old circle to celebrities – Elton John, Gianni Versace among them – and in particular to those who were as vulnerable to the price of fame as she was. She saw herself as a therapist, and she had certainly had plenty of experience on the receiving end. In May 1996 she introduced herself to Michael Barrymore, the popular British television star who was being treated for alcohol and drug addiction and who had recently come out as gay after twenty years of marriage. While he was in a clinic, Diana's office forwarded a note: 'She so understands what he and Cheryl [Barrymore's wife and manager] are going through. She hopes that people will let them have their own space and time. She also hopes they will be able to meet with her a little bit later. She sends lots of love.' Martin Bashir telephoned to make an appointment with Barrymore, then, when Diana was about to arrive, telephoned twice to ensure that Cheryl Barrymore would not be present at the interview.

Diana and Barrymore spent several hours in this first private meeting from which Cheryl Barrymore had been specifically excluded. Despite the prohibition, Cheryl checked up on them, to find them sprawled together on adjoining sofas, chatting away like old friends. 'It was very cosy for a first visit,' she noted. Neither of them looked up or noticed her entry: she went away leaving them together for a couple of hours until she heard Diana leave. The next morning Burrell arrived with a handwritten note to Barrymore saying how much Diana had enjoyed the visit, how much they had in common, and that they should meet again soon. 'It quickly became a regular thing,' Cheryl recalled. 'Martin Bashir would phone to make arrangements, a meeting would take place, and the following day Paul Burrell would deliver another gushing note saying how enjoyable it had been.'[24] It was somehow poignantly illustrative of Diana's estrangement from Establishment circles, that the Princess of Wales should make use of a television journalist and a butler for her confidential missions.

The theme of their conversations was their own problems in the context of celebrity. Significantly, Diana would say that only three people in England counted as far as the media was concerned: herself, Barrymore and 'Gazza' – Paul Gascoigne, a superbly talented but troubled England footballer, who had set off down the road to self-destruction. 'She seemed to think that there was a front-page rotation for stars with a problem, and saw Barrymore and Gazza as stand-ins to give her a break,' Cheryl wrote. Slowly it became clear that Diana was drawing Barrymore further and further into her world. She talked to him about her own problems and insecurities. 'She seemed to feel that, by opening up herself, she would help him unload his troubles,' Cheryl wrote, but to her the confidences seemed to be more than a cry for help. 'Diana seemed to believe they could achieve something truly great . . . together because they had the key weapon: massive public affection . . . [Diana was] telling Michael how they were really going to teach a few people some lessons . . .' Quite who she meant she did not say, at least not in front of Cheryl, but it could be surmised that the targets would be Charles and Camilla and their friends. Finally, to Barrymore's fury, Cheryl suggested Diana should leave and from then on their meetings took place at Kensington Palace.

Cheryl was kept in the dark about their conversations but, she alleged, Diana's influence caused him increasingly to lose any sense of reality. 'Over the year or so that Diana and Michael entertained each other, things got steadily worse,' she wrote. 'She encouraged a way of thinking that was hardly normal, and he was starting to lose the ability to see when something was nonsense . . . He would often have a distant look in his eyes, almost like a religious conversion . . .'[25] The words 'my public' were becoming all too frequent. Dangerously, both were beginning to believe too much in the huge power of celebrity legitimized by public affection.

In her role as international celebrity fund-raiser, Diana made two more trips to the United States that year: once to Washington to raise money for Katharine Graham's charity, the Nina Hyde Center for Breast Cancer Research, at a high-powered gala for eight hundred people from the worlds of society and fashion. Kay Graham gave a lunch in her honour, and Hillary Clinton a White House breakfast for 110, where Diana received a standing ovation. America increasingly became the focus of Diana's dreams of a new life of her own, deluding herself that in a country so rich in celebrities she might escape the constant press persecution which dogged her closer to home.

Over the years leading up to their final divorces in 1996 – Sarah's on 30 May and Diana's on 28 August – Diana and her sister-in-law had been close, in cahoots against 'the grey men' of the Queen's and the Prince of Wales's households. The unfortunate Sir Robert Fellowes happened to be related to both of them, being not only Diana's brother-in-law but also Sarah's cousin. But while he remained fond of Diana, whom he called by her nickname Duch, he and the other courtiers now detested Sarah on Andrew's behalf. The Duke of York remained obsessed with his wife and on the best of terms with her, despite her sexual relationship with the louche John Bryan, her 'financial adviser', he of the toe-sucking pictures which had caused such scandal. Unlike Diana, who maintained her star status and popularity with the public, Sarah was an object of ridicule for her relationship with Bryan, who was declared bankrupt in August 1996 (by which time his relationship with Sarah was over), for her debts and her frantic attempts to redeem herself by writing books – *Budgie the Helicopter* and a book on Queen Victoria's travels, actually written by the scholarly Benita Stoney, niece of the royal librarian, Oliver Everett. Her announcement on a charity visit to Portugal that she had twice taken AIDS tests – once before her marriage to Prince Andrew in 1986 – had not helped.

On one occasion the Palace had blocked Sarah's hopes of becoming a goodwill ambassador for refugees and the UNHCR, in the footsteps of Audrey Hepburn and Sophia Loren. Sarah had been thrilled at the prospect, which would have seen her upstaging 'the Blonde', as she called Diana. Beneath their friendship as 'the Wicked Wives of Windsor', as they called themselves, the old rivalry, however, survived. Both of them were therapy junkies, swapping the latest exciting forecast from their psychic mediums and fortune-tellers – Rita Rogers and astrologer Penny Thornton among them. A persistent shared delusion was that Charles would never become King, that he would die, or be forced to abdicate, leaving Prince Andrew as Regent until Prince William came of age. After one consultation, Sarah was reported as 'bursting with excitement': she had received a prediction that Charles was about to die – having survived one avalanche, he would not survive a second. She telephoned Diana to inform her she was about to become a widow. In Sarah's version of the Charles death scenario, the boys would be killed with him, leaving Andrew to become King, when she would definitely outrank 'the Blonde'. The Queen Mother, regarded by both Diana and Sarah as 'the Chief Leper in the Leper Colony', was another royal candidate predicted to succumb.[26] Both women happily shared this belief which would remove the chief obstacles to their royal futures.

It was basically an unequal relationship: Diana outranked Sarah in almost every way that mattered, in beauty and in status. Diana had always been rich in her own right, with an impeccable pedigree stretching back over the centuries. Sarah, although well connected, had always been relatively poor and was now desperately in debt.

There were old rivalries, notably the Queen's undoubted preference for Sarah in the early years of the York marriage: an identity
of interests which Diana would never achieve despite the Queen's
even-handed treatment of her daughters-in-law. The bottom line
now was that Sarah's misbehaviour had far eclipsed Diana's. Somehow, a letter from Princess Margaret to Sarah informing her in no
uncertain terms that she had let down the Royal Family came into
the public domain. John Bryan's former business partner and friend
Allan Starkie quoted Sarah as saying, 'One of the overriding reasons
I should go back to Andrew is simply to say "Fuck you" to all
those people who said it couldn't be done, and all those people
who have been backstabbing me. But it would mean returning to
a joyless life, living as a nun, and giving up JB [John Bryan].'[27]
Starkie, it must be said, had many reasons for wanting to get his
own back on both Sarah and Bryan.

One theme above all others illustrates the underlying rivalry
between Sarah and Diana and their obsession with celebrity – this
time with John F. Kennedy Jr, son of the assassinated President,
dubbed 'the Sexiest Man Alive', 'Hunk of the Year' and 'the
Handsomest Man in the World' by *People* magazine in 1988. Sarah
apparently had a dream that she would marry John Kennedy and
become First Lady of America. In pursuit of this dream, she had
obtained his telephone number on one of her visits to New York
and asked him if he would like to come round for drinks or dinner
at the Carlyle Hotel where she was staying. Two hours later,
however, a member of Kennedy's staff called back to say he would
be unavoidably detained and would have to cancel their date.
Sarah's mortification can only be imagined when she heard that
Diana and JFK Jr had had a meeting at the Carlyle when Diana
was in New York in December 1995. Kennedy had requested the
meeting, hoping to persuade Diana to appear on the cover of the
first issue of his magazine *George*. Diana turned him down. Rumour
later spread that they had had a brief but passionate encounter.
Unfortunately for rumour, Patrick Jephson had been present when
the meeting took place, a witness to its disappointingly platonic
nature. An absurd coda to the JFK Jr obsession came after Allan

Starkie attempted suicide in 1995. Sarah telephoned Rita Rogers with the news, to be told that he would try it again and this time would succeed. If Starkie is to be believed, and the story appears too bizarre to be invented, Sarah then asked him to do her a favour: 'When you're dead, would you find JFK and explain to him that I am destined to marry John–John and become the First Lady of the United States? But I would like him to help me with this and approach John–John in his dreams and try to explain it to him and convince him . . .'[28]

In 1996 three books about Sarah were published: one by Allan Starkie, one by the 'Pyramid Lady', Vasso Kortesis, the repository of many of Sarah's confidences over the years, and a self-justifying ghost-written autobiography by Sarah herself, *My Story*. The book and Sarah's tour of the United States to publicize it led to what was to be the final rift between her and Diana. The book contained various references to Diana which seemed to her to be breaches of confidence: that she was weepy and reclusive at Balmoral in 1986 where Sarah's radiance compared favourably with Diana's gloom. Annoying, too, was Sarah's stress on what she saw as her close and caring relationship with the Queen. Even more offensive to Diana was Sarah's reference to catching verrucas from Diana's borrowed shoes.[29] Petty though it may have been, in Diana's eyes it was disloyalty and in 'Duch's' world once you were gone you were gone. They never spoke again, nor were William and Harry allowed to visit their cousins, Beatrice and Eugenie. Despite Sarah's attempts at reconciliation, there was to be no way back. They would still be estranged when Diana died.

19. Stirring Beneath the Surface

'The divorce was more or less done and dusted – but she had very strong views on Charles's household . . . she used to tell me she was more concerned about Charles and the people around him'[1]

'It's the 28th August 1996 – 15 years of marriage have now been signed off,' Diana wrote on the day her divorce was finalized. 'I never wanted a divorce and always dreamed of a happy marriage with loving support from Charles. Although that was never meant to be, we do have two wonderful boys who are deeply loved by their parents. A part of me will always love Charles, but how I wish he'd looked after me and been proud of my work.

'It has been a turbulent 15 years, having to face the envy, jealousy and hatred from Charles's friends and family – they have so misunderstood me and that has been painful and brought enormous heartache.

'I want so much to be Charles's best friend as I understand more than anyone what he is about and what makes him tick . . .'[2]

'There was a big change after the divorce had come through, I somehow felt she was very much happier. She was on a much more even keel,' a former lady-in-waiting said.[3] Anthony Holden, who lunched with Diana in October, recalled her mood as she considered the possibility that Charles and Camilla might now get married.

'She said to me, "Oh, I don't care, they can get married, they probably ought to get married, it doesn't bother me now." She was in what I would call a fairly serene mood and I think genuinely wanted [it] for the children's sake. She would never have liked Camilla because she blamed Camilla, to my mind justifiably, for the break-up of her marriage with Charles. But she was in the sort of "Oh, what the hell, shrug shoulders, let them do what they want" mode but slightly more generous than that, actually. "Well, I hope they'll be very happy", she'd say, but she'd very much have the children in mind, I think.'[4]

'Diana was blooming after her divorce,' a friend said. The reason was directly linked to her passion for Hasnat Khan, which, although it was still secret, she pursued in her public as well as her private life. The doctor's absorption in his work and his hatred for the publicity which surrounded Diana only made him more attractive to her. Despite his comfortable background in Pakistan, Khan was not rich and Diana did everything she could to advance his career. Her idea appears to have been that he should find work outside England where they could marry and live together in peace. On 13 October 1996 she flew to Rimini to receive a humanitarian award at a conference on health, the annual congress of the Pio Manzù Centre, an international think tank presided over by the ex-President of the Soviet Union, Mikhail Gorbachev. Diana made a speech on the opening day of the congress on her chosen topic: 'The challenge of an ageing population'. Dr Christiaan Barnard, the famous South African surgeon who had carried out the first human heart transplant in 1967, also attended the congress to receive an award.

Sitting next to Barnard at dinner, Diana spoke to him about Hasnat and asked him to help get him a position in South Africa. Later, after her death, Barnard revealed that Diana had told him she wanted to marry Hasnat and have two daughters; she was, he said, obviously very much in love with him and would have married him if he had agreed.[5] On her return to London, she wrote to Barnard and telephoned him about job possibilities for Hasnat, and subsequently asked him to dinner twice at Kensington Palace to discuss it. The problem for her was that Hasnat was determined to finish the Ph.D. he was studying for under Dr Magdi Yacoub and was not remotely interested in leaving England until he had done so. He was quite unaware of Diana's campaign on his behalf and was furious when he later found out. Having, at Diana's suggestion, met Barnard on one of his London visits,

Hasnat had, at Barnard's request, sent him his CV under the impression that this might be for a position after he had taken his Ph.D. He only found out what Diana had been plotting when he received a job offer from an American hospital.

His anger did not deter Diana. She also considered Australia a possibility and later that month flew to Sydney for fund-raising events connected with the Victor Chang Institute, set up in memory of Hasnat's late mentor. Diana raised one million Australian dollars for the cardiac centre during her visit, a demonstration to Khan of how much her fame and her abilities could help him in his chosen career, and while she was there she arranged to meet old friends of Hasnat. She had even hoped Hasnat might fly out to Sydney, but the huge publicity surrounding her visit made this impossible. In terms of publicity Diana was reaping the consequences not only of her worldwide celebrity but of her previous visits to Australia where Di-mania had been born. Without the Royalty and Diplomatic Protection Department and with inadequate security provided by her hosts, Diana was hounded: women crowded round her table to stare and often to touch her; when she got up to dance, she was quickly surrounded by gawping couples, some of whom made sure they brushed against her. She was mobbed when she tried to go to the lavatory and forced to flee. In the hotel chosen for her she had to lie low with the curtains drawn even in daytime. If she had ever thought that her divorce from the Royal Family would bring her freedom and a normal life, this experience should have disabused her.

The Australian visit was a disaster in other ways. Her romance with Hasnat was outed by the *Sunday Mirror* (3 November 1996) which claimed to have made the connection between her midnight hospital visits, her interest in medicine expressed by her attendance at heart operations and the object of her current visit. The reason behind all this focused attention, the newspaper declared, was her love for Dr Hasnat Khan. Terrified of the effect this unwanted publicity might have on Hasnat, Diana tried to deflect it by her old method, leaking a counterstory to the press through Richard Kay, in Australia with the press pack. Her denial appeared in the

Daily Mail the following day in which she was described as upset at the effect these untrue allegations might have on William and Harry and as 'laughing herself silly' over them. Hasnat was deeply offended by the story and temporarily cut off relations with Diana. The incident underlined further what his life with Diana might be like. To woo him back Diana deployed her two confidants, Martin Bashir and Paul Burrell, to socialize with him and keep him on side.

Her relationship with Hasnat and the finality of the divorce had helped her distance herself from thoughts of Charles and Camilla. She no longer felt resentful of Camilla, even sympathizing with the bad publicity her relationship with Charles generated. Nevertheless, Charles and his household still featured large in her thoughts. Richard Aylard, whom she had regarded as the arch-enemy, was to depart at the end of the year, replaced by the assistant private secretary, Stephen Lamport. Of great interest to Diana was the arrival there in 1996 of Mark Bolland as deputy private secretary. Bolland, formerly of the Press Complaints Commission, was a man whose skill with the media was well known, and who had been recommended by friends of Camilla. Camilla's position in the life of the heir to the throne was the principal – but unspoken – cause of resentment between the households of the Queen and her heir. Bolland did little to diminish this; his chief preoccupation was to improve the Prince of Wales's image by subtly gaining public acceptance of the role of Camilla in his life. 'We were all trying to manoeuvre the Prince back into public life in a more respectable way, and trying to find a path for Camilla through it all,' Bolland said. 'At the time before Diana died, it was our view that the Prince was in such a bad position in terms of public reputation and esteem, he went through that ridicule stage . . . it was our view that one of the levers which would bring him up was Camilla, people starting to think better of Camilla would help him . . .' Bolland was clever enough to see that being perceived as trying to do down Diana, public idol number one, would be self-defeating. 'One of the things I went there at the beginning to do,' he recalled, 'was to end this War of the Waleses, the media war fought on their behalf by various people around them, which was also influenced directly by them, more so by her than by him but he was quite capable of nodding and winking to people when it suited, although he's not going to ring up a newspaper and do it himself like she did . . . One of the things that had to be done at that time was to try and disengage from all of that and having to reassure her [Diana] that I wasn't going to be souping up the campaign again but actually the reverse.'6

From his days with the PCC, Bolland had had experience of dealing behind the scenes with the various royal offices: 'One had a sense of what a mess the situation was . . . it was far more a mess on his side than on her side . . . at the time [when he was at the PCC] I was actually very friendly with Robert Fellowes and Charles Anson . . . and you know, St James's Palace was very much a poor relation, it was all a bit of a muddle . . . And when I went to work for the Prince of Wales those relationships broke up, particularly it seemed over the Camilla situation where they took a view and the Prince had a view and I had to choose but it was a shame . . . because if anything when we were at the PCC the relationships with Buckingham Palace were very important, then the Spencers and Kensington Palace to a lesser extent, and then St James's Palace way down the list . . . When William went to Eton [September 1995] the whole putting together of a contract with the press that kept the media away from William was actually a Buckingham Palace initiative, that Charles Anson started off . . . Diana, who must have been talked to by David English about it, played ball . . . was happy with the thing, and St James's Palace were very, very reluctant to participate and actually at Buckingham Palace, Charles and Robert very much made it in terms of the internal dynamic of the Palace, their initiative. You know the Queen wanted to stand up and look after her grandchildren, we know those two other offices hate each other and are dysfunctional but we are going to make sure that the right thing happens for the grandchildren.'

David English had great influence with Diana, and in Bolland's case helped reassure her that Bolland was not there to put her down. 'He had said to her, "You know who the enemy is, you know who are the people Mark needs to deal with and who you need to deal with as well . . .''; he said to her, "Mark is not there to run things against you and if he did I'd stop it anyway.'''" Reassured, Diana invited Bolland to Kensington Palace, which caused near panic at St James's Palace: 'There was a big, kind of, is this the right thing to do? Is Diana going to convert Mark into her way of thinking? They all had a view, even the Prince had a view. Anyway, they decided it was safe, I wasn't going to succumb to charm . . .'[7] Diana did indeed try to exercise her charm: 'She was always very kind, she was always incredibly polite – she'd send me notes, she'd send my mother notes, send my mother signed photographs, all those tricks she employed and every time anything [like that] happened, I was always told by the [St James's] staff, "You see, this is what she does." But my mother liked it – it was a sweet thing for her to do – [but] it wasn't going to change the world for me. She'd ring up – she was clearly sensitive about the outing of Camilla process and understood that had to happen but she didn't want it to happen in a way which overdid things.'[8]

Diana, he said, had very strong opinions about the children, 'how they should be portrayed, how much they should be portrayed with their father and all that'. Poignantly, Bolland recalled how she didn't want the children to end up in the situation she was in 'in terms of just being consumed every day'.

Lord Wakeham, as chairman of the Press Complaints Commission, dealt directly with Buckingham Palace and with Diana, always her own media expert. Treading a delicate tightrope between the palaces and the press, it was his concern to use the monarchy to establish an informal code of conduct which would avoid the necessity for draconian and unworkable privacy laws. In this context it had often been his unenviable job to deal with both Diana and Sarah, who would ring up with some complaint and then, a few hours later, withdraw it. 'We used to get telephone calls either from her or from some friend of hers or from Fergie who she was very close to at one time,' Wakeham recalled, 'and they would ring up and complain about something, and we would say, "You must get someone to write in so that we can deal with it; we can't deal with complaints just over the telephone like that", and there was all hell let loose while we rushed around . . . and then they'd just drop it, just forget about it. You'd hear nothing, they wouldn't give you any details – so there was this scatterbrained approach to it.'⁹ Of Diana's fabled skills in dealing with the press, Wakeham said, '. . . there was a certain schoolgirl idealism about her and a certain lack of practicality but, because she moved in high places with high things, she maybe gave her own thoughts more weight and value than perhaps they really had. And perhaps it's understandable, when you're living in that world – no ma'am, yes ma'am, what a wonderful thought ma'am and everything else type of business – the most trite remark can be thought wise . . . I think that was the problem she had . . .'¹⁰ At one point in 1995, when Diana was getting rough treatment from certain sections of the press, her private secretary came to see Wakeham: 'There was a lot going on,' Bolland, then at the PCC, recalled. 'She was working on too many fronts and his line was "You've got to do something, John, to calm everything down and Wakeham did then go off and talk to the chairman of News International, the chairman of this, the chairman of that. It did trigger a process . . .'¹¹

Bolland confirmed that Buckingham Palace had been sympathetic towards Diana. 'I don't think Buckingham Palace ever did brief against her,' Bolland said. 'Certainly when I knew Robert and Charles during my time at the PCC, we never heard anything that came from them other than a sort of care, no matter how exasperating she was. *Panorama* was around then and they were very disappointed about that. They would never be drawn on her. What St James's Palace did, what Richard Aylard did, I don't know.'¹² At the launch of the new policy to raise the profiles of Charles and Camilla without antagonizing Diana, Aylard had to go since he was seen by all the main media as architect of the campaign against Diana from St James's Palace. Also against Aylard was Camilla, a powerful force with the Prince. 'Camilla blamed

him entirely for the Dimbleby thing, for the adultery [admission],'
an aide said. 'She thinks it couldn't possibly be the Prince's fault
and that he was manipulated into doing it and she wasn't treated
properly about it or told about it properly. And the statement
that was put out later about the Prince having no intention of
remarrying, that was the final straw, but the Dimbleby thing really
made her marriage situation completely untenable. She, and the
people round her, never forgave him [Aylard]. And she will never
forgive him for that.'[13]

Diana still kept up her connection with Charles. 'Occasionally,
if she got in a fix with the media, which did happen from time to
time, she would ring him up. It was quite interesting; whenever
she really got into trouble she would ring him and he would always
be there, also he would ring her up and speak his mind – "I don't
want to be involved, I can't cope any more, I've had enough of
it" etc, etc, "do anything you can to deal with it, use my name,
spend my money, sort it out. I don't want to know but just deal
with it".'[14] Charles would still send her flowers on her birthday
with a card to 'Dearest Diana'.

Despite the divorce, there was no diminution in Diana's preoccupation with her ex-husband. This was best demonstrated by
a curious incident which was to have repercussions long after her
death. It concerned Prince Charles's personal staff. Valets and
dressers have traditionally had access to and influence with their
employers far exceeding that of principal officers of the household,
including private secretaries. Margaret MacDonald, always known
as 'Bobo', the Queen's childhood nursery maid and subsequently
her principal dresser, had been, until her death, the only person to
whom the Queen told 'everything'. Bobo's influence over the
Queen had been widely feared among the Palace staff and the
household; even the Queen's couturiers were bullied by her. 'Miss
MacDonald was the Queen's eyes and ears at the Palace and it
didn't do you any good to fall foul of Miss MacDonald,' said a
member of the Queen's domestic staff. 'If things went wrong Miss
MacDonald would make more fuss than the Queen would. If you
upset Miss MacDonald, it was for life . . .'[15] Staff on the royal yacht

who had to serve Bobo with champagne on a tray, or bring in her breakfast, used to call her 'the QE III'.

The story of the Prince of Wales's valets was rather different from the dominion of Bobo. James 'Jem' MacDonald, who had found the Prince's grandfather, King George VI, dead and who had 'coddled' the young Prince as he grew up, had been succeeded by the flamboyant Stephen Barry and Barry in turn by Ken Stronach, loyal until, shocked and appalled by the Prince's Dimbleby interview, he had talked to the newspapers. He had been replaced by the assistant valet, Michael Fawcett, who had entered royal service as one of the Queen's footmen in 1981. Fawcett, a far more dominant figure, had begun to assert himself as early as 1985. Protective, indeed exploitative, of the Prince and reputed to bully the other staff, Fawcett used his royal connection to obtain goods and favours. He became a director of the Prince's shirtmakers, Turnbull & Asser, and later was given permanent access to a suite at the Ritz. Suppliers who fell out with him were given short shrift. Staff who criticized him or his activities got the sack. 'He was quite ruthless and would get rid of anybody who stood in his way.'[16] 'He's very dangerous,' said a fellow member of staff. 'And the Princess could see that, she knew that . . . people like him butter the Prince up all the time. They created the Prince and they were expert at creating division between the two [Charles and Diana] and one wonders how much they were responsible for it.'[17] 'He's a big man who finds it easy to impose himself.'[18] 'That's how he got on really. It was his size that he was able to use to be so forceful.'[19] At one point Camilla, Fawcett and Mark Bolland formed a powerful trio at St James's Palace – 'Because between the three of them . . . nobody could put up a challenge . . .'[20]

Diana's chance, as she saw it, to make trouble at St James's Palace came through a conversation with the Prince's orderly, George Smith: 'George Smith was a veteran of the Falklands War, a corporal in the Welsh Guards, a loyal man, a squaddie who had put his life at risk to fight for his country . . .' said a member of Diana's staff.[21] 'He was a good man, a decent man that worked his butt off as a soldier and was recommended by his colonel to work as an orderly for the Prince of Wales. Now you don't get that recommendation if you're an absolute idiot, and you don't get it if you're a drunk . . .'[22] George Smith became caught up in a Palace web which was to destroy him mentally and physically. Diana was in the habit, which the Prince rightly regarded as dangerous, of picking up members of her staff for a chat in the kitchen. 'You could be walking in the corridor or the grounds of Kensington Palace and the Princess would say, "Oh, what are you doing, x?" And I'd say, "Nothing much." And she'd say, "I'm going to the kitchen, why don't you come and have a cup of tea?" And you don't turn it down. Similarly George Smith would be there and she'd say, "George." – "Oh, hello, Ma'am." "What are you doing, George? Are you going to see Mervyn [the chef]?" "I'll see you up there then." Of course, poor old George gets up there and it doesn't take long before he's cornered, locked in but feeling safe to talk . . .'[23]

Poor George Smith was simply not equipped to deal with the intricacy of life in the Waleses' household. 'George Smith arrived there in his uniform and was whisked off to Jermyn Street by Michael Fawcett and togged up with a three-piece suit, a Turnbull & Asser shirt and tie, and a pair of shoes from Trickers,' said a staff member. 'So suddenly you have this robot that's no longer George Smith . . . And then you have the open door to the drinks cupboard, you have the open door to the kitchen, so there's plenty of food, there's plenty of drink and plenty of travel, there's a car, there's Highgrove, and you get lost in all of this.'[24] In conversation with Smith, Diana picked up his claim that he had been the victim of homosexual rape by a member of the Prince's staff. In August 1996, armed with Richard Kay's tape recorder, Diana made two visits to Smith (accompanied on one occasion by her personal secretary, Victoria Mendham) to record his allegations.

Friends of Diana doubt that the contents of the tape were intended as ammunition against her husband. 'The divorce was more or less done and dusted – but she still had very strong views on Charles's household . . . she loved causing trouble for St James's Palace, and it did cause a lot of trouble . . .'[25] If, however, she had wanted to do real damage, then she would have handed the tape to the police; instead she told Charles about it. News of its existence did not surface until after the collapse of the Burrell trial in November 2002, when it became evident that the stone Diana had thrown into St James's complacent pool had had ever-widening consequences.

On 11 November 2002, Prince Charles requested his recently appointed private secretary Sir Michael Peat, together with Edmund Lawson QC, to investigate – among other matters – whether there had been 'an improper cover-up of the rape allegation made by Mr George Smith in 1996'. The Peat Report was made public on 13 March 2003. The inquiry was not directed at discovering the truth or otherwise of George Smith's allegations but only as to whether there had been a deliberate cover-up of the affair. Smith had been working for the Prince as a 'Travelling Orderly' after joining the household on secondment from the Welsh Guards in 1987, and was later promoted to 'Assistant Valet' in 1993.[26] In October 1995 Smith was described as 'chronically depressed', his wife having left him, and suffering from post-traumatic problems as a result of his service in the Falklands, where he had been on HMS *Galahad* when the ship was attacked and caught fire with horrific results. He apparently told an assistant personnel officer that he had been raped by 'AA' (the 'alleged assailant', whose identity was known to the Prince of Wales's office and to the press). According to Smith he made his first report of the rape allegation to the Princess of Wales and her personal secretary, Victoria Mendham, at Kensington Palace. He was quoted as describing his visit to Diana later to the police: 'I went to see her and she was just asking me about all different stuff about AA.'[27] He said that he had repeated his allegations to the Princess sometime in 1996 when she had visited him during his third stay at the Priory. He also said that the Princess had visited him at his home in Twickenham, when 'we definitely talked about both rapes'.[28] The first rape is said to have occurred in 1988 when he had only recently joined the household. The second rape of Smith by AA is alleged to have taken place in 1995 but this only emerged

later in an interview with Smith by the *Daily Mail* in 2002, by
which time Smith could have been said to have become unreliable
due to his problems.

Diana telephoned Mrs Yaxley, head of personnel in the Prince
of Wales's household, in the autumn of 1996 and told her of
a 'horrendous' allegation made by George Smith about another
member of staff. Having made sure that someone else knew of the
allegation, Diana then telephoned her husband. Charles reacted
fiercely and called his solicitor, Fiona Shackleton, from the royal
lawyers Farrer & Co., who made a note of their telephone conversation, reporting Charles's words: 'Diana has been interfering &
visiting George Smith, a valet who was suffering from post-
traumatic stress syndrome from Falklands – George was now alleging that AA had raped him years ago.' Charles told her he knew
this to be untrue and wanted the matter cleared up. George, he
said, must go: he was sorry for him because he was an alcoholic
but he could not have him causing trouble in the household 'by
spreading untruths about AA', adding that 'AA was in a terrible
state.' Fiona Shackleton was to telephone Diana's lawyer, Anthony
Julius, 'to tell him to stop Diana interfering & to sort out George
making sure he was properly looked after'.[29] Smith apparently
went to his local police at Hounslow and on '13th–15th' of
October (1996) told them of his background and personal problems
including the alleged rape in 1988 and identified the alleged rapist
by name. The police note read: 'Victim states that one night they
got very drunk and AA raped him.' In view of Smith's earlier –
apparently unfounded – allegations about an armed stalker who
had approached him at his home and in the street – and his
unwillingness to proceed with the rape allegation, the police did
not investigate further.

On 17 October Fiona Shackleton interviewed Mrs Yaxley who
told her that Smith had been 'reissuing' his rape allegations; Mrs
Yaxley also apparently told her that the Princess of Wales 'hates'
AA. Mrs Yaxley wrote that day to the Princess of Wales asking
her for a copy of the 'notes made in the summer' which Smith
told her had been given to her. Diana replied on 21 October: 'I

am afraid that I am unable to accede to your request because I have made a commitment of confidentiality to George', adding enigmatically, 'the purpose of my drawing this to your attention is so that you, with all your resources, might be able to deal with the matter.'

Fiona Shackleton noted to Anthony Julius that they wanted to find out the truth of the allegation 'without press involvement', adding 'we want minimal involvement between the two Households'. Somehow someone in the press had picked up on the story. Diana denied through her solicitor that she had been involved; as the story was well known – 'black rumours, very dangerous' – as one member of staff described it, the leak could have come from anybody. Colin Trimming, the Prince's eyes and ears at Kensington Palace, affirmed that Smith had 'a fairly close social or "drinking" relationship' with two members of Diana's staff. She also said she had not visited Smith since August.

Notes from Fiona Shackleton's meeting with George Smith state: 'Mr Smith did not convey that he "withdrew" his allegation. Rather he said that he did not wish to "press charges"; and he volunteered what was, apparently, his reason, namely that AA was "too powerful". AA's alleged "power" within the Household has been referred to by many of those interviewed by us and Mr Smith's view of this was clearly shared by others.'[30]

From early on Diana had taken what Michael Gibbins, her private secretary, described as 'a close personal interest' in what was happening. She and Gibbins had hired a solicitor for Smith, whose previous solicitor had backed out on the grounds that the matter was 'too big'. It had been decided that, as Charles had said from the beginning, 'George must go'. Gibbins told the solicitor, Chris Benson, that his understanding of the formal reason for the termination of his employment was his dependency on alcohol . . . but that Diana had told him that the substantive reason was the rape allegation. Gibbins advised Benson that, although he could not directly divulge his awareness of that allegation to the Prince's lawyers, he should use that knowledge to gain advantage in obtaining a favourable settlement.

The Peat Report admitted that, although Fiona Shackleton had suggested at the beginning that there should be a wider investigation of the truth of the allegations, there had been none for various reasons, which did not reflect well on St James's Palace. This started from the top, according to Fiona Shackleton, in a meeting on 30 April 2001 with the police and Lady Sarah McCorquodale during the investigations concerning the Burrell trial. Shackleton is recorded in notes by the investigating officer, Mrs De Brunner, as saying: 'I had written instructions from the boss, to make the whole business go away, which I did, but it was one of the lowest points of my professional career.'[31] Fiona Shackleton later denied that she had said this, specifically that she had had written instructions from the Prince 'to make the whole business go away'. She also denied saying that it had been one of the lowest points of her professional career. 'I may well have said "pretty sad about it generally" because of George and his predicament'; further, she said by way of clarification, 'by investigating the allegation I was exceeding the precise instructions I had been given and I was under pressure for a solution to be reached more speedily than I was able to achieve. To that extent it was a very difficult situation for me personally.'[32]

According to the Peat Report, interestingly, 'the fact that the allegation came to be reported initially via The Princess of Wales served to devalue it; the acrimony then existing between St James's and Kensington Palaces was such that this was suspected to be just another "shot" in the battle'. It was put to those charged with drawing up the report that: 'All we had was one poor, sad individual making an allegation of assault some years before to The Princess, who, at that time, quite frankly wanted to find ways of hurting/embarrassing her husband.'

On 18 October, Fiona Shackleton had advised that an investigation should be conducted. On 21 October at a 'Household' meeting with Sir Stephen Lamport, the incoming private secretary, and other senior officers, Mrs Shackleton noted, 'S[tephen] L[amport] wondered if some form of agreement could be reached with George to settle this matter which would avoid an investigation'. Lamport's explanation for this was that he was 'anxious to avoid unnecessary publicity in respect of an allegation believed to be untrue and "withdrawn"'. In fact, there was confusion as to whether or not George Smith had 'withdrawn' the allegation, rather than deciding not to proceed with it because of his 'terror' of AA. Again, it was stressed that no one at that level believed the rape allegation. Colin Trimming, as 'a high-ranking Police Officer and as a long-term associate of the Household', although apparently unaware that George Smith had made his allegation to anyone other than the Princess of Wales, or the Hounslow Police, did not advise any investigation either internally or by the police because 'he also disbelieved the allegation'.[33] Other explanations for the failure to investigate illuminated the general muddle and confusion in the Prince of Wales's household. Unsurprisingly, the report found that there had been no deliberate attempt at a cover-up: 'There was plainly an acute anxiety to prevent, insofar as was possible, the repetition and publication of what was believed to be a false allegation. There was not, however, as we conclude, a desire to suppress the truth.'[34]

The public remained unaware of this potentially sensational material until the Burrell trial when the existence of Diana's tape of Smith's allegations came out. According to police notes of a meeting on 12 June 2001 during the investigation of alleged theft of Diana's property, Lady Sarah McCorquodale said: 'Found box in Diana's apartment. PB [Paul Burrell] asked to look after it because I was going on a train and it was too cumbersome. PB's got the box. In the box: letters, tape. Tape about a rape.' Someone unnamed then said: 'Tape of GS balling [sic] about being raped by AA . . .' Shackleton then said, 'I know all about that. I was asked to make it go away.' She 'became muted' and said, 'It was a terrible business. He was paid. I had to go to Twickenham to see him. He was a pathetic figure. It was the low point of my 22-year legal career.' Later, the Crown Prosecution Service notes did not refer to 'making it go away' or to the 'low point' of Fiona Shackleton's career, giving as explanation that they were 'off the record', but they do mention Lady Sarah's reference to the tape, the box and its contents: 'There is a recording of a male, George Smith, raped by AA and his description of it, Patrick Jefferson's [sic] letter of resignation, James Hewitt's signet ring and documents relating to the divorce.'

In the end, George Smith got a settlement which was worth more than twice the amount he would have got in normal compensation for dismissal. Expelled from the existence he had enjoyed in the royal household, he split up with his wife and went to live with his father in Wales. Still suffering from post-traumatic stress when interviewed by a journalist in 2002 (*Daily Mail*, 9 November 2002), he renewed his rape allegations and added that the man who had attacked him had stolen the tape from Diana's apartment. The mystery concerning the tape and the box continued when Lady Sarah McCorquodale eventually recovered the box from the police – she said she had given it to Burrell but it was not found in the police raid on his Cheshire house looking for 'the Crown Jewels', as the mahogany box was known. George Smith died, aged only forty-five, in 2005.

Meanwhile, following complaints of bullying by other staff in 1998, Prince Charles's favourite servant, Michael Fawcett, resigned. Charles was extremely reluctant to see him go and, allegedly after the intervention of Mark Bolland and Camilla Parker Bowles, he was reinstated as 'Personal Consultant' to the Prince of Wales, with a retainer and the use of a £450,000 house, a grace-and-favour property of the Duchy of Cornwall. As the organizer of stylish events – 'he is a genius at organizing events,' a guest said [35] – for the Prince he became even more indispensable.

George Smith's story had also been material for Diana's teasing of Charles – something which she was always unable to resist. An aide to Charles remembers how, when 'all this was going on in the background, Diana said to the Prince: "Poor George . . . what ghastly people you employ . . . Poor darling . . . Such a shame for you", all that sort of thing, she was such a wonderful carer, she knew exactly which buttons to press . . . I always remember when she rang up, when we heard that Blair might become Prime Minister: "Oh I had dinner with Mr Blair and his wife last night

– they're so concerned about you, darling, they so much want to help . . . It's so kind of them but they don't want to upset me and I said to them 'I don't mind'." You can imagine it. Wonderful!'[36] Diana had certainly succeeded in stirring up the mud for St James's Palace; the details of the unsavoury affair were only to come to light more than five years after her death.

20. Diana the Hunted

'For photographers, Diana became the pot of gold at the end of the rainbow . . .'[1]

'The "third stage" of her life was the one between her divorce and her death,' a friend wrote. Diana was engaged in making a new life for herself. As a single woman she was enjoying a much freer social life; as a public figure she was making her compassion practically useful; she was continuing to be an excellent mother. Everything was beginning to fall into place . . .'[2]

As the new year of 1997 opened, Diana seemed to be standing on a pinnacle of celebrity which she herself had created, a remarkable achievement for the shy teenager who had captured the Prince of Wales just over fifteen years before. 'Diana was globally transformed in my view in that last year of her life,' her friend Richard Kay said. 'That's when she became the big figure that she was.'[3] At lunch with her in Kensington Palace, Anthony Holden was astounded by the people she knew or had met: 'She'd just come back from seeing Hillary Clinton in Washington; we talked about that. She'd been to see the Pope; we talked about that. Talked about the Queen Mother. We talked about, you know, the six most famous people in the world, all of whom she had seen in the last month or so.' They discussed the possibility of her setting up a charitable trust, the idea of which had cropped up at various times in recent years. Then she said: 'What if I gave you a name? I was speaking the other day to Colin Powell and he strongly advised me not to form a foundation. There are complicated this, you lose control of that, there are tax implications . . .' 'I was very much struck by the way she said, "If I gave you a name" – we'd already discussed everybody you'd ever heard of –'[4] Beyond the celebrities, she had a worldwide public not only for her beauty and charm, but for her compassion for the poor and sick which communicated itself to anyone who saw her. And, as she frequently said, she was determined to use this power to help people.

She had already taken a step which symbolized the sloughing off of her old life, deciding to auction her old wardrobe for charity. The idea had been William's. He had said, 'Mummy, you're running out of cupboard space and you're not going to wear any of those again, and I really think something should be done with them, and what will you do with them, send them to a charity shop?' Diana said, 'No, I can't do that. They're too well known, they're too well photographed, why don't we make some money for charity out of it?' When Meredith Etherington-Smith asked William if it had been his idea, 'He said, "Yes, it was my idea – we don't want Mummy wearing any of those again" – and he said it rather firmly.'[5] Some of the clothes were more than ten years old, dating from her earlier, frillier period, before Victor Edelstein had given her a more sophisticated look.

The vehicle was to be a Christie's sale of the clothes for the benefit of the National AIDS Trust, which included two of her friends, Marguerite Littman and Christopher Balfour, chairman of Christie's, with whom she had first discussed the project at lunch in July 1996. Meredith Etherington-Smith, then marketing director of Christie's Worldwide, was to be their representative for the sale, handling all aspects of it, including the cataloguing of each item.

'Christopher Balfour summoned me one morning and said, "Interesting project for you. The Princess of Wales wants to sell her clothes." I said, "Don't be stupid, what are you talking about?" And he said, "She wants to sell her clothes because she's not going to be wearing kind of big ball dresses any more, she's got a new life, she wants to sell them in aid of Marguerite's AIDS Crisis Trust and the Royal Marsden . . . You leg it down to Kensington Palace and meet her . . ."'[6] Wearing her good luck black jacket with starfish buttons, Meredith arrived at the Palace to be met by Burrell, 'smiling but looking slightly nervy'. He took her coat,

asking her to wait. 'He nips upstairs and I subsequently learned
from her that he'd actually gone to say, "She looks all right . . ."
because she was actually rather nervous, she was as nervous as
I was about meeting me for some reason. Apparently I passed
muster – I was filtered through by the butler and went up this very
grand staircase which was obviously part of the original baroque
KP, to see this amazing human being dressed in a white T-shirt
and sneakers and a navy blue cardigan, also looking rather
nervous . . .'

'It's very curious,' Meredith recalled. 'I've met a lot of very
famous people but no one as famous as Diana, visually famous
anyway. But there's a difference between visual fame and people
who are famous for who they really are. In the months after
September 1996 when we first met, I formed a very different
opinion of her from the one I had read about. What I'd thought
she was like was totally unlike the side of her she presented
to me.'[7]

Meredith surmised that Diana was very comfortable in the company of older women. 'I think possibly, without being too psycho-
therapeutic about it, because of the lack of a mother . . . most of
her confidantes apart from Rosa Monckton, were actually older
women – Annabel Goldsmith, Elsa, Marguerite – and I think she
felt very comfortable, they weren't competition, they were fun
and she could become slightly girly with them without the baggage
of "I'm the most beautiful person in the world" . . .' It was decided
that Diana should be involved all the time. ' "It's going to be
partners",' Meredith said. ' "I'll never do anything and make any
decision without referring to you." ' 'There wasn't one decision
that wasn't discussed with her, faxed to her, okayed by her . . .
And as a result of that, I worked with her for nine months, pretty
much, and we didn't have one what I call eyelash moment.' Asked
what she meant, Meredith explained: 'That sort of look, when she
kind of retreated into herself and that hair came over the forehead
and the head went down and she looked up [through her lashes]
. . . it was a very nice and fun working partnership.'[8]

Meredith bought a green leather book which Diana filled with the catalogue entries in her big loopy writing. 'That writing reminds me so much of so many people who were at West Heath . . . She was not a stupid Sloane, she was much more perceptive about herself than you would ever think from just looking at the image or reading the press or seeing her on television. I think she was one of the smartest people I've ever met. Because West Heath was basically knitting for Sloanes when she was there. In my generation we used to laugh at them, we used to say they did O levels in Hamster Husbandry, and I think it was a shame because she had great natural common sense . . .'[9]

Meredith realized that it would be wise to keep a certain distance between them. 'She was a tremendous charmer in the fact that she wanted to draw people into her web and then, having drawn them into the web, when they were totally enslaved by her, then she got bored . . . I felt my job was to always be slightly removed . . . At the second or third meeting, she said, "You must call me Diana." I said, "Actually no, I'd be happier with Ma'am, because as far as I'm concerned that's what you have been and you are . . ." Which went down really well. She said, "Come on, call me Diana", and I said "No", and a slight distance was maintained. Because she talked about other people, "so and so is getting kind of boring, she's ringing up the whole time", I said to her, "Your problem is you are too damn charming and they get completely enthralled by you and have to have the fix", and she laughed and said, "I suppose you're right." And I said, "It's a weapon isn't it, charm? You can convert people." And she said, "You're quite right, but I haven't had that many weapons in my life. What you've got you use." '[10]

Among other things, they discussed Diana's campaign against the use of landmines. Diana told Meredith that she had written to the Foreign Office asking them if she could become a roving ambassador – 'Of course they turned me down . . . I've decided to do it on my own and I'm going to do it for a cause and the cause is going to be landmines. It's appalling the damage they do, and no one cares and they just spray them all over the place like ghastly bulbs. At least I can do something good with this kind of presence, you know, the opportunities I have, well, they're not opportunities, they're huge open gateways . . .'[11]

'Discouraged from becoming a roving unofficial ambassador,' William Deedes, who accompanied her to both Angola and Bosnia on landmine research trips, wrote,

she sought to address herself to various issues in the world which were being neglected. There were millions of them [landmines] scattered round the world. They lurked wherever there had been conflict. A few charitable organisations were engaged in locating and lifting them, but it was discouraging as well as dangerous work because more mines were being constantly laid in the wars bedevilling Africa. The manufacturers of these mines represented a huge vested interest, which reduced the chances . . . of an international ban . . . defence forces in Britain, America and much of Europe saw the mines, properly laid and charted, as legitimate means of defence . . .[12]

Diana had been in discussion with Mike Whitlam, head of the British Red Cross, about renewing her work for the organization. The result was a visit in January 1997 to Angola, the scene of prolonged civil war, under the auspices of the Red Cross and with a BBC television crew in attendance to film a documentary to raise money for the British Red Cross Landmines Appeal. Lord Deedes, who had been an advocate of a landmines ban since 1992, travelled with her for the *Daily Telegraph*, accompanied by mostly unenthusiastic and cynical members of the press corps. Deedes, who had been briefing Diana about landmines on visits to Kensington Palace, paid tribute to the drawing power of Diana's presence: 'Nobody took a blind bit of interest in landmines until she came along,' he said. The journalists, accustomed to accompanying royal visits in daintier surroundings than Angola, were, Deedes said, 'dismayed' by the state of the capital, Luanda, with stinking rubbish piled high in the hot streets. *Sunday Times* reporter Christina Lamb, young but nonetheless a veteran war reporter, had certainly been cynical about Diana in Angola. She was impressed: despite the heat and the smells Diana had come to work and work she did. Angola, said Lamb, was one of the few remaining places in the world where most people had no idea who she was, and therefore it was all the more remarkable to see the effect she had on the amputees she went among. 'The Red Cross whisked us from one hospital to the next,' Lamb wrote,

each with ever more horrific scenes of skeletal figures with missing arms, missing legs, and blown off heads – victims of some of the 16m land-mines scattered round the country. Many of the injuries were so grue-some I could not bear to look, despite years of Third World reporting. But Diana never turned her head away. Instead, she had something I'd only ever seen before in Nelson Mandela – a kind of aura that made people want to be with her, and a completely natural, straight-from-the-heart sense of how to bring hope to those who seemed to us to have little to live for.[13]

Diana insisted on going to Huambo and Cuito where the war had left the countryside infested with mines. The television reporter Sandy Gall described Diana's action as extremely cour-ageous: he had encountered mines in Afghanistan and knew how dangerous it could be to walk through 'cleared' minefields. Just before it was reluctantly agreed to allow her to visit these 'hell-holes', as Deedes described them, in London two journalists from *The Times* and the *Daily Telegraph* had entertained a junior minister, Lord Howe, to lunch. Expressing the usual Establishment view of Diana, he had been critical of her visit and called it political interference – the usual cliché 'loose cannon' came up. The minis-ter's remark caused heightened interest in Diana's trip: as Deedes put it, 'if it was causing offence to the Tory Government, that doubled its news value'.[14] Diana's comment to Deedes when he approached her in private next morning was 'idiot minister': to the cameras she insisted more diplomatically that the purpose of her visit was humanitarian and in no way political.

By now, Christina Lamb admitted, the visit had 'wiped out' all her past cynicism about Diana. 'That Lady-with-the-Lamp performance wasn't just for the cameras,' she wrote.[15]

Once, at a hospital in Huambo when the photographers had all flown back to their air-conditioned hotels to wire their pictures, I watched Diana, unaware that any journalists were still present, sit and hold the hand of Helena Ussova, a seven-year-old who'd had her intestines blown to pieces by a mine. For what seemed an age the pair just sat, no words needed. When Diana finally left, the young girl struggled through her pain to ask me if the beautiful lady was an angel . . . At the end of the Angola trip Diana said that the lasting image she'd take away was of that terribly ill young girl.[16]

The Angola visit was not the end of Diana's involvement with landmines that year. In mid-June she spoke at a conference in London on landmines under the auspices of the Mines Advisory Group held at the Royal Geographical Society, chaired by Deedes, who helped her draft her speech. With Mike Whitlam's advice she had drawn up a chart of landmine sites across the world, marked with red pins, which she kept in a corner of her sitting room at Kensington Palace. She told Deedes they should make another landmines expedition that summer, and, with the cooperation of Norwegian People's Aid and Landmine Survivors Network (LSN) from Washington, a three-day visit to Bosnia was arranged from 8 to 10 August. The party, which included Bill Deedes and Paul Burrell, by now Diana's inseparable shadow, flew out on a private jet owned by multimillionaire philanthropist George Soros. On the drive to Sarajevo they were joined by two Americans, Jerry White and Ken Rutherford, who had formed LSN after being maimed by landmines. White had lost one leg, Rutherford both. As the two Americans climbed awkwardly into the back of the Landcruiser, Diana turned round from her front seat to say, 'You can take your legs off, boys!' That broke the ice, Burrell recorded; the men had felt that they should keep their artificial limbs on in the presence of royalty.[17] Burrell, the Boswell of the landmines visits, recorded one very significant remark. Landmine victims can recall exactly where and when their accident happened: as they were discussing this, Diana remarked, 'My accident was on 29 July 1981 . . .'[18]

Deedes recalled with amusement his memory of Burrell, the protector. 'We stayed in a brand new hotel in Bosnia, and our rooms were opposite – she was one side of the corridor and I was the other side and I came out of my room in the morning and met Burrell coming out having delivered her breakfast, so I said to him, "Are you going downstairs? Let's have breakfast together." He said, "Yes, sure." I went downstairs, had my breakfast, went up to my room and found Burrell with a chair against her door looking very determined. And I said, "Hi, I thought you were coming to breakfast?" And Burrell said in tones of outrage, "The manager of this hotel burst into her room to ask her whether she approved of it because it's new." I said, "That's very continental, in Paris managers do." Anyway, he was not pleased, he sat there and said, "I'm staying here until she's dressed and ready to go out." That was an indication of the relationship – he was her protector.'[19]

On the last day of the visit they toured the ruins of Sarajevo. 'It had suffered cruelly during the Bosnian war, with mortar bombs falling constantly on the city, and much of the open space had been given over to burial grounds. Diana saw a woman tending her son's grave in one of the huge cemeteries there, walked up to her and embraced her silently, the two touching each other's faces with complete empathy.'[20] The same scene had taken place previously with a young widow whose husband had been killed by a mine while fishing. 'There being no interpreter present there could be very little said. What passed between them is beyond reckoning. When we parted, the widow seemed restored to life.' Diana had the unique gift of silent empathy. Deedes saw the two sides of Diana – 'All this,' he said, 'in the middle of a fling with Dodi Fayed.'[21] The same Diana who stood quietly embracing the bereaved mother in the Sarajevo cemetery would, within hours, be on the jet giggling with Burrell at the tabloid frenzy over her new affair. Aboard the plane she discussed with Deedes the prospect of attending an Oslo conference on landmines with a view to calling for a ban. 'Be careful,' Deedes told her. 'It's political.' 'I was going to write the speech with her . . . saying exactly how to keep out of politics for her but to get the landmine ban.'[22] On

the plane, Diana made a toast: 'Here's to our next country . . .'
Cambodia and Vietnam were on the list for October. She never
got to Oslo or to Cambodia or Vietnam. It was 10 August 1997
and she had only twenty-one days of life to live. 'She was only
involved with landmines from January 1997 until her death in
August,' Bill Deedes said. 'And there's no doubt at all that while
she was on the job she woke the world up as nobody else has
done.' In December 1997, in the wake of a surge of opinion
after Diana's death in favour of a ban on landmines, the Ottawa
Landmine Accord banning landmines was drawn up, to be signed
by forty countries. Mike Whitlam said: 'They would not have
been talking at the Canadian meeting, where they ratified the
Convention later that year, had she not gone to Angola. I would
stake my life on that. They actually acknowledged what she'd done
– at that meeting.'[23]

The landmines campaign had given her a new purpose in life;
she publicly announced in a speech in May, about eating disorders,
that she had finally beaten bulimia. She looked radiantly healthy.
Even her physical appearance had changed 'from a puppy to a
gorgeous lady', as one of her designers, Jacques Azagury, put it.
Catherine Walker, who had dressed Diana for much of her adult
life, said, 'the demure phase was over and so was her marriage but
what I hadn't anticipated was how quickly she would change and
begin wearing my sexier evening wear . . . her looks had changed
dramatically since she had first come to see me as a pale, slightly
plump, fragile-looking girl. Now she was tanned, fitter, more
muscular. She had become a perfectionist, working hard on her
body because of the scrutiny it was under and to help keep her
sane through her marital upheaval . . .'[24] In keeping with this free,
independent image, her skirts became shorter, her heels higher,
the lines of her dresses simpler and sexier. Now outside the royal
circle she could wear black for the first time since the disastrous
outing in 'that dress' at the Guildhall.

'She was growing up in front of my eyes,' said Meredith Etherington-Smith, who saw her from September 1996 through to July
1997. 'It was the most amazing year seeing this person growing

up and making choices, really important kind of choices, about landmines, taking that on, being serious about it, being really serious about this [Christie's] sale. She was professional, she was serious, she was grown up.' Even Diana's posture had changed, from the shy upward glance and hunched shoulders, to sitting erect and standing up straight. She was even stopping chewing her nails. Her fingernails, Meredith observed, 'got better as we went on'. 'She was generally more confident, she became a different sort of person, less the Princess of Wales and more Diana.'[25]

One thing she did take seriously was her role first as mother to the boys and second, as Meredith put it, as the Queen Mother of the twenty-first century. 'Her relationship with the boys was patently a wonderful one . . . She was a very good mother.[26] I expected them to be more protective of her than they were, and they weren't, they weren't mewling and puking and clustering round her. They didn't have a neurotic relationship. It seemed to me to be perfectly healthy and normal and nice and a great tribute first of all to Diana and secondly to Charles.'[27] 'Constitutional plans – well, she felt her long-distance role was to be the Queen Mother of the twenty-first century, that the influence the Queen Mother had had on her grandchildren in a way, she felt that was the kind of role which in a curious way she had been chosen for and one did feel that there was a bit of divine right entering into this, a little bit of fate. And she felt that William should be a democratic King, that the boys needed to have friends, that they needed to know their generation, they needed to know politicians, not just Tory ones, that they needed to know the Blair children. They needed to be part of contemporary English life, not an English life that was really out of date by the end of the war – and I'm paraphrasing some quite long conversations about this. And her job was to make sure they were released from the glass cage, and that when he did come to the throne, a lot of people would know him, and he wouldn't be a mystery, wouldn't be a royal freak, that he would be a person.[28] I think that she very much thought she would be a power behind the throne . . .'[29] Diana emphasized her desire that William should be 'a very English King': she felt that her Spencer blood had a lot to contribute. 'She felt that because of the spider's web of marital alliances and blood they [the Royal Family] weren't English. "I come from an English family," she had said proudly, and "we [the Spencers] are a lot older than they are." She was very proud of the Duke of Marlborough, for instance.'[30]

Diana was very anxious that her boys should not become isolated as the previous royal generation had been, as indeed their father had been. That was why she had wanted the boys, and William in particular, to go to Eton because they would have proper friends there and not sycophants. 'Diana said, "There's no messing around at Eton about someone being the heir to the throne. If you're not popular, charming, intelligent, or good at games, you're not going to rate, are you?" And so William knows a lot of people. And the interesting thing about that she said, "I think they'll be protection, those friends too. They've grown up together and they'll be protective."[31] And they are. You don't see grab shots of William that often, and why? Because his friends don't utter. She'd thought all this through. That's what I mean by being smart.'[32] 'They had money which they carried and spent and they went shopping. In other words she was trying to provide as normal a life as possible – they could come out from behind the glass window, and that was her great legacy.'

Meredith helped her shape her new modern image, with photographs by Mario Testino. One day she had commented to Diana how much better she looked in real life – without make-up, in jeans and a T-shirt and natural hair. 'You know you look so much better like that rather than with all the lacquered hair and the make-up. You've got wonderful skin, you don't need to slap all that stuff on. It's not modern. Jewellery isn't modern except for one of those little Tiffany diamond crosses – those chokers – for God's sake!' A set of photographs in the grand manner had been taken by Snowdon for the sale. 'They were fine but I wanted much more the girl who walked through the minefields. I wanted the woman I saw who looked amazing and modern. Discussing who should do them, Diana asked Meredith to choose someone she hadn't worked with before: 'I want someone new and I want to look how I feel inside. I feel like I belong to the twentieth century now, I really do. I'm doing modern things and I'm trying to lead a modern life, and I'm a single woman and that's how I want to look.'[33]

At the shoot with Testino in a Battersea studio, Diana had enjoyed herself immensely. Afterwards, as they were packing up, with music booming in the background, she started playing around, arm in arm with Mario Testino, imitating Naomi Campbell doing catwalk and Kate Moss doing catwalk. 'Everyone was screaming with laughter, including her, and she went that amazing rose pink colour [Diana always had blushed easily] and she looked fantastic, so full of energy and life. It was so sweet and so sad when I took the work prints [of the photographs] back and she said, "It was one of the happiest days of my life – and I really mean it." Looking at them she said, musing, "But these are me. Really, really me." She also said, "God, I think I look like Marilyn Monroe in those pictures . . ."' She was quite obsessed with Marilyn Monroe, Meredith said, and in one of the pictures she did look like the young Marilyn. She often talked about her, and how she had fought the studio system in Hollywood on her own and won, because they had dumped her and then had to take her back. 'I think perhaps she felt there was another woman against the world,' Meredith said. 'I remember having a conversation about it with her once and her saying that she [Monroe] wasn't just a blonde fluffy thing, she was smart, and I think she identified with that.'[34]

Diana still felt beleaguered by court circles. She told Meredith she had 'a lot of enemies'. 'That sounds a bit paranoid,' Meredith replied. 'No, you know how it works. It's justification – I'm the baddie.' 'Well, all you have to do is to be a goodie, and you are a goodie by the example you set. That's why landmines – patently you have an enormous sympathy with people less fortunate than you are.' 'You call me fortunate?' 'I do, actually. I call you fortunate because you have the rest of your life in front of you and you have amazing opportunities to do amazing things . . .' 'Yes,' she said, repeating that she had enemies and felt very much on her own sometimes. 'But you have good friends.' She replied, 'Yes. But you try fighting them [the Establishment enemies].' She was right, of course. It took a great deal of courage to face down her powerful enemies who saw the Establishment threatened by her very existence. Despite her supportive friends in all walks of life, the hostile pressure was very much alive and relentless and ready to pounce when 'goodie' Diana fell back into the ways of 'baddie Diana'. Diana believed that there was an agenda among Camilla and her circle and certain jealous courtiers to paint her as mad and sideline her in public life. 'They would have preferred her to disappear,' a friend said; 'she was deeply inconvenient – and enjoyed being deeply inconvenient.'[35]

Unfortunately, Diana could not remain 'goodie' Diana for long, without tripping up on her needier, more foolish and self-indulgent instincts. She quarrelled with her staff, helpers and 'star' friends. She quarrelled with her personal assistant Victoria Mendham, presenting her with her bill at the K Club which represented an astronomical sum for the woman to pay (Prince Charles later settled it). She quarrelled with Martin Bashir, backing out of a book she had contemplated doing with him. Under the terms of her divorce agreement, with its confidentiality clause which did not allow her to discuss her life in royal circles, the huge sums quoted by her potential publisher did not seem realistic. Moreover, it was alleged that Paul Burrell had repeated to her some disobliging comments Bashir had made to him about her. She quarrelled with Gianni Versace and Elton John when she backed out of contributing a foreword she had written to a book of photographs to raise money for John's AIDS Foundation, because, just after her divorce came through, she became nervous of what the Queen would think when she saw the book's suggestive images next to pictures of the Royal Family. (She was reconciled with Elton John at Versace's funeral in Milan on 22 July after the designer's murder in Miami.)

She did not abandon hopes of Hasnat Khan, nor of her dream of marrying him. In May she flew to Pakistan again on the pretext of helping Imran Khan and his hospital. She intended to meet

52

Diana enjoys the freedom of Nevis – her first holiday after her separation.

53

Diana is painted by Nelson Shanks as she sits for her first portrait as a
separated woman.

In 1994 Diana gave up police protection, which made her increasingly vulnerable to the ever-merciless paparazzi.

Post-*Panorama*, December 1995: Diana accepts an award from Henry Kissinger at the 'Humanitarian of the Year' awards ceremony, New York.

1996: Diana watching heart surgery at Harefield Hospital, Middlesex.

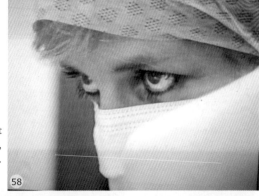

Diana with Imran and Jemima Khan and Lady Annabel Goldsmith at a fundraising gala for Imran's hospital charity in Lahore.

28 August 1996: Diana on the day of her
divorce from Charles, accompanied by
Lucia Flecha de Lima.

Hasnat Khan.

New York, June 1997: Diana at a gala party to launch the Christie's
auction of her dresses held in order to raise money for her charities.
She is wearing a dress by Catherine Walker.

63

Diana visiting the Lord Gage Centre for old people, a Guinness Trust home in Newham, East London. Despite her global success, Diana was always dedicated to home-grown charities.

London, June 1997: Diana at the Christie's pre-auction party.

64

1997: Diana comforts a grieving mother during her final campaign to ban the use of landmines in Bosnia.

65

Angola, January 1997: Diana at Neves Bendinha, an orthopaedic workshop in Luanda.

66

August 1997: Diana and Dodi on the yacht *Jonikal* in St Tropez.

Diana and Dodi leave the Ritz moments before their fatal accident.

6 September 1997: the funeral of Diana, Princess of Wales. Her coffin is followed by her ex-husband, her ex-father-in-law, her brother and her two sons.

Tribute to the 'People's Princess': flowers and wreaths outside Kensington Palace after the death of Diana – an expression of the extraordinary popularity of a princess who touched the lives of many.

Hasnat's parents, his mother in particular, and if possible to convince them that she would be a suitable wife for their son. She persuaded Jemima Khan to go with her and Jimmy Goldsmith to lend them his jet. This was Diana at her most selfish and inconsiderate; Jimmy Goldsmith, as all his close circle knew, was dying, in fact was soon to die, and the last thing a member of his family wanted to do was to leave him and fly to Pakistan. Jimmy apparently told Jemima to go but to have the jet in readiness to leave Pakistan at any moment if necessary. This time Cosima Somerset did not go with her; she had been the victim of one of Diana's cruelly abrupt breaks, the reason apparently relating to something within the Goldsmith circle.

Diana had done everything she could to get close to Hasnat Khan's family, visiting his uncle Omar and his English wife Jane at their home in Stratford, and inviting Jane to stay at Kensington Palace. Through them she had made friends with Hasnat's grandmother, Nanny Appa, and she hoped to follow Jane's example and win acceptance into the aristocratic Pathan clan. Above all she needed to win acceptance from Hasnat's mother, the formidable, university-educated Naheed, who had bitter memories of the British when, after Partition, her family had been uprooted from their home in India. In Muslim society the mother is given great respect in the close extended family where arranged marriages are the rule, and each member of the family supports the other, often sharing the same house. Naheed did not approve of Western cultural images and her son, for all his Western ways, at heart shared her cultural beliefs. Although Diana hoped to follow the example of her friend Jemima, who in marrying Imran had converted to Islam and lived in the family complex in Lahore, that marriage was eventually to fail. It was a complicated situation both for Diana and for Hasnat's parents, anxious to see their son married (two arranged engagements had not led to marriage) but nervous of the consequences where Diana was concerned. Diana was staying with Imran and Jemima in Lahore when she was invited to visit Khan's family at their Model Town home in Jhelum, some one hundred miles to the north of Lahore, to meet not only

Hasnat's mother and father but also eleven members of his family. She dressed in a blue shalwar kameez which Jemima had had made for her in Lahore, and travelled incognito with two of Hasnat's sisters in an old black Toyota Corolla to avoid press attention. Nothing was said about marriage during Diana's visit and Diana appeared sombre as she left, but in the car with one of Hasnat's sisters she seemed confident that she could continue with her modern life and her campaigns at the same time as being married to Hasnat. On her return she confessed to Imran Khan how much she wanted to marry Hasnat.

The Hasnat Khan relationship continued on and off through the summer. Although he loved her, he continued to be undecided about the prospect of marriage and Diana's needy behaviour – constant telephone calls, sitting in a car in the street outside his house – following the pattern of her previous affair with Oliver Hoare, unnerved him. When Diana tried the old tactic of jealousy, being seen and photographed with Sikh businessman Gulu Lalvani, he was so angry that he broke off relations with her, not for the first or the last time.

With her private life in turmoil, Diana had her public life to distract her. In late May she had taken William to lunch with the newly elected Prime Minister Tony Blair and his family at his official country residence, Chequers, when they had discussed a possible future role for her. Blair, who displayed a unique ability to gauge popular feeling, saw the promotional potential of Diana as other more conventional politicians had not. June was a busy month: on 19 June she was in Washington for a meeting with Hillary Clinton; she then flew to New York to see her idol, Mother Teresa. (She had met her in Rome in February 1992 after visiting her hospice and orphanage in Calcutta on her India trip with Charles. This had greatly inspired her.) They walked hand in hand through the Bronx. Two days later, back in England, she drove herself up to Stratford to see the Omar Khans and eleven members of the family over from Pakistan, including her particular friend, Hasnat's grandmother, Nanny Appa. Two days after that, on 23 June, she was back in New York for the pre-sale party at

Christie's, flying back before the auction took place on 25 June to avoid the media circus. The sale was a great success: all the dresses sold, for a total of $3,258,750; the catalogue sales alone accounted for $2.5 million. The top price of $222,500 was paid for the 'White House dress' by Victor Edelstein which she had worn dancing with John Travolta.

While in New York before the sale on 23 June, Diana had continued her campaign to win over – and perhaps to learn from – powerful women. After seeing Katharine Graham and Hillary Clinton in Washington, she lunched at the fashionable Four Seasons in New York on 23 June with Anna Wintour, editor of American *Vogue*, and the British journalist Tina Brown, then editor of the *New Yorker*. The lunch had been arranged by Anna Wintour, with whom she had worked on a breast cancer fashion benefit the previous September. Despite her brave talk of her 'strength', the joy of giving help to people who needed it and her purpose in life – speaking of the landmines campaign, apparently, with an 'eerie' expression in her eyes – Tina Brown perceptively diagnosed 'the frantic Diana' lurking beneath the shining surface, so soon to be revealed in her summer antics with Dodi Fayed.

Beneath the glitter of her public life, her worldwide celebrity, the beauty which bewitched everyone she met, she was still insecure and a prey to the sense of rejection which never left her, encapsulated in the failure of her marriage. Out of the limelight, she was lonely, shut up in the gloom of Kensington Palace with the butler and addicted to soaps (*Brookside* was a favourite). The loneliness struck hardest at weekends when the boys were with their father: 'I stay in town. If I go out, I keep my eyes down or straight ahead. Wherever I go the press find ways to spy. Often I visit a hospice.'[36] Evenings, again, were hard; sometimes accompanied, first by Patrick Jephson, then driven by Burrell, she toured the seedier parts of London, spotting drug dealers or prostitutes to whom she often gave money in an effort to make them go home. The media siege served further to isolate her; to escape them she sometimes went out sitting on the floor of a taxi; from the time she dispensed with her protection in 1994 the hunt was on. Often the paparazzi waiting outside places like her therapist Susie Orbach's house would shout obscenities at her, 'spraying her down', hoping to catch shots of her distress and tears. Her fame and her royalty made it worse; 'that three-foot royal aura' around her, which Meredith Etherington-Smith had observed, made her almost unapproachable in an intimate way. At times on private social occasions, such as a dinner party at Taki Theodoracopulos's house, she seemed almost desperate to make friends, zeroing in on people, reaching out and drawing them in. Then, in order to seem 'one of the girls', she would rivet, and sometimes repel, people with her indiscreet talk, 'inappropriate', sexual conversation, venomous remarks about former friends, and raucous 'common' laugh. She was sadly aware that the baggage of her past would make it difficult to find the Barbara Cartland married life she still yearned for. 'Who would take me on?' she said. Yet at times she concluded that she would be better off single, the mother of the future King and the promoter of great causes.

Again, she was alone, even as far as her family was concerned. Sarah McCorquodale was the closest to her and sometimes acted as her lady-in-waiting, but she lived with her family on a large farm in Lincolnshire and therefore was physically distant. Relations with Jane, who lived close by, were awkward: despite Robert Fellowes' friendly attitude to Diana, he was still the Queen's principal private secretary and could not afford to take sides. For almost all the past four years, relations with her brother Charles had been tense, first in the misunderstanding over the house and then as a result of an unkind letter written by him in April 1996 referring to Diana's 'mental problems' quoted by a ferociously loyal Paul Burrell.[37] In private conversations Charles had made no secret of his opinion that his sister was dangerous to know. The terms of Spencer's letter were bitter: 'After years of neglect on both sides, our relationship is the weakest I have with any of my sisters . . . perhaps you have more time to notice that we seldom speak . . . I will always be there for you . . . as a loving brother: albeit one that has, through fifteen years' absence, rather lost touch – to the extent I have to read Richard Kay to learn that you are coming to Althorp

. . . I long ago accepted that I was a peripheral part of your life, and that no longer saddens me. Indeed, it's easier for me and my family to be in that position as I view the consternation and hurt your fickle friendship has caused so many.' Worst of all, from Diana's point of view, went on to refer to her 'illness' (presumably bulimia) and 'mental problems': 'I fear for you. I know how manipulation and deceit are parts of the illness . . . I pray that you are getting appropriate and sympathetic treatment for your mental problems.'[38] Recently, however, they had had a rapprochement when Diana had flown to South Africa in March, ostensibly to see her brother but actually in pursuance of her campaign for Hasnat Khan, and to check out the possibilities of South Africa as a place where they could eventually live.

Saddest of all, Diana had not been on speaking terms with her mother since Frances had given an interview to *Hello!* (for charity) in which she had claimed that the withdrawal of the HRH title did not matter and made other observations to which Diana objected. Diana had not been consulted over the article but in any case their relationship had been difficult after a series of telephone calls in which Frances had criticized Diana's behaviour with men. Frances had been convicted of drink-driving the previous year and was in a fragile emotional state. She was so anguished by the breakdown of relations with Diana that she even telephoned William Tallon, the Queen Mother's page, imploring him to get Diana to speak to her. Diana, as always when she felt she had been betrayed or let down, was implacable and sadly they never spoke again.

21. Fatal Summer

'Whom the gods love, die young' (Lord Byron, *Don Juan*, Canto IV, xii, from the Greek)

At the lunch in New York in June with Tina Brown and Anna Wintour, Diana had displayed 'unease' when asked how she was going to spend the summer holidays. The truth was that at that moment she had nowhere to go. July and August are difficult months for fashionable people without an invitation to a villa or a yacht for the sun, or a country house estate in Ireland or Scotland for the fresh air and the shooting. In any case, country house life was no longer an option for Diana who had cut herself off from that set long ago. Diana and 'the boys', with their concomitant detectives and paparazzi, were not normal guests. For Diana, it was the Jackie Kennedy Onassis dilemma: how to combine great celebrity with a need for privacy and family life. Later that month, she thought she had found the answer.

Mohamed Fayed, or, as he preferred to be called, 'Al' Fayed, had been born in 1929 in a village near Alexandria, Egypt, into a modest background which he preferred to forget.[1] Fayed had risen from his lowly beginnings through his connection with the Kashoggi family, Saudis of Turkish descent, who owed their position to their connection with the rulers of Saudi Arabia. In 1954 he had married Samira, the sixteen-year-old sister of Adnan Kashoggi, his contemporary, son of the head of the family Dr Mohamed Kashoggi. Their son, Emad, always known as 'Dodi', had been born in 1955; after Fayed's divorce from Samira shortly afterwards, Dodi had been brought up in straitened circumstances by his uncle, Salah, his father's younger brother, and his Italian wife, and strictly forbidden to associate with his mother. While his father travelled the world in search of a fortune through a series of dubious enterprises, the wretched Dodi had been left at home in Alexandria. Fayed's biographer wrote that Dodi was the casualty of his father's unsuccessful ambitions. 'Barely literate, speaking poor Arabic . . . Dodi endured an isolated and loveless childhood. Frequently he cried, and he even screamed during the night. Anguished by the suffering, the father would comfort his son in a shared bed, and, the following morning, would spend over-generously on toys. Torn between earning his fortune and caring for his son, Fayed . . . did little to alleviate the boy's misery.'[2]

By 1969, through his connections with Dubai, Fayed had amassed a fortune of £2 million, a considerable sum for those days. Within two years he had acquired a Rolls-Royce with chauffeur, a chalet in Gstaad, apartments at 60 Park Lane and the honorific 'Al' before his name. By 1972 he was the proud owner of a Scottish castle, Balnagown, a villa in St Tropez, and a yacht named *Dodi*. Dodi himself had been enrolled at Sandhurst, the British military training college, attended not only by British officer candidates but also by the sons of Arab princes like King Hussein of Jordan. After only four weeks, uneducated, materially spoiled, hopelessly indolent and unathletic, the boy had begged to be withdrawn. Mohamed Fayed, meanwhile, had added Barrow Green Court, Oxted, Surrey, to his property portfolio, qualifying him to be considered as the owner of a country estate. In 1975 he bought shares in Lonrho, the company set up by 'Tiny' Rowland, a capitalist adventurer whose wealth surpassed even Fayed's. Alarmed by the Department of Trade and Industry inspectors' adverse report into Lonrho's dealings, Fayed sold out, having made £8 million on the transaction. In 1979, still in search of the social position and prestige which eluded him, he bought the Paris Ritz.

Dodi, meanwhile, was pursuing a playboy life of girls and nightclubs: his aimlessness both irritated and alarmed his father. Dodi dreamed of a career in films and, as a reward for introducing his father to a Finnish beauty queen, Heini Wathen, whom he later married, Fayed set up a film production company for Dodi. Interested only in girls and drugs, Dodi had little to contribute to the enterprise. Financial success came when Fayed's company, Allied Stars, invested 25 per cent in the Oscar-winning film *Chariots of Fire*. Dodi was billed as executive producer – in fact he had done nothing but spend money on friends, girls and cocaine, even succeeding in getting himself thrown off the set of *Chariots*. Mohamed, furious at his son's decadent lifestyle, cut off his financial support. It was not for lack of love: 'Mohamed only wanted the best for him but the way in which he went about achieving the best for him, didn't help,' said a friend. 'But he loved him, worshipped him, adored him and if anybody tells you differently, they're wrong.'[3] In 1984, Mohamed Fayed had found a new source of wealth, becoming financial adviser to the Sultan of Brunei. In 1985, after a protracted war with his old partner, Tiny Rowland, Fayed bought the House of Fraser and became the owner of what was then a British national treasure, Harrods.

By then, Mohamed and Dodi had become reconciled; when Dodi's mother Samira died in March 1986, his father forbade him from attending her funeral, definitively cutting him off from his Kashoggi relations. He gave Dodi a £150,000 monthly allowance, free accommodation in Park Lane, Paris, St Tropez and his suite at the Pierre in New York and use of his fleet of cars, including a Mercedes, a Lagonda and two Aston Martins.[4] Meanwhile, a vengeful Rowland had asked that Fayed's purchase of Harrods should be referred to the Monopolies Commission, alleging dishonesty in its financing. Questions were asked by MPs friendly to Rowland in the House of Commons and another investigation, once again by the Department of Trade and Industry, loomed. Fayed gave donations to the ruling Conservative Party and, in tandem with a parliamentary lobbyist, Ian Greer, payments for questions to MPs. This, however, did not prevent the DTI from launching an investigation into the Harrods purchase. The investigation branded the Fayed brothers, Mohamed and Ali, 'liars' but the behaviour of Rowland in pursuing his vendetta led Lord Young at the DTI to decide neither to refer the case to the Monopolies Commission nor to release the inspectors' hostile report. The report was eventually released but Fayed's devious behaviour and

that of Rowland had tarnished both of them. As a result of the
DTI report, when the Fayed brothers applied for British passports
in 1993 their application was rejected. Fayed had been deeply
offended and, as a result, turned against what he liked to imagine
was the corrupt British Establishment. Despite his wealth, he was
a deeply controversial figure.

And the wealth was, to say the least, ostentatious. Fayed's Gulfstream jet was decorated in deep pink with Egyptian motifs and
hieroglyphics woven into the fabrics covering the walls and floors.
A penthouse in the style of a Roman villa adorned the new eighth
floor of 60 Park Lane, with solid gold fittings on his double
bath. In Harrods, the escalator was decorated with gilded Egyptian
statues cast with Mohamed Fayed's features. He had nine houses
to commute to with his Gulfstream, a Sikorski helicopter and
a fleet of red armoured Mercedes limousines. Yet the British
Establishment, shocked by his vendetta against the Conservative
government which had refused him his passport, began to turn
their backs on Fayed. By 1996 he needed Diana to add to Harrods,
the Villa Windsor in Paris which he had acquired in 1986, Turnbull
& Asser, the Prince's shirtmakers, and *Punch* magazine.

Fayed was determined to rise to the top in British society after
his acquisition of Harrods. He relished his annual meeting with
the Queen at the Royal Windsor Horse Show, contriving to be
photographed with the monarch even if he had to retreat to the
stands as a mere spectator afterwards. Cleverly, he had diagnosed
that the route into the British Royal Family lay through polo:
sponsorship of a Harrods polo match in July 1986 would, he knew,
lead to an introduction to the Prince and Princess of Wales (a
photograph shows Diana at the event with Dodi in the background). In September 1996 he had offered Diana a directorship
of Harrods; when she refused it, he offered it to Raine, who
accepted.

Diana was the ultimate prize and the honey trap was his wealth.
Diana had persuaded him to sponsor *The Nutcracker* for the English
National Ballet. 'It was at a gala,' Pamela Harlech remembered,
'and she just said to him, "Come on, you can afford it, come on,

just give it!" It was something like £400,000 – and she said, "You can afford it. It'll be good for you." And of course it was, it was terrific for Harrods because it was Christmas.'[5] At another ballet gala dinner in early June, Fayed was sitting between Pamela Harlech and Diana when he saw his chance. 'He said, "What are you doing this summer?" And she said, "I don't know, I haven't decided what to do with the boys." He said, "Why don't you come and stay with us?" Pamela and Derek Deane, who was sitting on her other side, winced. "Don't do it. Really bad idea." But she said something like, "Well, how lovely . . .".'[6] Dismissing her friends' warning about Fayed's reputation, she later sent a message that she would be delighted to accept.

As always with Diana, there were several reasons for her decision to take her children to stay at St Tropez with Fayed. Much as she might talk about not worrying about Camilla any more, she could not restrain her natural reaction to her old rival. Camilla's success raised the old nightmare feelings of helplessness, jealousy and despair, always potent triggers for some of her most misguided actions. July 1997 was to be Camilla month in the Prince of Wales's household. ITV were to screen a documentary about her. 'When I got to know Diana,' Richard Kay said, 'Camilla as far as she was concerned was a fading influence on her life. She was obviously always going to be there and she would always blame her [for the failure of her marriage] but she developed almost a sense of pity towards her . . . She felt that Camilla was now having a pretty hellish life in the mid-1990s because she was now undergoing the same level of interest that she herself had had many years earlier, and yet she wasn't getting anything back from it. She was getting a very bad press which I'm sure Diana was delighted about. But there were certain things that did freak her out. She was very unhappy when Channel 5 decided to do the first television biography of Camilla which ran in July 1997 and that upset her a lot. She wanted to know why television would be interested in her.'[7] Worse, on 18 July Charles was giving a fiftieth birthday ball for Camilla at Highgrove, staged, of course, by Michael Fawcett. Two days before, on 16 July, Diana with William and Harry took

Fayed's helicopter from Kensington Palace to lunch at Barrow Green Court, then went on to Stansted for the flight to Nice on Fayed's jet, and from there via his yacht, the *Jonikal*, to the Castel Sainte Hélène, a ten-acre estate on a cliff overlooking St Tropez.

Having secured his prize, Fayed had pulled out all the stops. He even invested something in the region of £15 million buying the *Jonikal*, a 195-foot yacht built in 1991 and requiring a crew of sixteen, from a Milanese textile tycoon, just to entertain Diana.[8] More, he now saw Dodi as the ideal companion for his prized princess. Despite failure in almost all the other areas of his life, notably the business positions his father had procured for him, Dodi had had success with women. He was charming, kind and generous, reputedly good in bed, and had the ability to focus his entire attention on a woman who interested him. He had had affairs with several beautiful and well-known women and indeed would find women for his father and uncle. His principal drawback was a well-known cocaine habit. Now aged forty-two, he had one failed marriage behind him and, as Fayed well knew, a fiancée, the American model Kelly Fisher; he was due to marry her three weeks later in Los Angeles where Fayed had just paid $7.3 million for Paradise Cove, a six-bedroom seaside house in Malibu, formerly the property of Julie Andrews and her husband Blake Edwards. Determined to bring Dodi to entertain Diana, Fayed telephoned him in Paris, ordering him to dump Kelly Fisher, and sent his Gulfstream to bring him to St Tropez on 14 July. In fact, Fisher was brought down by Dodi two days later and installed to alternate between his father's lesser yachts, moored near the *Jonikal*, the 'love boat' destined to woo Diana. In London society the rumour ran that Fayed had promised Dodi $30 million if he could land Diana – but not for himself, for his father.[9]

On the morning of 18 July, the day of the Highgrove party, the tabloids were full of pictures of Diana, as she had intended they should be. She had taken particular care to make herself known to the accompanying press party, moored offshore from the Fayed villa. Wearing a sexy leopard-print bathing suit, she posed beside the swimming pool, occasionally breaking off to execute a gracefully athletic dive, in the 'look-at-me' fashion of her childhood. She rode behind Harry on a jet ski, showing a handsome cleavage. The press, assembled in boats off Fayed's beach, had no idea what was going on. They had not yet picked up on Dodi who, when he was seen with Diana and the boys in St Tropez, they assumed to be a sailor off the Fayed yacht. 'Why the press was so excited about it all,' Richard Kay recalled, 'was because they just didn't know what the hell was happening. They never knew where the story was going. In fact James Whitaker admitted that he was on the verge of a nervous breakdown and if it had carried on he would probably have cracked up. He said he just couldn't cope with the sheer stress.' Diana was not about to enlighten them but to mystify them further. Commandeering one of Fayed's speedboats, she dashed up to the press boat to announce that they should wait for something great: 'I'm going to surprise the world . . .' Questioned later by Richard Kay, she more or less admitted that it had been a meaningless stunt and a tease. Asked what this 'great' thing was, she shrugged, 'Oh, it's nothing . . . I've just had enough of everything . . .'[10] That same day, photographs flashed round the world of Fayed on the deck of the *Jonikal* with his arm round Diana, she – several inches taller than her host – with her hand resting on his shoulder. Fayed then gave an interview with a journalist in which he claimed that Diana saw him as a father figure, that her attitude to all the criticism of her stay was that these people 'can go to hell if they don't like it'. He boasted of his superb security for her to keep the press away, that he was on good terms with the Royal Family, yet was unable to resist a dig at Camilla. Diana, he said, 'doesn't think or care about Camilla Parker Bowles. She is something out of a Dracula film . . .'[11]

What, indeed, was Diana doing accepting Fayed's hospitality for herself and even more for her son, the future King of England, and his brother? When advised by friends not to go, she had replied, 'Oh, he's very naughty . . .' Fayed's speech was normally littered with his version of the English expletive 'fuggin', and he was happy to retail lurid details of his sexual exploits even to other women who didn't want to hear them. But he was expansive, a cheerful figure on holiday surrounded by his wife, Heini, and their four children, with the kind of family atmosphere that appealed to Diana. Moreover, it was a Muslim family, even if not quite on the lines of her still beloved Khans. The fact that the Establishment might look askance at Fayed made no difference whatsoever to her. Diana had never thought along Establishment lines; indeed, their disapproval may indeed have enhanced his appeal. 'Fayed has always been very nice and courteous to her and she had nowhere to go and he offered his house and she accepted,' said an old friend.[12] 'But she had a very good sense of the ridiculous and she knew how ridiculous Al Fayed is with his plane and his house and his bad taste. He gave her a watch with pearls, the kind of watch that had a pearl bracelet. And she hated it.'[13]

Diana returned to London on 20 July to face what appeared to be the final showdown with Hasnat Khan. Despite their previous troubles she had by no means given up on him and had telephoned his London flat to tell him the date of her return. Sometime during the few days she spent in London in late July – she flew to Milan on 22 July for Gianni Versace's funeral – they parted, seemingly for ever, Hasnat having told her that their marriage was impossible. Diana had told close friends that she wanted to marry Hasnat. 'He was a wonderful person and he was in love with her, he was completely besotted with her but he did not want to marry her,' said one.[14] 'Hasnat Khan has only one interest in life,' Richard Kay said. 'He was very fond of Diana but he wanted to be a very good doctor and his ultimate aim is to take the skills he's learned here back to Pakistan. And the idea that he could become Mr Diana of Wales and still be a practising doctor was just absurd, it was never going to happen. And I think she knew that too. I mean, who do you marry if you've once been married to the future King? She went almost from the sublime to the ridiculous. The idea that she could marry an impoverished hospital doctor was a wonderful Mills and Boonish sort of story line.'[15] Diana persisted, despite having told two of her mother figures that, on her Pakistan mission to meet his parents, they had been horrified at the thought of the marriage and had told her it was impossible.[16]

But now, in late July, with London emptying as people went off on their summer holidays and the boys departed with their father, romance with Dodi offered an escape. On 26 July she flew to Paris for twenty-four hours to be met by Dodi and enveloped in the Fayeds' world – private helicopter to the centre of Paris, then on to the Ritz Hotel where she was given the Imperial Suite. After dinner at Lucas Carton, the couple returned briefly to Dodi's flat in his father's apartment block on rue Arsène Houssaye, its windows overlooking the Champs-Elysées, then took a romantic walk along the Seine, hand in hand, and for once alone (the trip had been kept secret). Diana spent the night by herself in the Ritz, breakfasted with Dodi and then flew back to London. Diana was exhilarated, touched by Dodi, the first man ever to cherish her with so much thought and attention.

On 31 July she was back on the *Jonikal* for a cruise alone with Dodi (if you except numerous crew and bodyguards, butler, chef and masseuses), cruising off the coasts of Corsica and Sardinia. Dodi Fayed was simple, gentle and considerate of her every need. On this, and subsequent trips, the two of them talked unceasingly of loveless childhoods, the cinema and gossip. Importantly for Diana, Dodi was intellectually unchallenging and never made her feel inferior; at the same time he looked after her in the way she had always dreamed of and never hitherto found. It was a stress-free experience where Diana could behave in a relaxed, almost childlike way. Significantly, numbers of furry stuffed animals figured prominently in both their bedrooms: in Dodi's Paris apartment three Harrods bears sat on a table in the bedroom, three more on chairs in the dining room. He also had a collection of model aeroplanes on display in his bedroom. They played the soundtrack from the film *The English Patient* over and over again, watched DVDs and television; sometimes Diana played the piano: 'All my family play,' she told the astonished butler, René Delorm. When Dodi was busy, Diana read. She was reading, Delorm noted, a book entitled *On Being Jewish*, a curious choice for Muslim company.

Unwittingly, however, she had become caught up in a Fayed-controlled environment from which she would not escape.

Mohamed Fayed monitored the romance from afar: Dodi was in high favour owing to his obvious success with the Princess. Father and son spoke daily on the telephone, sometimes more often. Fayed was determined to extract the maximum good publicity for his son's coup. He employed the publicist Max Clifford as his adviser to supplement the skilful efforts of his spokesman, former BBC royal reporter Michael Cole. The results of his campaign were to dog the remainder of Diana and Dodi's days. On 4 August, a noted photographer, Mario Brenna, arrived in Sardinia from Monaco following a tip-off. Fayed's biographer, Tom Bower, suspected a Fayed employee was responsible; another well-informed author, Kate Snell, however, claims that Brenna was acting on a tip-off from another notorious paparazzo, Jason Fraser, who had obtained the information from a different source. Brenna had spotted the *Jonikal* moored off the bay of Cala di Volpe on the Costa Smeralda, but subsequently lost her. Later, however, he spotted the yacht travelling between Corsica and Sardinia. Using a tender, Dodi and Diana left the *Jonikal* to swim in various places, snapped and tracked by Brenna. Later, from the shore, he obtained the famous photographs of Dodi and Diana embracing on the yacht, later entitled 'the Kiss'. Back in London, Jason Fraser sold the set of pictures for huge sums – a quarter of a million pounds was paid for the first rights by the *Sunday Mirror* which published them on 10 August. The *Sun* and the *Daily Mail* paid one hundred thousand pounds each for second rights. Diana seemed no less willing than Mohamed Fayed to publicize her new affair: Richard Kay, no doubt acting on information passed to him by Diana, confirmed that it was 'her first serious romance' since the divorce.[17] It was obvious that she wanted the world to know, her specific targets probably being Hasnat Khan and her ex-husband. On 7 August, when Diana dined with Dodi at 60 Park Lane on their return to London, a horde of photographers, doubtless acting on a tip-off, were there to record her arrival. Dodi at least was innocent of having given the information: when snapped boarding a boat to take them to the *Jonikal*, he looked genuinely surprised. Diana calmly looked the other way.

Diana left for Bosnia on 8 August for the landmines campaign with Bill Deedes, returning on the 11th when, still in the Fayed embrace, she and Dodi spent a romantic night at Oxted. Ten paparazzi were waiting outside the gates as they left guarded by Trevor Rees-Jones, an ex-soldier who had become Dodi's favourite bodyguard. Giving them the slip, they drove to 60 Park Lane for dinner. 60 Park Lane was the Fayed London headquarters, the complex in which Fayed occupied the lavish seventh floor with various other relations, including Dodi, dispersed around the other floors. It was like a hotel, with centralized service from one kitchen for all the apartments. It was also the headquarters of Fayed's security operations, a private army of some thirty armed ex-soldiers from the Military Police, the SAS and the Parachute Regiment. Unlike the highly trained Royalty and Diplomatic Protection Department, which had been taught specifically how to protect its principals and had a strict code of conduct, Fayed's bodyguards were under the direct control of whichever of the Fayeds, Mohamed or Dodi, they happened to be accompanying. It was well known among Fayed's employees that disobeying Fayed meant instant dismissal, an unspoken rule that was to have fatal results. When asked to do things of which they disapproved, the saying among the men was 'It's paying the mortgage'. 'You never challenged the Boss, even if you thought professional procedures were being compromised,' Trevor Rees-Jones said.[18]

That evening Diana and Dodi went to a private screening of *Air Force One*; as Trevor Rees-Jones drove out of the underground garage of the apartment, the car was besieged by cameramen. Dodi and Diana escaped being photographed by practically lying, giggling, on the floor. A few days later, on 15 August, when Diana left for a short holiday on a boat in Greece with Rosa Monckton, Fayed saw to it that they flew out and returned on his Gulfstream. For five days they managed to escape the notice of the paparazzi, with the sole exception of a tourist who snapped them. Next day his photograph was on the front page of the *Sun*. 'It's a hunt, Rosa, it's a hunt,' Diana told her friend.

The hunt was now on in earnest, partly orchestrated by the

distant Fayed but more closely, it would appear, by Diana herself. On 21 August, the day Diana returned on the Fayed jet to Stansted, Fayed had alerted not only Nigel Dempster but also the *Sun*. That same evening Diana flew to Nice to join Dodi for a second holiday on the *Jonikal*. At the jetty in the small port of St Laurent-du-Var, where they were to join the yacht, Jason Fraser and two French showbusiness photographers were waiting. Later they were joined by more. At Monte Carlo on 25 August Dodi and Diana decided to walk in the town, accompanied by Delorm and the two body-guards, Rees-Jones and 'Kez' Wingfield. They lost their way but remained unbothered by the media. It was on this expedition that Fayed would claim that Diana and Dodi picked out a special ring from the 'Tell Me Yes' range at the jewellers Repossi, which was later, according to him, to be presented to Diana as an engagement ring. Rees-Jones emphatically denied that they visited Repossi. (They had done so, however, on the earlier *Jonikal* trip on 5 August.) A fleet of paparazzi boats dogged the *Jonikal* from then on. After Monte Carlo Dodi was beginning to panic about the paparazzi, suspecting the crew of tipping them off. The two British bodyguards, Kez and Trevor, were telephoning requests for reinforcements, only to be turned down. Later, when the couple were trying to have a quiet romantic walk on the beach at Porto Venere, they were surprised by a single paparazzo; by now even Diana seemed upset and was seen in tears by the crew. On 27 August helicopters made three sorties to hover over the *Jonikal*, driving Diana below. Dodi began to fantasize about night-vision laser devices to disrupt the cameras or blind their operators. There was a sense that Diana was beginning to be bothered about his overreaction to things like mosquitoes, asking their stewardess, 'What are these Arab men like?'[19] Later, it was to be suggested by Diana's friends that, fiercely opposed as she was to drug use, she was beginning to be suspicious about Dodi's disappearances to the bathroom. On Friday 29 August they were at Cala di Volpe, on Sardinia, again when news filtered through that they would be leaving for Paris the following day.

Arriving at Le Bourget on a stifling hot August day, the party found the paparazzi waiting and this time in their most aggressive form – on motorbikes. Diana's face was set as she got into the Mercedes to drive to the city centre. They set off in two cars, Dodi and Diana in the Mercedes guarded by Rees-Jones and driven by the usual chauffeur, Philippe Dorneau. The back-up Range Rover with the luggage, valet, maid and masseuse, guarded by Wingfield, was driven by Henri Paul, assistant head of security at the Ritz, who had been personally greeted by Dodi. Outside the airport they were buzzed by paparazzi on motorbikes darting round them, oblivious to safety. An agitated Dodi told Dorneau to accelerate and lose them and at one stage Diana screamed at the driver to 'slow down' as she was worried there might be a collision with the bikes.[20] She tried to soothe Dodi. Outdistancing their pursuers, the couple stopped to visit the Villa Windsor, the home of Diana's ex-husband's great-uncle, the Duke of Windsor, and his wife for the last thirty and more years of their lives. Diana jumped out of the car without waiting for the door to be opened for her. According to the villa's security chief, Ben Murrell, 'Diana looked flustered and her face was red. She didn't look happy. Dodi was still sitting in the car by the time Diana walked into the house. It was obvious something had occurred during the journey ... Diana looked shaken.'[21] The villa now stood empty of the furniture, which had been sent for auction. They spent precisely twenty-eight minutes there: Diana found it creepy, as she was to tell Richard Kay. Later Fayed was to claim that they spent two hours touring what he said was to be their future home together, accompanied at one stage by an interior decorator. Security cameras later proved this to be untrue. They then drove to the Ritz where Diana once again had use of the Imperial Suite. She had her hair done while Dodi visited the nearby Repossi jewellery shop, apparently to complete arrangements for the ring he had ordered for her and to inspect designs for more jewellery. The ring was then taken to the Ritz and given to Dodi who put it in his pocket.

Later, they left for Dodi's apartment on rue Arsène Houssaye to dress for dinner. There they were met by a noisy and aggressive troop of paparazzi shouting and pushing. 'This really upset the

Princess even though she was used to it,' one of the bodyguards recalled. 'The paparazzi were shouting which made them even more threatening. Dodi was particularly annoyed by their behaviour. He wasn't used to it and he asked me what could be done to get rid of them. I told him it was impossible to escape from them just like that.'[22] Similar scenes occurred when they left the apartment, as a witness testified. 'Despite the agreement made with the paparazzi, they didn't respect anything we had asked them to do . . . as soon as the couple's car moved off they behaved like real devils. They called their bikes and sped off like fools, trying to stick to the car. They could have knocked over pedestrians. People flattened themselves against walls as the paparazzi's bikes mounted the pavements and sped past.'[23] Dodi, by now thoroughly unnerved, made a change of plan. Instead of dining at the Left Bank restaurant Chez Benoît, where they were booked, he decided to switch to the Ritz to avoid the photographers. The atmosphere was becoming strained and chaotic: Dodi would not reveal his plans to the bodyguards until the last minute. Despite their best efforts there was an ugly scene on arrival at the hotel. As the mob closed in, Diana and Dodi hesitated. Cameras surrounded the car: 'The couple were engulfed. Dodi's hand went up to shield his face, the Princess looked anguished as she took a running stride towards the door. The results of Dodi's hesitation had enormously bothered the couple,' Rees-Jones recalled.[24] Inside the hotel, it was hardly any better. This was August, a deeply unfashionable time when smart people would not be seen in Paris, let alone at the Ritz. In the restaurant people stared at the couple, forcing them to break off to dine upstairs. Diana, one of the bodyguards noted, was in tears.

Yet, earlier that evening she had been on the telephone to her friends. According to Richard Kay, 'that evening Diana was as happy as I have ever known her'. She did not mention marriage; indeed, to Annabel Goldsmith she said that she needed another marriage like she needed a rash, and to Rosa Monckton in Greece she had said, 'Whatever happens in this relationship, I will continue to do my work, and to help where I am needed.' She would need the connection with reality – something lacking in Dodi's world. Speaking to Rosa on her mobile on 27 August, she had described her holiday as 'bliss'. Later Rosa Monckton wrote of Diana's holiday romance with Dodi: 'She was happy, enjoying herself, and liked the feeling of having someone who not only so obviously cared for her, but was not afraid to be seen to be doing so.'[25] But she was looking forward to being home and seeing her boys. 'I'm coming home tomorrow and the boys will be back from Scotland in the evening,' she told Kay. 'I will have a few days with them before they're back at school.' She was, he said, 'a bit troubled' because William had called her that Saturday to say that Buckingham Palace had told him he must 'perform', and present a photo call at the beginning of his third year at Eton. Both Diana and William disliked having the spotlight shone directly on him to the exclusion of Harry. Diana had once said how hard it was for Harry being overshadowed as a second son and how she and Charles had tried to ensure that everything was shared.[26] At some point she had also arranged to meet Hasnat on the Tuesday of the following week, perhaps hoping to sort out their future. Michael Gibbins had called the office of her driver/security guard, Colin Tebbutt, formerly of the protection squad, to tell him to be at Stansted on Sunday morning as she would be coming in around 10 a.m. 'She'll come back with you', he was told. 'She doesn't want to come back with the circus . . . two cars roaring through London and drawing attention to herself.'[27]

While Dodi and Diana were having dinner in the Imperial Suite at the Ritz, Dodi made a decision that would cost them their lives. To escape the paparazzi outside the front of the hotel, he decided that they would leave the hotel by the rear entrance on the rue Cambon while the limousine and the Range Rover should be seen waiting outside the front exit to give the impression they would be leaving that way. They would then go to the rue Arsène Houssaye apartment. Dodi specifically required that Henri Paul should be their driver and had confirmed his plan in a telephone call to his father, or so he said. The limousine at the back exit, a Mercedes S-280, had been hired from the nearby Etoile Limousine;

it had originally been bought second hand and did not have tinted windows which would have protected the passengers from being photographed by the paparazzi. The driver Henri Paul had been claimed by Murrell to have acted strangely, his breath smelling 'of wine and onions'. The two trained bodyguards, however, had noticed nothing when Paul sat with them as they ate in the Bar Vendôme and he drank two Pastis. Paul, it appears, had been taunting the paparazzi outside the front door which had led them to believe something would happen at the back. It later emerged that he was not a qualified chauffeur and did not have the licence required by law to drive a car registered as a limousine.

Kez Wingfield, the bodyguard who went in the other Mercedes, recalled that Diana and Dodi seemed happy when they left the Imperial Suite. 'It was obvious they'd had a glass of wine or two.'[28] But according to Colin Tebbutt and an ex-Special Branch colleague, when they later examined the CCTV tape covering the Ritz exit, Diana's manner showed that she was not happy with what was going on. As a protection squad policeman he had always taught his trainees to look at their principal's 'hands and eyes and face'. Examining the tape carefully, despite Dodi's protective arm round Diana, he said, 'she was p . . . off. You look at the face and she was taut, "Why all this fuss" . . . She'd been living with this for twenty years, she knew protection, she knew how to do things . . .' Poignantly, he added: 'I never went fast with her. She always used to scream, "Don't run over anybody, don't hit anybody" . . . always used to worry.'[29]

The bodyguard Trevor Rees-Jones, who was to accompany them, preceded Diana out of the door, followed by Dodi. Henri Paul was in the driving seat. Rees-Jones ushered Diana into the right rear seat, with Dodi on her left. Rees-Jones got into the front passenger seat. None of them fastened seat belts. Just before 12.20 a.m., Paul drove off down the rue Cambon. A small crowd of photographers observed the departure: hunting as a pack, they alerted their colleagues waiting outside the hotel's front entrance on the Place Vendôme. Paul turned into the rue de Rivoli; by the time he had reached the Place de la Concorde, both sets of paparazzi had joined the chase. Here he came to the fateful decision not to turn right on to the Champs-Elysées, the most direct route to the apartment, as he would have had to stop at several traffic lights en route, giving the pursuing paparazzi time to catch up and grab photographs of the couple through the untinted windows. Instead he decided to take the back route down the Cours La Reine/Cours Albert 1er, a stretch of dual carriageway leading to the tunnel beneath the Place d'Alma, which would enable him to pick up speed and shake off the paparazzi. In the approach to the tunnel there is a hump followed by a dip before the road bends sharply to the left at the tunnel entrance. Paul had by now shaken off the photographers. As he approached the tunnel travelling at between 118 kmh (74 mph) and 155 kmh (97 mph) he overtook a much slower white Fiat Uno in the right-hand lane, brushing its left-hand rear with his right wing just as they passed over the notorious hump. Oversteering to the left he then understeered to the right as the car reached the dip at the mouth of the tunnel. At 12.23 a.m., three minutes after leaving the Ritz, the Mercedes, out of control, slammed into the thirteenth concrete pillar dividing the roadway in the tunnel. Henri Paul and Dodi died instantly from their injuries; the inflated airbag saved Rees-Jones from death, if not disfigurement; Diana was left semi-conscious. Within seconds the paparazzi had surrounded the stricken Mercedes, now in clouds of smoke, its horn blaring, and zoomed in on their prey.

22. Death in Paris

'This is going to unleash grief like no one has ever seen anywhere in the world'
(Tony Blair to Alastair Campbell)

It took almost an hour to free Diana from the wrecked car. She appeared to her rescuers to be the least injured of the four: only a slight trickle of blood from mouth and nose indicated that anything was wrong. Yet her internal injuries were life-threatening. After the initial impact the Mercedes had spun away, rotating at high speed before crashing into the tunnel wall on the right. At the first impact Dodi and Diana had been thrown violently forward against the backs of the front seats, then the rotation of the car had flung them around against the interior. When the Mercedes finally stopped, pointing back towards the mouth of the tunnel, Diana was slumped on the floor, against the back of Rees-Jones's seat, facing down the tunnel. Her legs were twisted, one under her, the other on the seat. With her eyes closed and her face undamaged apart from a cut on her forehead, she looked beautiful and as if she were asleep. But the shock of the impact and deceleration on her body had displaced her heart from the left to the right side, severing the pulmonary vein and rupturing the pericardium (the protective sac round the heart), flooding her chest cavity with blood. She was dying, suffocating in a foreign country just as one of her psychics had predicted would be the fate of Charles.

Yet to the first doctor on the scene, Frédéric Mailliez, who had been driving through the tunnel in the opposite direction, she 'looked pretty fine . . . I thought this woman had a chance.' He put an oxygen mask over her face while attempting to clear her air passages. When the ambulance arrived, Dr Jan-Marc Martino, a surgical anaesthetist and resuscitation specialist, worked on Diana.

Before they could transfer her to the ambulance, she suffered a heart attack. She was given cardiac massage and a respiratory tube was inserted into her mouth. Then she was lifted on to a stretcher and placed in the ambulance which crawled its way with a police escort to La Pitié-Salpêtrière Hospital, stopping once on the way as Diana's blood pressure dropped to a dangerous level. She was put on a ventilator. 'She was unconscious and under artificial respiration. Her arterial blood pressure was very low but her heart was still beating.[1] X-rays revealed the horrific state of her internal injuries and afterwards she suffered a second heart attack. An incision in her chest revealed that bleeding was coming through a hole in the membrane round her heart and later that her superior left pulmonary vein was torn. Adrenalin was administered and cardiac massage kept her heart going but only just; there was no independent rhythm. Diana was to all intents and purposes already beyond help. Electric-shock therapy was administered, to no effect. At 4 a.m. (3 a.m. British time) on the morning of 31 August, she was pronounced dead.[2]

Even before the doctor had begun his treatment of Diana in the wrecked car, the paparazzi, headed by the oddly named Romuald Rat, who arrived first, began snapping the scene. In total some ten or fifteen photographers gathered, their flashes going off like machine guns. Only two of them had thought to call for assistance and even they turned immediately to photograph the grisly scene. Members of the public were appalled by their greed and insensitivity – two of their victims were, after all, dead. Shocked onlookers attacked the paparazzi; when the police arrived, it was assumed that the photographers had directly caused the accident by their pursuit of the car and seven were arrested, to be charged with involuntary manslaughter and non-assistance. The police confiscated the cameras, but when the rolls of film were developed it became obvious that no photographs had been taken before the arrival of the paparazzi on the scene, when the accident had already happened. Nonetheless, people were already trying to profit from Diana's death. Two internet websites revealed that the asking price for photographs of Diana in the car was over £600,000. In London,

Piers Morgan of the *Daily Mirror* viewed a collection of agency pictures and realized the impossibility of running them. He knew, as did every other editor, that the press was going to be accused of killing Diana.

At the hospital, the British Ambassador in Paris, Sir Michael Jay, had been waiting with the French Interior Minister, Jean-Pierre Chevènement, outside the operating theatre and had reported the accident to the Queen's deputy private secretary, Sir Robin Janvrin. At Balmoral Diana had dropped so far from the Royal Family's mental radar that Janvrin was not even aware she was in Paris. When told of her death he informed the Queen and Prince Charles, who decided that 'the boys' should not be told immediately until the situation was absolutely clear. Diana's death was officially announced at 5.45 a.m. Paris time, and flashed to an incredulous world.

Meanwhile, Colin Tebbutt and Paul Burrell had flown in with Prince Charles's security man, Ian von Tanz. At the British Embassy they were met by Sir Michael and Lady Jay and the Military Attaché, Brigadier Charles Ritchie. It was Lady Jay who produced a black cocktail frock to dress Diana's body. Burrell, contrary to the calm, controlled figure featured in his somewhat self-serving book, was shaken and sobbing. At the embassy Tebbutt and Brigadier Ritchie took charge, arranging an interpreter and a car to take Tebbutt and Burrell to the Ritz to pick up Diana's things. At the Ritz, where they were apparently treated with total disdain, they discovered that Fayed had already had Diana's possessions packed up and sent to London. At La Pitié-Salpêtrière Hospital they were shown into the room where Diana lay. 'She looked calm,' Tebbutt recalled.[3] The press had got on to a nearby roof and were trying to shoot into the room, so Tebbutt found some blankets and pinned them over the windows. The room was very hot and the air stifling; Tebbutt switched on additional air conditioning and 'Diana's hair moved and so did her eyelashes – I actually thought she was alive,' Tebbutt recalled, 'and so did Paul.'[4] '[She] just looked like she was asleep . . . her face just had little scratches and her hair was hiding the injuries on her head. I didn't see the injuries although I was close, right next to her.'[5] Two undertakers stood like statues in the corner: they were to prepare the body before the arrival of the royal undertakers from London. Leadington's, as the London undertakers were called, were to arrive later, marching down the corridor ready equipped with a lead-lined coffin and the royal standard to drape over it.

Confusion at La Pitié-Salpêtrière was echoed by similar confusion at the Palace, Balmoral and Downing Street. At first it was thought that Diana had survived, then that there was a possibility of brain damage; at last it was confirmed that she had died. There was no precedent for the sudden death of a divorced Princess of Wales. At Balmoral a devastated Prince Charles braced himself to tell William and Harry the terrible news. William, apparently, said that he thought something dreadful had happened as he had kept waking up during the night. Charles, no doubt racked with guilt over his wife's fate, kept saying – presciently as it turned out – 'They're all going to blame me, aren't they?'[6] With equal prescience, Tony Blair, at home in his Sedgefield constituency, told Alastair Campbell, 'This is going to unleash grief like no one has ever seen anywhere in the world.' Again, Blair showed the sureness of his popular touch in his statement issued that morning on what Diana had meant to the nation: 'They liked her, they loved her, they regarded her as one of the people. She was the People's Princess and that is how she will stay, how she will remain in all our hearts and memories for ever.'[7]

'There were rows almost immediately Diana died,' said a royal aide. At Balmoral there was confusion as to whether Charles should stay with his sons or go to Paris to collect Diana's body and whether a Queen's Flight would be arranged to take him. Charles's aides, Stephen Lamport and Mark Bolland, convinced that the right thing to do was for him to go to Paris and bring Diana back, urged him to follow his instincts and go, even threatening to book the Prince on to a scheduled flight from Aberdeen if the Queen's Flight would not be made available.[8] There was doubt, too, whether Diana should be treated as one of the Royal Family and the mother of the future King, or whether she should be returned to the care of the Spencers. The Queen's instinct was for a private family funeral at Windsor and interment at Frogmore (in the same plot as that other royal embarrassment, the Duchess of Windsor). The Spencers would have preferred a quiet family funeral at Althorp. Somehow a consensus was reached that only a state funeral would satisfy public feeling. At Balmoral, as usual, the Royal Family carried on as if nothing had happened. They attended the customary Sunday service in Crathie Church, where Diana's name was not mentioned and had not been since the royal ruling that, with the loss of her HRH, her name should be dropped from the prayers for the Royal Family. Even the minister went ahead with the sermon he had planned to deliver before the accident, which included unsuitably jokey references to Billy Connolly. The absence of any reference to Diana apparently prompted Prince Harry to ask, 'Are you sure Mummy's really dead?' The press was equally taken aback: 'No mention of Accident' *The Times* remarked on Monday morning. The *Sun* would follow this up, asking 'DO THEY CARE?' It was the beginning of a mounting wave of criticism directed at the Queen and her family which was to reach dangerous levels of hostility by the end of the week.

On Sunday afternoon, Charles, joined at Aberdeen by Diana's sisters, flew to Paris in a BAe 146 of the Queen's Flight. Her brother Charles had been at his house in Cape Town when he heard the news. 'The telephone went in the middle of the night,' Spencer recalled:

It was the manager who runs this place [Althorp] and he said, 'We've heard there's been a car crash in Paris and Dodi Fayed's dead but your sister's just injured. We thought you should know straight away.' I went downstairs and flicked between the various satellite news stations. They were saying much the same actually. They were saying she'd been seen walking away and I thought, well, I'd better stay up and see just how bad it is and then my sister Sarah rang me and she said: 'Look, I'm afraid it's really bad news. It looks like she's got brain damage.' I was totally shaken. I couldn't believe it. And then I rang my sister Jane, whose husband worked for the Queen. He [Robert Fellowes] was on another line in the background and he went 'Oh, no' and then my sister Jane said, 'I'm afraid that's it, she's died.'[9]

Before flying home, he issued a statement praising his 'unique sister', adding ominously that he always believed the press would kill her in the end. He declared that 'every proprietor and every editor of every publication' that had paid for intrusive and exploitative photographs of her 'has blood on his hands today'. His charges set the scene for the mood of public anger against the press. Diana's mother was isolated on the Isle of Seil, in a desperate state over the fate of her daughter with whom she had not been on speaking terms for the past three months. Neither Prince Charles nor the Queen telephoned her to express their condolences.

When Prince Charles and Diana's sisters arrived in Paris, they found Diana looking serene and composed in death, wearing Lady Jay's black cocktail dress and shoes, her hair freshly blow-dried, the rosary which Mother Teresa had given her in her hand. After Charles and the sisters had spent time alone with her, she was placed in a coffin for the return journey. Colin Tebbutt and Burrell accompanied the hearse on its journey through Paris: 'It was just fantastic,' Tebbutt recalled. 'They do it differently in Paris – they applaud. With the coffin, Prince Charles, the President, millions of police by now, me, Paul and the vicar [the Rev. Martin Draper], the whole of Paris was applauding . . .'[10] Prince Charles flew back to Balmoral from Northolt, apparently preferring not to accompany the family on into London. On the drive from Northolt airport to Fulham where Diana was to be deposited at the mortuary, the road was lined with thousands of people. 'I couldn't believe what we were seeing,' Tebbutt recalled. 'Lady Sarah [McCorquodale] said, "We'll have a little private funeral at Althorp", and we turned on to the A40 and Paris was moving but I just couldn't believe what we were seeing, there were thousands upon thousands of people, no traffic.' Tebbutt sent one of his drivers to take Sarah home again via the A40. This time she exclaimed, 'We're not going to get a quiet funeral!'[11] Leaving Diana's body to undergo the obligatory autopsy in Fulham (there had already been one in Paris to conform with French law), Charles flew back to Balmoral. Isolated up on Deeside, the Royal Family remained unaware of the gathering hysteria in the capital. The crowds of people of all conditions, black, white, old and young queuing for up to seven hours to sign the condolence book at St James's Palace, the mountains of flowers outside Kensington Palace, the sorrowing notes and poems pinned to the railings, represented above all Diana's constituency, the ordinary people of Britain.

Diana's body was taken from Fulham to lie in the Chapel Royal at St James's Palace. Lucia Flecha de Lima, who had set off for London as soon as she heard of Diana's death, found her coffin lying there in lonely state, without flowers: 'The first day when I arrived at the chapel there was not one single flower on her coffin. Then I said to the chaplain that if he didn't allow flowers in, I would throw open the doors of the chapel so everyone could see her there without a single flower and all the flowers outside that people had brought. I said, "Tomorrow I'll come back with my flowers for her." And I came every day. And from then on I brought flowers, not only mine but from friends and people who knew her. And I went to a flower van outside the Michelin restaurant [Bibendum in the Fulham Road] and he said: "What are they for?" And I told him, and every day after that he insisted I take flowers to her for nothing . . .'[12] 'And they [the flowers] were around her, over her coffin representing the flowers of the world, and I said to Prince Charles, "These flowers represent the people, thousands and millions of flowers all around the world that people want to give to Princess Diana." I've never felt like that in my life. I have experienced personal loss . . . but the public's reaction was extraordinary . . .'[13]

Diana was taken home to Kensington Palace for the last night before the funeral. Earlier, Lucia had been with Paul Burrell when a devastating reminder was delivered: a forensics bag containing the clothes Diana had been wearing at the time of the accident, a black top and white trousers. The black blazer was missing. Paul Burrell had spent the day arranging flowers left by the public outside the Palace and flowers sent by friends – her favourite white lilies, tulips and roses – on the floor of the hallway where the coffin would rest. The Catholic priest, Father Tony Parsons from the Carmelite Church in Kensington where Diana used to go and pray, arrived with two large church candles. That evening Frances visited with Sarah and Jane and the grandchildren to spend some time beside the coffin. Charles Spencer did not appear. Burrell had asked Sarah McCorquodale, at Lucia's request, if she could spend the vigil at Diana's coffin. The request was refused. '. . . when I told Lady Sarah how important Lucia was to the Princess, and how much she needed to be there that night, Lucia's request was denied. Lady Sarah felt it appropriate for only family to attend. The one woman,' Burrell wrote, 'who was more family than any of them was refused her final, most personal farewell.'[14]

'WHERE IS THE QUEEN WHEN THE COUNTRY NEEDS HER?' the *Sun*'s front page asked on 4 September (Thursday) after four emotional days of unofficial grief for Diana. The Queen was on holiday 550 miles away from the capital and, the newspaper said, only intended to fly in for the day on Saturday for the funeral and fly back afterwards. The Queen had overruled her senior courtiers who believed that there should be a flag flying half-mast over the Palace. The empty flagpole at the end of the Mall was 'a stark insult to Diana's memory'. Why hadn't the Queen broadcast a personal statement of sympathy to the nation? the *Sun* asked. 'The people want the Monarchy to join publicly in their mourning for Diana . . . Every hour the Palace remains empty adds to the public anger at what they perceive to be a snub to the People's Princess . . .'

'It was sometimes difficult to get across to the people up there [Balmoral] that there actually was a sort of head of feeling building on that [the flag issue] or there was a real sort of crisis brewing on such and such,' said a former aide. 'If they had all been down here, they would have sensed just driving down the Mall that there was a very ugly feeling around and they actually needed to be a bit careful.'[15] The inevitable search for a scapegoat was on: how could such a terrible tragedy have happened? Someone must be to blame.

The first target was the paparazzi and by implication the press who had paid them, then it was the drunk driver Henri Paul, and then the Royal Family who had cast Diana out. If they had not done so, the argument went, she would not have been in the Alma Tunnel with a playboy boyfriend at the end of August. And what was more, the thinking (newspaper-led, it might be pointed out) was that the Royal Family, by remaining on holiday at Balmoral rather than returning to the capital to share the nation's grief, had shown themselves to be uncaring of the People's Princess. An early focus was the empty flagpole over Buckingham Palace, head-quarters of the Royal Family, where in popular opinion a flag should have been drooping half-mast in the traditional expression of mourning.

'The Queen is a traditionalist on things like that,' the aide said. 'If it's been a precedent in the monarchy it's quite hard to change. It's nothing to do with insensitivity, it's just there is a logic to a personal Standard or flag. I mean if you [the Queen] are there it's up and if you're not, it's not.'[16] After considerable pressure, the Palace, or rather the Queen, reluctantly yielded. The Union Jack was to be flown half-mast until she was in residence. The deputy private secretary Sir Robin Janvrin emerged from a meeting to tell a member of the 'haul-up-the-Union-Jack party': 'I'm covered in blood, but you've got your flag . . .'[17] A compromise was reached whereby when the Queen came down from Balmoral, her standard went up; it came down on the Saturday, the day of the funeral, and was substituted by the Union flag at half-mast which stayed there until midnight on Sunday.[18] 'I think there was a conscious decision that on the day of the funeral there had to be a symbolic move and that was it,' said Dickie Arbiter, the most experienced royal press officer, who had also worked for the Waleses before the split. Contrary to public perception, the Queen was, Arbiter said, 'very grief-stricken' by Diana's death. 'On the day of the funeral when the Royal Family came out of Buckingham Palace as the gun carriage carrying Diana's coffin passed, the Queen bowed. And the only other time that the Queen bows is at the Cenotaph.'[19]

Finally the Royal Family seemed to have perceived that tectonic plates of emotion and grief were shifting beneath their feet. The Queen and her family flew down to London on Friday 5 September: only then did they get first-hand experience of what Diana's death meant to the people at large. Walking out of the Palace gates to mingle with the crowds they could sense the strange atmosphere, the open grief and, for the first time, an undercurrent of hostility.

That week, television journalist Jon Snow taking the public temperature among the crowds on the Mall had found a high level of anger that the Queen was not there to share their grief. The state of public feeling was such, it is alleged, that the Metropolitan Police panicked under the weight of media hype. Fearing attacks on the funeral procession and other disorder, senior police officers went so far as to telephone the army to ask if they were bringing troops into London. The army refused to contemplate any such action, but the police brought in large vans loaded with riot squads which were concealed in side streets on the day of the funeral.[20]

On the Friday evening before the funeral the Queen gave a televised broadcast about Diana and the meaning of her life. The first paragraph amounted almost to an apology: 'We have all been trying in our different ways to cope,' she said. 'It is not easy to express a sense of loss, since the initial shock is often succeeded by a mixture of other feelings – disbelief, incomprehension, anger and concern for those who remain.

'We have all felt those emotions in these last few days. So what I say to you now, as your Queen and as a grandmother, I say from my heart.'

Then she paid tribute to Diana as 'an exceptional and gifted human being', concluding that there were 'lessons to be drawn from her life and from the extraordinary and moving reaction to her death . . .'

Dressed in black, the Queen sat at a window through which the grieving crowds could be seen outside the Palace. Her delivery was firm, solemn and moving, perhaps the most personal statement she had ever publicly uttered. Her speech had been written for her by Sir Robert Fellowes, Diana's brother-in-law. Downing Street, which had been in active communication with the Palace over the week, was involved in only one phrase of the broadcast draft, 'speaking as a grandmother . . .'. 'That was their only input,' Dickie Arbiter recalled. 'That was the only real input of the funeral arrangements. They said "two minutes" silence at the Abbey – one minute was done – but they came up with nothing else. They did say to Hayden Phillips who was Permanent Secretary at what was still the Department of National Heritage – "Money is no object" – because they [the government] had to pick up the bill for the stands for the media and everything else. So they were very much on board but at the same time realized probably within half an hour of the meeting starting at Buckingham Palace on the Monday morning that these guys at Buckingham Palace knew what they were talking about.'[21]

In the event, Diana's funeral, organized at relatively short notice, showed British royal ceremonial at its best. Diana's family had been wrong to suggest a quiet family interment at Althorp. The world demanded that Diana be properly recognized and she was – with a perfectly organized spectacular but dignified ceremonial orchestrated by Palace officials from start to finish. The original blueprint for the funeral was one designed for the state funeral of the Queen Mother along a route from the Chapel Royal in St James's Palace to Westminster Abbey, down the Mall, Horse Guards Approach Road, through the Horse Guards archway into Whitehall and then down to the Abbey. On advice from the police about the huge numbers of watching people who would be involved, the route was lengthened. Diana would be brought back from her temporary resting place in the Chapel Royal, St James's Palace, to spend her last night in Kensington Palace, and the procession would start instead from there before following the usual route. Screens with speakers following her progress were set up in Hyde Park, allowing the public to witness Diana's funeral until the very end. An estimated one million people or more had travelled to London to be present on the day.

At 9.08 a.m., as the bells of Westminster Abbey began to toll,

Diana's coffin emerged from the gates of Kensington Palace on a horse-drawn gun carriage. It was draped in the royal standard and there were three bouquets laid on it: a sheaf of white tulips from William, of white longiflorum lilies from Charles Spencer and, most moving of all, a bunch of Diana's favourite white roses with the simple card inscribed 'Mummy' in Harry's twelve-year-old hand. Slowly the procession advanced down the Kensington Road to Hyde Park Corner and down Constitution Hill to Buckingham Palace where the Queen stood with other members of the family, including Princess Margaret, to honour Diana as she passed. Then it went down the Mall to be joined by Charles, Prince Philip, Charles Spencer and the two boys. Apparently, the evening before, Prince Philip had said to William that if he wanted to walk behind his mother's coffin, he would walk with him. It was a terrible ordeal for William, aged fifteen, and Harry, only twelve. As they walked they could hear people shouting 'God bless you' to them and others wailing and throwing flowers into the road.

At Westminster Abbey, a two-thousand-strong congregation waited, an extraordinary mixture of people representing the range of Diana's life, charities and friendships. The Royal Family was out in strength, Bill and Hillary Clinton were there, and Bernadette Chirac representing her husband, the President of France. There was a clutch of celebrities – Sting, Valentino, Shirley Bassey, George Michael and Elton John – and Hollywood – Tom Hanks, Steven Spielberg, Tom Cruise and Nicole Kidman. There were friends who were also celebrities like David Frost and Clive James. There were old friends like Carolyn Bartholomew and Laura Lonsdale. There were the Flecha de Limas, Annabel Goldsmith, Imran Khan and Jemima. Ruth Rudge, headmistress of West Heath, was there. The largest single contingent was made up from her charities. 'It's interesting how Diana's life became extremely compartmentalized,' said Richard Kay, 'so much so that at her funeral they put all her friends in one area of Westminster Abbey and most of them had never met each other. A lot of them didn't even know who the others were, it was quite extraordinary.' Among the congregation was Hasnat Khan who, returning home from Pakistan, had found a birthday card from Diana on his doormat and at the same time the invitation to her funeral.

'What I remember about it,' said Meredith Etherington-Smith, who was in the Abbey, 'was the utter pin-dropping silence when the coffin came in. It was obviously very, very heavy, it was lead-lined, and all you could hear was the squeaking of the soldiers' boots as they carried it. They were shaking and I thought, Christ, they're going to drop it.' Diana's favourite music was played, the hymn 'I Vow to Thee, My Country' which had been played at her wedding, the 'Libera me Domine', from Verdi's Requiem. Perhaps most moving of all was Elton John's rendition of his requiem for Marilyn Monroe, 'Candle in the Wind', rewritten for Diana, 'Goodbye England's rose . . .'. 'God knows how he pulled that off,' Etherington-Smith recalled, 'the man was shaking like a jelly . . .' Nothing could have been more appropriate for Diana who had empathized with Monroe and now had died at exactly the same age. (Her other idol, Princess Grace, whose funeral she had attended, poignantly had also died as a result of a car crash in September 1982, just fifteen years before.) The most dramatic moment was provided by Charles Spencer, whose eloquent speech electrified everyone who heard it.

It was addressed to Diana, whose name had signified the huntress but who had become 'the most hunted woman in the world'. His eulogy to his sister could hardly have been bettered: 'Diana was the very essence of compassion, of duty, of style, of beauty. All over the world she was a symbol of selfless humanity: a standard-bearer for the truly downtrodden: a very British girl whose concerns transcended nationality: someone with a natural nobility who was classless and' – here he could not resist a hit at the Royal Family who had divested her of her HRH – 'who proved in the last year that she needed no royal title to continue to generate her particular brand of magic.' He praised her for her 'wonderfully mischievous sense of humour', her energy and her 'joy for life, transmitted wherever you took your smile and the sparkle in those unforgettable eyes . . .' 'Without your God-given sensitivity,' he declared, 'we would be immersed in greater ignorance at the anguish of AIDS and HIV sufferers, the plight of the homeless, the isolation of lepers, the random destruction of landmines.' Perhaps most movingly of all was when he emphasized how, beneath the glitter of the international celebrity, Diana was still an insecure little girl at heart. 'Diana explained to me once that it was her innermost feelings of suffering that made it possible for her to connect with her constituency of the rejected. And here we come to another truth about her – for all the status, the glamour, the applause, Diana remained throughout a very insecure person at heart, almost childlike in her desire to do good for others so she could release herself from deep feelings of unworthiness . . .'

Passages in the speech were undoubtedly not just directed at the media who had hounded Diana but implicitly criticized the Royal Family and its traditions. 'On behalf of your mother and sisters we pledge that we, your blood family, will do all we can to continue the imaginative and loving way in which you were steering these two exceptional young men, so that their souls are not simply immersed by duty and tradition, but can sing openly, as you planned . . .' Many people thought that the underlying bitterness and the implied attack on the Royal Family were inappropriate for a funeral which should be a time for mutual grief and forgiveness. Others, knowing the family background at the time, considered the 'blood family' pledge to be hypocritical. But at the time, Spencer's words touched a chord with the public.

There was dead silence in the Abbey when Spencer finished his speech. 'All you could hear was far, far down beyond the door this sound like raindrops, and then that it was actually people clapping,' said one of those present.[22] A distinguished journalist also used the raindrops simile:

A sound like a distant shower of rain penetrated the walls of Westminster Abbey . . . it rolled towards us. Then it was inside the church. It rolled up the nave like a great wave. It was people clapping, first the crowds outside and then the two thousand inside . . . People don't clap at funerals; and they don't clap because people outside are clapping. But they did. It was desire, serious applause, and it marked the moment at which the meaning of what was happening on this incredible day was made plain . . . the masses listening outside, who had been claiming their own place . . . broke into the abbey. The people wanted to make their feelings felt. It wasn't enough to be one of the millions on the streets of London. It certainly wasn't enough to be one of the billion watching on television. They wanted to be in the abbey and the applause was their way of getting in.[23]

Diana had transcended celebrity, she had touched people's hearts and not only in Britain but across the world.

As the coffin began its journey to Althorp at midday, the clapping continued. So many flowers were thrown at the hearse on its way out of London that the driver had to use his windscreen wipers to clear them. At the gates of Althorp the hearse broke down, a contretemps which would certainly have appealed to Diana's sense of humour. Meanwhile, the royal train with its smart burgundy carriages pulled by two locomotives named *Prince William* and *Prince Henry* left London for Northamptonshire. On board were Prince Charles, William and Harry. Paul Burrell and Colin Tebbutt were also on the train and were invited to the subsequent family lunch at Althorp. At some point during the journey, a member of the royal household apparently offered to restore Diana's title, Her Royal Highness. It was by now a meaningless gesture. Charles Spencer refused it. (Charles Spencer had deposited his South African girlfriend with the Burrells to avoid embarrassment but she, with Burrell and Tebbutt, was the only non-family member to be present at Diana's interment on the island.)

As they were finishing lunch, Spencer announced, 'Diana is home'. The royal standard was replaced by the white, red, black and gold of the Spencer flag. In death the Spencers were reclaiming Diana just as the Royal Family had rejected her. In truth, neither side had given her the support she deserved. The small party crossed the park for the interment on the island in the centre of the small, tree-lined lake. The eight Welsh guardsmen, accompanied by their officer, carried the coffin gingerly over the temporary pontoon crossing the water to the island where a grave had been prepared and the ground consecrated. After a thirty-minute burial service, the mourners left Diana, alone on the isolated island as she had been alone in life.

Source Notes

Chapter 1. The Country Girl (pp. 1–11)

1 Interview with the author 3/4/01.
2 Charles Spencer, *The Spencer Family*, p. 315.
3 Ibid., p. 321.
4 Ibid., p. 314.
5 Interview with the author 3/4/01.
6 Interview with the author 16/11/05.
7 Interview with the author 16/11/05.

Chapter 2. A Norfolk Childhood (pp. 12–28)

1 William Deedes interview with the author.
2 Interview with the author.
3 Private information.
4 Interview with the author 5/5/04.
5 Interview with the author 16/11/04.
6 Mary Clarke, *Little Girl Lost: The Troubled Childhood of Princess Diana by the Woman who Raised Her*, p. 25.
7 Ibid., p. 19.
8 Andrew Morton, *Diana: Her True Story – In Her Own Words*, p. 30.
9 Charles Spencer, *The Spencer Family*, p. 310.
10 Andrew Morton, *Diana: Her True Story – In Her Own Words*, p. 26.
11 Interview with the author 16/11/05.
12 Mary Clarke, *Little Girl Lost: The Troubled Childhood of Princess Diana by the Woman who Raised Her*, p. 178.
13 Andrew Morton, *Diana: Her True Story – In Her Own Words*, p. 26.
14 Rosalind Coward, *Diana: The Portrait*, p. 56.

15 Sarah Bradford, *Elizabeth: A Biography of Her Majesty The Queen*, p. 424.

16 Andrew Morton, *Diana: Her True Story – In Her Own Words*, p. 25.

17 Rosalind Coward, *Diana: The Portrait*, p. 47.

18 Ibid., p. 49.

19 Sally Bedell Smith, *Diana: The Life of a Troubled Princess*, p. 46.

20 Ibid., p. 47.

21 Ibid., p. 48.

22 Ibid.

23 Angela Levin, *Raine and Johnnie: The Spencers and the Scandal of Althorp*, p. 115.

Chapter 3. 'I'm Lady Diana' (pp. 29–47)

1 Andrew Morton, *Diana: Her True Story – In Her Own Words*, p. 31.

2 Ibid, p. 28.

3 Charles Spencer, *Althorp: The Story of an English House*, p. 2.

4 Interview with the author 2/1/05.

5 Rosalind Coward, *Diana: The Portrait*, p. 36.

6 Interview with the author 2/1/05.

7 Angela Levin, *Raine and Johnnie: The Spencers and the Scandal of Althorp*, p. 138.

8 Ibid., p. 140.

9 Settelen tapes.

10 Interview with the author 11/4/01.

11 Andrew Morton, *Diana: Her True Story – In Her Own Words*, p. 24.

12 Settelen tapes.

13 Letter to author 25/2/05.

14 Angela Levin, *Raine and Johnnie: The Spencers and the Scandal of Althorp*, p. 149.

15 Ibid., p. 143.

16 Ibid., p. 150.

17 Rosalind Coward, *Diana: The Portrait*, p. 70.

18 Andrew Morton, *Diana: Her True Story – In Her Own Words*, p. 29.

19 Ibid., p. 31.

20 Rosalind Coward, *Diana: The Portrait*, p. 72.
21 Ibid., p. 69.
22 James Whitaker interview with the author June 2001.
23 Andrew Morton, *Diana: Her True Story – In Her Own Words*, p. 31.
24 Mary Robertson, *The Diana I Knew*, p. 33.
25 Private information.
26 Andrew Morton, *Diana: Her True Story – In Her Own Words*, p. 105.

Chapter 4. Enter the Prince (pp. 48–62)

1 Philip Ziegler, *Mountbatten*, p. 687.
2 Anthony Holden, *Charles, Prince of Wales*, p. 22.
3 Interview with the author 5/4/05.
4 Jonathan Dimbleby, *The Prince of Wales: A Biography*, p. 243.
5 Philip Ziegler, *Mountbatten*, p. 686.
6 Ibid., p. 687.
7 Ibid.
8 Interview with the author 16/11/05.
9 Interview with the author 5/5/04.
10 Interview with the author 7/3/05.
11 Stephen Barry, *Royal Service: My Twelve Years as Valet to Prince Charles*, p. 180.
12 Interview with the author 7/3/06.
13 Christopher Wilson, *The Windsor Knot: Charles, Camilla and the Legacy of Diana*, pp. 90–91.
14 James Whitaker interview with the author June 2001.
15 James Whitaker interview with the author June 2001.
16 Interview with the author 9/3/94.
17 Jonathan Dimbleby, *The Prince of Wales: A Biography*, p. 267.
18 Ibid., p. 261.

Chapter 5. 'Whatever Love Means' (pp. 63–90)

1 Andrew Morton, *Diana: Her True Story – In Her Own Words*, p. 32.
2 Ibid.
3 Jonathan Dimbleby, *The Prince of Wales: A Biography*, pp. 279–80.
4 Stephen Barry, *Royal Service: My Twelve Years as Valet to Prince Charles*, p. 216.
5 Andrew Morton, *Diana: Her True Story – In Her Own Words*, p. 33.
6 Jonathan Dimbleby, *The Prince of Wales: A Biography*, p. 280.
7 Interview with the author.
8 Interview with the author.
9 Jonathan Dimbleby, *The Prince of Wales: A Biography*, p. 282.
10 Sally Bedell Smith, *Diana: The Life of a Troubled Princess*, p. 83.
11 Ibid., p. 87.
12 Ibid., p. 85.
13 James Whitaker interview with the author June 2001.
14 Roy Greenslade interview with the author 20/9/05.
15 Jonathan Dimbleby, *The Prince of Wales: A Biography*, p. 282.
16 Interview with the author 16/11/05.
17 Interview with the author 29/12/93.
18 Private information.
19 Stephen Barry, *Royal Service: My Twelve Years as Valet to Prince Charles*, p. 225.
20 Jonathan Dimbleby, *The Prince of Wales: A Biography*, p. 283.
21 Andrew Morton, *Diana: Her True Story – In Her Own Words*, p. 34.
22 Ibid., p. 33.
23 Letter from private collection.
24 Interview with William Tallon 24/2/04.
25 Hugo Vickers, unpublished diary, Toronto, 2 June 1981 © Hugo Vickers.
26 Andrew Morton, *Diana: Her True Story – In Her Own Words*, p. 34.
27 Ibid., p. 47.
28 Interview with the author 5/4/05.
29 Andrew Morton, *Diana: Her True Story – In Her Own Words*, p. 37.
30 Letter from private collection.

31 Ibid.

32 Interview with the author 6/4/05.

33 William Tallon interview with the author 24/2/04.

34 Interview with the author 9/3/04.

35 Andrew Morton, *Diana: Her True Story – In Her Own Words*, pp. 36, 37.

36 Andrew Morton, *Diana: Her True Story – In Her Own Words*, p. 119.

37 Sarah Bradford, *Elizabeth: A Biography of Her Majesty The Queen*, p. 431.

38 Ibid., pp. 431–2.

39 Jonathan Dimbleby, *The Prince of Wales: A Biography*, p. 284.

40 Sarah Bradford, *Elizabeth: A Biography of Her Majesty The Queen*, p. 429.

41 Robert Spencer interview with the author, 26 June 2001.

42 Hugo Vickers, unpublished diary, 26 November 2004.

43 Jonathan Dimbleby, *The Prince of Wales: A Biography*, p. 287.

44 Robert Spencer interview with the author 26/6/01.

45 Andrew Morton, *Diana: Her True Story – In Her Own Words*, pp. 40, 41.

46 Rosalind Coward, *Diana: The Portrait*, p. 84.

47 Private information.

Chapter 6. The Beginning of the 'Fairy Tale'
(pp. 91–106)

1 Andrew Morton, *Diana: Her True Story – In Her Own Words*, p. 41.

2 Ibid., p. 42.

3 Rosalind Coward, *Diana: The Portrait*, pp. 98–9.

4 Ibid., p. 99.

5 Ibid., p. 91.

6 Jonathan Dimbleby, *The Prince of Wales: A Biography*, p. 293.

7 Andrew Morton, *Diana: Her True Story – In Her Own Words*, p. 42.

8 Interview with the author 16/11/05.

9 Jonathan Dimbleby, *The Prince of Wales: A Biography*, p. 294.

10 Interview with the author 7/3/06.

11 Private information.

12 Interview with the author 9/5/01.

13 Interview with the author 9/5/01.

14 Jonathan Dimbleby, *The Prince of Wales: A Biography*, p. 294.

15 James Whitaker interview with the author June 2001.

16 Andrew Morton, *Diana: Her True Story – In Her Own Words*, p. 43.

17 Ibid., p. 43.

18 Interview with the author 9/5/01.

19 Interview with the author 9/5/01.

20 Interview with the author 16/11/05.

21 Private information.

22 Private information.

23 Andrew Morton, *Diana: Her True Story – In Her Own Words*, p. 43.

24 Ibid., p. 43.

25 Interview with the author 23/2/04.

26 Colin Tebbutt interview with the author 3/3/04.

27 Private information.

28 Interview with the author 16/11/05.

29 Interview with the author 16/11/05.

30 Interview with the author 16/11/05.

31 Interview with the author 16/11/05.

32 Interview with the author.

33 Interview with the author 25/10/05.

34 Jonathan Dimbleby, *The Prince of Wales: A Biography*, p. 298.

35 Andrew Morton, *Diana: Her True Story – In Her Own Words*, p. 45.

36 Private information.

37 Roy Greenslade interview with the author 20/9/05.

38 Andrew Morton, *Diana: Her True Story – In Her Own Words*, p. 45.

39 Private information.

40 Jonathan Dimbleby, *The Prince of Wales: A Biography*, p. 304.

Chapter 7. 'Di-mania' (pp. 107–25)

1 Interview with the author 25/10/05.
2 Patrick Jephson, *Shadows of a Princess. Diana, Princess of Wales 1987–1996*, p. 7.
3 Ibid.
4 David Hicks interview with author 2/6/93.
5 Stephen Barry, *Royal Service: My Twelve Years as Valet to Prince Charles*, p. 219.
6 Interview with the author 16/11/05.
7 Jonathan Dimbleby, *The Prince of Wales: A Biography*, p. 331.
8 Roy Greenslade interview with the author September 2005.
9 Sally Bedell Smith, *Diana: The Life of a Troubled Princess*, p. 140.
10 Ibid.
11 Private information.
12 Andrew Morton, *Diana, Her True Story – In Her Own Words*, p. 37.
13 Tim Clayton and Phil Craig, *Diana: Story of a Princess*, p. 15.
14 Jonathan Dimbleby, *The Prince of Wales: A Biography*, p. 332.
15 Ibid.
16 Ibid., p. 333.
17 Interview with the author 25/10/05.
18 Interview with the author 25/10/05.
19 Interview with the author 6/4/05.
20 Interview with the author 6/4/05.
21 Anthony Holden, *Charles, Prince of Wales*, pp. 204–5.
22 Private information.
23 Interview with the author 16/11/05.
24 Interview with the author 25/10/05.
25 Sally Bedell Smith, *Diana: The Life of a Troubled Princess*, p. 151.
26 Interview with the author 25/10/05.
27 Andrew Morton, *Diana: Her True Story – In Her Own Words*, p. 51.

Chapter 8. 'The Best Double Act in the World'
(pp. 126–43)

1 Jonathan Dimbleby, *The Prince of Wales: A Biography*, letter from Charles to friends p. 395.
2 Interview with the author 25/10/05.
3 Letter from private collection.
4 Interview with the author 6/4/05.
5 Rosalind Coward, *Diana: The Portrait*, pp. 141–2.
6 Ibid., pp. 144–5.
7 Ibid.
8 Ibid., p. 142.
9 Ibid., p. 132.
10 Interview with the author 25/10/05.
11 Rosalind Coward, *Diana: The Portrait*, p. 156.
12 Patrick Jephson, *Shadows of a Princess*, p. 18.
13 Ibid.
14 Letter from private collection.
15 Interview with the author 15/5/04.
16 Sally Bedell Smith, *Diana: The Life of a Troubled Princess*, p. 134.
17 Interview with the author 25/10/05.
18 Mary Roberston, *The Diana I Knew*, p. 111.
19 Ibid., p. 108.
20 Jonathan Dimbleby, *The Prince of Wales: A Biography*, p. 381.
21 Ibid., p. 382.
22 Ibid., pp. 386–7.
23 Interview with the author September 2004.
24 Interview with the author September 2004.
25 Interview with the author 20/2/06.
26 *Time* magazine, 11 November 1985.
27 Interview with the author 25/10/05.

Chapter 9. 'Charles has gone back to his Lady' (pp. 144–59)

1 Ken Wharfe interview with the author 11/4/05.
2 Settelen tapes.
3 Ken Wharfe interview with the author 11/4/05.
4 Ken Wharfe interview with the author 11/4/05.
5 Settelen tapes.
6 Ibid.
7 Interview with the author 14/4/05.
8 Andrew Morton, *Diana: Her True Story – In Her Own Words*, p. 58.
9 Interview with the author 10/4/06.
10 Interview with the author 7/12/05.
11 Interview with the author 7/9/05.
12 Andrew Morton, *Diana: Her True Story – In Her Own Words*, p. 58.
13 Jonathan Dimbleby, *The Prince of Wales: A Biography*, p. 393.
14 Ibid., p. 394.
15 Ibid., p. 395.
16 Ibid.
17 Ken Wharfe interview with the author 11/4/05.
18 James Hewitt interview with the author 11/1/06.
19 James Hewitt interview with the author 11/1/06.
20 James Hewitt interview with the author 11/1/06.
21 James Hewitt interview with the author 11/1/06.
22 James Hewitt interview with the author 11/1/06.
23 James Hewitt, *Love and War*, p. 23.
24 Ibid., p. 20.
25 Ibid., p. 27.
26 Settelen tapes.
27 Interview with the author 11/1/06.
28 Interview with the author 25/10/05.

Chapter 10. A Dying Marriage (pp. 160–79)

1 Patrick Jephson, *Shadows of a Princess*, p. 63.
2 James Hewitt interview with the author 11/1/06.
3 Ken Wharfe, with Robert Jobson, *Diana: Closely Guarded Secret*, p. 77.
4 Interview with the author.
5 Andrew Morton, *Diana: Her True Story – In Her Own Words*, pp. 59, 59.
6 Interview with the author 16/11/05.
7 Jonathan Dimbleby, *The Prince of Wales: A Biography*, p. 397.
8 Interview with the author 9/11/05.
9 Mike Adler quoted in Rosalind Coward, *Diana: The Portrait*, p. 178.
10 Baroness Jay quoted in Rosalind Coward, *Diana: The Portrait*, p. 178.
11 Rosalind Coward, *Diana: The Portrait*, p. 179.
12 Interview with the author 23/2/04.
13 Rosalind Coward, *Diana: The Portrait*, pp. 183–4.
14 Ibid., p. 184.
15 Ibid.
16 Marguerite Littman interview with the author 8/12/04.
17 Victor Edelstein interview with author 22/5/01.
18 Private information.
19 Interview with the author 14/4/05.
20 *Sunday Times*.
21 Roy Strong, *The Roy Strong Diaries 1967–1997*, 10 December 1987, p. 431.
22 Dickie Arbiter interview with author 23/2/04.

Chapter 11. Diana Fights Back (pp. 180–96)

1 Squidgygate tapes 1989.
2 Sarah Bradford, *Elizabeth: A Biography of Her Majesty The Queen*, p. 444.
3 James Hewitt interview with the author 11/1/06.

4 James Hewitt, *Love and War*, p. 48.

5 Sally Bedell Smith, *Diana: The Life of a Troubled Princess*, p. 197.

6 Anthony Holden, *Charles, Prince of Wales*, p. 260.

7 Ken Wharfe, with Robert Jobson, *Diana: Closely Guarded Secret*, pp. 96–7.

8 Interview with the author 5/5/04.

9 Patrick Jephson, *Shadows of a Princess*, pp. 34–5.

10 Ibid., p. 37.

11 Ibid., pp. 38–9.

12 Ibid., p. 40.

13 Ibid.

14 Interview with the author 16/11/05.

15 Andrew Morton, *Diana: Her True Story – In Her Own Words*, p. 60.

16 Interview with the author 21/6/05.

17 Rosa Monckton, in Brian MacArthur (ed.), *Requiem: Diana, Princess of Wales 1961–1997*, pp. 64–5.

18 Patrick Jephson interview with author March 2004.

19 Sally Bedell Smith, *Diana: The Life of a Troubled Princess*, p. 189.

20 Andrew Morton, *Diana: Her True Story – In Her Own Words*, p. 29.

21 Patrick Jephson, *Shadows of a Princess*, p. 67.

Chapter 12. The War of the Waleses (pp. 197–215)

1 Close friend of Diana's in an interview with the author 16/11/05.

2 Sally Bedell Smith, *Diana: The Life of a Troubled Princess*, p. 203.

3 Interview with the author 30/10/04.

4 Patrick Jephson, *Shadows of a Princess*, p. 137.

5 Ibid., p. 147.

6 Ibid., p. 138.

7 Ibid., p. 141.

8 Sir William Heseltine interview with the author 15/7/96.

9 Patrick Jephson, *Shadows of a Princess*, pp. 131–2.

10 Sally Bedell Smith, *Diana: The Life of a Troubled Princess*, p. 205.

11 Richard Kay interview with the author 16/3/04.

12 James Hewitt, *Love and War*, p. 151.

13 Interview with the author 16/11/05.
14 James Hewitt, *Love and War*, p. 151.
15 Interview with the author 16/11/05.
16 Interview with the author 16/11/05.
17 Andrew Morton interview with the author 20/3/01.
18 Andrew Morton interview with the author 20/3/01.
19 Andrew Morton interview with the author 20/3/01.
20 Patrick Jephson interview with the author March 2004.
21 Patrick Jephson interview with the author March 2004.
22 Patrick Jephson interview with the author March 2004.
23 Patrick Jephson interview with the author March 2004.
24 Patrick Jephson interview with the author March 2004.
25 Andrew Morton interview with the author 20/3/01.
26 James Whitaker interview with the author June 2001.
27 Sally Bedell Smith, *Diana: The Life of a Troubled Princess*, p. 210.
28 Andrew Morton interview with the author 20/3/01.
29 Interview with the author 7/3/06.
30 Dickie Arbiter interview with the author 23/2/04.
31 Interview with the author 16/11/05.

Chapter 13. The Volcano Erupts (pp. 216–32)

1 Andrew Morton interview with the author 20/3/01.
2 Sarah Bradford, *Elizabeth: A Biography of Her Majesty the Queen*, p. 360.
3 Dickie Arbiter interview with the author 23/2/04.
4 Interview with the author 3/4/01.
5 Interview with the author February 2005.
6 Sally Bedell Smith, *Diana: The Life of a Troubled Princess*, p. 222.
7 Interview with the author 23/2/04.
8 Patrick Jephson, *Shadows of a Princess*, p. 235.
9 Ibid.
10 Interview with the author.
11 Jean Willis interview with the author.
12 Patrick Jephson interview with the author March 2004.

13 Jonathan Dimbleby, *The Prince of Wales: A Biography*, p. 484.

14 Interview with the author 29/12/93.

15 Sally Bedell Smith, *Diana: The Life of a Troubled Princess*, p. 228.

16 Sarah Bradford, *Elizabeth: A Biography of Her Majesty The Queen*, p. 467.

17 Patrick Jephson, *Shadows of a Princess*, p. 248.

18 Interview with the author 8/9/93.

19 Jonathan Dimbleby, *The Prince of Wales: A Biography*, p. 487.

20 Ibid., p. 488.

21 Patrick Jephson interview with the author March 2004.

22 Jonathan Dimbleby, *The Prince of Wales: A Biography*, p. 488.

23 Patrick Jephson, *Shadows of a Princess*, p. 267.

24 Patrick Jephson interview with the author March 2004.

25 Jonathan Dimbleby, *The Prince of Wales: A Biography*, p. 489.

26 Patrick Jephson, *Shadows of a Princess*, p. 272.

27 Jonathan Dimbleby, *The Prince of Wales: A Biography*, p. 491.

Chapter 14. The First Step Towards the Abyss
(pp. 233–53)

1 Patrick Jephson, *Shadows of a Princess*, p. 278.

2 Ken Wharfe, with Robert Jobson, *Closely Guarded Secret*, p. 265.

3 Interview with the author 5/5/04.

4 Interview with the author 16/11/05.

5 Interview with the author 5/5/04.

6 Interview with the author 16/11/05.

7 Interview with the author March 2005.

8 Interview with the author 30/10/04.

9 Interview with the author 30/10/04.

10 Sally Bedell Smith, *Diana: The Life of a Troubled Princess*, p. 258.

11 Interview with the author 4/11/04.

12 Interview with the author 4/11/04.

13 Ken Wharfe interview with the author 11/4/05.

14 Ken Wharfe, with Robert Jobson, *Closely Guarded Secret*, p. 186.

15 Ibid.

16 Ken Wharfe interview with the author 11/4/05.
17 Interview with the author.
18 Max Hastings, *Editor: An Inside Story of Newspapers*, pp. 336–7.
19 Patrick Jephson, *Shadows of a Princess*, p. 412.
20 Douglas Hurd, *Memoirs*, p. 474.
21 Ibid., p. 556.
22 Interview with the author February 2005.
23 Patrick Jephson, *Shadows of a Princess*, p. 297.
24 Ibid., p. 297.
25 Ibid., pp. 297–8.
26 Ken Wharfe, with Robert Jobson, *Closely Guarded Secret*, p. 231.
27 Patrick Jephson, *Shadows of a Princess*, p. 307.
28 Andrew Morton, *Diana: Her True Story – In Her Own Words*, p. 57.
29 Paul Burrell, *A Royal Duty*, p. 183.
30 Ken Wharfe interview with the author 11/4/05.
31 Ken Wharfe, with Robert Jobson, *Closely Guarded Secret*, p. 218.
32 Ibid., p. 221.
33 Ibid., p. 241.
34 Ibid., p. 229.
35 Ibid., p. 248.

Chapter 15. The Inconsequential Years (pp. 254–68)

1 Patrick Jephson, *Shadows of a Princess*, p. 293.
2 Interview with the author 27/6/05.
3 Interview with the author 16/11/05.
4 Sally Bedell Smith, *Diana: The Life of a Troubled Princess*, p. 258.
5 Ibid.
6 Interview with the author 16/11/05.
7 Sally Bedell Smith, *Diana: The Life of a Troubled Princess*, p. 260.
8 Ibid., p. 259.
9 Andrew Morton interview with the author 20/3/01.
10 Sister Bridie Dowd interview with the author 20/1/06.
11 Sister Bridie Dowd interview with the author 20/1/06.
12 Sister Bridie Dowd interview with the author 20/1/06.

13 Interview with the author.

14 Interview with the author.

15 Patrick Jephson, *Shadows of a Princess*, p. 293.

16 Interview with the author February 2004.

17 Interview with the author 5/5/04.

18 Interview with the author 23/2/95.

19 Sally Bedell Smith, *Diana: The Life of a Troubled Princess*, p. 265.

20 Jonathan Dimbleby, *The Prince of Wales: A Biography*, p. 608.

Chapter 16. Towards a New World (pp. 269–80)

1 Brian MacArthur (ed.), *Requiem: Diana, Princess of Wales 1961–1997*, p. 102.

2 Interview with the author 16/11/05.

3 Patrick Jephson, *Shadows of a Princess*, p. 343.

4 Brian MacArthur (ed.), *Requiem: Diana, Princess of Wales 1961–1997*, p. 102.

5 Ibid., p. 101.

6 Ibid., p. 102.

7 Ibid., pp. 99–100.

8 Patrick Jephson, *Shadows of a Princess*, p. 345.

9 Ibid., p. 346.

10 Interview with the author 28/9/94.

11 Interview with the author 15/11/94.

12 Interview with the author 20/7/05.

13 Michael Shea interview with the author 1/2/95.

14 Patrick Jephson, *Shadows of a Princess*, p. 345.

15 Interview with the author 2/2/04.

16 Interview with the author 2/2/04.

17 Interview with the author 2/2/04.

18 Interview with the author 2/2/04.

19 Piers Morgan, *The Insider*, p. 106.

20 Ibid., p. 115.

21 Ibid., p. 118.

22 Ibid., p. 157.

23 Brian MacArthur (ed.), *Requiem: Diana, Princess of Wales 1961–1997*,
    p. 123.

24 Ibid., p. 124.

25 Paul Burrell, *A Royal Duty*, p. 203.

26 Ibid., p. 203.

27 Brian MacArthur (ed.), *Requiem: Diana, Princess of Wales 1961–1997*,
    p. 89.

28 Ibid., p. 96.

29 Interview with the author February 2005.

30 Interview with the author February 2005.

31 Brian MacArthur (ed.), *Requiem: Diana, Princess of Wales 1961–1997*,
    p. 89.

Chapter 17. Fall from Grace (pp. 281–300)

1   *Mail on Sunday*, 20 August 1995.

2   Patrick Jephson, *Shadows of a Princess*, p. 351.

3   Interview with the author November 1994.

4   Patrick Jephson, *Shadows of a Princess*, p. 356.

5   Brian MacArthur (ed.), *Requiem: Diana, Princess of Wales 1961–1997*,
    p. 97.

6   Patrick Jephson, *Shadows of a Princess*, p. 354.

7   Ibid., p. 356.

8   Interview with the author 4/11/04.

9   Judy Wade, *The Truth: The Friends of Diana, Princess of Wales, Tell
    Their Stories*, p. 87.

10 Sally Bedell Smith, *Diana: The Life of a Troubled Princess*, p. 283.

11 Interview with the author 23/2/04.

12 Interview with the author March 2005.

13 Richard Kay interview with the author 16/3/04.

14 Interview with the author 4/11/04.

15 Interview with the author 4/11/04.

16 Paul Burrell, *A Royal Duty*, p. 322.

17 Colin Tebbutt interview with the author 3/4/04.

18 Ken Wharfe interview with the author 11/4/05.

19 Andrew Morton, *Diana: In Pursuit of Love*, p. 179.

20 Ibid., p. 178.

21 Sally Bedell Smith, *Diana: The Life of a Troubled Princess*, p. 282.

22 Interview with the author February 2005.

23 Interview with the author February 2005.

24 Brian MacArthur (ed.), *Requiem: Diana, Princess of Wales 1961–1997*, p. 96.

25 Sally Bedell Smith, *Diana: The Life of a Troubled Princess*, p. 284.

26 Sarah Bradford, *Elizabeth: A Biography of Her Majesty The Queen*, p. 481.

27 Interview with the author 5/5/04.

28 Patrick Jephson, *Shadows of a Princess*, p. 367.

29 Ibid., p. 369.

30 Paul Burrell, *A Royal Duty*, p. 219.

31 Interview with the author 6/1/05.

32 Paul Burrell, *A Royal Duty*, pp. 221–2.

Chapter 18. Out on a Limb (pp. 301–20)

1 Patrick Jephson, *Shadows of a Princess*, p. 552.

2 Ibid., p. 560.

3 Paul Burrell, *A Royal Duty*, p. 222.

4 Ibid., pp. 225–6.

5 Ibid., p. 226.

6 Ibid.

7 Ibid., pp. 226–7.

8 Interview with the author 5/5/04.

9 Interview with the author 27/6/05.

10 Interview with the author 6/1/06.

11 Interview with the author June 2005.

12 Brian MacArthur (ed.), *Requiem: Diana, Princess of Wales 1961–1997*, p. 80.

13 Ibid., p. 80.

14 Ibid., p. 81.

15 Ibid., pp. 81–2.

16 Ibid., p. 83.
17 Kate Snell, *Diana: Her Last Love*, p. 86.
18 Ibid., p. 67.
19 Interview with the author 5/5/04.
20 Interview with the author 5/5/04.
21 Interview with the author 5/5/04.
22 Colin Tebbutt interview with the author 3/3/04.
23 Pamela Harlech interview with the author October 2004.
24 Cheryl Barrymore interview in the *Daily Mail* (21 October 2002).
25 Ibid.
26 Allan Starkie, *Fergie: Her Secret Life*, p. 76.
27 Ibid., p. 117.
28 Ibid., p. 206.
29 Sarah, The Duchess of York, *My Story*, p. 72.

Chapter 19. Stirring Beneath the Surface (pp. 321–37)

1 Richard Kay interview with the author 16/3/04.
2 Cited in Paul Burrell, *A Royal Duty*, p. 242.
3 Interview with the author 25/10/05.
4 Interview with the author February 2005.
5 Kate Snell, *Diana: Her Last Love*, p. 135.
6 Interview with the author February 2004.
7 Interview with the author February 2004.
8 Interview with the author February 2004.
9 Interview with the author January 2004.
10 Interview with the author January 2004.
11 Interview with the author February 2004.
12 Interview with the author February 2004.
13 Interview with the author 23/2/05.
14 Private information.
15 Sarah Bradford, *Elizabeth: A Biography of Her Majesty The Queen*, pp. 244–5.
16 Interview with the author February 2004.
17 Interview with the author September 2004.

18 Interview with the author September 2004.
19 Interview with the author September 2004.
20 Interview with the author 14/4/05.
21 Interview with the author 11/4/05.
22 Interview with the author 11/4/05.
23 Interview with the author 11/4/05.
24 Interview with the author 11/4/05.
25 Interview with Richard Kay 16/3/04.
26 *Report to His Royal Highness The Prince of Wales by Sir Michael Peat and Edmund Lawson QC*, 13 March 2003, p. 10.
27 Ibid., p. 11.
28 Ibid., p. 12.
29 Ibid., p. 13.
30 Ibid., p. 25.
31 Ibid., p. 36.
32 Ibid., p. 39.
33 Ibid., p. 43.
34 Ibid., p. 49.
35 Interview with author 6/2/04.
36 Interview with author 7/2/04.

Chapter 20. Diana the Hunted (pp. 338–55)

1 William Deedes.
2 William Rees-Mogg, in Rosalind Coward, *Diana: The Portrait*, p. 260.
3 Richard Kay interview with the author 16/3/04.
4 Interview with the author February 2006.
5 Meredith Etherington-Smith interview with the author 25/1/03.
6 Meredith Etherington-Smith interview with the author 25/1/03.
7 Meredith Etherington-Smith interview with the author 25/1/03.
8 Meredith Etherington-Smith interview with the author 25/1/03.
9 Meredith Etherington-Smith interview with the author 25/1/03.
10 Meredith Etherington-Smith interview with the author 25/1/03.
11 Meredith Etherington-Smith interview with the author 25/1/03.

12 William Deedes interview with the author 19/1/04.

13 Brian MacArthur (ed.), *Requiem: Diana, Princess of Wales 1961–1997*, p. 135.

14 William Deedes interview with the author 19/1/04.

15 Brian MacArthur (ed.), *Requiem: Diana, Princess of Wales 1961–1997*, p. 136.

16 Ibid.

17 Paul Burrell, *A Royal Duty*, p. 281.

18 Ibid.

19 William Deedes interview with the author 19/1/04.

20 Interview with the author March 2004.

21 Interview with the author March 2004.

22 William Deedes interview with the author 19/1/04.

23 Rosalind Coward, *Diana: The Portrait*, p. 294.

24 Ibid., p. 266.

25 Meredith Etherington-Smith interview with the author 25/1/03.

26 Meredith Etherington-Smith interview with the author 25/1/03.

27 Meredith Etherington-Smith interview with the author 25/1/03.

28 Meredith Etherington-Smith interview with the author 25/1/03.

29 Meredith Etherington-Smith interview with the author 25/1/03.

30 Meredith Etherington-Smith interview with the author 25/1/03.

31 Meredith Etherington-Smith interview with the author 25/1/03.

32 Meredith Etherington-Smith interview with the author 25/1/03.

33 Meredith Etherington-Smith interview with the author 25/1/03.

34 Meredith Etherington-Smith interview with the author 25/1/03.

35 Meredith Etherington-Smith interview with the author 25/1/03.

36 Brian MacArthur (ed.), *Requiem: Diana, Princess of Wales 1961–1997*, p. 113.

37 Paul Burrell, *A Royal Duty*, p. 300.

38 Ibid.

Chapter 21. Fatal Summer (pp. 356–72)

1 Tom Bower, *Fayed: The Unauthorized Biography*, pp. 6–7.
2 Ibid., p. 25.
3 Interview with the author February 2005.
4 Tom Bower, *Fayed: The Unauthorized Biography*, p. 159.
5 Pamela Harlech interview with the author October 2004.
6 Pamela Harlech interview with the author October 2004.
7 Richard Kay interview with the author 16/3/04.
8 Tom Bower, *Fayed: The Unauthorized Biography*, p. 413.
9 Interview with the author 18/2/04.
10 Richard Kay interview with the author 16/3/04.
11 Tom Bower, *Fayed: The Unauthorized Biography*, pp. 416–17.
12 Interview with the author 16/11/05.
13 Interview with the author 16/11/05.
14 Interview with the author 16/11/05.
15 Richard Kay interview with the author 16/3/04.
16 Interview with the author 16/11/05.
17 Interview with the author.
18 Trevor Rees-Jones, *The Bodyguard's Story: Diana, the Crash and the Sole Survivor*, p. 15.
19 Ibid., p. 72.
20 Martyn Gregory, *Diana: The Last Days*, p. 50.
21 Ibid., p. 49.
22 Ibid., p. 56.
23 Ibid., p. 57.
24 Trevor Rees-Jones, *The Bodyguard's Story: Diana, the Crash and the Sole Survivor*, p. 79.
25 Brian MacArthur (ed.), *Requiem: Diana, Princess of Wales 1961–1997*, p. 63.
26 Ibid., p. 55.
27 Colin Tebbut interview with the author 3/3/04.
28 Trevor Rees-Jones, *The Bodyguard's Story: Diana, the Crash and the Sole Survivor*, p. 86.
29 Colin Tebbutt interview with the author 3/3/04.

Chapter 22. Death in Paris (pp. 373–88)

1 Daniel Eyraud, vascular surgery team, cited in Martyn Gregory, *Diana: The Last Days*, p. 74.
2 Martyn Gregory, *Diana: The Last Days*, pp. 74–5.
3 Colin Tebbutt interview with the author 3/3/04.
4 Colin Tebbutt interview with the author 3/3/04.
5 Colin Tebbutt interview with the author 3/3/04.
6 Andrew Morton, *Diana: In Pursuit of Love*, p. 250.
7 Ibid., p. 251.
8 Interview with the author February 2004.
9 Rosalind Coward, *Diana: The Portrait*, p. 302.
10 Colin Tebbutt interview with the author 3/3/04.
11 Colin Tebbutt interview with the author 3/3/04.
12 Rosalind Coward, *Diana: The Portrait*, p. 304.
13 Ibid.
14 Paul Burrell, *A Royal Duty*, p. 297.
15 Interview with the author 20/7/05.
16 Interview with the author 20/7/05.
17 Interview with the author 23/2/04.
18 Dickie Arbiter interview with the author 23/2/04.
19 Dickie Arbiter interview with the author 23/2/04.
20 Private information.
21 Dickie Arbiter interview with the author 23/2/04.
22 Meredith Etherington-Smith interview with the author 25/1/03.
23 Brian MacArthur (ed.), *Requiem: Diana, Princess of Wales 1961–1997*, p. 6.

Select Bibliography

Barry, Stephen P., *Royal Service: My Twelve Years as Valet to Prince Charles*, Avon Books, New York, 1984

Bedell Smith, Sally, *Diana: The Life of a Troubled Princess*, Aurum Press, 1999

Berry, Wendy, *The Housekeeper's Diary: Charles and Diana Before the Breakup*, Barricade Books, Inc., New York, 1995

Bower, Tom, *Fayed: The Unauthorized Biography*, Pan Books, 2001

Bradford, Sarah, *Elizabeth: A Biography of Her Majesty The Queen*, rev. edn, Penguin Books, 2002

Burchill, Julie, *Diana*, Weidenfeld & Nicolson, 1998

Burrell, Paul, *A Royal Duty*, Michael Joseph, 2003

Campbell, Lady Colin, *Diana in Private: The Princess Nobody Knows*, Smith Gryphon, 1992

Clarke, Mary, *Little Girl Lost: The Troubled Childhood of Princess Diana by the Woman who Raised Her*, Birch Lane Press, New York, 1996

Clayton, Tim, and Phil Craig, *Diana: Story of a Princess*, Hodder & Stoughton, 2001

Courtney, Nicholas, *Diana: Princess of Wales*, Park Lane Press, 1982

Coward, Rosalind, *Diana: The Portrait*, HarperCollins, n.d.

Deedes, William, *Brief Lives*, Macmillan, 2004

Delorm, René, with Barry Fox and Nadine Taylor, *Diana & Dodi: A Love Story*, Tallfellow Press, Los Angeles, 1998

Dimbleby, Jonathan, *The Prince of Wales: A Biography*, Little, Brown, 1994

Ferguson, Ronald, *The Galloping Major: My Life and Singular Times*, Macmillan, 1994

Goldsmith, Lady Annabel, *Annabel: An Unconventional Life*, Phoenix, 2004

Graham, Caroline, *Camilla – The King's Mistress: A Love Story*, Blake Publishing, 1994

Graham, Tim, with text by Tom Corby, *Diana, Princess of Wales: A Tribute*, Weidenfeld & Nicolson, n.d.

Greenslade, Roy, *Press Gang: The True Story of How Papers Make Profits from Propaganda*, Macmillan, 2003

Gregory, Martyn, *Diana: The Last Days*, Virgin Publishing, 1999, revised and updated by Virgin Books, 2004

Hastings, Max, *Editor: An Inside Story of Newspapers*, Pan Books, 2003

Hewitt, James, *Love and War*, Blake Publishing, 1999

——, *Moving On*, Blake Publishing, 2005

Holden, Anthony, *Charles, Prince of Wales*, Weidenfeld & Nicolson, 1979

——, *Charles: A Biography*, Fontana Paperbacks, 1989

——, *Charles: A Biography*, Corgi Books, 1999

Hurd, Douglas, *Memoirs*, Abacus Books, 2004

Jephson, Patrick, *Shadows of a Princess. Diana, Princess of Wales 1987–1996*, HarperCollins, 2000

——, photographs by Kent Gavin, *Portraits of a Princess: Travels with Diana*, Sidgwick & Jackson, 2004

Junor, Penny, *Diana, Princess of Wales*, Sidgwick & Jackson, 1982

——, *Charles, Victim or Villain?*, HarperCollins, 1998

Kortesis, Vasso, *The Duchess of York*, Blake Publishing, 1996

Levin, Angela, *Raine and Johnnie: The Spencers and the Scandal of Althorp*, Weidenfeld & Nicolson, 1993

MacArthur, Brian, ed., *Requiem: Diana, Princess of Wales 1961–1997 – Memories and Tributes*, Arcade Publishing, 1997

Morgan, Piers, *The Insider*, Ebury Press, 2005

Morton, Andrew, *Inside Kensington Palace*, Michael O'Mara Books, 1987

——, *Diana: Her True Story – In Her Own Words*, revised edn, Michael O'Mara Books, 1997

——, *Diana: Her New Life*, Michael O'Mara Books, 1994

——, *Diana: In Pursuit of Love*, Michael O'Mara Books, 2004

Pasternak, Anna, *Princess in Love*, Bloomsbury, 1994

Pontaut, Jean-Marie, and Jerome Dupuis, *Enquête sur la mort de Diana*, Editions Stock, Paris, 1998

Rees-Jones, Trevor, with Moira Johnston, *The Bodyguard's Story: Diana, the Crash and the Sole Survivor*, Little, Brown, 2000

Report to His Royal Highness The Prince of Wales by Sir Michael Peat and Edmund Lawson QC, 13 March 2003

Riddington, Max, and Gavan Naden, *Frances: The Remarkable Story of Diana's Mother*, Michael O'Mara Books, 2003

Robertson, Mary, *The Diana I Knew*, Judy Piatkus, 1998

Rogers, Rita, *From One World to Another . . .*, Pan Books, 1998

Sancton, Thomas, and Scott MacLeod, *Death of a Princess: An Investigation*, Weidenfeld & Nicolson, 1998

Sarah, The Duchess of York, with Jeff Coplon, *My Story*, Simon & Schuster, 1996

Seward, Ingrid, *The Queen and Di*, HarperCollins, 2000

Shanley-Toffolo, Oonagh, *The Voice of Silence: A Life of Love, Healing and Inspiration*, Rider, 2002

Simmons, Simone, with Susan Hill, *Diana: The Secret Years*, Michael O'Mara Books, 1998

Snell, Kate, *Diana: Her Last Love*, Granada Media, 2000

Souhami, Diana, *Mrs Keppel and Her Daughter*, HarperCollins, 1996

Spencer, Charles, *Althorp: The Story of an English House*, Viking, 1998

——, *The Spencer Family*, Viking, 1999

Starkie, Allan, *Fergie: Her Secret Life*, Michael O'Mara Books, 1996

Strong, Roy, *The Roy Strong Diaries 1967–1997*, Weidenfeld & Nicolson, 1997

Wade, Judy, *The Truth: The Friends of Diana, Princess of Wales, Tell Their Stories*, Blake Publishing, 2001

Wharfe, Ken, with Robert Jobson, *Diana: Closely Guarded Secret*, revised and expanded paperback edn, Michael O'Mara Books, 2003

Whitaker, James, *Diana v. Charles*, Signet, 1993

Wilson, Christopher, *The Windsor Knot: Charles, Camilla and the Legacy of Diana*, Citadel Press, New York, 2002

Ziegler, Philip, *Mountbatten*, HarperCollins, 1985

Permissions

The author and publisher are grateful for permission to reproduce the following copyright material:

From *Diana: The Portrait* edited by Rosalind Coward. Reprinted by permission of HarperCollins*Publishers* Ltd. Copyright Rosalind Coward 2004

From *The Prince of Wales: A Biography* by Jonathan Dimbleby. Reprinted by permission of David Higham Associates. Copyright Jonathan Dimbleby, Little, Brown 1996

From *Diana: The Last Days* by Martyn Gregory. Reprinted by permission of Virgin Books. Copyright Martyn Gregory 1999, 2000, 2004, Virgin Books Ltd.

From *Shadows of a Princess: Diana, Princess of Wales 1987–1996* by Patrick Jephson. Reprinted by permission of HarperCollins*Publishers* Ltd. Copyright Patrick Jephson 2001

From *Diana: Her True Story – In Her Own Words* by Andrew Morton. Reprinted by permission of Michael O'Mara Books Ltd. Copyright Andrew Morton 2003

From *Diana: Closely Guarded Secret* by Ken Wharfe. Reprinted by permission of Michael O'Mara Books Ltd. Copyright Ken Wharfe 2002

From *The Insider* by Piers Morgan, published by Ebury Press. Reprinted by permission of The Random House Group Ltd. Copyright Piers Morgan 2005

From *Raine and Johnnie: The Spencers and the Scandal of Althorp* by Angela Levin. Reprinted by permission of Weidenfeld & Nicolson, an imprint of The Orion Publishing Group. Copyright Angela Levin 1993

Acknowledgements

I owe a great debt of gratitude to all those people who have been kind enough to help me with this book, those named below and those who have preferred not to be named. I have also been fortunate to have the taped memories of members of the royal circle recorded over a decade ago when the events described in this book and people's reactions to them were still fresh. If I have omitted anyone who should have been included, I ask their forgiveness.

A&H Associates; Dickie Arbiter LVO; Sally Bedell Smith; Michael Bentley; Mark Bolland; Tom Bower; Lord Carlile of Berriew QC; Phil Craig; Sir Geoffrey Dear QPM, DL; The Rt Hon. Lord Deedes; Sister Bridie Dowd DC, OBE; Victor Edelstein; Meredith Etherington-Smith; Tess Gilder; Robert Golden; Roy Greenslade; Geordie Greig; David Griffin RVM; Linda Hall; Pamela, Lady Harlech; Nicholas Haslam; James Hewitt; Stuart Higgins; Anthony Holden; Patrick Jephson; Richard Kay; Timothy Leese; Brian Lapping; Marguerite Littman; Christopher Loyd CVO; Robert Low; Colin and Annabel Mackay; Andrew Morton; M.J. Rockall for his kindness in making available to me his collection of Diana letters; the Reverend Michael Seed SA; Ian Shapiro of Argyll Etkin Ltd, London for giving me access to Diana documents and letters; James Sherwin; Robert Spencer; Dr Will Swift; William Tallon RVM★ Gold; Colin Tebbutt MVO; Hugo Vickers for kindly making available to me his unpublished diary and extensive collection of royal newspaper cuttings covering the Diana years; Judy Wade; Lord Wakeham PC, JP, DL, FCA; Christopher Warwick; Nigel West; Kenneth A. Wharfe MVO; James Whitaker.

I am grateful to Martin Morse Wooster for his help with American sources, Lucy Pullan for her research in newspaper archives, to Camilla Eadie and Lizzie Grant for their skilful transcriptions and general help, to Lynda Marshall for her help in picture research, and to Douglas Matthews for compiling the index.

My agent, Gillon Aitken, has been a great support, assisted by Ayesha Karim and Sally Riley. At my publishers, Viking in London, I should like to express my gratitude to Helen Fraser, Tom Weldon and Keith Taylor. Above all, Carly Cook has accompanied me almost every step of the way, going far beyond the call of duty in collecting and designing the pictures illustrating Diana's life, editing the book and seeing its completion down to the most minute and often tedious detail. Richard Collins has once again proved the most intelligent and skilful of editors. In the early stages of the book no one could have done more to encourage me than Antonia Till. Above all my husband, William Bangor, has provided me with moral support throughout and practical expertise on proof checking.

Index

He just wanted a decent book to read ...

Not too much to ask, is it? It was in 1935 when Allen Lane, Managing Director of Bodley Head Publishers, stood on a platform at Exeter railway station looking for something good to read on his journey back to London. His choice was limited to popular magazines and poor-quality paperbacks – the same choice faced every day by the vast majority of readers, few of whom could afford hardbacks. Lane's disappointment and subsequent anger at the range of books generally available led him to found a company – and change the world.

'We believed in the existence in this country of a vast reading public for intelligent books at a low price, and staked everything on it'
Sir Allen Lane, 1902–1970, founder of Penguin Books

The quality paperback had arrived – and not just in bookshops. Lane was adamant that his Penguins should appear in chain stores and tobacconists, and should cost no more than a packet of cigarettes.

Reading habits (and cigarette prices) have changed since 1935, but Penguin still believes in publishing the best books for everybody to enjoy. We still believe that good design costs no more than bad design, and we still believe that quality books published passionately and responsibly make the world a better place.

So wherever you see the little bird – whether it's on a piece of prize-winning literary fiction or a celebrity autobiography, political tour de force or historical masterpiece, a serial-killer thriller, reference book, world classic or a piece of pure escapism – you can bet that it represents the very best that the genre has to offer.

Whatever you like to read – trust Penguin.